"This subtle, learned, and intriguing analysis not only invites us to ponder anew some of the ultimate mysteries of the Christian revelation, but to see how the concept of paradox can encompass a wide range of apparently contradictory scriptural truths in order to underscore God's gracious salvation in Christ. Those who follow David Griffith's reasoning in this highly accomplished study will be enlightened and enriched."

—D. DENSIL MORGAN
University of Wales Trinity Saint David, Lampeter, emeritus

"Griffith's innovative take on the Christian paradox of exclusive or universal salvation is to find the paradox applied to every individual. A person's eternal life and character are divisible and thus subject to both divine acceptance and judgment. This is a fascinating exercise in constructive theology and in defining a person in relationship to the eternal God."

—J. ANDREW DEARMAN
Fuller Theological Seminary

"'Who then can be saved?' The question reverberates through Christian history from New Testament times. Taking Scripture seriously and employing a whole host of ancient as well as modern sources, David Griffith offers a fresh and original approach to the Bible's apparent advocacy of both a universal and an exclusive salvation. Erudite, stimulating, and lucid, the discussion is both constructive and provocative. Careful reading will yield insights into theological anthropology as well as Christian soteriology."

—ROBERT POPE
Westminster College, Cambridge

"This is a novel book with a fascinating argument. As Griffith indicates, the stalemate in Christianity between universal and limited salvation seems to be an intractable issue without resolution. However, Griffith has provided an original way forward that deserves recognition and careful consideration. A timely piece and a tour de force."

—MICHAEL BURDETT
University of Nottingham

The Great Divide
and the Salvation Paradox

The Great Divide
and the Salvation Paradox

David P. Griffith

PICKWICK Publications • Eugene, Oregon

THE GREAT DIVIDE AND THE SALVATION PARADOX

Copyright © 2022 David P. Griffith. All rights reserved. Except for brief quotations in critical publications or reviews, no part of this book may be reproduced in any manner without prior written permission from the publisher. Write: Permissions, Wipf and Stock Publishers, 199 W. 8th Ave., Suite 3, Eugene, OR 97401.

Pickwick Publications
An Imprint of Wipf and Stock Publishers
199 W. 8th Ave., Suite 3
Eugene, OR 97401

www.wipfandstock.com

PAPERBACK ISBN: 978-1-6667-3173-6
HARDCOVER ISBN: 978-1-6667-2450-9
EBOOK ISBN: 978-1-6667-2459-2

Cataloguing-in-Publication data:

Names: Griffith, David P. [author].

Title: The great divide and the salvation paradox / David P. Griffith.

Description: Eugene, OR: Pickwick Publications, 2022 | Includes bibliographical references.

Identifiers: ISBN 978-1-6667-3173-6 (paperback) | ISBN 978-1-6667-2450-9 (hardcover) | ISBN 978-1-6667-2459-2 (ebook)

Subjects: LCSH: Universalism—Biblical teaching | Universalism | Universalism—History of doctrines | Salvation—Christianity | Paradox—Religious aspects—Christianity

Classification: BS680.U55 G75 2022 (print) | BS680.U55 (ebook)

04/01/22

To those still here at the end.

Contents

Acknowledgments | xi
Abbreviations | xiii

Introduction | 1

1   Prolegomena | 12
    1. The Issue Is Ultimate Salvation | 13
    2. Salvation's Extent Matters | 16
    3. The Salvation Paradox Infringes Commonplace Logic | 21
    4. "Individual" Is the Lesser Embarrassment | 25
    5. Models Suit Paradoxes | 33
    6. Scripture Is the Signal Data | 37
    7. Understanding Requires Whatever It Takes | 40

2   Decease, Decrease, Increase | 45
    1. Everyone Dies, Followed by More | 46
    2. The Godly Are Separated from the Perishing | 49
    3. The Godly Are Completed | 58

3   Scripture's Salvation Paradox | 60
    1. Everyone Is Ultimately Saved | 61
    2. Only Some Are Ultimately Saved | 74
    3. Contradictions Reveal Fallacies | 81

4 The Responses | 85
    1. Universalism Began Strong and Resurges | 86
    2. Exclusivism Is Orthodox | 108
    3. Potentialism Hedges | 116

5 Unconvincing Treatments | 123
    1. Tradition Lacks Consensus | 124
    2. Each Response Is Problematic | 125
    3. The Responses Undervalue Paradox | 137

6 Divisibility's Coherence | 143
    1. The Individual Takes Personal Identity and Character | 145
    2. Most Any Metaphysic Works | 147
    3. Anthropology Historically and Currently Reflects the Essential *I* | 154
    4. We Each Live through an Indivisible Personal Identity | 165
    5. We Each Live as a Multilateral Personal Character | 169
    6. The Personal Character Is Divided | 173
    7. Scripture Reflects Personal Identity Centering Divided Character | 177
    8. Each Individual Is Oriented Both Towards and Away from God | 180
    9. Life Forms Personal Character, Which Forms Life | 189
    10. Evil Exists | 192
    11. Dividing an Individual in the Afterlife Is Realizable | 195
    12. A Divided Individual Can Be Modeled | 203

7 Preserving the Paradox | 214
    1. After This Life, Godly Is Divided from Ungodly | 215
    2. Individual Afterlife Divisibility Allows the Salvation Paradox | 228
    3. The Divisible Individual Transitions into the Afterlife | 231

8 Christianity's Divisible Individual | 235
    1. Scriptural Hints of Afterlife Divisibility Are Ignored | 236
    2. Theologians Approach Paradoxism | 255

9   Systemic Truth | 263
       1. Paradoxism Conserves Anthropology | 264
       2. The Good News Remains God's for Us | 265
       3. Paradoxism Handles Binary Problems | 268
       4. Proportional Justice Survives | 270
       5. Paradoxism Values Grace | 273
       6. Afterlife Decision-Making Is Unneeded | 275
       7. The Community Is Eternal | 277

Concludings | 281
Bibliography | 289

Acknowledgments

This book's inception can be traced to an assignment by a professor whose name I cannot recall. He assigned a one-page essay with no footnotes or citations concerning an eschatological question of our choosing. Because so little work was required, I risked the question that thoroughly confronted me. I knew, as we all do, people who were semi-saved and asked what ultimately happened to them—those of us who are variously faithful, righteous, godly, those like my dad, like me. Indeed, almost everyone seemed semi-saved. Humanity's nature, unlike God's, did not match salvation's nature. One was a mixed bag, and the other was either-or. So, I asked could a person be saved to an extent. My philistine answer amounted to another question: Could a person be divided between saved and not saved? Thanks, professor.

The question about salvation's extent stayed with me, which I later figured was the point. Scripture was not yielding the clear answer I sought because it clearly says both that everyone is saved ultimately and that not everyone is. The church's greats could, of course, make Scripture say just one or the other, and anyone of the greats could be nearly convincing, but only until the next one took the opposite position. For over five years, I pursued this nagging question whatever the academic assignment. Whether it nominally concerned Jeremiah, Ephesians, Augustine, Barth, or a literature review, I found a way to make salvation's extent the topic. Accordingly, the second set of people I wish to thank are all the professors at Fuller Theological Seminary and the University of Wales Trinity Saint David, who, often unbeknownst to them, put up with my underlying question regardless of what they assigned and who knowingly helped me nonetheless.

While I was in this way chipping away at the question about salvation's extent, the absence of a real answer vexed. To reach for that, I required more work and definitely more obvious direction. I realized that, though most students have to develop a thesis to obtain a PhD in theology, I had to obtain a PhD in theology to develop my thesis. Enter Conor Cunningham, who mysteriously agreed to take on a research student proposing to divide a person in the afterlife so as to address the prolonged rivalry between the contestants over salvation's extent, the universalists and the orthodox. Under Conor's supervision at the University of Nottingham and several Midland pubs, this conflict came to be seen through the prism of a paradox, the life-blood of a lived truth. With that, I found an answer to how Scripture appeared to be contradicting itself in expressing both universal salvation and exclusive salvation and to how someone could be saved and not saved.

I should also thank my viva examiners, who posed genuine questions at the heart of the paradox, which better exposed the answer, and who encouraged the publishing of that answer.

Finally, I thank my wife, who has for close on forty years been educating me about paradoxes without ever using the word.

In short, I thank in order of appearance my dad, my wife, the unnamed professor, Andy Dearman, R. P. Pope, Densil Morgan, Conor Cunningham, Michael Burdett, Robert Song, and those now reading this. Hosanna, which is my plea when I remember.

Abbreviations

AHD	*American Heritage Dictionary of the English Language* 4th ed.: Boston: Houghton Mifflin, 2000.
BDAG	Danker, Bauers, Aland, and Gingrich, eds. *Greek-English Lexicon of the NT and Other Early Christian Literature*. 3rd ed: Chicago: University of Chicago Press, 2000.
BDB	Brown, Driver, and Briggs. *Brown-Driver-Briggs Hebrew and English Lexicon*. Peabody, MA: Hendrickson, 2012.
BDF	Blass, F., and A. Debrunner. *Greek Grammar of the NT and Other Early Christian Literature*. Translated by Robert W. Funk. Chicago: University of Chicago Press, 1962.
CD	*Church Dogmatics*
JP	Journal and Papers
LSJ	Liddell, Henry George, Robert Scott, Henry Stuart Jones, and Roderick McKenzie. *A Greek-English Lexicon*. Oxford: Clarendon, 1968.
NIDNTTE	*New International Dictionary of NT Theology and Exegesis*. 2nd ed. 5 vols. Grand Rapids: Zondervan, 2014.
NT	New Testament
OED	*Oxford English Dictionary*. 2nd ed. 20 vols. Oxford: Clarendon, 1989.
ST	Systematic Theology or, for citations to Thomas Aquinas, *Summa Theologica/Theologiae*

Introduction

God turned to speak to me
(Don't anybody laugh);
God found I wasn't there—
At least not over half.

—Frost, "Ten Mills"

THE EXTENT OF SALVATION is a Christian aporia because Christians have not entirely agreed on whether Christ saves all of us or saves only some of us, but they all agree on the obvious: Not even Christ can truly do both. Their disagreement is based on what Christians find in Scripture, which sets out both accounts of salvation's extent and also justifies the notion, if a justification were needed, that contradicting accounts cannot be entirely true. As a result, the scriptural traditions have had to dissolve creatively what Scripture says and choose which account to embrace and which to refrain from embracing. A common shorthand for the competing positions that Christians (and others) have arrived at on salvation's extent is exclusivism and universalism. Exclusivism is the belief that not everyone is saved and has been orthodox longer than dyothelitism and since before Muhammad, but exclusivism must reconstrue all the scriptural texts that say everyone is saved so that Scripture can be interpreted in such a way that it never really says that. Universalism, the dissenting position, is the belief that everyone is ultimately saved and is a persistent heresy, but, so as to prefer wherever Scripture expresses universalism, it must negate the repeated scriptural depictions to the contrary. And, so, that is the problem: Scripture offers a paradox that says *both* everyone will be saved *and* not everyone will be, and all sides have reformulated those accounts into a contradiction so that Scripture, once the exegeting is done, can say only one account or the other.

This is not how the church typically handles scriptural paradoxes. Rather than adopting the tempting nuances that heresies have offered to simplify the scriptural answers, the church has usually offered greater wit. It has accepted such enigmas as God being both one and three and as Christ being both truly divine and truly human, but, unfortunately, by the sixth century, the church had exhausted itself on such paradoxes before understanding salvation's extent and, after recuperating, was beyond fighting over additional ones. As a result, the church settled for the simplicity of contradiction and choose exclusivism, and the second-place finisher, universalism, was only simpler. No part of the church has ever acknowledged that somehow all of Scripture is actually true in saying that both everyone will be saved and not everyone will be. This book purports to do that—accept both contraries on salvation's extent—without unlearning the principle of noncontradiction, and, to do that, the thesis must model the individual as divisible. With this divisibility, each person can be both saved *and* not saved, it is argued, which would then leave Scripture's salvation paradox as it aspires to be, true. Admittedly, dividing the individual, who is practically, normally, and etymologically *in*divisible, is a high price to pay to preserve the paradox, but it is no higher than that paid in order to understand the other scriptural paradoxes. Being both saved and unsaved is not much different from being both one and three or being both human and divine. Each scriptural paradox has been worth the cost of rethinking the irrefutable.

The divisibility of the individual as proposed here is not the conventional one associated with biological death, where the vanishing cadaver leaves an afterlife remainder, typically labeled the soul. What constitutes the personal remainder that may persist after biological death, which is presumably spiritual and definitely not zoological, is left to those dealing with that topic. The thesis in this book divides, rather, whatever the particulars of that remainder turn out to be. Though what is substantively the remainder is not declared, what functionally continues after death is declared and that out of necessity. If we are to live after biological life, what continues must include that which has lived that life, which is usually called our character. Without the continuation of the personal character, those who are saved in eternal life would be none of us, just other people altogether. This personal character, given how we each live, has roughly two paramount outlooks, directions, alignments, mindsets (φρόνημα), or, as broadly termed here, orientations.[1] Our dueling as-lived orientations are roughly that of being godly and of being selfish, whether relating to God favorably or, from pride or cowardice, sinning.[2] The two orientations cohabitate in each of us. This is absolutely incontrovertible for one person and, given the good authority from many others, is confidently presumed of nearly everyone else. To this widely shared observation that the personal character is conflicted in this life, the thesis proposed here adds the novelty that it is divisible afterwards. This unconventional idea takes nine chapters to explain.

Chapter 1 clarifies several preparatory issues required for understanding the salvation paradox, including the meaning of the central issue—ultimate[3] salvation. Ultimate (or final) salvation specifies a quality of this life but also a quality of the life beyond it. That is, salvation is eschatological,[4] "the fulfilment of all time," Karl Barth's phrase.[5] Salvation, while it applies to every moment, is critical in the *ultimate* because it is as of then that everyone is or is not saved and is the context in which the answers of universalism and exclusivism diverge. The first chapter also justifies devoting precious attention to the issue of salvation's extent despite the contemporary sheepishness about preserving paradoxes, including the meaning of death and the objectivity of truth. The dispute about salvation's extent is often deemed too contentious for polite society or too speculative for practical company, but its extent must be

---

1. Fromm, *Man for Himself*, 57–59.

2. Unless explained otherwise, the words used here have their common meanings and usually their most useful ones. "Sin" is no exception. Sin is both relational, which is that which is unloving, and forensic, which is that which violates the standard, but is fundamentally theological, which is that which is contrary to God's will (Jas 2:8–13). McKnight, *James*, 121.

3. "Ultimate" has qualitative and quantitative meanings. Robinson, *In the End, God . . .*, 37. Here, it includes both meanings—fulfillment of purpose and the ending.

4. "Eschatology" is similarly understood here inclusively. Moltmann, *Theology of Hope*, 112. It is both what lasts and what comes last. Harding, *Paul's Eschatological Anthropology*, 68–69, 96.

5. Barth, *Romans*, 498 (13:11–12).

understood because questions demand answers. If questions are not answered intelligently, we have only answers of the other variety. The fundamental hurdle for understanding salvation's extent is that its paradox consists of two scriptural propositions pointing in opposite directions. Happily, scriptural propositions in paradox do not generally intimidate Christians, who believe ideas like dying to live. The paradox of salvation's extent suffers in particular because it pertains to individuals, and this can be associated with "individualism," which Christians can find problematic. Yet too, this association is unavoidable because, as Thomas Aquinas reminds us, individuals cannot be reduced to universals.[6] This is especially true in salvation. We can, Søren Kierkegaard noted, be treated like a herd on other subjects such as innoculations, but not on subjects like salvation.[7] Finally, this chapter identifies the authority for addressing salvation's extent, which means tackling such issues as the relationship of tradition to Scripture.[8]

Chapter 2 outlines the conceptual framework of ultimate salvation in which its paradox rests. While salvation's *extent* is paradoxical, its bewildering *content* has, to the limit of the information available to us, mostly been settled among the Christian faithful: We live with death, then die, and experience the binaries of eternal life for the godly or of perdition for the ungodly. These parameters triangulate the salvation paradox, which is delivered by Jesus, who is a sign of contradiction (ἀντιλεγόμενον) and who produces our division (διαμερισμόν, Luke 2:34; 12:51), which bisects us (διχάσαι, Matt 10:34–35). Though universalists and exclusivists agree that salvation relates to this life and that at least some of us experience eternal life, they disagree whether any of us suffer its negation. This is of course not the only salvation dispute, but the others are left undisturbed because, no matter how they are resolved, the salvation paradox abides in them. For example, whether salvation extends to faith-alone or to faith-plus-works leaves the Christian consensus that godliness, broadly understood, relates to salvation's extent.

Chapter 3 lays out the two scriptural accounts of salvation's extent, and they are, if not paradoxical, undeniably contradictory. The universalism account is well represented in Scripture. There is "one God and

---

6. Schaff, *Marxism and the Human*, 49–50, 53, 84, 107.

7. Kierkegaard, *Sickness unto Death*, 123.

8. "Scripture" refers to the Hebrew Scriptures and the NT. Elwell, ed., *Scripture*, 1915; Geisler, *ST*, 383–402.

Father of *all* who is over *all*, through *all*, and in *all*"⁹ (Eph 4:6), with each "all" being a substantive of πᾶς, the most natural way that the NT has to refer to *everyone*. Because Christ "wills *all* men saved" and "gave himself ransom exchange for *all*" (1 Tim 2:4, 6), "God's grace, saving to all men, *has appeared*" (Titus 2:11), the aorist indicative verb actualizing universal salvation. Paul explains: The salvation of the God-man must be as thorough as the thoroughly infectious sin of the first-man and thereby reach "all men" (Rom 5:12–21). So, God saves "all men, most especially [μάλιστα] those believing" (1 Tim 4:10), which emphasizes that none fewer than everyone is saved. Scripture is, however, equally expressive on exclusivism. The evil are "gathered and burned in" the consummation's "fiery furnace" (Matt 13:24–50). Christ will "separate men from each other" and the cursed will suffer "eternal castigation," a "torment" in "fire" (25:31–46; Luke 16:19–31). Those not abiding in Christ are "like the branch cast away to wither" (John 15:6). While "many" traverse "the way leading to the destruction," only "a few" traverse "the way leading to the life" (Matt 7:13–14). In the end, God's wrath inundates the cosmos, which is likened to Sodom's brimstone and Noah's cataclysm (Luke 17:26–30//Matt 24:37–39), "an example of suffering eternal fire's punishment" (Jude 7). Given these seemingly contradictory accounts, both cannot be true, at least not without more comment. So, both exclusivists and universalists must, in adhering to their respective positions, unwind the paradox by downgrading its opponent's scriptural basis to something that is only facially true, not authentically true. Exclusivists take *all people* as *all believers* so that, wherever Scripture says all people are saved, only all believers are, and universalists take God's wrath as a passing phase so that, wherever Scripture speaks of the damned, no one truly is. This chapter, in contrast, takes the accounts as written without anticipating the logic collision towards which they are evidently bound.

Chapter 4 presents the church's responses to the paradox of salvation's extent. The contesting responses have throughout history been roughly two, and, not coincidently, they follow the two accounts found in Scripture. The two positions were competitive among Christians until the sixth century, which was when exclusivism abruptly prevailed and universalism was anathematized. Because Christians have since grown accustomed to the orthodoxy of that resolution, the chapter must give an extended survey of Christian universalists to counterbalance exclusivism's obvious dominance,

---

9. Scriptural translations are mine.

and confirmation of that dominance comes primarily from Christianity's creeds, which chapter 4 also presents. In reviewing the universalism and exclusivism in the church, the chapter strives for evenhandedness while juggling thoroughness and brevity. The overview finds that 1) universalism gained strength in the second century and lasted until the sixth century, convincing luminaries like Origen of Alexandria, Athanasius the Great, Hilary of Poitiers, Gregory of Nyssa, John Cassian, and Maximus the Confessor, and has more recently flourished as a minority, whose notables have included Friedrich Schleiermacher, Paul Tillich, William Barclay, Jürgen Moltmann, and David Bentley Hart, and 2) exclusivism has more or less predominated since the beginning and has been led by such greats as Justin Martyr, Irenaeus, Cyril of Jerusalem, Basil of Caesarea, Augustine, Chrysostom, Jerome, Gregory the Great, John Damascene, Thomas, Martin Luther, John Calvin, and the authors of every extant Christian confession for over one thousand years and nearly every church order since the *Didache*. No one has yet taken any but these two positions, though a twentieth-century exclusivist subset, with worthies like Barth and Hans Urs von Balthasar, has claimed that universalism is *potentially*, though not actually, true (here designated "potentialism").

Chapter 5 explains why these positions have failed to maintain a consensus, much less extinguish its competition. Each response, in treating its preferred scriptural account as sincerely true, treats its opposite account as only superficially true, all to make Scripture intelligible, though some potentialists say Scripture is unintelligible on this subject. Exclusivists, who are grounded in how obviously Scripture says eternal life is not for everyone, suffer a sort of semantic anomia whenever they encounter scriptural words like *all* in connection with *salvation*. Universalists, on the other hand, have the same sort of motivated perception when it comes to scriptural words like *hell*, *wrath*, *perishing*, *remnant*, or any unqualified imperative. As for potentialists, they mostly say that everyone is saved potentially, which optimistic exclusivists espousing unlimited atonement have been saying all along. The chapter does not referee the theological conflict so much as find that no side convinces when rejecting its opposition. Said differently, much like heresies had tried with the paradoxes of the Trinity and of Christ's natures, each position has deflated Scripture's paradox to one account, while treating the other account as a misdirect, which inevitably gives each position a nagging sense of imbalance. On the positive side, the persistence of each position in the church confirms what a fair read of Scripture clearly yields—both positions on salvation's extent are obviously present.

Chapter 6, the longest, sets the table for the proposal to preserve the salvation paradox as Scripture has presented it, and that argument depends on the individual's divisibility. The chapter reviews the thought history and current perspectives on what we think we know about who we are in this life and about what of this life that perdures into the next. Addressed but found wanting are the views that say the self is a fiction or an organic robot. Instead, the subject is as Richard Wollheim aptly described it after appropriating Kierkegaard—it is one who *leads a life*.[10] And this self is all too reasonably assumed to be indivisible. The body partly explains this assumption, but the body can divide even in this life (*e.g.*, amputation) and always does, at least eventually and then thoroughly, in death. The natural body's most pertinent limitation is that an afterlife[11] lacks one. The individual after death is, if anything, either discarnate[12] or preternatural. This supposed belittlement of the terrestrial physique sounds antiquated and must therefore be addressed repeatedly.[13] Irrespective of the natural body or any other ontological inventory, an individual is incurably a personal character, which consists of memories, beliefs, and preferences from leading a life, and is inherently centered on a personal identity's first-person awareness of that life. Accordingly, an afterlife, to be the self from this life, must include the personal character and, to be experienced, must include the personal identity. And certainly in this life, the personal character is manifestly semi-divided for the healthy (*e.g.*, internal dialogue) and can be pathologically divided for the unhealthy (*e.g.*, dissociative identity disorder). Scripture likewise describes the personal character's orientations as divided in this life: Two

---

10. Wollheim, *Thread of Life*, 1.

11. "Afterlife" has two common meanings: a broad meaning that refers to every existence after this life or a specific meaning that refers to only the intermediate existence between this life and the resurrection. N. T. Wright, *Resurrection*, 30–31. It has the broad meaning here. "Heaven" is avoided as a reference to the afterlife because it tends to refer to the dwelling of God, not of the dead, at least in Scripture (1 Thess 4:16). Gooder, *Heaven*, 79–80. "Afterlife" definitely does not here refer to others continuing to live after a death. Scheffler, *Death and the Afterlife*, 15, 64. That is simply death. Dalferth, *Creatures of Possibility*, 143.

12. "Discarnate" means not having a natural body, but can include having a "subtle body," such as any finite extent from which existence is experienced. Moore, *Where Are the Dead?* 186.

13. Song, *Covenant and Calling*, xv.

ways are choosable, and we each choose both. We are not two beings, but *two modes of being*. As Paul observed, the self is metaphorically two selves by literally living two ways (Rom 7:19–21). So, our character develops as we each live, and, because it is conflicted in this life, the character's divisibility afterwards is almost plausible.

Chapter 7, to finalize the argument, takes what the prior chapters have established. First, according to Scripture, everyone is ultimately saved and not everyone is. Second, according to those whose thoughts find traction in reality, contradictions entail falsehood. So, according to everyone interpreting Scripture, either everyone is ultimately saved or not everyone is. Third, according to those who have candidly explored the individual, each one of them is conceptually, though not actually, divisible in what orients them. These verities, this chapter argues, lead to the ineluctable but unprecedented conclusion: The individual suffers divisibility in the next life. Rather than godly individuals being separated from ungodly ones as tradition sees the separation then, the godly can be separated from the ungodly as to each individual. Accordingly, a single individual can have both eternal life and perdition. In other words, because Scripture says that everyone is saved and that not everyone is saved and because the principle of noncontradiction is adamant, something must give, and that something is the weak link. The *individual* splits. The individual's divisibility differs critically from its purging, which is traditional. Purging is what removes ungodliness from the individual, and, as a consequence, purging does not address the salvation paradox—it damns no one. Dividing an individual, in contrast, results in one who is saved and one who is not. Thus, the thesis, in striving for the orthodoxy of honoring what Scripture says in its entirety, is thereby unorthodox in the sense of beyond belief. Like Christianity generally, the thesis foolishly chooses both sides of Scripture's paradox and scandalously arrives at the incredible. As a result, Scripture's accounts of salvation's extent are not as they have been taken—poorly worded—but are utterly true.

Chapter 8 is defensive. While the thesis is built on the salvation paradox that Scripture presents, this chapter sets out how Scripture hints at the answer that the thesis offers. The scriptural exegesis is mostly original and, hence, probationary, but it exploits the greater literalness that the thesis of afterlife individual divisibility allows. For instance, when Jesus says self-amputation is better than perdition entirely, might he have meant something like that, such as perdition partly (Mark 9:43–49//Matt 18:8–9; 5:29–30)? Jesus adds that he will bring about personal division (διαμερισμόν), which tradition has understood as dividing persons into two groups, one consisting of the unbelieving, but Jesus adds that his division involves one person being divided into two (διχοτομήσει), with one part (μέρος) for the unbelieving (Luke 12:46, 51). The NT also frequently uses ἐάν, which combines *if* (εἰ) with the generally untranslatable contingency of ἄν, and this combination could express a condition in both kind (from *if*) and degree (from ἄν), which English expresses with *to the extent*. So understood, Scripture is explaining that salvation is "to the extent," not merely "if," godly. Further, certain grammar oddities in Scripture, conventionally taken as unproductive, are reexamined and found suggestive. To illustrate, the NT uses *comparative* adjectives for those who are saved and those who are damned, thus expressing degrees of salvation and damnation, though traditionally understood as not really meaning that. The NT also uses neuter nouns (*e.g.*, πᾶν and αὐτὸ), not personal nouns, to describe *what*, not *who*, is saved and damned. In one instance, Jesus says he wants fellowship with *what* (ὃ) the Father has given him (John 17:24). Correct grammar here demands *who* (οὕς), which a few early copyists "corrected" John to, but the best manuscripts kept *what*, which just forced exegetes to interpret it as *who* anyway. Individual division, however, justifies the canonical wording, which is that personal qualities, not persons altogether, are saved. So, dividing a person, which may have at first seemed deranged, is, upon reflection, earnestly so (2 Cor 5:13). The chapter ends with an examination of several theologians, such as universalists like Sergei Bulgakov, potentialists like Balthasar, and exclusivists like Wolfhart Pannenberg, who, without dividing the individual to account for the salvation paradox, resort to descriptions of purging that are similar to division as a way to account for how persons have eternal life despite their endemic ungodliness.

Chapter 9 reviews whether the individual divisibility that is being proposed disturbs any Christian doctrines other than that of salvation's extent, and, conveniently, the thesis requires no further innovations. Dividing the individual after this life changes only those doctrines it intends to, which is actually none. And that includes anthropology because the proposal does nothing to anthropology as it relates to this life, which is naturally the primary focus in both Scripture and tradition, and, as for the afterlife, which is traditionally conceived as involving the individual's purgation and transformation, the proposal merely discerns divisibility among all that metamorphosis. Related to every chapter, but especially this last, are the numerous doctrines that the proposed model leaves undisturbed. For example, not developed here is soteriology, whether its nature or means, or the resurrection, whether Christ's or generally, because addressing such issues is unnecessary for the salvation paradox. More generally, the thesis sidesteps any issue not directly implicated in the paradox of salvation's extent, even when the issue is in the same doctrinal domain, such as what constitutes, comprises, or accounts for being human, the extent to which eschatology is realized or not-yet, whether there is an intermediate state, whether perdition is torment or annihilation, or how the final judgment is administered. One paradox per book is enough.

As this introduction manifests, the approach will be conceptual. That is, while pertinent scholarship will be extensively relied on for premises and context, the book is not a critical evaluation of what any particular theologian thinks or what any comparison or combination of certain theologians produces. While some theologians will rightfully contribute more here than others, none has negotiated the salvation paradox *as a paradox*. On that issue, the position, if the theologian has taken one, has always been either that everyone will be saved, that not everyone will be, or, a purported compromise, that everyone will be saved potentially. In reaching these positions, each side must retreat to its favored ghetto, which is fortified by the obvious Scripture for its preferred expression and is protected by the well-rehearsed exegetics for pounding the other side, but, to nonpartisans, this theological shadowboxing has been unconvincing because Scripture clearly takes both sides, at least until the exegetes do their magic. Therefore, focusing on any theologian or any handful would miss the point, and, so, numerous authorities from a wide variety of backgrounds are counted upon instead. As a further result of what the thesis strives to accomplish, it cannot circumscribe its focus by isolating on any specific set of theologians. The thesis instead relies on the singularity of the salvation paradox for that focus. This means citing broadly the expressed insights of various theologians (and others) without trying to determine with confidence what they thought comprehensively. For us the auditors, the truth comes from the artwork, not the artist,[14] and the truth from the artwork is found without exegeting the rest of the corpus.[15]

And the citations will be unapologetically generous, but they are not presented to make the reasoning more persuasive, though they might

---

14. Heidegger, "Origin of the Work," 167.

15. Greggs, *Barth, Origen, and Universalism*, 13; Jenson, ST, II: vi; Lash, *Easter in Ordinary*, 7.

help those needing a nudge. Rather, the authorities serve as arbiters of the reasoning so as to ensure that the proposal reaches for the outlandish only in its titular conclusion. The reasoning therefore surveys broadly, distilling the scholarship and treating its convergence, but is always motivated by the cultural embarrassment in how the salvation paradox has everywhere been reduced to a mere contradiction. Even if individual divisibility is the wrong approach, this project is called for, certainly beforehand and definitely after. The Gregorys anticipated the sentiment of both the project and the approach. "I do not wish the Word to save only half of me,"[16] even if this means I must be "at once conjoined and separated."[17]

---

16. Gregory of Nazianzus, "Concerning His Own Life," 58–59 (ln 626).
17. Gregory of Nyssa, "Letter 35," ¶ 4 (p. 255).

1

Prolegomena

The ancients used to say: Animals are instructed by their organs. I will add: Men are too, but they have the advantage of being able to instruct their organs in their turn.

—Goethe, 17 Mar. 1832 letter[1]

THIS FIRST CHAPTER STRIVES for a shared beginning on how to approach salvation's extent by obtaining agreement on several preliminary issues through either convincing or concession. To that end, the issue that every chapter explores, which is *salvation*, is defined, because meaning is inseparable from understanding. Then the unruly understanding with which the second half of this discourse works, which is a *paradox*, is upheld because, if true paradoxes are not profoundly true, there has been a misunderstanding, and what the salvation paradox abuses, as it does particularly in chapter 6, which is an *individual*, is explained because, no matter how annoyingly selfish we are, individuals are the selves we are. This first chapter also justifies what abuses the individual as will be seen in chapter 7, which is a *model*, because, whether explicit or implicit, a model is always our best entrance into a new understanding. Finally, this

1. Fairley, "Goethe's Last Letter," 1.

Prolegomena 13

first chapter recognizes the authoritative resources to be used throughout the discourse, which are *Scripture* and any other truth, because not to admit one's starting point is to conceal it. While the issues are several, what unites them beyond their pertinence to salvation's extent is that their affirmations have been dependably true everywhere except for the occasional scholar.

1. The Issue Is Ultimate Salvation

"There is only one way," Socrates observed, "for those to begin who are to take counsel wisely about anything. One must know what the counsel is about, or it is sure to be utterly futile.... [S]ince we are to discuss the question, ... let us first agree on a definition."[2] All sorts of learners have concurred openly with this approach,[3] including Calvin: "I certainly am dull enough to refer everything to the definition as the hinge and foundation of the whole discussion."[4] This is because meaning, which is what a definition aims at, and understanding, which is here the aim, are interrelated.[5] If we are unable or unwilling to explain what we mean when we are trying to contribute with words, then the contribution is bound to get misplaced by the listener, if not the speaker.

So, at the beginning here, the meaning of *salvation* is offered, and the finest definition, at least since Luke the Evangelist contributed to Scripture, is "eternal life" (18:18, 30; Acts 13:46, 48).[6] That is, salvation is what has been given to us, and eternal life is what we then experience. Eternal life is also the meaning that Paul gives salvation,[7] and, more generally, this is the meaning that the NT articulates (*e.g.*, John 6:40).[8] Christian salvation is rightly relating to God, and eternal life is its

---

2. Plato, *Phaedrus* (2017), 237C-D.

3. Allen, *Extent of Atonement*, xxi; Epictetus, *Discourses*, I: I,xvii,12, II,xvii,5–13 (pp. 117, 339–41); Hamann, "Essay on an Academic Question," 11–12 & note a; John, "Fount of Knowledge," I,8 (p. 26).

4. Calvin, *Institutes*, III,4,1 (p. 407).

5. Caputo, *Radical Hermeneutics*, 72, 172–73.

6. Bock, *Acts*, 463; Stein, *Luke*, 315–16.

7. Matera, *Romans*, 142.

8. Bultmann, *Theology of the NT*, II: 41.2 (p. 7).

content.[9] In short, salvation is our living with the Eternal One.[10] Fittingly, in Christ's spoken language of Aramaic, *salvation* and *life* are the same word (*chayyē*).[11]

Like life generally, salvation's eternal life has a beginning and a completion, and, in more theological terms, it is one event with two aspects—justification and sanctification, or being holy and becoming holy.[12] The earthly life experiences salvation fractionally, but that life is in a continuum with salvation ultimately.[13] As widely accepted, therefore, salvation requires not just this life but its end.[14] Said another way, salvation is thoroughly eschatological.[15] While grounded in the present, salvation is future leaning,[16] "the fulfilment of all time," Barth formulated.[17] This does not confuse the way of salvation with its destination,[18] but just makes explicit that salvation is the way to the destination (1 Pet 1:9).[19] One need not side with the mystic's conclusion, "Death is the entrance to eternal life,"[20] to realize that salvation, while beginning with faith in this life, is completed with promise in the next.[21]

With salvation meaning "eternal" life, the rendering of αἰώνιος, the Greek term found in the NT, must be considered because its rendering can be theologically motivated.[22] "Eternal" is its traditional rendering, and using it avoids the lexical detour of another translation. Its use here, however, has more in its favor than tradition and simplicity because "eternal"

---

9. Berkouwer, *Man: Image of God*, 99, 144, 243; Gunton, *Father, Son and Holy Spirit*, 90.

10. Leget, "Eschatology," 369–70; Lossky, *Mystical Theology*, 135.

11. Bruce, *Romans*, 76.

12. Barth, *CD IV/2*, § 66.1 (p. 503); Nichols, *Death and Afterlife*, 153, 160.

13. Mostert, *God and the Future*, 113; O'Collins, "Salvation," 911.

14. Barth, *Romans*, 167 (5:12); Grenz, *Theology for the Community*, 446–47; Gschwandtner, "Fully Alive?" 72; Novello, "New Life," 99, 115, 119; O'Collins, "Salvation," 911–12.

15. Congdon, *God Who Saves*, 64.

16. Colijn, *Images of Salvation*, 125.

17. Barth, *Romans*, 498 (13:11–12).

18. Hoff, "Rise and Fall," 190.

19. Ziegler, *Militant Grace*, 10–11.

20. Speyr, *Mystery of Death*, 82.

21. Boer, *Defeat of Death*, 177; Kierkegaard, *Eighteen Upbuilding Discourses*, 28–29; N. T. Wright, *Surprised by Hope*, 197.

22. D. Hart, *New Testament*, 537–43.

does a decent job of reflecting the range of meaning that αἰώνιος has (at least when that range is acknowledged, as it is here).²³ Αἰώνιος originally meant something like *live much* and came to mean either *unending* or *prolonged* (unlike the metaphysics term ἀΐδιος, which always means *endless*), and, as a result, at least for universalists, αἰώνιος is flexible enough to mean *permanent* when modifying salvation and to mean *temporary* when modifying perdition.²⁴ Such definitional flexibility, however, is not really translating but exegeting, if not subjectifying. The translation issue is what word or, if necessary, words best render αἰώνιος's range of meaning, and "eternal" adequately does that because, by all accounts, αἰώνιος in the NT refers to *eschatological duration*²⁵ or *the world to come*.²⁶ That suits *eternal* because it is derived from the Latin *aeternus*, which means "of an age [*aevum*]," and this gives *eternal* the meaning of perpetual or seemingly so.²⁷ Most importantly, the dispute about the exact meaning and proper translation of αἰώνιος is beside the point when debating the extent of salvation because the contested issue is not how "eternal" salvation's life is, but whether there is a true *obverse* to salvation's eternal life. That is, the issue is whether there is any ultimate outcome that is *not* eternal life, no matter what "eternal" is understood to be precisely. The key word in the context of salvation's extent is thus "life," regardless of how extended in time "eternal" is in that context.

That the contested extent of salvation is not about eternal life, but about its opposite, is made conspicuous by the fact that salvation, though entirely good, implies the opposite of good. Salvation is being saved from something, whether from ourselves or another force. That is, salvation in itself means that there is at least a theoretical alternative to it, indeed an obverse to it, because salvation, while omitting anything negative,²⁸ also evokes the existence of that negation.²⁹ This is consistent with the fact that salvation involves a process leading to a judgment that fixes one's relation to eternal life, an individual's existence in God.³⁰ Thus, the

---

23. Crouzel, *Origen*, 244.
24. Ramelli and Konstan, *Terms for Eternity*, 5–70, 82, 94–95, 114–17, 237–39.
25. BDAG, 33; Guhrt, "Time-αἰών," 826–33; *NIDNTTE*, s.v. "αἰών."
26. Ramelli and Konstan, *Terms for Eternity*, 19.
27. *AHD*, s.v. "eternal"; *OED*, s.v. "eternal."
28. Long, *Perfectly Simple Triune God*, 170.
29. Colijn, *Images of Salvation*, 122, 141; Demarest, *Cross and Salvation*, 26–27; Lossky, *Mystical Theology*, 135.
30. Guardini, *Freedom, Grace, and Destiny*, 226–28.

opposite of salvation—that is, the alternative to eternal life, no matter what "eternal" means exactly—is exclusion from eternal life. Said differently, the obverse of salvation is the ultimate negation (*e.g.*, John 3:16), which is variously termed as perishing, perdition, doom, annihilation, damnation, or the second death.[31] In short, salvation is eternal life, and the absence of salvation is eternal life's negation. And the disputed issue here involves the latter.

2. Salvation's Extent Matters

Despite the acknowledged importance that salvation has for Christians, avoiding the troublesome issue of its extent is de rigueur in contemporary societies, including Christian ones.[32] Previously, the question of who has eternal life was deadly serious.[33] As late as three centuries ago, Joseph Butler could assert, "Whether we are to live in a future state . . . is the most important question which can possibly be asked,"[34] but, after a century of further enlightenment, Kierkegaard detected that "eternal salvation seems to have become what the thought of it has become, a loose and idle phrase, at times virtually forgotten, or arbitrarily left out of the language, or indifferently set aside as an old-fashioned turn of speech," and it is "retained only because it is so quaint."[35] After another century and in the thick of postmodernism, Dietrich Bonhoeffer asked rhetorically, "Hasn't the individualistic question about personal salvation almost completely left us all?"[36] When Balthasar looked back from the other side of the twentieth century's halfway mark, he concluded, "Modern theological thought has largely abandoned the attempt to document this final phase of all theology."[37] The hubris implicit in debating who is and is not saved has become, Moltmann sensed, "'confessional witch-hunting' and banished from public life."[38]

---

31. Demarest, *Cross and Salvation*, 31; Tillich, *ST*, II: 165.
32. Bavinck, *Reformed Dogmatics*, 704; White, *Life Beyond Death*, 2.
33. Bray, *God Has Spoken*, 494.
34. Butler, *Analogy of Religion*, 298.
35. Kierkegaard, *Eighteen Upbuilding Discourses*, 254.
36. Bonhoeffer, *Letters and Papers*, 286.
37. Balthasar, *Theo-Drama*, V: 373.
38. Moltmann, *Theology of Hope*, 307.

The late-modern apathy partly derived from the staleness in the stalemate between universalism and exclusivism.[39] No side in the debate about salvation's extent had so carried the day that the also-rans had to concede the field, and, so, to avoid another *filioque*, Scripture's antimony on salvation's extent became a *mokita*, an unspoken but well-known truth.[40] Honest observers of this conflict, if made to confront the debate, could only concede the obvious: Each side has much in its favor. Yet, both universalism and exclusivism cannot be true. Therefore, Christians, if they treat the issue at all, root for their chosen side based on a tiebreaker, such as a perceived hegemonic hermeneutic.[41]

Whether any answer to salvation's extent is even true became evadable when the skepticism in Pilate's "what's truth?" reappeared.[42] The Nietzscheans answered that truth is nothing, only styles are real,[43] but the straightforward answer to the question has always been that truth is the way things are.[44] None of us, not even a Nietzschean, lives to the contrary, at least not for very long.[45] Whenever anyone claims that the way things are is nonexistent or unknowable, Hegel's reminder that beasts can find food suffices for anyone without a death wish.[46] Truth, though basic, drives thinking,[47] and less truth is less reality.[48] For Christians anyway, truth is apprehending reality.[49] They are to study all that is true (Phil 4:8) and then defend the truth (2 Cor 6:4–7; 1 Tim 3:15) while turning from what is not (Titus 1:13–14). The Spirit of truth is their guide (John 14:17, 26; 15:26; 16:13), and it is Christ, "the Amen" (Rev 3:14), that witnesses to the truth (John 18:37). Thus, Ceslas Spicq with good grounds

---

39. Edwards, *After Death?* 1; D. Hart, *That All Shall Be Saved*, 4–5, 28.

40. Naselli, "Conclusion," 222–23.

41. McClymond, *Devil's Redemption*, II: 1049.

42. Ratzinger, *Truth and Tolerance*, 72.

43. Caputo, *Radical Hermeneutics*, 156–57.

44. Gilson, *Spirit of Mediaeval Philosophy*, 267; Hartshorne, *Logic of Perfection*, 165; Horst, *Cognitive Pluralism*, 12; Locke, *Essay Concerning Human Understanding*, IV,V,2, 9.

45. McGilchrist, *Master and His Emissary*, 151.

46. Arendt, "Willing," 116, 119; Taylor, *Hegel*, 353.

47. Balthasar, *Theo-Logic*, I: 25–27, 35–36, 39, 208; Hamann, "Golgotha and Sheblimini!," 176–77; Rawls, *Theory of Justice*, 3.

48. Plato, *Republic*, 585c.

49. Elster, *Sour Grapes*, 148; Gregory of Nyssa, *Life of Moses*, Bk II (p. 38).

called Christianity "a cult of the truth."[50] For Christians, "Truth is the measure of being and, therefore, the expression of what *is*," Balthasar summarized.[51] What is *not* truth is anything else. Truth is not what works well, though it helps.[52] Nor is truth relative,[53] what feels good,[54] or always pretty.[55] Admittedly, as Nietzsche bemoaned, this understanding of truth restricts human freedom,[56] but reality is like that, obstinately resisting both humanity's reductionism and its relativism.

The better explanation for the modern social censorship surrounding salvation's extent lies in religion's concession to secularism: being judgmental has, without shame, been judged and been judged as oppressive.[57] "The question of our destiny is terrifying, even painful, when we have the naiveté of believing in it," Maurice Blondel complained.[58] So, damnation joined the devil as either a scriptural image or an outmoded distraction, and the extent of damnation joined the Crusades and the Inquisition as Christian evils.[59] As William James discerned when the twentieth century was beginning, "the old-fashioned Christian" concerned "with the salvation of his soul" has become "something sickly and reprehensible rather than admirable...."[60] Even actual death, at least its non-gratuitous variety, has become taboo.[61] The dying are now cordoned off, and the dead are even more hermetically so. Therefore, in the intellectual movements that are the Enlightenment's progeny, salvation's extent is argued wholeheartedly only on scholarship's margins.[62] Polite systematic theologians, when they are not arguing about what another thinker has meant or should have meant, focus on fundamentals like ontology, meaning, or Trinity and

---

50. Spicq, *Theological Lexicon*, I:75.
51. Balthasar, *Theo-Logic*, I: 75.
52. Lash, *Easter in Ordinary*, 87.
53. Moltmann, *Theology of Hope*, 271.
54. James, *Varieties of Religious Experience*, 17.
55. Pater, *Marius the Epicurean*, 263.
56. Nietzsche, "Genealogy of Morals," 3rd, XXIV (p. 287).
57. Moore, *Where Are the Dead?* 220, 225.
58. Blondel, *Action (1893)*, 16 [1].
59. Sedgwick, *Life of Marcus Aurelius*, 247.
60. James, *Varieties of Religious Experience*, 89.
61. Schumacher, *Death and Mortality*, 1.
62. Walls, *Oxford Handbook of Eschatology*, 14–15.

on applications like ecclesiology, liberation, or ethics.[63] Salvation's extent drops between the fundamentals and the applications.[64]

Further, the Nietzschean error that what counts must have utility, which the issue of salvation's extent seemingly lacks, discourages the debate.[65] Salvation's hope is escapism,[66] Marx's opium.[67] When the issue of salvation's extent does surface, pragmatists can respond, "What is its cash-value?"[68] To be worth discussing now, a question must deal with our happiness.[69] But an understanding, even when it lacks an immediate application, is irresistible.[70] So, despite the intellectual headwinds, salvation's extent flares periodically as a topic, and recent decades seem to be one of those times, especially where doctrines are debated more than enforced.[71] Perhaps in reaction to how it had begun, the twentieth century ended up as "the century of eschatology."[72] Interest in salvation's extent has been renewed, which is opportune because each truth matters.[73] Any void in thinking fills with error, not open-mindedness.[74] "It is one of the peculiar qualities of the human mind that, when confronted with a contradiction, it cannot remain passive," Erich Fromm saw.[75] As Franz Rosenzweig observed, "better the rashest hypothesis than a question with a question mark."[76]

More to the point, truth is theology's purpose.[77] "There is nothing," Gregory of Nyssa recognized, "more saving for Christians than true

63. Milbank, *Word Made Strange*, 1–4.
64. Balthasar, *Theo-Drama*, V: 373.
65. Erickson, *Christian Theology*, 45; Guardini, *Freedom, Grace, and Destiny*, 37.
66. Freud, *Future of an Illusion*, 36–38, 63, 69; Pannenberg, "Task of Christian Eschatology," 1 (reporting modern view).
67. Marx, "Contribution to the Critique," 131.
68. James, *Varieties of Religious Experience*, 433.
69. Harari, *Sapiens*, 376–77.
70. Aquinas, *ST*, Part II-II, Q. 180, art. 7, co; Aristotle, *Metaphysics: Books 1–9*, 980a 22; Candler and Cunningham, eds., *Grandeur of Reason*, 2.
71. J. Sanders, "Raising Hell," 267–81.
72. Schwobel, "Last Things First," 217.
73. Gunton, *Father, Son and Holy Spirit*, 74; James, *Essays in Radical Empiricism*, 81.
74. Barth, "Preface to Second Edition," 4.
75. Fromm, *Man for Himself*, 44.
76. Rosenzweig, "Life," 8 (diary 15 Mar. 1906).
77. Grenz, *Theology for the Community*, 1, 4; Martin, *Will Many Be Saved?* 172; Milbank, *Theology and Social Theory*, 217.

theology,"[78] and salvation's extent is no exception. Salvation is not "God's secret will and counsel," Luther wrote, but "revealed to us in His Word."[79] Salvation is the "end of faith" (1 Pet 1:9). Hence, salvation cannot be the McGuffin in the faith story, a prop like the Maltese Falcon that motivates the plot but that is left unexplained.[80] Salvation's extent *is* the plot. It asks *What happens to my relationship with God?*[81] And, if everyone is saved or only some are, this portrays the God doing the saving, whether his holiness or charity, whether his justice or mercy, whether his will or love.[82]

Perhaps as importantly and definitely more immediately, salvation's extent matters to how we live.[83] "The future determines the present," Johann Georg Hamann noted.[84] Only the aspirations in life that are viable serve the outcomes of life.[85] Even in games where the scoring is clear and proximate, the end determines victory or defeat no matter how many ups and downs there are beforehand.[86] The "fundamental structure of our present life can only be understood on the basis of its reaching out towards the future," Karl Rahner reasoned.[87] History fills with the lesson: Whether apostles, medieval greats, or abolitionist evangelicals, those doing the most good in this life think the most about the next.[88] This is because, no matter how difficult life is, its path is endurable when it ends in triumph.[89] Thus, individual eschatology, while it addresses an individual's ending,[90] does not end with the individual.[91] Instead, salvation's extent

---

78. Gregory of Nyssa, "Letter 34," ¶ 1 (p. 246).

79. Luther, *Genesis*, II: 19 (22:15–19).

80. Kristensen, *Body and Hope*, 15–16.

81. Leget, "Eschatology," 373.

82. Badham, *Christian Beliefs*, 74; Congdon, *God Who Saves*, 24; White, *Life Beyond Death*, 37.

83. Balthasar, *Life out of Death*, 14–17; Gillman, *Death of Death*, 247; Moore, *Where Are the Dead?* 218–19.

84. Hamann, "Cloverleaf," 46.

85. Milbank, *Theology and Social Theory*, 173; Mostert, *God and the Future*, 23; Watkin, "Kierkegaard—Dying," 52–55.

86. Pannenberg, "Constructive and Critical Functions," 124; *What Is Man?* 43–44.

87. Rahner, "Eschatology," 435.

88. Jobes, "Remember These Things," 202; Lewis, *Mere Christianity*, 104.

89. Kierkegaard, *Upbuilding Discourses*, 304; Walsh, *Living Christianly*, 125.

90. Walls, *Oxford Handbook of Eschatology*, 4.

91. Yu, *Being and Relation*, 171, 180.

tells each of us, the self-absorbed, what lasts to the end.[92] "Read your own obituary notice," Joyce teased, "you live longer."[93] Sensing the end enables us to work towards it.[94]

Otherwise human destiny is nothingness.[95] James observed, "Back of everything is the great spectre of universal death, the all-encompassing blackness.... This sadness lies at the heart of every merely positivistic, agnostic, or naturalistic scheme of philosophy."[96] Atheists accept that "Absolute peace prevails only in the graveyard," but, for blatant reasons, also accept that "To a believer,... life is always meaningful."[97] Paul agreed (1 Cor 15:19).[98] Kierkegaard discerned, "the most appalling meaning is not as appalling as meaninglessness, and this is all the more dreadful, the more thoughtlessly it smiles."[99] Life, therefore, is richer when goodness is known to last.[100] Accordingly, ultimate salvation exposes the meaning in this life, not devalues that life.[101]

3. The Salvation Paradox Infringes Commonplace Logic

Like all paradoxes, the paradox of salvation's extent consists of propositions, which can put off those who deny that propositions express truth, at least important ones,[102] but, if we are to engage in the critical task of communicating truths, we must use propositions.[103] Indeed, propositions are inescapable when pursuing truth, including that proposition, whether true or false. To forsake propositions is like forsaking

---

92. Becker, *Denial of Death*, 2, 5; Kempis, *Imitation of Christ*, I,XXI,5, XXIV,1, XXV,10; Scheffler, *Death and the Afterlife*, 22.

93. Joyce, *Ulysses*, 109.

94. Frankl, *Man's Search for Meaning*, 73; Kierkegaard, *Eighteen Upbuilding Discourses*, 70, 347.

95. Brunner, *Eternal Hope*, 96.

96. James, *Varieties of Religious Experience*, 136–38.

97. Schaff, *Marxism and the Human*, 243, 253.

98. Kierkegaard, *Upbuilding Discourses*, 228–29.

99. Kierkegaard, *Stages*, 359.

100. Küng, *Eternal Life?* 197.

101. Kierkegaard, *Purity of Heart*, 120; Ratzinger, *Eschatology*, 100–101.

102. Gilson, *Being and Some Philosophers*, 190; A. Williams, *Architecture of Theology*, 164.

103. Hobbes, *Leviathan*, I,4 (p. 12); Wittgenstein, *Philosophische Untersuchungen*, §§ 136, 225.

questions, right? The forming of propositions may be our brain's signature achievement,[104] and reality without propositions certainly becomes even more hazardous because, it can be said, *crocodiles are lethal*.[105] Anti-propositionalists, at least those expressing themselves, usually prove the value of propositions when they use them to repudiate them and also when they offer a replacement that amounts to another proposition. The anti-propositionalist Stanley Grenz, for instance, says "propositionalists" do "not give adequate attention to the contextual nature of theology" and, so, prefers that "the propositions of systematic theology find their source and aim in the identity and life of the community it serves."[106] Barth, who understood God's revelation as personal, not propositional,[107] took six million words and an untold number of propositions to dogmatize that revelation.[108] Thus, this writing, like those of propositionalists and of anti-propositionalists, uses propositions and, unlike the latter, does not offer the bait-and-switch of a proposition-free safe-space.[109] "[A] man must delight in assertions or he will be no Christian," Luther concluded, "Take away assertions and you take away Christianity."[110] Propositions follow from belief (2 Cor 4:13), and God speaks them to us.[111]

Admittedly, even avid users of propositions can be discouraged by the particular proposition that is being proposed here to preserve the salvation paradox, which is that individuals are divisible after this life such that each can be saved to the extent godly (or righteous, faithful, justified, or whatever brands that which bears eternal life) and not saved as to the remainder. The discouragement is coincident with the fact that no one in the church has ever corroborated that proposition.[112] Not even a heretic has corroborated it. This is no brag about the novelty of the thesis to justify its contribution to scholarship, but is a concession of profound

---

104. Panksepp, *Affective Neuroscience*, 332.

105. Chomsky, *Reflections on Language*, 184–85; Pinker, *Enlightenment Now*, 353–55; Wittgenstein, *Philosophische Untersuchungen*, § 241.

106. Grenz, *Theology for the Community*, 5–8.

107. Barth, *CD I/1*, § 5.2 (esp. p. 137).

108. Ramm, *Pattern of Authority*, 98.

109. Henry, *God, Revelation and Authority*, I: 190.

110. Luther, "De Servo Arbitrio," 105–6.

111. Carson, *Divine Sovereignty*, 22.

112. Olson, *Mosaic of Christian Belief*, 200, 225; Ratzinger, *Eschatology*, 130; W. Taylor, "Humanity, NT View," 321.

unease.[113] Outside of fiction, the loner who claims that the well-dressed emperor is naked is bound to be mistaken, if not also demented. Certainly, that Christian tradition has gone two millennia without employing or even disavowing individual divisibility for the salvation paradox should disallow the thesis—the hedge "should" is necessary only because tradition remains open.[114] The etymology of *individual* (the indivisible) also seemingly disqualifies the thesis.[115] Indeed, that any one person could be two persons sounds more like science fiction, even comedy, than theology.[116] These all express the same sensible objection: Theologians, users of *individual*, and anyone with a sense of self naturally expect one individual per individual.

This sensible view has, however, sensible limits, as will be discussed thoroughly in chapter 6. True, the body's one face and other singularities resist the individual's non-destructive division, and each first-person perspective is inherently indivisible. The thesis here denies neither observation. Rather, the thesis will divide who the individual is, which is the personal character, but this individual divisibility is only barely less counterintuitive. That the divisibility of the individual infringes our intuition is, however, only an internal alert of strangeness,[117] and strangeness, fortunately, indicates falsehood inconsistently and is especially unreliable in paradoxes and other God disclosures.[118] Christians are, as examples, to celebrate God's death by drinking his blood (John 6:53–56)[119] and, more incredibly, to love their enemies (Matt 5:44; Luke 6:27).[120] Counterintuitive is clearly no problem for Christians.[121] They also die and yet live, retaining identity without contradiction,[122] which is, Luther noted,

---

113. Fudge, *Fire That Consumes*, 5.

114. Blondel, "History and Dogma," 276; Long, *Perfectly Simple Triune God*, xi; Lossky, *Mystical Theology*, 112.

115. Gilson, *Spirit of Mediaeval Philosophy*, 198; Mitchell, *Being and Participation*, I: 379.

116. Crosby, *Selfhood*, 65; Guardini, *World and the Person*, 114–15.

117. Horst, *Cognitive Pluralism*, 249.

118. Dunning, *Grace, Faith, and Holiness*, 178.

119. Kierkegaard, *Concluding Unscientific Postscript*, I: 176.

120. Boyd, "Christus Victor View," 38.

121. Kierkegaard, *Practice in Christianity*, 79, 82; Nicholas, "Learned Ignorance," 158 [III,Ltr,264].

122. Lewis, *Between Cross and Resurrection*, 76.

a "monstrous manner of speaking."[123] Christians are in particular no stranger to strange arithmetic involving the first whole number: God is three in *one*, Christ is two in *one*,[124] the many faithful are *one* in Christ,[125] and a married couple is *one*.[126] Two individuals from *one* should fit in nicely. For the Christian, as well as for the scientist or philosopher, facts are not rejected when they are counterintuitive,[127] but only when they are counterfeit (1 John 2:27).[128]

Strangeness, therefore, should not discourage the quest and might even be a positive. Whether through Copernicus, Galileo, Newton, Einstein, or Paul, strangeness is inane until insightful.[129] To the anti-Christian, "Christianity sides with everything idiotic,"[130] but, to Montaigne, "A man must be a little mad if he does not want to be even more stupid."[131] The master of the absurd recognized that "there is nothing that requires as gentle a treatment as the removal of an illusion,"[132] while the master of the lucid concluded that Christian claims "about something behind the world" are "bound to be difficult—at least as difficult as modern Physics, and for the same reason."[133] Hence, paradoxes appear as madness,[134] as does Christian salvation itself, which has been deemed humorous,[135] even folly (1 Cor 1:18). Salvation by its nature, Josephine Gabelman observed, "involves wandering beyond the given, and straying outside the possible," and its ultimate, where "the limits of reality are altered," must appear now very much like "nonsense."[136] This is challenging, but

---

123. Luther, *Galatians*, 169 [WA401,283 (2:20)].
124. Fagerberg, "Foreword," ii.
125. Zizioulas, *Being as Communion*, 145–47.
126. Schindler, *Perfection of Freedom*, 383.
127. Aquinas, *Faith, Reason and Theology*, Q. 1, art. 4, s.c. 2 (p. 31); Hartshorne, *Logic of Perfection*, 29.
128. Lewis, *Mere Christianity*, 33; Moore, *Where Are the Dead?* 222.
129. Fraassen, *Empirical Stance*, 65, 111–15, 151; Wiles, *Making of Christian Doctrine*, 174.
130. Nietzsche, "Anti-Christ," 52 (p. 51).
131. Montaigne, "Essays," III,9 (p. 761).
132. Kierkegaard, *Point of View*, 43.
133. Lewis, *Mere Christianity*, 121.
134. Westphal, *Becoming a Self*, 68.
135. J. Betz, *After Enlightenment*, 69.
136. Gabelman, *Theology of Nonsense*, 183–84.

so be it. "Christianity is the paradoxical truth," Kierkegaard reminded.[137] "Although it may be beautiful," he conceded, "to want to help people to become Christians by making it easy, I venture according to my poor ability to take on the responsibility of making it difficult, as difficult as possible, yet without making it more difficult than it is."[138]

4. "Individual" Is the Lesser Embarrassment

The issue of salvation's extent pertains to individual eschatology, which means the thesis uses the concept of "individual." Though the term may discomfort some, it fits here, certainly better than the alternatives, and any neologism for a concept that is expressed every day is offensive literarily. The term's lexical target is a familiar one: It is who I am, who you are, and, if anyone else is listening in, them too.[139] For this idea, the standard alternatives to *individual* are *person*, *self*, or *human* [being].[140] The concept of *person* and *self* can be considered together here because *person* implies *self*-awareness.[141] For the topic at hand, this concept of the person/self is both overinclusive and underinclusive. It is overinclusive for including such entities as divines, angels, martians, and corporations[142] and possibly certain non-human primates and cetaceans[143] and extremely advanced artificial intelligences.[144] The noun *individual* desirably excludes these.[145] The person/self is also underinclusive by connoting rationality or moral responsibility,[146] which, if consistently applied independent of the human species (discussed next), excludes incompetents

---

137. Kierkegaard, *Book on Adler*, 37.
138. Kierkegaard, *Concluding Unscientific Postscript*, I: 381.
139. Baker, *Persons and Bodies*, 11.
140. Olson, *Mosaic of Christian Belief*, 266; Schaff, *Marxism and the Human*, 94; Zizioulas, *Being as Communion*, 105–6, 226.
141. Crosby, *Selfhood of the Human*, 1; Gerson, *Knowing Persons*, 14; Perry, *Identity*, 189–91.
142. Baker, "Materialism with a Human Face," 162; Jenson, *ST*, II: 95–96; Lee, "Standing Accused," 90–114.
143. LeDoux, *Synaptic Self*, 27–28.
144. Hafner et al., "Prerequisites for an Artificial Self," 1–10.
145. Baker, *Persons and Bodies*, 10 n.19.
146. Baker, *Persons and Bodies*, 148–49; Boethius, "Contra Eutychen," III,5, 87 (pp. 84–85, 90–91); Eshleman, "Moral Responsibility."

like infants,[147] and incompetents are clearly part of the group at issue in salvation's extent, at least historically. *Individual* as a noun, in contrast, only necessitates creaturely experience.[148]

A *human*, when not synonymous with a person or self,[149] is a member of a specific species of animal, classically the rational or religious kind[150] or, more profanely, "an animal belonging to the genus *Homo*."[151] Yet, because our topic includes the afterlife, which is when none of us are likely to be confused for mammals with large brainpans procreating fertile homo sapiens,[152] *human* needlessly engages with those disagreeing about that concept's parameters. Even those who agree that someone previously human continues in the afterlife will debate whether a human *qua* human is continuable then given the obvious discontinuance of its defining characteristic, the human body.[153] *Individual*, in contrast, usefully references the continuity, whatever it is understood to be, without positing human continuation.[154] And what it means to be human is contentious because the concept derives from *universalizing* who we are,[155] while what an individual is derives from *extrapolating* who we are, which is easier and less dogmatic.[156] *Individual* is you, me, and anyone else joining our group without disputing about the hard cases, but *human* universalizes that group, which requires ascertaining human nature, which is a disputed issue.[157] *Individual* conceptually reserves that dispute, and this is another reason why *individual* works so well here since our taxon is inconsequential to the central issue of salvation's extent.

Combining these alternative terms could be worth considering as the reference, but such combinations are wordy and can invite the

---

147. Brookins, "Greco-Roman Perspectives," 57–58.
148. Schiller, "Letters on the Aesthetical," 92 (Ltr XX); Volf, *After Our Likeness*, 82.
149. Eastman, *Paul and the Person*, 12–14.
150. Dalferth, *Creatures of Possibility*, 9, 19; Visala, "Human Cognition," 93.
151. Harari, *Sapiens*, 5.
152. Crosby, *Selfhood of the Human*, 11; Perry, *Identity*, 148; Pieper, *Death and Immortality*, 35–36.
153. Brower, *Aquinas's Ontology*, 280–87; Toner, "Thomas Aquinas on Death," 587–99.
154. Adorno, *Minima Moralia*, 150 [ch 97]; Brower, *Aquinas's Ontology*, 292–300.
155. Stuurman, *Invention of Humanity*, 553.
156. Kierkegaard, *Concluding Unscientific Postscript*, I: 490; *Two Ages*, 82–83; *Stages*, 488–89.
157. Chomsky, *Reflections on Language*, 125–34; Perry, *Identity*, 148–51.

components' respective problems. That said, *each human person* identifies the target normally, but English has a single word that does the same job at least as well as this amalgamation without the wordiness.[158] In a sense, *individual* bridges the two competing but similar concepts of *human* and *person*[159] and thereby compensates for their respective weaknesses. At least as importantly, *individual* also continues to work, as noted above, under the abnormal circumstance of the afterlife, which is here not a peripheral issue. A human or a person, either of whom may become incomplete through death's destruction of the earthly body because it is a part of what it means to be a human or a person, can still be an individual.[160] Therefore, *individual* best fits the subject here.

Despite being the best term, *individual* can nevertheless be problematic when it is associated with individualism—the belief that the individual is the center of existence.[161] Avoiding individual because of individualism, however, is word bigotry,[162] like avoiding science because of scientism. Christianity, even if no other ideology does, both elevates the self and renounces the supremacy of selfishness.[163] Christianity rejects narcissism, not Narcissus.[164] Indeed, it is the individual as a concept that recognizes that the individual as a reality is not a means to a collective.[165] Christianity's great advocate praised "self-sacrificing unselfishness,"[166] as its great detractor accepted that it was "heathens" who had difficulty with *individual*.[167] Christians, therefore, can safely use *individual* because they know it is neither the be-all nor nothing at all.[168]

Some Christians nonetheless worry that focusing on the individual occasions an individualistic focus, which dethrones the community as

---

158. *AHD*, s.v. "Individual."

159. Schumacher, *Death and Mortality*, 20–23.

160. Haan and Dahm, "Aquinas on Separated Souls," 589–637.

161. Gergen, "Social Construction of Self," 644; Williams and Bengtsson, "Personalism."

162. Pfuetze, *Self, Society, Existence*, 335.

163. Barth, *Romans*, 467 (12:16); Basil, "Asketikon," LR 7 ¶ 1; Maston, "Enlivened Slaves," 158.

164. A Narcissus was patriarch of Jerusalem (Aelia Capitolina) from 185 to 212. Crouzel, *Origen*, 15.

165. Buber, *Way of Man*, 31–32; Hartshorne, *Logic of Perfection*, 121, 145.

166. Kierkegaard, *Works of Love*, 335.

167. Feuerbach, *Essence of Christianity*, I,XVI (p. 151).

168. Peguy, *Temporal and Eternal*, 117.

the premier consideration and leads to sinning against others.[169] In a view traceable to Hegel,[170] Christians can argue that everything, even God and certainly creatures, exists only via relationships, which basically means that individuals are merely the components in what really exists.[171] This view, however, that the individual lacks an independent existence or that the idea of *individual* should be suppressed for communal reasons does not match the reality that individuals everywhere have lived in and descanted for millennia.[172] The distinction between one's self and everything else seems to be humanity's most basic thought.[173] We experience *I am* different from *you are* or *it is*.[174] Though both arrive as experience, the first arrives as existence, and the rest arrives as knowledge.[175]

Even in life's first few months, we appreciate attention given to ourselves as compared to others, and we sense how to return individually the attention we have received individually.[176] Already in infancy, we singularize solid objects and recognize that the discontinuously moving solids are agents, and, before age five, we realize that some agents have different beliefs than we do.[177] Ever onward throughout life, individuals experience individually, even in experiencing others.[178] The conundrum of *Do others see what I see?* such as *Is your blue the same color as mine?* seems to be *no*,[179] but, even if the answer were later to change, the fact that we thought to ask the question at all says enough to realize that we each are an individual. "That unsharable feeling which each one of us has of the pinch of his individual destiny," James noted, "may be disparaged for its egotism, may be sneered at as unscientific, but it is the one thing that fills up the measure of our concrete actuality, and any would-be existent that should lack such a feeling, or its analogue, would be a piece of reality only

---

169. Caldecott, *Radiance of Being*, 91; Cavanaugh, "Beyond Secular Parodies," 184; Oakes, *Theology of Grace*, 82–91.

170. C. Taylor, *Hegel*, 40.

171. Eastman, *Paul and the Person*, 19, 75; McInroy, *Balthasar on the Spiritual*, 180; Zizioulas, *Being as Communion*, 17–18, 36–37, 87–88.

172. Arendt, "Karl Jaspers," 88–89; Dalferth, *Creatures of Possibility*, 169–70.

173. Fichte, *Vocation of Man*, 63; Wiles, *Making of Christian Doctrine*, 18.

174. Husserl, *Ideas*, 80 (pp. 214–15); Krapiec, *I-Man*, 324.

175. Kierkegaard, *Concluding Unscientific Postscript*, I: 316.

176. Reddy, *How Infants Know Minds*, 115, 124.

177. Horst, *Cognitive Pluralism*, 49–57, 141.

178. Ludlow, *Universal Salvation*, 149; R. Williams, *Christian Theology*, 153.

179. Lafer-Sousa et al., "Striking Individual Differences," R545–46.

half made up."[180] This sense of individuality, which chapter 6 explores in depth, is common to humans everywhere at all times, though it can be nearly lost *in extremis* such as in the conditions of Nazi concentration camps,[181] severe schizophrenia,[182] and, taking their objections as sincerely held, a few schools of thought.

Because of the common sense that we are individuals, ancient philosophy's *Know thyself* is in the singular, both to whom and about whom it speaks.[183] It is also why no one but you is taking in this thought now for you. "A self is not a thing that may or may not exist," wrote Tillich, but "an original phenomenon."[184] "We cannot literally bring into being another person that was not there before simply by relating to the thing that is there," W. N. Clarke agreed, "Try doing this with a rock...."[185] Individuals establish relationships and not the converse.[186] An autistic child, a practical example, can have a well-developed self-awareness without well-developed relationships.[187] Individuals, not groups, are sentient.[188] And individuals actually live; relationships do so only metaphorically.[189] Accordingly, the claim, "You have to be addressed as a subject to become one,"[190] is as false as its refinement is true: You have to be addressed as a subject to realize it.[191] We are addressed *as* subjects because we *are* subjects. Our sense of self "arises from the betweenness," psychiatrist Iain McGilchrist observed, "Yet the paradox is that those feelings only arise because of our distinctness, our ability to be separate, distinct individuals,

---

180. James, *Varieties of Religious Experience*, 489–90.

181. Frankl, *Man's Search for Meaning*, 50.

182. McGilchrist, *Master and His Emissary*, 332.

183. Epictetus, *Discourses*, II: III,i,25 (p. 15).

184. Tillich, *ST*, I: 169.

185. Clarke, *Person and Being*, 58.

186. Highet, *Man's Unconquerable Mind*, 80; Kapriev, "Conceptual Apparatus of Maximus," 179; Watkin, "Kierkegaard—Dying," 3.

187. Hobson, "Autism and the Self," 572–74, 585; Reddy, *How Infants Know Minds*, 146.

188. Pinker, *Enlightenment Now*, 10–11.

189. Crosby, *Selfhood of the Human*, 122–23; Hartshorne, *Logic of Perfection*, 16, 122, 212; Henry, *Material Phenomenology*, 119–21.

190. Reddy, *How Infants Know Minds*, 32.

191. Jopling, *Self Knowledge*, 166; Pannenberg, *Anthropology in Theological Perspective*, 516.

that come, that go, in separation and death."[192] The individual "possesses its act of existing," Thomas discerned, "For universals do not exist in the universe of things insofar as they are universals, but only inasmuch as they are individuated."[193] The individual, even if a relations ensemble, is the baseline.[194] John Rawls, who set out to rationalize a regime of policed social justice, thus accepted that the individual's "inviolability" was such that "even the welfare of everyone else cannot override" it.[195]

Admittedly, living as an individual requires others.[196] The more ladened concept behind *person* or *self* certainly requires others for the concept to emerge.[197] Even imagining a relationless individual looks impossible.[198] Those forswearing the individual's existence often confuse this organic limitation for its existential dependency,[199] but individuals can exist apart from actuating relationships.[200] A child whose existence absolutely depends on a parent, at least at some point, can exist without her, as most of us prove eventually. Similarly, entities owing their existence to God can exist opposed to him.[201] It is said too often that "conceiv[ing] of an entirely isolated individual" is "impossible,"[202] but we know this is false because we reject solipsism only after conceiving of it. Furthermore, relating personally requires a person.[203] Meister Eckhart observed, "'The other' is the *terminus a quo*, 'the self' is the *terminus ad quem*."[204]

If the complaint against *individual* is merely that one must use another concept to explain it, then the complaint is unresolvable because

---

192. McGilchrist, *Master and His Emissary*, 303.

193. Aquinas, *Quaestiones De Anima*, Q. 1, ad. 2 (p. 49).

194. Schaff, *Marxism and the Human*, 49–50, 53, 84, 107.

195. Rawls, *Theory of Justice*, 28.

196. Kreppner et al., "Normality and Impairment," 931–46; Mooney, "Pseudonyms and 'Style,'" 201.

197. Buber, *I and Thou*, 62–65; Dalferth, *Creatures of Possibility*, 30–31.

198. Zizioulas, *Being as Communion*, 105.

199. Hartshorne, *Logic of Perfection*, 136; Wallenfang, *Human and Divine Being*, 174–77.

200. Dalferth, *Creatures of Possibility*, 6; Guardini, *World and the Person*, 129; Pfuetze, *Self, Society, Existence*, 254, 300.

201. Aquinas, *De Potentia*, Q. 5, art. 1 (p. 134); Dahl, *Resurrection of the Body*, 101; Volf, *After Our Likeness*, 184–85.

202. McConville, *Being Human*, 58.

203. Pfuetze, *Self, Society, Existence*, 334.

204. Eckhart, "John," 146.

Prolegomena

no other concept does better. Apart from explanations, however, conceiving of a coherent idea such as *individual* (contra *married bachelor*) is a matter of will. Even conceiving of a concept's inconceivability involves conceiving it. Those having trouble in this case can conceive of two individuals in one relationship and then subtract one individual. When this happens, though what remains has lost a great deal, what remains is still an individual.²⁰⁵ No mathematics, nor any other operation, yields one relationship of zero individuals. It cannot be done, Rudolf Bultmann noted, because, as an individual, "I am I, of course, not as an isolable and objectifiable world-phenomenon but I am I in my particular existence . . . ."²⁰⁶

Scripture, while never using the word *individual* (e.g., ἄτομος),²⁰⁷ uses a thousand times its passé locution—*man*²⁰⁸ or, to emphasize individuality, *son of man*.²⁰⁹ Scripture also uses countlessly the primary words that every language has for an individual—*you* and *I*.²¹⁰ Accordingly, all the personages are singular in the first divine command to love *your* God, in the second command to love the other as *yourself* (Matt 22:37–39//Mark 12:30–31//Luke 10:27; also Deut 6:5; Lev 19:18), and in Paul's proclamation that "I [ἐγώ]" live in the faith and "this Son of God loved me [με] and gave himself over for me [ἐμοῦ]" (Gal 2:20).²¹¹ God loves singularly,²¹² reaching the self's *con-science* (συν-είδησις, 2 Cor 1:12; Heb 9:14; 1 Pet 2:19).²¹³ This explains Jesus' extraordinary attention to the individual and why he advised evaluation of the self (Matt 7:3–5// Luke 6:41–42).²¹⁴ It is over the one, not the ninety-nine, that is the greater joy (15:4–7//Matt 18:12–14). Jesus too, according to every account, was

---

205. Epictetus, *Discourses*, I: II,v,26 (p. 245).

206. Bultmann, *Theology of the NT*, II: epil. 1 (p. 239).

207. The NT does use once an inflection of the root, but it is in the neuter so that it means, not an individual person, but an individual thing, specifically an indivisible unit of time, a moment (1 Cor 15:52).

208. Gerson, *Knowing Persons*, 14; Gundry, *Soma in Biblical Theology*, 84, 156. The NT and the Septuagint use ἄνθρωπος 1,950 times. *NIDNTTE*, s.v. "anthropos."

209. Nickelsburg, *Resurrection, Immortality, and Eternal Life*, 281, 293.

210. Goddard, "Natural Semantic Metalanguage Approach," 462; McConville, *Being Human*, 202; Zizioulas, "On Being a Person," 35.

211. Demarest, *Cross and Salvation*, 194.

212. Barth, *CD II/2*, § 35.1 (p. 313).

213. Arendt, "Thinking," 5; Hahn, "Conscience," 348–51; Wall, "Conscience," 1128.

214. Henry, *Incarnation*, 248; Sloterdijk, *Critique of Cynical Reason*, 40.

an individual.[215] As Balthasar recognized, "community must begin in particularity; moreover, it must continue in particularity, for this is how Christ's path began, proceeded—and ended."[216] Günther Bornkamm summarized, "in principle it is not proper to speak of man and his concerns in collective and general terms, but only of him as an individual."[217] Barth similarly, "the individual is not a 'part,' but is himself the 'whole.'"[218] Christian responsibility for the importance of the individual is, therefore, no coincidence.[219]

The individual has enhanced importance in the understanding of salvation because the consensus is that Christian salvation concerns individuals.[220] Without individuals, no *One* saves any*one*. To illustrate, when God gave his Son to save "everyone," it was to save the singular (πᾶς, John 3:16). Jesus' salvation parables also emphasize this individualized understanding of salvation (Matt 13:47–50; 25:1–13).[221] As Kierkegaard observed, salvation is not "distributed in bulk."[222] "In eternity you will look in vain for the crowd."[223] The "Omniscient One, even though he surely can maintain an overview better than anyone else, does not want the crowd. He wants only the single individual."[224] God wills "to have Is."[225] "People can be put to death *en masse*, sprayed *en masse*, flattered *en masse*—in short, in many ways they can be treated as cattle, but they cannot be judged as cattle, for cattle cannot come under judgment. No matter how many are judged, if the judging is to have any earnestness and truth, then each individual is judged."[226]

While it has been argued here that *individual* is the best term for the topic, this argument has also proven in an indirect way that tolerance is

---

215. Blondel, "History and Dogma," 244.
216. Balthasar, *Theo-Drama*, III: 447 (emphasis removed).
217. Bornkamm, *Paulus*, 129.
218. Barth, *Romans*, 441, 443 (12:3–5).
219. Lash, *Easter in Ordinary*, 148; Pannenberg, *Human Nature*, 14, 26.
220. Brunner, *Eternal Hope*, 148, 168–69; Grenz, *Theology for the Community*, 581; Lubac, *Catholicism*, 326; Pannenberg, *ST*, III: 541–43.
221. Bulgakov, "Lamb of God," 114; Lubac, *Catholicism*, 206–7.
222. Kierkegaard, *Concluding Unscientific Postscript*, I: 130.
223. Kierkegaard, *Purity of Heart*, 185, 191.
224. Kierkegaard, *Upbuilding Discourses*, 127.
225. Kierkegaard, *JP*, IV: ¶ 4350.
226. Kierkegaard, *Sickness Unto Death*, 123.

a virtue when the issue is terminology.[227] Consistently using even a well-distinguished term in this area is intractable, if not pointless,[228] as Locke also unwittingly demonstrated.[229] Therefore, the hobgoblin of little minds will be shunned on this concept, and various terms, such as person, self, I/me, you, human, ego, soul, spirit, heart, or mind, will be (and have been) used for the same lexical reference for what is the unanimously felt pocket outside of which is everything else.[230] That said, this calibrates best in English to "individual," and, so, that is the primary term, *sit venia verbo*.

5. Models Suit Paradoxes

If an individual is who we each are, then dividing one can seem grotesque,[231] though perhaps no more so than the passion. Any sense of revulsion from the thesis, however, is likely from taking the proposed division too lightly, as if it merely involved the guillotining of flesh. The individual's divisibility as proposed here is deeper, and, for that reason, what is proposed has to be a model. The cognitive dissonance comes not from using a model, but derives from replacing the ordinary model of an *in*divisible individual. Using a model of some kind is unavoidable when trying to understand the hardly understood,[232] which is what the *individual* clearly is.[233] As chapter 6 discusses, it is by violating the *in*divisibility version of the model, which works so well in daily life, that makes the proposed model of individual divisibility counterintuitive.[234] A model of some variety is unavoidable, whether explicitly or implicitly, because individual divisibility involves the not (yet) understood and because models connect truth and understanding by using a relatively

---

227. Fraassen, *Scientific Representation*, 86; Plato, *Republic*, 533e.

228. Barresi and Martin, "History as Prologue," 33–34; Noonan, "Personal Identity and Its Perplexities," 89.

229. Locke, *Essay Concerning Human Understanding*, II,xxvii,9.

230. Gregor, *Philosophical Anthropology*, 14; Husserl, "Author's Preface," 14; Pannenberg, *Anthropology in Theological Perspective*, 128.

231. "[G]rotesqueness is constituted by . . . the paradoxical . . . ." Kayser, *Grotesque in Art*, 53.

232. Lonergan, *Method in Theology*, 285; Morrison, *Reconstructing Reality*, 122–23; Soskice, *Metaphor and Religious Language*, 60.

233. Aquinas, *Division and Methods*, Q. 6, art. 2, reply to opp. arg. 1 (p. 70).

234. Horst, *Cognitive Pluralism*, 255–56.

known thing so as to explain a relatively unknown thing, which is to link ontology and metaphor.[235]

Words themselves, Aristotle noted, come in three basic types: *ordinary* ones that impart existing knowledge, *strange* ones that simply puzzle, and *metaphorical* ones that "get hold of something fresh."[236] The last type is a must in discussions concerning God because the first is hardly ever sufficient and the second is hardly ever helpful.[237] Instead, God-related discussions must probe the ultimate without infringing its invisibility.[238] As a result, mere words glance off the Absolute,[239] which has forced scriptural words into metaphors like the divine *he*,[240] the *Begotten*,[241] or the *Way, Word*, and *Truth*.[242] Metaphors are acutely required in taking on paradoxes,[243] whether they pertain to the afterlife[244] or salvation,[245] and underlying any such metaphor is a model.[246] Models and their metaphors are needed to explain because, without them, too much is going on to *under-stand*, which itself represented once upon a time a model-based metaphor.[247] Scripture, as it communicates at one level to penetrate to another, is itself a model.[248] Scripture, Jüngel noted, is "The translation of the model of human speech to God," and its parables are similar to models, except that parables are metaphors with plot while models are metaphors with architecture.[249]

---

235. Lakoff and Johnson, *Metaphors We Live By*, 5; Soskice, *Metaphor and Religious Language*, 1, 6, 15.

236. Aristotle, *Rhetoric*, III.10, 1410b10–13.

237. Bray, *God Has Spoken*, 304; Jüngel, *God as the Mystery*, 6, 281.

238. Charlton, *Non-Dualism*, 1; Hamann, "Socratic Memorabilia," NII,64,14 (p. 382).

239. Barth, *Romans*, 530 (15:15).

240. Lash, *Easter in Ordinary*, 277.

241. Gunton, *Father, Son and Holy Spirit*, 61.

242. Milbank, *Word Made Strange*, 149.

243. Pabst, *Metaphysics: Creation of Hierarchy*, 440–41.

244. Brunner, *Eternal Hope*, 117, 139–40; Küng, *Eternal Life?* 109.

245. Russell, *Doctrine of Deification*, 1; Spezzano, *Glory of God's Grace*, 6.

246. Black, "More About Metaphor," 31.

247. Horst, *Cognitive Pluralism*, 5, 48, 77, 83, 184–85; Soskice, *Metaphor and Religious Language*, 115.

248. Martens, "Kierkegaard and the Bible," 155.

249. Jüngel, *God as the Mystery*, 288–89.

Models come in substantively different sorts.[250] The thesis here does not use the sort of model that expresses what we know already, like those we use internally to navigate our bedroom in the dark or like the scientific ones we use to teach natural mechanisms.[251] Instead, the thesis is of the sort that models what are ineffable structural relations.[252] Such models are "fundamental units of understanding," as philosopher of cognition Steven Horst observed. "We *believe* propositions, but we *understand*" these models.[253] Religious discourse necessitates them in particular.[254] Luke Timothy Johnson explained, "A model is a paradigm within which the data appropriate to a discipline make sense." It is an "imaginative construal of the materials being studied, a structured picture of both process and product, within which the parts are seen not only to fit but also to function."[255]

Models, while they do not express reality exactly, unveil reality usefully.[256] Their continued use confirms this.[257] Models that knowingly exceed reality might even be best.[258] This is because representation, to serve its purpose of understanding the known data, relates imperfectly to that data.[259] The particle and wave models, for example, explain light without confusing it for corpuscular masses or liquid swells.[260] Models of the Lord and the Father similarly use earthly owners and sires to understand God without losing the distinction between them and their reference.[261] Models not only reflect reality but also reflect humility towards that reality, which well serves theology, especially eschatology,[262] most especially this thesis. In pursuing the inconspicuous, theology is innately provisional.[263]

---

250. Dilworth, *Metaphysics of Science*, 110 & n.1.
251. Harre, *Principles of Scientific Thinking*, 34–35.
252. Grenz, *Theology for the Community*, 11–13; Pannenberg, *ST*, II: 421.
253. Horst, *Cognitive Pluralism*, 5.
254. Guarini et al., "Resources for Research," 93.
255. Johnson, *Writings of the NT*, 4.
256. Hawking and Mlodinow, *Grand Design*, 46.
257. Dunning, *Grace, Faith, and Holiness*, 52; Horst, *Cognitive Pluralism*, 6; Lonergan, *Insight*, 18.
258. Soskice, *Metaphor and Religious Language*, 118.
259. T. Hart, "Redemption and Fall," 192.
260. Horst, *Cognitive Pluralism*, 230; Küng, *Eternal Life?* 109.
261. Kierkegaard, *Eighteen Upbuilding Discourses*, 100; Tillich, *ST*, I: 288.
262. Robinson, *In the End, God . . .* , 27, 31.
263. Westphal, *Becoming a Self*, 91; A. Williams, *Architecture of Theology*, 22.

So, a theological model anticipates understanding.[264] In Gilbert Highet's phrasing, a model "combines the wish to know with the knowledge that all cannot be known."[265] Models thereby helpfully avoid subjecting the ultimate to reduction.[266] They are a careful mixture of facts and surmise, maximizing truth and minimizing error, like epistemology generally.[267] Models are necessary because "This moment, we see by a mirror darkly" what we will see "thereafter face to face" (1 Cor 13:12).

The term *model* can admittedly sound scientific,[268] but, as Hamann protested, "A careful interpreter must imitate the scientists."[269] Trying to avoid the use of *model*, however, leads only to substitutes, two in particular, that are unattractive in our context, which are *myth* and the previously mentioned *metaphor* (or *analogy* if broadened to include *simile*). *Myth* is inappropriate because myths relate unreliably to truth.[270] The twentieth-century fascists confirmed this by using myths to convince cultivated peoples of falsehoods.[271] Accordingly, *myth* is rarely countenanced as something that is truthful, certainly when used by those outside liberal art departments. Unheard, for example, is the myth of radioactivity.[272] This is because myths are what we call things we do not entirely believe or do not believe at all. *Myth* is an artifact that intentionally disavows objective truth in some sense, either generally or specifically—a fairytale with a message.[273] So, even the positive meaning of *myth* would wrongly imply here that the afterlife is not about an objective truth like the more accessible truths such as radioactivity.[274] Christianity relegated such myths to the ideological dustbin, as Balthasar recognized.[275] Paul definitely thought so (1 Tim 1:4, 4:7; 2 Tim 4:4). Theology and mythology are opposites.[276] Of course, myths as fictional stories that expose grand truths

264. Mostert, *God and the Future*, 117.
265. Highet, *Man's Unconquerable Mind*, 67.
266. Tillich, *ST*, III: 422.
267. Fraassen, *Empirical Stance*, 86–87; Mountcastle, "Brain Science," 29.
268. Horst, *Cognitive Pluralism*, 99.
269. Hamann, "Socratic Memorabilia," NII,71,25 (p. 389).
270. Honko, "Problem of Defining Myth," 7.
271. Cassirer, *Myth of the State*, 282; Orlow, "Conversion of Myths," 906–24.
272. Harari, *Sapiens*, 108–11, 117.
273. Gillman, *Death of Death*, 27–30, 250–51.
274. Lewis, "Is Theology Poetry?" 119, 136.
275. Balthasar, *Theo-Logic*, II: 262.
276. Torrance, *Atonement*, 446.

have been employed responsibly,[277] such as how Plato used them,[278] but this usage of *myth* is inapposite here because ultimate salvation purports to be a grand truth, not an instructive fiction about it.

Metaphor, the other alternative to *model*, shares a similar purpose as noted above and this similarity can confuse theologians, particularly those unaccustomed to models, but metaphors express a state of affairs to suggest another, while models explain a state of affairs with another.[279] Here the divisible individual is modeled as explanation, not offered as analogy. A model exceeds a metaphor by adding structure to the understanding being explored,[280] which means that *metaphor* is inadequate here because the divisibility being modeled describes what is happening, not parallels what is described. Many analogies will of course be used to help explain the model of individual divisibility, but the model itself is not one of them. While metaphors, at least good ones, can be more vivid than models, a metaphor is inevitably more limited in its application. The metaphor of *God is my fortress* (Ps 18:2), though picturesque, suffers if subjected to too much interpretive pressure, but the model of *God is the Trinity* does not have this problem (nor does it offer the metaphor's vividness). Likewise, the divisible individual is intended to model what is going on, not be a figure of speech. So, *model* it is.

6. Scripture Is the Signal Data

A model explains data,[281] which are the observations, deductions, and other facts that are available for any understanding.[282] Thus, another preliminary question is what are the data for the proposed model. The answer is both simple and complex. In the latter sense, the answer is Scripture.[283] Every inquiry begins,[284] and Christians begin there, at least

---

277. Bultmann, "New Testament and Mythology," 32, 42–43 n.5; "Problem of Demythologizing (1961)," 161.

278. Smith, "Plato's Use of Myth," 20–34.

279. Soskice, *Metaphor and Religious Language*, 50–51, 55, 101.

280. Bailer-Jones, "Models, Metaphors and Analogies," 123; Horst, *Cognitive Pluralism*, 207.

281. Johnson, *Writings of the NT*, 4.

282. Dilworth, *Metaphysics of Science*, 79; Lopez, *Gift and Unity*, 27–28.

283. Barth, *CD* II/2, § 32.2 (p. 36); T. Hart, "Redemption and Fall," 189; Henry, *God, Revelation and Authority*, I: 229, 238–39.

284. C. Taylor, *Hegel*, 139.

for salvation.[285] Scripture records Christianity's founding events and therefore founds its theology.[286] "Christianity knows and recognizes no other shackles of faith," Hamann allowed.[287] This is particularly applicable to the NT.[288] This is not from any added authority or inspiration, but is from the NT's added development without losing its authority or inspiration.[289] Scripture so understood binds all Christian confessions.[290] It also binds, Roger Olson quipped, "nearly all Christian thinkers throughout history—unless one counts modern liberal theologians as 'Christian thinkers.'"[291] Scripture is thus the uniquely divine authority, which is why it cannot be "treated so scientifically that it could just as well be by anonymities," Kierkegaard warned.[292] Scripture is God's authority[293] and is loved in proportion to its Giver.[294] The gospel "truly is the Word of God" (1 Thess 2:4, 13).

The reliance on Scripture obtains acutely here because reliable afterlife experiences are currently unavailable to us.[295] Sources such as visitations or near-death experiences, while certainly numerous and nominally empirical,[296] reveal the notoriously private.[297] For this reason, they are ignored here except in passing. Because afterlife experiences are beyond nearly all of us for now,[298] eschatological authority must depend on Scripture, not experience.[299] Accordingly, less Scripture and more

---

285. Barth, *CD I/1*, § 1.2 (p. 16); Henry, *I Am the Truth*, 1–2, 216–17.

286. Tillich, *ST*, I: 35; A. Williams, *Architecture of Theology*, 129.

287. Hamann, "Golgotha and Sheblimini!," 185.

288. Kierkegaard, *JP*, III: ¶¶ 2870, 3568; Lonergan, *Method in Theology*, 312–13.

289. Augustine, "Against an Adversary," 143 [1, 17, 35]; Williamson, *Death and the Afterlife*, 49 & n.56.

290. Hillerbrand, *Division of Christendom*, 386; Marsilius, *Defensor Pacis*, II: II,XIX,2 (p. 274).

291. Olson, *Mosaic of Christian Belief*, 71.

292. Kierkegaard, *Book on Adler*, 35.

293. Bulgakov, *Orthodox Church*, 18; Richardson, *Christian Apologetics*, 220.

294. Wycliffe, *Truth of Holy Scripture*, xx,129.

295. Brunner, *Eternal Hope*, 98; Küng, *Eternal Life?* 75.

296. Moore, *Where Are the Dead?* 226.

297. J. Cooper, *Body, Soul, and Life*, 235; White, *Life Beyond Death*, 61–62; Zaleski, "Near-Death Experiences," 614–28.

298. Schumacher, *Death and Mortality*, 118, 126, 129.

299. Abraham, "Eschatology and Epistemology," 587; Pieper, *Death and Immortality*, 7–8; Williamson, *Death and the Afterlife*, 28.

experience, which some advocate,[300] is no option on the central topic at issue.[301] Instead, rededication to what Scripture teaches is required,[302] and Scripture urges us to know (γνῶναί), even grasp (καταλαβέσθαι), the knowledge (γνώσεως) of Christ's saving love (Eph 3:18–19). Hence, for the model, the data feed is Scripture, even when it is figurative.[303]

Saying Scripture is the input can be misleading, however, if it is not appreciated that Scripture reveals what is true, not lists what is true. As a result, Scripture's authority cannot involve either inputting only some of its pieces or inputting it only in pieces. The first problem involves rejecting Scripture whenever it says whatever the auditor senses it ought not to,[304] and, given what has just been said, this is entirely unjustified. Rejecting Scripture wholesale is preferable to doing so piecemeal because either way the real authority is the auditor but a wholesale rejection of Scripture is more honest about the usurpation.[305] The second problem involves treating Scripture not as the authority, but treating its pieces that way.[306] Though in this discourse scriptural *passages* are what are exegeted, and this tends to be done one passage at a time, this is because such an approach is all that finite minds can handle.[307] Although this is the form of the presentation, Scripture in its entirety remains the authority. While not all of its expressions are true in the literal sense, all of it expresses truth in that sense.[308] Indeed, Scripture is mistaken only when misunderstood.[309] Thus, to avoid misunderstanding Scripture, more than Scripture is required, which has been consistently acknowledged throughout its existence.[310] None of us

---

300. Cooper, *Holy Eros*, 5–6; Schaff, *Marxism and the Human*, 245.

301. Henry, *Words of Christ*, 8; Marsilius, *Defensor Pacis*, II: I,IV,3, XIX,4 (pp. 13, 91–92).

302. Bowles, "Does Revelation Teach?" 154.

303. Constable, "Divine Justice," 203.

304. Congdon, *God Who Saves*, 55–57, 102; J. Cooper, "Whose Interpretation? Which Anthropology?" 249.

305. Augustine, "Against Faustus," 58 [17, 3].

306. Balthasar, *Theo-Drama*, III: 11; Bonhoeffer, *Life Together*, 52; Erickson, *Christian Theology*, 23.

307. Barth, "Preface to Second Edition," 12–13.

308. Geisler, *ST*, 1320.

309. Augustine, "Letters," 82,1,3; Wycliffe, *Truth of Holy Scripture*, viii,159.

310. Caldecott, *Radiance of Being*, 117; Erickson, *Christian Theology*, 283; D. Hart, *Experience of God*, 233; Kierkegaard, *JP*, IV: 452 (entry 4751) & 734 n.999; Rosenzweig, *Star of Redemption*, 117.

understands anything without help, and this is especially the case when addressing Scripture's paradoxes[311] or its eschatology.[312] So, described next is the simple answer to the data used here—anything true.

7. Understanding Requires Whatever It Takes

Theology, which is the human inquiry into everything as it relates to God, is what exalts Scripture from words merely carried around to words actually carried on.[313] Scripture, though it founds theology, is misunderstood without theology.[314] Scripture, therefore, to be understood, needs the philosophizing implicit in theology, which involves the intelligible expression of reality.[315] When philosophy is understood not as a discipline but as a set of deeds, it means the love of wisdom, and, because the love of God is true wisdom, theology is true philosophy.[316] "The objects" of both theology and philosophy, Hegel noted, "are upon the whole the same" because "In both the object is Truth . . . ."[317] Hence, as Christians reflect on truth, they philosophize.[318] A Christian's only choices in this regard are philosophizing well or wrong.[319]

Some theologians may object to philosophy's intrusion here by repeating some version of Tertullian's rhetorical question, "What indeed has Athens to do with Jerusalem?"[320] The problem with any such hostility to philosophy is not merely that the original question came from a Sophistic lawyer with Stoic, Platonic, and Aristotelian tendencies,[321] but that the answer is so transparent. To Tertullian's specific question, the answer is that both Athens and Jerusalem are Mediterranean cities filled

---

311. Lubac, *Catholicism*, 165.

312. Bulgakov, *Bride of the Lamb*, 382.

313. Bultmann, "Theology as Science," 57–58, 65; Candler, *Theology, Rhetoric, Manuduction*, 38; Montemaggi, *Reading Dante's Commedia*, 46.

314. Bray, *God Has Spoken*, 1225.

315. Merleau-Ponty, *Signs*, 101; Pieper, *Death and Immortality*, 1–2; Sloterdijk, *Critique of Cynical Reason*, xxxviii.

316. Gregor, *Philosophical Anthropology*, 12; John, "Fount of Knowledge," I,3 (p. 11).

317. Hegel, *Logic*, I.1 (p. 3).

318. Blondel, *Action*, 358 [389]; Gilson, *Spirit of Mediaeval Philosophy*, 419.

319. Richardson, *Christian Apologetics*, 38.

320. Tertullian, "Prescription against Heretics," ch VII (p. 246).

321. MacDonald, *History of the Concept*, 137, 141.

with sages and simpletons. The answer to the broader question is that Scripture does not ever oppose the ideas coming from Athens per se, just sophistries (Acts 17:15–34; Rom 14:1; 1 Cor 2:6; Col 2:8; Jas 1:5; 3:17; 1 Pet 2:2),[322] and Scripture's take on the ideas coming from Jerusalem can hardly be called consistently flattering (*e.g.*, Ezek 22). So, philosophy, until wrong, serves theology.[323] Indeed, using best practices, theology *is* philosophy, just with all the data.[324]

Theology's all-inclusiveness follows from the reality that to hear Scripture is to interpret it.[325] As an intelligible address to everyone, Scripture ratifies the dearness of common sense and logic—namely reason.[326] Through reasoning we understand, especially scriptural revelation (1 John 5:20).[327] Preferring "mystery" over "proud reason" as some advocate[328] is a false choice, as Hart explained: "to believe solely because one thinks faith demands it, in [spite] of all the counsels of reason, is actually a form of disbelief, of faithlessness. . . . Submission of that kind could not be sincere, because it would make 'true faith' and 'bad faith'—devotion to truth and betrayal of truth—one and the same thing."[329] Therefore, added always to any message, most especially Scripture, is thinking.[330] Hamann observed, "Reason and scripture are basically the same species: the language of God."[331] "Faith needs reason just as much as reason needs faith."[332] Whether it is the Augustinian "understanding completes

---

322. Augustine, *On Christian Teaching*, II,117–18; Beale, *Colossians and Philemon*, 174–75; Kooton, *Paul's Anthropology in Context*, 264–65.

323. Wycliffe, *Truth of Holy Scripture*, ii,31–32.

324. Blondel, "Letter on Apologetics," 185; Henry, *Essence of Manifestation*, 727; Justin, *First and Second Apologies*, II,13 (p. 83).

325. Bonhoeffer, *Christ the Center*, 75; Welz, *Humanity in God's Image*, 106.

326. Augustine, *On Christian Teaching*, II,142; Henry, *God, Revelation and Authority*, I: 35; Lewis, "Why I Am Not a Pacifist," 65–66; Richardson, *Christian Apologetics*, 222.

327. Blondel, "History and Dogma," 275; Milbank, *Word Made Strange*, 25; Pannenberg, "Faith and Reason," 54 n.15.

328. Torrance, *Atonement*, 187.

329. D. Hart, *That All Shall Be Saved*, 61.

330. Pabst, *Metaphysics*, 55–57; Pannenberg, "Task of Christian Eschatology," 2; Temple, *Nature, Man and God*, 317.

331. Alexander, *Johann Georg Hamann*, 129.

332. Hamann, "Letter to Jacobi," 255.

faith"[333] or the Anselmian "faith seeking understanding,"[334] *how* faith and understanding relate can be disputed, but not *that* they do.[335]

Scripture thus invites consideration of facts that it does not explicitly exhibit. Hamann again, "Whoever studies the ancients without knowing nature is reading the notes without the text."[336] Both creation and Scripture are God-breathed (Gen 1:3, 6, 9, 14–15, 20, 24; 2:7; 2 Tim 3:16), and this demands, in John Milbank's words, "the unavoidable need for interpretative abduction"[337] or Paul Blowers' more extravagant "multidimensional participation in the polymorphous epiphany of the Word in Scripture, in the fabric of creation, and preeminently in historical flesh . . . ."[338] "God is in the facts themselves," Bonhoeffer abstracted.[339] "Whoever says that the words of the Torah are one thing and the words of the world another," Martin Buber concluded, "must be regarded as a man who denies God."[340] Among the essential sources of truth are life's experiences,[341] and this is particularly true for salvation[342] and, indirectly, for the afterlife.[343]

Because experiencing involves introspecting, truthfully expressing our experiences requires the grammatical first-person. Given that the understanding that results also derives from relating to others, which is the second-person,[344] and given that the first- and second-persons combine, the viewpoint is more comprehensively and literally the first-person plural. Theology and philosophy probably require this perspective on all issues, as truth is implicitly accessed there.[345] Regardless, the understand-

---

333. Vaught, *Access to God*, 35.

334. Rausch, *ST*: 1.

335. Gregor, *Philosophical Anthropology*, 13; Pabst, "Sovereign Reason Unbound," 137; Sutton, *Heaven Opens*, 240.

336. Hamann, "Cloverleaf," 48.

337. Milbank, *Beyond Secular Order*, 2.

338. Blowers, *Maximus the Confessor*, 78.

339. Bonhoeffer, *Letters and Papers*, 191.

340. Buber, *Ten Rungs*, 63.

341. Blondel, "History and Dogma," 286; Erickson, *Christian Theology*, 23; Moltmann, *Theology of Hope*, 76.

342. Erickson, *Christian Theology*, 76.

343. Bulgakov, *Bride of the Lamb*, 349.

344. Reddy, *How Infants Know Minds*, 26–42.

345. Montemaggi, *Reading Dante's Commedia*, 71, 168, 223, 247; Rosenzweig, "New Thinking," 179 (Briefe, 597).

ing of *self*, a central topic, most definitely requires the first-person because it derives primarily, if not exclusively, from personal experience.[346] It is this perspective that awakens, Balthasar noted, "the elementary insight that I am . . . ."[347] From this understanding of the *I*, the universally practiced principle of the world's consistency is applied,[348] and, so, our introspection is extrapolated to others.[349] "For he who knows himself," Anthony the Great saw, "knows all men."[350] Accordingly, as chapter 6 will explore, the first-person and our commonalities yield our understanding of *individual*.[351]

Because nearly all facts, and all of our scriptural ones,[352] reach us through our forbearers[353] and because much is needed to preserve the salvation paradox, eclectic scholars contribute here to its understanding. If, as Barth advised, we are to "listen as unreservedly as possible to the witness of Scripture,"[354] we must shun answers that soothe, guarding against both mendacity and favoritism.[355] To this end, we are obliged to provoke interpretations not our own, and, to do that, assorted coteries of tradition have to be consulted, but not as authorities independent of Scripture, forgetting from where they too originated their ideas.[356] Instead, as the church fathers understood, tradition seeks truth out of, not outside of, Scripture.[357] Therefore, theologians have relied on human tradition to understand God's revelation.[358] To avoid bias, they must listen to

---

346. Johnston, *Surviving Death*, 139; McDonald, "Kierkegaard and Romanticism," 101.

347. Balthasar, *Theo-Logic*, II: 255.

348. Dilworth, *Metaphysics of Science*, 53.

349. Crick, *Astonishing Hypothesis*, 107; Husserl, *Cartesian Meditations*, 110, 113; Sartre, *Between Existentialism and Marxism*, 155.

350. Anthony, *Letters*, Ltr VI (p. 20).

351. Bergson, *Two Sources*, 14–15; Schaff, *Marxism and the Human*, 87.

352. Behr, *Mystery of Christ*, 64–70; A. Williams, *Architecture of Theology*, 222.

353. Candler, *Theology, Rhetoric, Manuduction*, 35.

354. Barth, *CD IV/2*, xi.

355. T. Hart, "Redemption and Fall," 191; Wycliffe, *Truth of Holy Scripture*, xxiii,208.

356. Berkhof, *Christian Faith*, 98; Bulgakov, *Orthodox Church*, 18; Merleau-Ponty, *Signs*, 159.

357. Kelly, *Early Christian Doctrines*, 39, 42–43, 46–49; Wiles, *Making of Christian Doctrine*, 114 n.1.

358. J. Betz, "Radically Orthodox Reformer," 674; Bulgakov, *Orthodox Church*, 10–11; Geisler, *ST*, 163.

all sides, and, to avoid falsehood, they must cross-examine their claims with tradition's findings.[359] Following this approach here, the testimony of divergent experts are tendered.[360] And, on common issues, even "infidels," when competent, testify because, as Anselm recognized, both they and Christians "appeal to reason," "the thing sought is one and the same."[361] "He talking on his own seeks his own glory" (John 7:18).

This consideration of anything true, Hans Hillerbrand remarked, is not merely "Protestant self-confidence" in "the conviction that all pursuit of truth would confirm rather than deny religious truth," but is fully endorsed by its sparring partner, Thomas, and the other medieval scholastics.[362] It is "an 'abiding wonder'" at the "peaceful coexistence" of "every form of practical cognition," Bas van Fraassen explained.[363] Theological and secular insights correspond particularly on the subject of *individual*,[364] and, so, insights from all quarters are gathered, including artists, whose eloquence on the universal experience benefit ideation.[365] On topics more explicitly reliant on special revelation,[366] such as almost everything concerning the afterlife, learned Christians are then the source, but they too are of all sorts, not "too papistic" or "too evangelical" (or too Lutheran).[367] Such eclecticism is desirable even when the cited thinkers make other claims that are spurious and are left uncited.[368] Truth is what matters, Kierkegaard affirmed, whether from "Balaam's ass or a sniggering wag or an apostle or an angel."[369]

---

359. Heidegger, "What Calls for Thinking?" 354; Pannenberg, *ST*, II: xiii.

360. O'Meara, *Thomas Aquinas Theologian*, 72.

361. Anselm, *Cur Deus Homo*, 15 (Bk I, ch 2). Accord Al-Ghazali, "Deliverance from Error," 39.

362. Hillerbrand, *Division of Christendom*, 430.

363. Fraassen, *Empirical Stance*, 155.

364. Grant, "What Is Man?" 6; Kelsey, "Personal Bodies," 141; Radner, "Mystery of Christian Anthropology," 243–44, 257.

365. Husserl, *Ideas*, 70 (pp. 183–84); Jung, *Modern Man*, 155–56.

366. O'Meara, *Thomas Aquinas Theologian*, 72.

367. Luther, *Word and Sacrament II*, 237.

368. Bulgakov, "By Jacob's Well," 103; Erickson, *Christian Theology*, 69.

369. Kierkegaard, *JP*, V: ¶ 5646.

2

Decease, Decrease, Increase

> *Mainly [for heaven] I just think about the splendors of the world and multiply by two. I'd multiply by ten or twelve if I had the energy. But two is much more than sufficient for my purposes.*
>
> —Robinson, *Gilead*

While the first chapter has cleared out several preliminary issues concerning ultimate salvation, including clarity on its meaning, a few relatively uncontested convictions that Christians hold about ultimate salvation also need to be outlined before proceeding to its paradox, if for no other reason than situating what is agreed-upon should, before the more difficult issue is undertaken, minimize the risk that any understanding that results might transgress its more certain context.[1] This chapter thus presents the three well-established moments of ultimate salvation that are true regardless of its extent: Death ends this life; the godly and ungodly are separated for eternal life or perishing, respectively; and those in eternal life are completed.

---

1. Aquinas, *Division and Methods*, Q. VI, art. 1, reply to opp. arg. 3 (p. 61).

1. Everyone Dies, Followed by More

All human life bestrides death.[2] We live warily and then die (Gal 2:19–20).[3] Because we see every living thing everywhere go out this way, each of us noetically accepts that we will each join them sooner or later.[4] Of every human who has ever lived, 100 percent have already died or will within about 120 years, which is corroborated scripturally (Gen 6:3; Job 30:23; Rom 5:12),[5] scientifically,[6] and empirically.[7] Three instances in Scripture have sometimes been suggested as exceptions to death's universality because a description of biological death is skipped as earthly life ends: Enoch was suddenly "not there," "snatched up" (Gen 5:24); Elijah "was taken up to heaven in the tempest" (2 Kgs 2:11); and humanity's last generation will be "snatched in clouds into the receiving of the Lord" (1 Thess 4:16–17). These aberrational ends to earthly life are, however, not said to be skipping the act of death, but appear to be skipping the act of dying, and, therefore, they are properly understood, not as exceptions to death, but as exceptional deaths.[8]

While death is thorough for humans, no human has entirely self-authenticated it.[9] Not only are the witnesses who have genuinely died beyond our jurisdiction, the living cannot comprehend their testimony, as Vladimir Nabokov syllogized: "other men die; but I / Am not another; therefore I'll not die."[10] No one has yet to figure out how to be conscious of nonconsciousness.[11] Even when we imagine the world after we die,

---

2. Augustine, *City of God*, I,11, XIII,10 (pp. 20, 518); Balthasar, *Theo-Drama*, I: 370; Barth, *Romans*, 89 (3:20).

3. Eastman, *Paul and the Person*, 153, 159.

4. Bergson, *Two Sources*, 130.

5. Grant, "What Is Man?" 21.

6. Aging science says death is inexorable. Nelson and Masel, "Inevitability of Multicellular Aging," 12982–87; Pinker, *Enlightenment Now*, 61.

7. About 94 percent of all humans that have ever lived have died already, and the remaining 6 percent are just those who have been born within the last 120 years and not died yet. Haub, "How Many People Have Ever Lived?"; Gerontology Research, "GRG World Supercentenarian Rankings."

8. Aquinas, *ST*, Part III (Suppl.), XX, Q. 78, art. 1, co. (pp. 149–50); Wanamaker, *Thessalonians*, 176; N.T. Wright, *Resurrection*, 94–95.

9. Krapiec, *I-Man*, 349.

10. Nabokov, *Pale Fire*, lns 213–14.

11. Davies, "Immortality," 34; Tolstoy, *Death of Ivan Ilyich*, 137; Watkin, "Kierkegaard—Dying," 80.

this usually consists of imagining the world without us in it, but we can be certain that our death is even more of a negation than that. The world before we got here is the world without us, and it is that benign world that has invited our life; in sharp contrast, this world that we depart from will be intent on entirely obliterating our life.[12] Our post-life nullification is thus unimaginably beyond our pre-life personal absence (Eccl 4:2–3).[13]

As a result, though human death happens definitely, what happens is indefinite,[14] except for two things. First, the Christian consensus is that the individual, as chapter 6 will detail, may continue after biological life.[15] Regardless of the truth of this belief, death as it ends life completes life.[16] The world tells each of us, "Death is the condition of your creation," Montaigne interprets, "This being of yours that you enjoy is equally divided between death and life." "The constant work of your life is to build death."[17] Life, accordingly, takes a lifetime, and life's accumulations are the individual.[18] Though death then follows, the life that leads up to it, by nearly all accounts, retains meaning for death, reflecting the ultimate difference between biological life ending and its never having been.[19]

Second, by dominant tradition and common experience, any individual existence after biological death must outlast the biological body.[20] "We brought nothing into the world, nor, so, can we take anything out" (1 Tim 6:7). This remains true even when our treasures are in our bodies, whether our gold fillings or digested delicacies. It is not that an afterlife lacks any sort of body, but it is that death positively discontinues the earthly body (Eccl 12:7; Phil 1:21–23). This body's discontinuity is

---

12. Arendt, *Love and St Augustine*, 51–52, 55, 70–72.
13. Wollheim, *Thread of Life*, 257.
14. Kierkegaard, *For Self-Examination*, 18.
15. Berkouwer, *Man: Image of God*, 269; Shields and Pasnau, *Philosophy of Aquinas*, 206.
16. Krapiec, *I-Man*, 335, 350; Watkin, "Kierkegaard—Dying," 268.
17. Montaigne, "Essays," I,20 (p. 65).
18. Kierkegaard, *Concluding Unscientific Postscript*, I: 345; Westphal, *Becoming a Self*, 154.
19. Balthasar, *Theo-Drama*, IV: 490; D. Hart, "Death, Final Judgment," 477; Kierkegaard, *Book on Adler*, 7; Pieper, *Death and Immortality*, 78; Williamson, *Death and the Afterlife*, 28–29.
20. Bulgakov, *Bride of the Lamb*, 357; J. Cooper, "Whose Interpretation? Which Anthropology?" 239, 248–49; Wallenfang, *Human and Divine Being*, 165. As will be discussed in chapter 6, Christ's resurrected body is not to the contrary.

what biological death fundamentally is.[21] What we have in this life, Käsemann noted, "is always the evanescent circumstance which is shattered in death."[22] Even when scholars strongly identify this body with the self, they mostly accept this understanding of death.[23] The resurrected life, which is notoriously corporeal for Christians, does not change this understanding of the earthly body because, also as explained in chapter 6, the resurrection does not rely on the body's revivification, but involves a *new* body (1 Cor 15:44–46).[24]

Given the stark corporeal discontinuity between this life and whatever the next is, some theologians can struggle with whether our *identity* in this life is *identical* to that in the next, presuming that identity relates to identicalness, and, so, they argue the loss of the earthly body, which is here all-important to identity, means our identity is lost too.[25] Yet, this is disproven every time we remain us after we change, whether we change our appearance or our mind.[26] Those who believe a changed person is a different person are suffering from Capgras syndrome, and they are constantly misplacing their ever-changing friends and family.[27] The rest of us realize that identity tracks the individual despite the changes to the individual and that the changes are the opposite of identicalness.[28]

While the understanding of an afterlife has evolved since humanity first began to appreciate its existence, even the earliest scriptural sources understood that corpses were not the end.[29] The dead were "gathered to" their deceased "peoples" in such a way that was separate from the body's interment, and this was "the way of all the earth" (Josh 23:14; 1 Kgs 2:2).[30]

---

21. Arendt, *Love and Augustine*, 78; Schumacher, *Death and Mortality*, 48; Vidal, "Brains, Bodies, Selves, and Science," 938.

22. Käsemann, *Perspectives on Paul*, 25.

23. Walker, "Lived Body," 214.

24. Balthasar, *Theo-Logic*, III: 295; Bovon, "Soul's Comeback," 401; Finlan, "Can We Speak of Theosis?" 70–73.

25. E.g., Hershenov and Koch-Hershenov, "Personal Identity and Purgatory," 439–51.

26. Bergson, *Time and Free Will*, 209.

27. McGilchrist, *Master and His Emissary*, 53.

28. Rips et al., "Tracing the Identity," 1–30; Turner, *Theology, Psychology and Plural Self*, 145.

29. J. Cooper, "Biblical Anthropology," 220; Ratzinger, *Eschatology*, 89.

30. Gundry, *Soma in Biblical Theology*, 128–29; Johnson, "Life, Disease and Death," 536; Williamson, *Death and the Afterlife*, 39–40.

This afterlife gathering is specified in nearly every scriptural stratum.[31] This uncluttered understanding of the afterlife matured as the faithful reflected on how death separates us from the body without separating us from God (Ps 73:24–26; Rom 8:38–39).[32] The author of Isaiah saw that God's "dead will live; my corpses will rise. You who lie in dust, wake and shout for joy . . . ; the earth will birth the specters" (26:19). Samuel in death, for instance, communicated with the living and foretold the future (1 Sam 28:7–19). In the NT, the departed Moses and Elijah conversed with Jesus (Matt 17:3//Mark 9:4//Luke 9:30), and Jesus argued that God was of the living because the long-since perished patriarchs still lived in an existence similar to the angels (Matt 22:30–32//Mark 12:25–27//Luke 20:36–38).[33] Jesus called those in hell more than dead (Matt 10:26–28; Luke 12:1–5), and he assured the thief of immediate postmortem existence after his execution (Luke 23:42–43).[34] Paul too saw afterlife existence as not only a reality but a superior one (Phil 1:20–24), and the slaughtered martyrs are reported to be still active (Rev 6:9–10).

Thus, we live with death and then die, and Scripture, even when it is figurative, refers to some sort of existence afterwards. Our terrestrial body is transcended then, but something essential continues.[35] This well-acknowledged view sets up the salvation paradox.

2. The Godly Are Separated from the Perishing

According to every Christian faith, every human, in addition to potentially undergoing an experience after dying, is distinguished between the godly, who have eternal life, and the ungodly, who have perishing. This moment involving the binary division of humanity is the one that holds the salvation paradox, and, so, the outline of the second moment cannot be as brief as the others.

---

31. Gen 25:8–9, 17; 35:29; 49:29, 33—50:2; Num 20:24–26; 27:13; 31:2; Deut 32:50; Judg 2:10; 2 Kgs 22:20; 2 Chr 34:28; Acts 13:36–37.

32. Badham, *Christian Beliefs*, 5–7; Williamson, *Death and the Afterlife*, 22.

33. Gillman, *Death of Death*, 121; Williamson, *Death and the Afterlife*, 51–52; N. T. Wright, *Resurrection*, 424–26.

34. Brown, *Death of the Messiah*, II: 1005–13.

35. Bergson, *Two Sources*, 134.

a. The Division

A common Christian doctrine is that judgment comes, in life and with death, based on godliness.[36] "God is nowhere and never neutral, resting in an attitude of indifference with regard to the antithesis holy-unholy, resistance to God and obedience to God," Emil Brunner summarized. "This non-neutral positive purposefulness is so consistently and piercingly the Biblical idea of God that we cannot be surprised that the thought of judgment penetrates unequivocally every section and layer of Holy Scripture."[37] Christians can dispute the precise predicate that serves the divine judgment, whether *righteousness*, including rightly relating to God, or *faith*, including living for God,[38] or any permutation, but all such concepts related to the personal character that are relevant to salvation are here frequently given the inclusive shorthand *godliness*.[39]

The divine judgment's division of humanity based on this godliness distinction begins in this life (Ps 1:5–6). "The Lord tries the righteous and evil," and the first group obtains God while the second obtains "fiery coals; brimstone and scorching wind" (11:5–7). The prophetic future involves separating the godly for the ungodly's destruction (Jer 12:15–17, 36:3, 31; Amos 9:8–11; Mic 7:18–19; Zech 5:1–4, 8:14–17; Mal 3:1–3). Among God's people, "two parts will be cut off, expire; yet the third will remain in it. This third I will bring through the fire" (13:8–9). The separating of the godly from the doomed, though it has begun, has no expiry (Hab 2:2–4). The coming day of the Lord, which likely originated with Holy War, foreshadows God decisively intervening to protect the godly remnant as the ungodly perish (Joel 1:15; 2:2–3, 28, 32; 3:12–13, 20–21; Amos 5:18–20; Zeph 1:2–3, 14, 17; 2:2–3).[40] Those who rebel against God perish as the godly live in a new creation (Isa 65–66). Ultimately, everyone is resurrected so that some of them have eternal life and others of them do not, having something like eternal abomination (Dan 12:2).

---

36. Behr, *Irenaeus of Lyons*, 182; Daley, *Hope of the Early Church*, 219–20; Nichols, *Death and Afterlife*, 37–38; Swinburne, "Future of the Totally Corrupt," 238; Williamson, *Death and the Afterlife*, 98–99.

37. Brunner, *Eternal Hope*, 173–74.

38. Martin, "Faith," 246–47; Seifrid, "Righteousness, Justice and Justification," 740–45; S. Taylor, "Faith, Faithfulness," 487–93; N. T. Wright, "Righteousness," 590–92.

39. Gouvea, "Godliness," 508–9; Vinson, "Godly," 620–21; *OED*, s.v. "godly."

40. Arnold, "OT Eschatology," 27.

The NT retains the depiction of the godly, who perdure, as separated from the ungodly, who perish.[41] Christ's followers continue; the rest do not (Matt 7:24–27//Luke 6:47–49).[42] The sheep-goat parable depicts this particularly: the righteous are eternally living, and the unrighteous are eternally castigated (Matt 25:31–46). This dividing of the godly for eternal life from the ungodly for eternal destruction is not in spite of Jesus, but he brings it: "I came not to cast peace," but "to bisect [διχάσαι]" (10:34–35). He is "a sign of contradiction [ἀντιλεγόμενον]," bringing "a sword" that pierces even the noblest (Luke 2:34–35). "Fire I came to cast on the earth, and would it were already kindled." "Think I came to give the earth peace? No, I tell you, but division [διαμερισμόν]" (12:49, 51). The Shepherd's door, through whom those experiencing eternal life enter, safeguards them from what is outside that life (John 10:9, 26–28). As for those outside the door, "they're gathered, cast into the fire, and burned" (15:2, 6). This separation that is part of death and of eternal life is expressed non-pastorally too: "all in the tombs will hear his voice and come out—those doing goods into a resurrection of life and those practicing evils into a resurrection of judgment" (5:28–29). "Whoever comes to me I'll never ever cast out, ... for my Father wills that all who note and believe in the Son have eternal life" (6:37–40).

The NT continues the Hebrew Scriptures' portrayal of the day of the Lord as an occasion of ungodly destruction and godly salvation (2 Pet 3:10–15).[43] Everyone is resurrected, and, when God judges, he saves the godly from evil (Acts 24:15–16; 2 Tim 4:18; Heb 4:9–14; 1 Pet 1:3–9). As the godly endures, the ungodly does not (2:9–10; 2 Cor 9:9). In the end, the godly are segregated from the ungodly such that the former eternally live and the latter perish (Rev 19:20–21; 20:6, 10; 22:11–15). Being named in the Book of Life, which is also referenced throughout Scripture, reflects the godliness division as well, particularly in the end (Exod 32:31–33; Ps 69:28; Dan 12:1; Luke 10:20; Phil 4:3). The godly are listed in the Book, while those not listed, those against God, have the second death (Rev 3:5; 13:8; 17:8; 20:12–15; 21:27).

This division between the godly who are saved and the ungodly who perish is embraced across all the understandings of salvation's extent, including universalism, except that universalists say the ungodly only

---

41. Brunner, *Eternal Hope*, 168; Küng, *Eternal Life?* 141; Moltmann, *Crucified God*, 174.

42. Irenaeus, *Against Heresies*, 4:4,3 (p. 88).

43. Williamson, *Death and the Afterlife*, 98.

"perish" at an intermediate eschatological horizon so that their perishing is provisional, which allows everyone to avoid actually perishing and to then be saved at a later eschatological horizon, when everyone has eternal life.[44] Subsequent chapters, particularly 7 and 8, will further discuss this godliness division in the context of the salvation paradox.

b. The Individual's Role

The division of humanity based on godliness pertains to something about the humans because salvation has divine *and* human dimensions, involving both the gift by God and the reception by the individual.[45] God draws each of us by grace with our reason and will.[46] While it is God who promises, empowers, and provisions, it is the individual who repents, believes, and obeys.[47] Salvation is bequeathed, not inflicted.[48] Hence, the Christian concurrence shuns both Pelagianism's self-salvation where individuals earn it and cheap-grace mechanical-salvation where individuals do nothing.[49] Christians need not agree on our role to acknowledge that Scripture gives us one (Matt 5:7; 6:14–24; 18:26–35).[50] That role, Nicholas Lash noted, is at least *"making a difference,"* whether to our community, our family, our neighbor, ourselves, something.[51]

The infamous denominational breach concerning whether salvation is by faith plus works or by faith alone, Scripture reflects.[52] On the one hand, it says too frequently to be sure of completeness that our response includes deeds.[53] Faithful actions, not assertions of faith, are repaid

---

44. D. Hart, *That All Shall Be Saved*, 103–4, 129.

45. Demarest, *Cross and Salvation*, 43, 45, 461; Ludlow, *Universal Salvation*, 252; Olson, *Mosaic of Christian Belief*, 267, 272–73, 286.

46. Blondel, "Letter on Apologetics," 141.

47. Demarest, *Cross and Salvation*, 461; Finney, *Memoirs*, 273 (MS522, JHF264); Harris, "Salvation," 765.

48. Ambrosiaster, "Commentaries on Pauline Epistles," 179 [1 Tim 2:4]; Colijn, *Images of Salvation*, 140.

49. Geisler, *ST*, 779; Pannenberg, *ST*, III: 444–45.

50. Balthasar, *Dare We Hope*, 94–95.

51. Lash, *Easter in Ordinary*, 284.

52. Oakes, *Theology of Grace*, 77–81; Rausch, *ST*, 155.

53. 2 Chr 6:23; Ps. 62:12; Prov 24:12; Jer 17:10; Ezek 18:20; Matt 16:27; Acts 10:35; Rom 2:6, 14:12; 1 Cor 3:12–15; 2 Cor 5:10; 11:15; 2 Tim 4:14; 1 Pet 1:17; Rev 2:23, 14:13; 18:6; 20:12–13; 22:12.

(Matt 21:28–31; Luke 14:13–14; 16:19–31; John 5:28–30; 1 Cor 6:9–11). Salvation is worked out (Phil 2:12–13). Forgiveness too is like for like (Matt 6:12–15; 7:1–2; 18:23–35; Luke 6:37–38; 11:4; Jas 2:13).[54] Acts are all that anyone can literally contribute.[55] On the other hand, Scripture says, "God's electing purpose" stands, "not by works" (Rom 9:11–12), but "through our Lord Jesus' grace" (Acts 15:11). The only work is faith (16:30–31)—that is, "only [μόνον] believe" (Luke 8:50). The key is "believing in the one he sent" (John 6:28–29). Faith equals eternal life, and faith's absence equals dying (3:15–16, 36; 5:22–24; 8:23–24). "To the extent you confess in your mouth Jesus 'Lord' and believe in your heart God raised him from among the dead, you will be saved, for with the heart one believes into righteousness and with the mouth one confesses into salvation" (Rom 10:9–10).

The theological energy devoted to the faith-plus or faith-alone dispute seems therefore to displace faith's centrality, which seems to be Scripture's point. In living, which is an entirety, we represent God.[56] Adding anything to *faith*, even *alone*, thus likely undersells what faith is (Rom 14:23; Eph 2:8–9). If a summarizing slogan is needed, Bonhoeffer's "what is the will of God?" should suffice.[57] Scripture certainly urges holiness.[58] To begin with the most obvious examples, Jesus' parables reveal the ultimate importance of the individual's response in faith (Matt 13:24–30, 36–43; 21:28–32; 25:1–13, 31–46; 22:1–14//Luke 14:16–24; 18:9–14).[59] Even Jesus' contrasting parable of the vineyard laborers requires that they accept employment (Matt 20:1–16). In a different metaphor, the sheep must follow the shepherd (John 10:9–16). Paul too understood that the Christian transformation that is called for involves a response.[60] "Continue working out your salvation with fear and trembling" (Phil 2:12). "Be not conformed to this age, but be transformed by your mind's renewing into attesting what God wills, the good, pleasing, and complete" (Rom 12:1–2). We are frequently exhorted to respond because responding matters (8:13–17; Eph 4:22–32; Col 3:1—4:6; 1 Thess 4:1–12; Heb

---

54. Kierkegaard, *Works of Love*, 380; McKnight, *James*, 222.
55. Geisler, *ST*, 822, 825; Lohr, "Role of Eschatology," 661.
56. Schwarz, *Human Being*, 24.
57. Bonhoeffer, *Ethics*, 47–48 [31].
58. Sprinkle, *Four Views on Hell*, 203.
59. Behr, *Irenaeus of Lyons*, 97; C. Taylor, *Secular Age*, 646.
60. Finlan, "Can We Speak of Theosis?" 77; Lewis, *Mere Christianity*, 115.

12:14; 2 Pet 1:5–11).[61] Otherwise, the apostles summon us in vain (2 Cor 5:20).[62] Faith is integral and, when done by humans, requires an answer.

The disputations about faith-plus or faith-alone may not only misplace the scriptural point, but they distract from what Christians agree upon—it is a *lived* faith that is called for,[63] an "allegiance."[64] "What counts before God is not simply the substantial, verifiable deed," Bultmann noticed, "but how a man is disposed . . . ."[65] Even when salvific deeds are denied, participation is not.[66] Calvin realized that "faith . . . alone . . . is not destitute of good works" and, therefore, "can admit not only a partial righteousness in works (as our adversaries maintain), but that they are approved by God as if there were absolutely perfect."[67] To God's will, we add our own will.[68] We work for God, not God for us.[69] Even the most grace alone Christians, who affirm that God "wholly and completely" achieves salvation, recognize that this requires a "self-surrendering response."[70] Barth summarized, "God acts in His free grace, but He also wills and expects and demands something from His covenant-partner," and this is "the parallel but opposing fulfillment of two great movements," "a human action" "in participation" with Christ.[71] While atoning is God-based,[72] the individual must accept its acceptance.[73] To "not destroy the grace that we have received," Nicholas Cabasilas concluded, "there is need of something human," and "This alone we contribute to this life—that we submit to His gifts, retain His graces, and do not reject the crown which God by many toils and labors has prepared for us."[74] Christians thus understand

---

61. Bornkamm, *Paulus*, 202; Erasmus, "De Libero Arbitrio," 87; Lohr, "Role of Eschatology," 661.

62. Bernstein, *Formation of Hell*, 216.

63. Geisler, *ST*, 870, 1050; Lewis, *Mere Christianity*, 114–16; Ratzinger, *Eschatology*, 99–100.

64. Bates, *Salvation by Allegiance Alone*, 5, 8, 92, 101, 109, 213.

65. Bultmann, *Theology of the NT*, I: 2.2 (p. 13).

66. Gorman, *Inhabiting the Cruciform*, 80, 93, 102, 161–62.

67. Calvin, *Institutes*, III,11,1, 13,2, 17,10 (pp. 475, 499, 534).

68. J. Betz, *After Enlightenment*, 310.

69. Peguy, *Temporal and Eternal*, 99.

70. McCoy, "Gospel Truth," 174–75.

71. Barth, *CD* II/2, § 32.1 (p. 11); *CD* IV/3.1, §§ 69.1, 69.3 (pp. 4–7, 220).

72. Long, *Perfectly Simple Triune God*, 26.

73. Tillich, *ST*, II: 170, 173, 179.

74. Cabasilas, *Life in Christ*, Bk VI § 1 (p. 159), Bk I § 11 (p. 63).

that God does not will to save us without us.[75] Our role involves at least relinquishing our role.[76]

Any of these approaches to the relationship between who we are and our ultimate destiny is admissible here so long as it admits of a relationship.[77] What we are, whether a result, cause, or correspondence, is integral to the godliness separation, and, as further discussed in chapter 6, living changes us in a way relevant to that separation.[78] So, the paradox of salvation's extent arises from the benchmark that the separation between godly and ungodly is based on something about our lives, whether done by us, to us, or some combination.

c. The Binaries

Another scriptural certainty is that our destiny is binary—eternal life or perishing.[79] "Risky though it always is to speak of a consensus among theologians," Brian Daley distilled one issue on which a consensus seems to exist: that God's judgment renders "permanent and perfect happiness for the good, and permanent, all-consuming misery for the wicked."[80] The Second Temple texts articulated these binaries explicitly: "multitudes sleeping in the soil's dust will wake: these to eternal life and these to shames, eternal contempt" (Dan 12:2). This Janus-faced resurrection tied to God's final reward and condemnation matured in the intertestamental Jewish literature.[81] It was upon these insights that the NT then built.[82]

While believers have eternal life, there is another outcome, which believers elude (John 3:16). Humanity as a whole has two ultimates applicable to its members, which is being saved *and* being annihilated, and, so, humans as members fall into two ultimate groups, which are the saved *and* the annihilated (2 Cor 2:15; 2 Thess 2:10; Jas 4:12). The binary outcomes track the as-lived separation noted above: "man reaps to the extent he sows. The one sowing into his flesh will from the flesh reap corruption,

---

75. Bates, *Salvation by Allegiance Alone*, 103; Lubac, *Catholicism*, 226.
76. Jenson, *ST*, I: 167, 224–25, 232–33; Lewis, *Mere Christianity*, 150.
77. McKnight, *James*, 226.
78. Harrison, *God's Many-Splendored Image*, 16.
79. Ludlow, *Universal Salvation*, 13.
80. Daley, *Hope of the Early Church*, 219–21 (emphasis removed).
81. Henze, "Anthropology of Early Judaism," 40–42.
82. Balthasar, "Epilogue: Apokatastasis," 236.

but the one sowing into the Spirit will from the Spirit reap eternal life" (Gal 6:7–8).[83] "[T]o the one who thirsts I will give freely from the spring of life's water," "but, the cowards, unfaithful," etc., "their part is in the lake that burns fire and brimstone" (Rev 21:6, 8). And the binary outcomes suffer no third outcome. Any purgatory, for instance, is a penultimate.[84]

Theologians can decide that the two outcomes have degrees,[85] but they uniformly agree that there are only two outcomes: unmitigatedly wonderful eternal life and wholly undesirable perishing.[86] It is this dual destiny that occasions the salvation-extent dispute. Scripture demonstrates that some of us definitely obtain the positive ultimate.[87] Passages could be catalogued to establish this (*e.g.,* Heb 12:23; Rev 6:9), but, because Christ undeniably atoned with effect (Rom 5:9),[88] no Christian doubts that some people are saved. Whether the negative ultimate outcome is also populated is, however, disputed, which is the subject of chapter 4, and this is what forms the paradox of salvation's extent, the next chapter's subject.

Two contested issues about the binary outcomes are independent of the salvation paradox and thus of the thesis. The first is of what the negative binary consists. It is usually denominated something like "perish" (ἀπόληται, John 3:16), which is understood as either eternal torment or final oblivion.[89] Eternal torment has been the traditional understanding,[90] but the terms that Scripture uses for the negative outcome point to annihilation of some kind.[91] The difference between torment and annihilation is at best subtle. Neither outcome is any less endless in that both last forever, and both are wholly undesirable in that each is total in its negation.[92] Indeed, neither outcome is obviously worse than the other since torment offers a continued existence with its allure of hope while annihilation's

---

83. Oakes, *Galatians*, 38, 182; Schwarz, *Human Being*, 19.
84. Griffiths, "Purgatory," 427–29; Nichols, *Death and Afterlife*, 173.
85. *E.g.,* Bridges, "Degrees of Punishment," 81–86.
86. Balthasar, *Dare We Hope*, 133.
87. Marshall, "Divine and Human Punishment," 226.
88. Lewis, *Mere Christianity*, 42; Ludlow, *Universal Salvation*, 186.
89. Caldecott, *Radiance of Being*, 245; Johnson, "Wideness in God's Mercy," 77–78.
90. Froom, "Conditionalism in the Early Church," 260–75; Williamson, *Death and the Afterlife*, 26.
91. Fudge, *Fire That Consumes*, 51–84, 116–69, 187–252; Pinnock, "Annihilationism," 464–66; Stackhouse, "Terminal Punishment," 61–81.
92. Marshall, "Divine and Human Punishment," 223.

cessation of existence offers a final peace.[93] In addressing salvation's extent, however, what "perishing" means exactly, whether eternal torment or final oblivion (or any combination), can be left unanswered. The given is that "perishing" is the only stated alternative to salvation.

The second independent issue is whether there is an intermediate state.[94] Tradition recognizes two afterlives—a resurrected life, which has a body radically different from this one, and, for all those who die before the eschaton, an intermediate existence, which is discarnate.[95] Scripture suggests these two afterlives,[96] but some, like Luther reputedly,[97] have argued that there is no intermediate existence experienced after this life but before the resurrected life.[98] Thomism has a middle approach: The intermediate state is a diminished experience that lacks sense imagery.[99] Others see the intermediate state as undiminished.[100] The proposed model accommodates all such approaches because the issue of salvation's extent is about the antithetical outcomes of the afterlife, not about another stage, if any, to be experienced along the way.

※

Scripture sets out two, and only two, possible outcomes for all of humanity—wonderfully good eternal life for the godly and horribly bad perishing for the ungodly.[101] No specifics about either are relevant here because the nonparadoxical given is that the ultimate for humanity is binary, regardless of what the negative outcome consists or whether any intermediate state exists. As subsequent chapters will discuss, particularly chapter 9, the binary outcomes can cause problems for how to

---

93. Kierkegaard, *Stages*, 260.

94. Griffiths, "Purgatory," 431; Yates, *Between Death and Resurrection*, 1–5.

95. International Theological Commission, "Some Current Questions on Eschatology," 4.1; Murphy, *Bodies and Souls*, 7.

96. J. Cooper, "Biblical Anthropology," 220–26; Williamson, *Death and the Afterlife*, 61–62.

97. Secker, "Martin Luther's Views," 422–35.

98. Davis, "Eschatology and Resurrection," 388; Küng, *Eternal Life?* 138; Murphy, *Bodies and Souls*, 10.

99. Fitzpatrick, *Aquinas on Bodily Identity*, 155; M. Rousseau, "Elements of Thomastic Philosophy," 581–602; Yates, *Between Death and Resurrection*, 240.

100. Blosser, *Become Like the Angels*, 246 (discussing Origen); Lewis, "Transposition," 111.

101. Balthasar, *Dare We Hope*, 14–15, 133.

understand salvation's extent, but the paradox itself pertains to getting to the binary outcomes, not being in them.

3. The Godly Are Completed

The final relevant scriptural certainty regarding ultimate salvation is that, because we each lack to an extent in this life what God desires for us,[102] we are afterwards completed.[103] So, in addition to the unrighteous among us being carved out at least by the end, the righteous are consummated at least by then (Rom 9:27–28). This is often called glorification.[104] "Simply to look at people with any degree of realism at all," Joseph Ratzinger discerned, "is to grasp the necessity of such a process."[105] Given the conspicuousness of our failings, afterlife completion might be the easiest Christian tenet to verify empirically, at least the need it addresses.[106] Thus, salvation, to be complete, must involve completion (Matt 5:48).[107] We "are being transformed into the same icon" as "the Lord's glory," "from glory into glory, even as from Lord into Spirit" (2 Cor 3:18) to "commune with divine nature" (2 Pet 1:4). What continues from this life to be transformed for the next includes the individual,[108] and it is only then that God's children are made complete like the Father (1 Cor 2:6; 1 John 3:1–2). In addition to glorification, this can be called theosis, deification,[109] be gods with God,[110] or, from Greek philosophy, assimilation to God (or the gods).[111] Irrespective, the Christian accord is that any resurrected individual, after losing some of this life, will gain what

---

102. Talbott, "Reply to My Critics," 252.
103. Pannenberg, "Modernity, History, and Eschatology," 498.
104. Cabasilas, *Life in Christ*, Bk I § 1 (p. 43); Cooper, *Naturally Human, Supernaturally God*, 2; Keating, *Deification and Grace*, 39–40, 60–63, 87, 110.
105. Ratzinger, *Eschatology*, 230–31.
106. A. Williams, *Architecture of Theology*, 13.
107. Spezzano, *Glory of God's Grace*, 1.
108. Pannenberg, *ST*, III: 574, 639–40; Volf, *After Our Likeness*, 187.
109. Christensen, "Problem, Promise, and Process," 25–27.
110. Cabasilas, *Life in Christ*, Bk I § 11 (p. 63).
111. Kooton, *Paul's Anthropology in Context*, 92, 206, 210–11, 214.

is needed for the next.¹¹² That is, though not all of who we are in this life makes it to the other side, whatever continues requires completing.¹¹³

The completion in the afterlife has significance to the position that the individual can then be divisible as the thesis proposes, which chapter 7 considers, but the paradox of who all are ultimately saved occurs explanatorily before this completion. The paradox of salvation's extent is about *who* is completed, not about *what* happens to them when they are. The completion moment awaits Christ's day (1 Cor 15:23; 1 Thess 4:16–17; Phil 1:6).¹¹⁴ The moment in which salvation's extent is reached is the issue upcoming.

---

112. McGuckin, "Strategic Adaptation of Deification," 95–110; Starr, "Does 2 Peter Speak of Deification?" 81–90; Williamson, *Death and the Afterlife*, 88; Winslow, *Dynamics of Salvation*, 193.

113. Basil, "Asketikon," LR Pro. ¶ 4 (p. 159).

114. Bornkamm, *Paulus*, 204; Demarest, *Cross and Salvation*, 382, 411, 467–68, 474; Harding, *Paul's Eschatological Anthropology*, 320; Peeler, "Eschatological Son," 172.

3

Scripture's Salvation Paradox

When you come to the point, it does go against the grain to kill an Archbishop, especially when you have been brought up in good Church traditions.

—T. S. Eliot, *Murder in the Cathedral*

As the last chapter showed, the scripturally described *co*ntent of salvation is bewildering but not contradictory: Salvation is wonderful, starts in this life, and completes in the next. In contrast, as this chapter will show, the scripturally described *ex*tent of salvation consists of accounts that seemingly contradict—one that is universalist and one that is exclusivist. To convince nearly all Christians of this, at least half of the argument is a must, and which half tends to depend on the side with which the reader starts out on the salvation-extent issue. For most Christians, the required half is universalism's scriptural basis because it is underappreciated for two reasons, as will be detailed in this chapter and the next. The first is that exclusivism has had a long-running currency in the church, which familiarity can convey the impression that universalism is not really Christian but is an alien implant from a philosophy based on wishful thinking. The second reason is that universalists tend to justify their position based on God's unadulterated loving nature, which lends itself to an absolutistic position, rather than on Scripture's messier account of how God and humans interact.¹ For these reasons, this chapter cannot truncate the presentation of Scripture's universalism. That presentation, along with that of Scripture's exclusivism afterwards, is designed to disturb the reader who may be untroubled by how Scripture ostensibly contradicts itself.

Despite its length, the presentation cannot be in-depth like the article-length exegeses of each universalist or exclusivist scriptural passage that can be found wherever biblical studies are practiced, nor can it be like the book-length defenses of the scripturalism of either universalism and exclusivism that materialize wherever salvation's extent is debated among theologians. Instead of offering such detail, the presentation relies on the cumulative effect of what Scripture says literally for each account and on the next chapter's confirmation of the coexistence of both scriptural accounts given how the respective parties in the church have understood that cumulative effect.

1. Everyone Is Ultimately Saved

Before addressing universalism's scriptural basis, a few rationales need to be identified as outside Scripture's salvation paradox because such a paradox is from what Scripture says and, in the case at hand, what it says about universalism and not from what might otherwise justify universalism. Christians have at times justified universalism, as well as exclusivism, independent of Scripture, but the issue at the moment is to demonstrate that Scripture has taken both contrary positions, not that theologians have.

The first excluded rationale for universalism is the argument that, because God's creation began with all things saved (Gen 1:31), it has to end that way too. The idea that everything will ultimately be restored to its beginning is sometimes called the *apokatastasis*, the transliterated Greek for *full restoration*, and this term can at times be used more broadly for any type of universalism.² The word appears in Scripture once (Acts 3:21), but universalists do not generally use this aberration to validate their position, which is no oversight on their part, because, while the verse does say that Christ's parousia involves "restoring [ἀποκαταστάσεως] all" to God, the reference is part of the call in Peter's second sermon for his

---

1. D. Hart, "Christ's Rabble," 18.
2. Oepke, "Ἀποκατάστασις," 389–93; Ramelli, "Procus and Apokatastasis," 95.

audience to repent so as to avoid obliteration (3:19, 23), which call would hardly exhort if the threatened obliteration was not really a threat.³ Instead, the *restoring* of *all* that Peter is referring to plainly includes the exclusion from eternal life in conjunction with God's wrathful judgment.⁴ Therefore, this unique *apokatastasis* verse does not shape the scriptural argument for universalism.

Two universalist deductions are also disqualified. The perennial question, *why would God not save everyone?* faces Origen's elementary answer: "If he is unwilling, then he will not be good; if he is willing but cannot, he will not be almighty."⁵ This philosophically attractive argument is a universalist favorite because its stated premises are sound—God is good and God is almighty.⁶ The argument is not, however, part of the universalist scriptural basis because it rests on an unstated premise that is not found in Scripture—God's goodness means he ensures the ultimate welfare of everyone.⁷ To the extent Scripture says anything about God ensuring anyone's welfare, it seems to be that of the godly (Isa 40:11; Jer 29:11; Rom 8:28). From the deluge in Genesis to the cataclysm in Revelation, Scripture presents the exact opposite of God ensuring everyone's welfare. The will that God has for utilitarian goodness has stated exclusions (Matt 23:37–38//Luke 13:34).⁸ Most relevantly, God wills that his creatures not reject him, yet they still do (Col 3:23–25).⁹ The existence of his will and the doing of his will are different or else we would not petition for his will to be done (Matt 6:10).¹⁰ In particular, God's loving goodness, though unrelenting and undiluted, does not mean that salvation is forced on the impenitent.¹¹ And to reject his love does not remove or even limit his love, but it does mean that we are not forced to accept his

---

3. Trumbower, *Rescue for the Dead*, 109.

4. Ludlow, *Universal Salvation*, 41 & n.90.

5. Origen, *On First Principles*, II,5,2 (p. 102).

6. Grenz, *Theology for the Community*, 635; D. Hart, *That All Shall Be Saved*, 90–91; Talbott, "Pauline Interpretation," 32.

7. Kierkegaard, *JP*, II: 47 (entry 1210); Strange, "Calvinist Response to Talbott," 156–60; Talbott, "Pauline Interpretation," 32.

8. McClymond, *Devil's Redemption*, II: 951.

9. Strange, "Calvinist Response," 164–65; Walls, "Philosophical Critique," 122.

10. Davis, *Risen Indeed*, 157.

11. Finney, *Memoirs*, 549 (MS935, JHF436); Geisler, *ST*, 587; Torrance, *Atonement*, 158.

love, meaning that we can incur his wrath as a result.[12] God's all-powerful love is, accordingly, not part of the *scriptural* paradox despite the argument's *ipso facto* appeal.

The second excluded universalist deduction is similar: The saved, it is argued, would empathetically suffer if anyone were damned, which would mean the saved can never be in bliss if everyone is not there with them.[13] Universalists occasionally cite in support of this argument Jesus' concern for the needy (Matt 25:40) or Paul's concern for others (Rom 9:2–3; Phil 2:27), but no such concern warrants the conclusion that the saved cannot live without everyone else living too. Scripture certainly never says the saved *require* that everyone else be saved too. Universalists, rather, take such tenderheartedness as an obvious inference—that is, those who are saved, if they are truly godly, will have to hurt for the unsaved.[14] This inference is unwarranted as well, at least based on Scripture. The godly can positively crave divine vengeance (Neh 4:4–5; Jer 17:18). The Psalmist certainly does,[15] including in the psalms that Jesus prophetically fulfilled (Pss 41:9–10, 69:21, 24, 28). Jesus, for his part, favorably described Abraham resting peacefully as Dives looked on in torment (Luke 16:19–31). The thought of divine vengeance comforted Paul as well (Rom 2:5–6; 12:19; 1 Thess 4:6; 2 Tim 4:14–15), and the godly martyrs were similarly reassured (Rev 6:10; 18:20; 20:12–15). God too proves daily his willingness to endure suffering.[16] This ability of the godly to endure the suffering of the reprobate obviously continues outside of Scripture, whether Tertullian, Thomas, or Luther, which universalists acknowledge.[17] The saved, it is therefore safe to say, are apparently not so delicate as to find eternal life any less if those rejecting it are not made to join them.[18] Presumably this is because eternal life entails relating to the Savior, and this is joyful superabundantly.[19]

---

12. Edwards, *After Death?* 153–54; Grenz, *Theology for the Community*, 74; Matera, *Romans*, 48, 55.

13. Talbott, "Christ Victorious," 15–18; "Reply to My Critics," 266.

14. D. Hart, *That All Shall Be Saved*, 31, 78–79, 166–67.

15. Pss 7:6–9; 10:15; 31:17; 58:10–11; 71:13; 79:6, 10, 12; 137:7–9; 140:8–10; 143:12; 149:5–7, 9.

16. Koehn, *Nature of Evil*, 15.

17. D. Hart, *That All Shall Be Saved*, 78.

18. Caldecott, *Radiance of Being*, 243; Gregory the Great, *Forty Gospel Homilies*, hom. 40 (p. 381); Kierkegaard, *Eighteen Upbuilding Discourses*, 256–57.

19. Jobes, "Remember These Things," 198–99.

Even with these three exclusions, universalism has broad scriptural support. Though universalism was not articulated before Christ,[20] the Hebrew Scriptures suggested it. Its first chapters established humanity's universality (Gen 1–11), which implies a universal human destiny.[21] Accordingly, God appointed Abraham and his seed to bless *all* clans on earth (12:2–3; 18:18; 22:18; 26:4; 28:14) and told Moses that God's glory will fill *all* the earth (Num 14:21). Later, the Psalmist sung of God's "salvation among all nations" (67:1–3), and the prophets foretold of God's "salvation to the end of the earth" (Isa 49:6). "I will pour out My Spirit on all flesh" (Joel 2:28). It is the NT, however, that makes universal salvation explicit.[22] To present this adequately requires addressing each universalist passage, at least in a synopsis, but, instead of taking the NT passages in canonical order, they can be grouped by emphasis: God's will for universalism, God's achievement of it, the rationale for universalism, and salvation's explicit application to the ungodly.

a. God's Will

Scripture frequently says that God wills that his salvation extend universally. John's gospel, for instance, says Christ was "sent to save the world [ὁ κόσμος]" (3:16–17; 12:47–50), which expresses universalism unless Christ was a failure.[23] Exclusivists cannot bring themselves to say that Christ was a failure, but they nonetheless concede that he failed to save that part of the world that disbelieves in him.[24] Understanding the world as the world per se, they say, is to not fully appreciate John's exclusivist passages elsewhere.[25] This common strategy is patently not derived from what John is saying here, but, rather, is derived from giving priority to the exclusivist verses discussed in the next section. This common exclusivist rule of construction is based on starting with the chosen winner of salvation's extent, instead of starting with the scriptural paradox itself.

---

20. McClymond, *Devil's Redemption*, I: 130; Ramelli, *Christian Doctrine of Apokatastasis*, 819.

21. Glasser et al., *Announcing the Kingdom*, 29; Wallenfang, *Human and Divine Being*, 8.

22. Balthasar, *Dare We Hope*, 21; Johnson, "Wideness in God's Mercy," 94.

23. Allen, *Extent of Atonement*, 777.

24. Morris, *John*, 205–6.

25. Carson, *John*, 206–7.

First Timothy confirms that Christ "entered the world to save sinners," "wills all men saved," and "gave himself ransom exchange for all" (1:15; 2:4, 6). Most exclusivists admit the obvious, which is that these express God's intent to save everyone in the world, but, using one of their usual gambits, draw the line at God actually realizing his intent; the best that God can manage is saving a scattered assortment from around the world.[26] Nothing in these verses, however, expresses this boundary limit on Christ's salvation.[27] John's main epistle adds, the Father "has sent" "the world's Savior" (4:14; also John 4:42). Exclusivists notice that the "has sent" is in the perfect tense, which means it is referring to Christ's saving of the world as a historical event, but exclusivists posit its achievement by Christ is still not achievable by Christ.[28]

Second Corinthians expands on these simple universalist formulas: Christ "died for all and therefore they all died, and he died for all so that the living live no more to themselves but to him who for them died and was raised." "God in Christ was reconciling the world to himself" (5:14–15, 19). "This," Bornkamm observed, "makes clear that God's saving act in the death of Christ embraces the whole world."[29] Exclusivists naturally acknowledge that Paul's *all* is universal when written in such phrases as Christ "died for all" and certainly in the phrase "they all died," but exclusivists must deny that Paul intends for *all* to have the same meaning in his parallel phrases identifying those living in Christ. Paul Barnett, to illustrate, argues that the *all*'s "clearly emphasize the universal and inclusive nature of Christ's death," meaning "none is excluded," but the *all* in salvation "is in actuality limited." Similarly, *the world* refers, not to something as obvious as the world, but just to believers around the world.[30]

Second Peter ties God's repeatedly expressed will for universalism to God's actual accomplishment of it: Since God does "not resolv[e]" even "some to perish," his patience will "accommodate all" (3:9). Yet, exclusivists take this to mean, not that God resolves to accommodate all so none perish, but that he wants to, which human freewill trumps.[31] If that does

26. Knight, *Pastoral Epistles*, 101, 119, 122; Mounce, *Pastoral Epistles*, 84–86, 89; Towner, *Timothy and Titus*, 146, 177–78.

27. Allen, *Extent of Atonement*, 777.

28. Smalley, *1,2,3 John*, 253; Stott, *Epistles of John*, 167.

29. Bornkamm, *Paulus*, 141.

30. Barnett, *Second Corinthians*, 289–91, 307 & n.25.

31. Davids, *2 Peter and Jude*, 281–82; Green, *2 Peter and Jude*, 148; Schreiner, *1,2 Peter, Jude*, 381–83.

not work, exclusivists modify the unmodified "all" so it pertains only to the letter's addressees—that is, believers.[32] This limitation of Scripture to only those who believe in it before reading from it belittles its authority (2 Tim 3:15). A Barth is not required to appreciate that Scripture "veritably speaks to all men of every age"[33] or, per Hamann, to "the entire human race."[34] Scripture's audience has certainly included nonbelievers such as Augustine, who came to belief afterwards.[35] Besides, the scriptural writers have demonstrated the ability to choose words that can limit a point to believers when that is their intent (Acts 28:2; Rom 4:16; 8:32; 2 Cor 3:18), but, in 2 Peter, no such words appear. God's accommodating "all" so that not even some perish is not limited to, say, a few churches in Asia Minor. God has clearly accommodated more than that.

b. Reality

According to Scripture, universalism is, not only God's active *will* for humanity, but also his *work*. In Philippians, God exalts "the Name above every name, *so that* [ἵνα] in Jesus' name every knee may bow in the heaven, earth, and underworld and every tongue may confess Jesus Christ 'Lord'" (2:9–11). Though *bow* and *confess* are in the subjunctive, a mood which suggests uncertainty, the ἵνα clause for the verbs is what provides the purpose-result of Christ's exaltation—that is, "*both the intention and its sure accomplishment.*"[36] Everyone is, accordingly, said to be ultimately worshipping Christ.[37] To confine universal salvation to God's never achieved purpose, however, exclusivists once more elevate their preferred account in the paradox so as to outmaneuver this verse's stated point.[38]

Titus makes the same point using a different grammatical device: "God's grace, saving to all men, *has appeared*" (2:11). The aorist indicative verb relates saving everyone to Christ's historical appearance and, so, is actualizing universalistic salvation by inflection, but exclusivists

---

32. Bauckham, *Jude, 2 Peter*, 313.
33. Barth, "Preface to First Edition," 1.
34. Hamann, "Golgotha and Sheblimini!" 189.
35. Augustine, *Confessions*, VIII,xii,29 (pp. 152–53). See Chadwick, *Augustine of Hippo*, 27.
36. Wallace, *Greek Grammar*, 473–74.
37. Thompson, "Philippians," 73.
38. Marshall, "NT Does Not Teach Universalism," 68–69.

respond with their go-to defense: Because "all men" is the specified extent of God's salvation, the phrase has to mean "all sorts of men."[39] For added variety, if not cogency, some exclusivists say that God's referenced universal "grace" is not related to the "saving" and conclude that, while the grace extends to everyone, the salvation extends only to representatives from every tribe,[40] but this separation of concepts is not a promising solution since in the original Greek nothing at all separates the words "grace" and "saving." None of these strategies, therefore, detracts from the verse's literal universalism.[41]

Construing *all* as *all sorts* buckles particularly under the universalist aphorism, "God and Father [of] πάντων, who is over πάντων, through πάντων, and in πᾶσιν" (Eph 4:6). The four πᾶς substantive plurals mean "all" and does not mean "all sorts" as it can when used adjectively.[42] Exclusivists nevertheless read each "all" as "all believers" for the same two reasons they usually give: 1) the aphorism would otherwise conflict with Scripture's exclusivist account and 2) Paul addressed these words to believers.[43] But these reasons are especially inapposite here. The first reason of just siding with Scripture's exclusivism ignores that the *all*'s apply to *who* God *is*, not merely *what* he *does*. If *all* were taken to mean only *all believers*, then God is the God of only believers, not the God of everyone, which is a high price to pay to avoid its stated universalism. Scripture certainly rejects, at least eventually, such a henotheistic understanding (Ps 24:1; Rom 11:36; 1 Cor 8:6,; 10:26; Col 1:16; Heb 2:10). As for the second reason, this verse's textual history exposes the inapplicability of restricting its scriptural authority to believers. A few scribes of Ephesians added the second person plural pronoun (ὑμῖν) to the verse so that God would in fact be only *in all of you*, and, by this addition, the letter would be specifying that it was limited to its audience—that is, the saved, not all of humanity—but the certain reading excludes this exclusivist addition.[44] The belated "fix," therefore, accentuates the original intent to state the universality of God's salvation without limiting it to the addressees.

---

39. Knight, *Pastoral Epistles*, 318–19.
40. Mounce, *Pastoral Epistles*, 422.
41. F. Sanders, "Wesleyan View," 156–57.
42. BDAG, 782–84.
43. Hoehner, *Ephesians*, 518–21.
44. Metzger, *Textual Commentary*, 536.

Revelation's presentation of the cosmic consummation, despite that book's heavy emphasis on the eschatological doom, also manages to recognize universalism. After the godly have worshipped God, everyone else, "every creature [πᾶν κτίσμα] in the heaven, on the earth, under the earth, and in the sea," will join in the worshipping, "singing: To him enthroned and to the Lamb the praise and honor, the glory and dominion, into the ages!" (5:11–13). Since this worshipping by "every creature" in the end is being contrasted with the worshipping by those already aligned with God, to suggest that this is not everyone worshipping, but just a subset, defies the words. So, exegetes acknowledge that this passage expresses "universal acclamation," "universal praise in an absolute sense," "not only from God's willing subjects but also from his opponents," and that this "ideal purpose" is "actually . . . fulfilled."[45] Revelation relates the "Universal Worship" of God[46] by "the whole created world,"[47] for which "The universality of Christ's great redemptive work calls."[48] Thus, even in the book most prolific in its description of the negative outcome for the ungodly, God still somehow achieves in the end his stated objective of bringing all to him.

c. Rationale

Scripture not only asserts the reality of universalism as both willed and accomplished by God, but Paul explains *why* salvation is universally achieved: Adam's thoroughly infectious sin, which to the sentient is unquestionably universal, is perforce overmatched by Christ's even mightier salvation. That is, "through one man, sin entered the world, and through sin death, and thus to all men death passed, on which all have sinned," but, "if the many died by the trespass of the one, how much more God's grace and the gift by grace of the one man, Jesus Christ, abound to the many" (Rom 5:12, 15). The "many" in the last verse, a Hebraism for "all,"[49] is by parallelism "all men" from the first verse to whom death passed—namely, everyone.[50] "The world," the exclusivist Augustine accepted, refers

---

45. Beale, *Revelation*, 332, 365–66.
46. Osborne, *Revelation*, 264–66.
47. Gooder, *Heaven*, 67.
48. Mounce, *Revelation*, 137–38.
49. Ringgren, "Rab, Inclusive Plural," 293; Torrance, *Atonement*, 183.
50. Edwards, *Mark*, 61 & n.34.

to "the whole human race."[51] Just as Adam doomed "all men," Christ gave "eternal life" to "all men" (Rom 5:18–19, 21), which is of course literally universalism.[52] Because the same terms are used here for those who have death and those who have eternal life, to deny that salvation is universal is to deny that the need for salvation is universal. As is obvious to every exegete and anyone looking around, Adam's sin-effect is effectively inescapable for all humans, and, to this self-evident point, Paul merely adds that Christ's grace-effect is responsively more, which makes sense given the personages being compared, the first man and the God-man.[53]

Exclusivists demur: While of course Adam's sin includes everyone, Christ's more potent grace cannot include everyone because this just cannot be what Paul meant.[54] The *many* within the Adam-effect has its usual meaning of *all people*, but the *many* within the Christ-effect, which is connected by "how much more" in the same clause position twenty words later, has to be fewer people—just *believers*.[55] Paul supposedly uses *all* to mean *all* for the Adam-effect but *all* to mean only *all the justified* for the Christ-effect.[56] This, if a proper understanding, is certainly poor composition from someone who has, according to NT scholarship, "a strong track record of choosing his vocabulary with great care."[57] Paul's competing exclusivist passages once again rationalize the grammatical gymnastics.[58] Yet, the *all* condemned through Adam and the *all* justified through Christ are clearly the same set—everyone.[59] Exclusivists who realize this and who can navigate the most sublime passages elsewhere claim an inability to disambiguate here.[60]

---

51. Augustine, *Enchiridion*, 8,26 (p. 59).

52. Dunn, *Romans 1–8*, 280, 285, 293–94, 297; Moo, *Romans*, 349; Schreiner, *Romans*, 286–87, 290–92.

53. Cranfield, *Romans 1–8*, 295; Moo, *Romans*, 362–63, 369–70; Trueman, "Definite Atonement View," 51.

54. Marshall, "NT Does Not Teach Universalism," 65–66.

55. Moo, *Romans*, 363, 369–70.

56. Cranfield, *Romans 1–8*, 290.

57. Weima, *1–2 Thessalonians*, 477.

58. Trueman, "Definite Atonement View," 51.

59. Bell, "Rom 5.18–19," 417–32; Boer, *Defeat of Death*, 174–75; D. Hart, *New Testament*, 298 note 2.

60. Dunn, *Romans 1–8*, 298.

d. The Ungodly

To attentive ears universalism is contrary to attentive eyes because much of humanity has noticeably been refusing salvation's offer, but Christ has an answer: "I will drag [ἑλκύσω] all to myself" (John 12:32). Ἑλκύσω means to pull something to somewhere else, such as when captured fish resist their fate in a net (21:6, 11).[61] *All* translates πάντας, which needs no comment except for how exclusivists treat it. If it were modifying a noun, it can mean *all kinds of*, but here it is an anarthrous substantive, so it has its normal meaning of *all*.[62] Still, exclusivists interpret πάντας as *all kinds of persons* because of, once more, the exclusivist passages that are found elsewhere.[63] Nothing, however, in commonsense or the passage's wording, which is how writers normally curtail *all*,[64] indicates πάντας is less than that. Rather, the passage says that Christ draws everyone to himself, whether or not they are resisting their fate.[65]

Paul speaks similarly in discussing Israel's ultimate salvation: God graces "all," though "all" disobey (Rom 11:25–36). Notwithstanding that grace is for *all* and disobedience is by *all*,[66] exclusivists read the first *all* as *some*, but reverse course to give the parallel *all* appearing five words later its ordinary meaning.[67] Alternatively, exclusivists "resolve . . . the paradox" by "assum[ing]" Paul is only speaking "in general terms," which is code for his not really meaning what he is saying.[68] Because nothing here actually limits salvation's extent,[69] the best exclusivist resort is God's "mysterious" "dark" way,[70] but that characterizes Paul's topic, not his insight.

Colossians repeats the observation that salvation includes those opting out: Christ is "to reconcile fully all things into him, whether those on the earth or in the heavens" (1:20). What is rendered "to reconcile fully"

---

61. *BDAG*, 318.
62. *BDAG*, 783–84.
63. Carson, *John*, 443–44; Keener, *John*, II: 881; Morris, *John*, 532–33.
64. Allen, *Extent of Atonement*, 777; Hammett, "Response to General Atonement," 138; Luther, *Galatians*, 226 [WA 401,513 (3:22)].
65. Balthasar, *Dare We Hope*, 39–40; D. Hart, *That All Shall Be Saved*, 98.
66. Trumbower, *Rescue for the Dead*, 39–40.
67. Marshall, "NT Does Not Teach Universalism," 67–68; Moo, *Romans*, 751; Schreiner, *Romans*, 629, 631.
68. Dunn, *Romans 9–16*, 689, 696–97.
69. Talbott, "Pauline Interpretation," 34.
70. Cranfield, *Romans 9–16*, 587–88.

reflects the infinitive of ἀποκαταλλάσσω, which is an emphatic ἀπό prefixing καταλλάσσω, which by itself means "exchange hostility for a friendly relationship," such as what Christ's death achieves for us with God (Rom 5:10).[71] What is so thoroughly befriended is the neuter plural τὰ πάντα, "all things." The universality of these terms plus "the earth [τῆς γῆς]" is difficult to surpass.[72] Undeterred, exclusivists redeploy their reinterpretation of *all things* on *earth* as just the faithful scattered about.[73] They also say the verb only means *pacification*, not *reconciliation*—the unfaithful are subjugated but nonsalvifically.[74] This, however, dodges the word's actual meaning of emphatically friendly.[75] The verb is contorted because otherwise it expresses the idea that God fully reconciles everyone, which, given the exclusivist account, is ruled out as too paradoxical.[76]

Paul's treatise on resurrection in 1 Corinthians' fifteenth chapter has at its heart one of universalism's strongest citations:

> [S]ince by a man came death, by a man too comes the dead's resurrection. For, as in Adam, *all* die, so, in Christ, *all* will live, but each in its own corps: Christ the firstfruit, thereafter those of Christ at his presentment—then the end, whenever he gives over the reign to the God and Father, whenever nullifying *all* rule, *all* liberty and force, for he must reign till he has put *all* his enemies under his feet. A last enemy is being nullified, the Death, for *all* he has committed under his feet.... Whenever *all* has been committed to him, the Son himself will be committed to him committing *all*, so God may be *all* in *all*. (15:20–28)

Paul here makes emphatic the all-ness of Christ's work of salvation.[77] As exclusivists understand Paul, however, he is only hoping for universalism because he is not explicit enough, but this is just refusing to accept

---

71. *BDAG*, 521.

72. Talbott, "Christ Victorious," 22.

73. Marshall, "NT Does Not Teach Universalism," 70–71.

74. Bruce, *Colossians, Philemon, and Ephesians*, 75–76; O'Brien, *Colossians, Philemon*, 56; N. T. Wright, *Colossians and Philemon*, 77.

75. It is not that Paul does not employ the concept of subjugation, but he does it elsewhere (Phil 3:20–21), using the word (ὑποτάξαι) that has that meaning. *BDAG*, 1042; Silva, *Philippians*, 185.

76. Bruce, *Colossians, Philemon, and Ephesians*, 75; Dunn, *Colossians and Philemon*, 104; N. T. Wright, *Colossians and Philemon*, 77.

77. Ramelli, *Christian Doctrine of Apokatastasis*, 38–39; Robinson, *In the End, God . . .*, 93–94; Talbott, "Christ Victorious," 25.

what he writes.⁷⁸ Despite seeing that *all* dying in Adam means every human and that Paul has secured the parallel between Adam and Christ, *all* living in Christ just cannot mean "all humans," because a "reference to the resurrection of non-Christians would only confuse matters."⁷⁹ The confusion stems, of course, from this passage being read along with the exclusivist account, which Paul has presented elsewhere.⁸⁰ Why an exclusivist is confused is therefore easy to appreciate, but the clarity of Paul's "all in all" is easy to appreciate too.⁸¹

This key 1 Corinthians passage also makes explicit the central point regarding the salvation of the ungodly because it says that both "those of Christ" and "his enemies" attain the preferred outcome in the resurrection—"all" in the end live in Christ. The only stated difference in the outcomes between the two groups is their sequencing: Christ's followers enter eschatological life before his enemies do.⁸² This explicit comparison between the faithful and the rest of us, where both categories are said to eternally live, is perhaps the clearest way to establish universalism.⁸³ The NT does this twice more.

According to 1 John, Jesus "is reconciliation [ἱλασμός]⁸⁴ for our sins, and not ours only but all the world's" (2:2). Though this verse establishes an unmistakable equivalency in the divine reconciliation between those who are faithful and everyone else in the world, to exclusivists this "cannot mean that all people's sins are automatically forgiven so that all are the inheritors of eternal life, even if they do not believe," but this refusal to accept the apparent meaning is only because it conflicts with the exclusivist account, which, therefore, leaves exclusivists in "difficulty."⁸⁵ Their difficulty is understandable because "not ours only but all the world's" conveys universality and universal reconciliation implies universal

---

78. Boer, *Defeat of Death*, 112, 126; Fee, *First Corinthians*, 760; Ludlow, *Universal Salvation*, 241.

79. Garland, *1 Corinthians*, 709. Accord Thiselton, *First Corinthians*, 1224–25.

80. Ludlow, *Universal Salvation*, 241.

81. D. Hart, *That All Shall Be Saved*, 193–94; Origen, *On First Principles*, III,6,3 (p. 248).

82. D. Hart, *New Testament*, 348 note ab; Talbott, "Reply to My Critics," 254.

83. Boer, *Defeat of Death*, 113, 136, 139, 174.

84. This term's rarity generates scholarship. Kruse, *Letters of John*, 75–76. Two meanings compete—expiation and propitiation. *BDAG*, 474. "Reconciliation" is intended to accommodate either.

85. Kruse, *Letters of John*, 75. Accord Stott, *Epistles of John*, 84.

salvation, particularly from the pen of someone writing before theologians had separated reconciliation from salvation.[86]

Yet, the simplest and surest expression of salvation's all-inclusiveness may be in 1 Timothy: God is "the Savior of all men—most especially those believing" (4:9–10). "Most especially" translates μάλιστα, which is the superlative of μάλα ("very"), and this gives it the meaning of "to an unusual degree" or "most assuredly."[87] Because μάλιστα denotes an emphasis that is non-exclusive, the understanding of the saving of "all men" as *everyone* is unavoidable.[88] If "believers" are saved *especially*, the adjacent phrase cannot be limited, even implicitly, to believers because the two groups are distinguished in a way that does not involve whether they are saved—everyone is saved, but the faithful are saved particularly.[89]

A few secular papyri apparently use μάλιστα to mean "that is" or "specifically," which meaning if applied to 1 Timothy would yield the loutish but exclusivist: The saved are "all men—that is, believers."[90] Unexplained is why any author, much less one scripturally enshrined, would first refer to the full 100 percent of humanity and then explain that what he actually means is only something like one hundredth of 1 percent of it, which was Christianity's approximate extent as of about then.[91] Unexplained too is why the author of 1 Timothy would pick the superlative of the extreme "very" to express something that is neither superlative nor extreme when he had several other Greek terms that could more surely express "that is."[92] Unexplained also is why μάλιστα does not mean "that is" in Paul's injunction "let's do good to all, but μάλιστα to the house of the faith" (Gal 6:10). Presumably this does not mean that we are to do good only to the faithful, and when the Pastoral Paul said, "bring . . .

---

86. D. Hart, *That All Shall Be Saved*, 101; McClymond, *Devil's Redemption*, I: 259; Owen, *Death of Death*, 173–74.

87. BDAG, 613.

88. D. Hart, *That All Shall Be Saved*, 102; Ramelli, *Christian Doctrine of Apokatastasis*, 41.

89. Balthasar, *Dare We Hope*, 36–38.

90. Hutson, *First . . . Timothy*, 113–14; Knight, *Pastoral Epistles*, 203–4.

91. Poythress, "Meaning of Malista," 523–32. Christians numbered about 7,530 by the end of the first century. Stark, *Rise of Christianity*, 6–8. The world's population was then hundreds of millions. U.S. Census, "Historical Estimates of World Population."

92. Candidate Greek words that might convey the meaning of *to restate something in a different way* are τοῦτ' ἐστί (this is), λέγω (I mean), σάφως (clearly), διαρρήδην (expressly), or ὀνομαστί (by name). Woodhouse, *English-Greek Dictionary*, s.vv. "namely" and "specifically." Other possibilities could be δηλαδή (in essence) or even just γάρ (for).

the books, μάλιστα the parchments" (2 Tim 4:13), presumably Timothy would understand not to leave behind the more common papyri while grabbing the parchments.

As a result, exclusivists who recognize that 1 Timothy says on its face that everyone is saved, even non-believers, must help its author along with his thinking through their exegesis. For example, Christ "is the Savior of all men [potentially], and especially [actually] of those who believe."[93] Scripture invites such Herculean exegesis, exclusivists argue, because otherwise Scripture is in paradox.[94] Indeed.

2. Only Some Are Ultimately Saved

Scripture is universalist except where it isn't,[95] but its exclusivism is expressed more descriptively, thematically, and thoroughly. Thus, the presentation of exclusivism can and must be less of a catalogue. Before setting out its scriptural account, however, three arguments need to be culled from the presentation. First, Scripture often says believers are saved,[96] and, while such verses can sound exclusivist, the passages are immaterial to the salvation paradox if they do not also refer to the unsaved because only damnation forms the paradox.[97] Confusing the truth of a proposition, such as that believers are saved, for the truth of its converse, such as that unbelievers are not saved, is the negative inference fallacy.[98] Second, passages that merely warn of the "soul" perishing are excluded because, by themselves, they are not exclusivist unless referring to the "soul" as meant by Greek philosophy, which is an enduring metaphysical entity, but these passages may reflect the Hebrew understanding of the "soul," which refers to the perishable life in an entity; and, given this, the passages can be saying that *natural* life ends, not that *eternal* life is lost (*e.g.*, Mark 8:36, 38//Matt 10:33; 16:26//Luke 9:25, 26; 12:9). Third, the instances where Scripture says that salvation is only through Christ are excluded because,

---

93. Geisler, *ST*, 863.

94. Knight, *Pastoral Epistles*, 203; Towner, *Timothy and Titus*, 311–12; Trueman, "Definite Atonement View," 35.

95. Marshall, "NT Does Not Teach Universalism," 56.

96. John 3:16; 6:37–40; 10:26–29; 11:26; 14:6; 17:6–10; Rom 3:21, 26; 11:5; 1 Cor 1:21; Eph 5:25–27; Titus 2:14.

97. Osborne, "General Atonement View," 89.

98. Allen, *Extent of Atonement*, 20–21.

while they express salvation's exclusive *agent*, they do not express salvation's exclusive *extent* (*e.g.*, John 10:7–10; Acts 4:12). Stating who is doing the saving does not by itself state who all is being saved. Depriving exclusivism of these points, however, still leaves it plenty.

a. Descriptions

The Hebrew Scriptures, when depicting the cosmic climax, consistently portray some people as not saved. In "the new heavens and new earth," for instance, the evildoers receive "caprice" and "dread," "their worm will not die nor their fire quench" (Isa 65:17; 66:4, 22, 24). "Behold, the Day comes, burning furnace-like: All the arrogant and each evildoer will be chaff, and the coming day will set them afire, says the Lord of Forces. No root or branch will remain to them" (Mal 4:1). The clearest reference to resurrection in the Hebrew Scriptures also clearly specifies two ultimate destinies, one "to eternal life" and one "to shames, eternal contempt" (Dan 12:1–4). This anticipates the NT's depiction of two populated ultimates—"those doing goods into a resurrection of life and those practicing evils into a resurrection of judgment" (John 5:28–29).

The NT adds little to the binary outcomes referenced in the Hebrew Scriptures other than to elaborate on the negative one, particularly when Jesus is the speaker.[99] In heavens' reign, a parabolic dragnet captures everyone, where "the sons of the evil," or those who are "unsound," are segregated and "burned in" "the fiery furnace, a place of weeping and gnashing" (Matt 13:24–30, 36–43, 47–50).[100] Christ's sheep-goats parable, among the most explicit descriptions concerning salvation,[101] similarly teaches exclusivity: The Son of Man will "separate men from each other" such that the blessed are in "eternal life" and the cursed are in "eternal castigation" (25:31–46). His Lazarus parable also portrays two eternal destinies, one that is "tormented" "agony" in "fire" (Luke 16:19–31), which is, if nothing else, inhabited negativity.[102] Christ's eschatological feast likewise has the unprepared evicted "into the outer darkness, where weeping and gnashing will be" because "many are called but few elected"

---

99. Geisler, *ST*, 1268.
100. Dulles, "Population of Hell," 36.
101. Nichols, *Death and Afterlife*, 154.
102. Ratzinger, *Eschatology*, 124; Stein, *Luke*, 424; Witherington, "Equally Orthodox Christians," 295.

(Matt 22:1–14). Even when the point of one of his parables is inclusivity, still not everyone enters (Luke 14:15–24). Accordingly, Jesus describes the alternative to salvation as something like torturous imprisonment, and his numerous mentions of an eschatological hell make it difficult to ignore it as an ultimate (Mark 9:43–47//Matt 18:8–9; 5:22, 25, 29–30; 10:28; 18:34; 23:33; 11:23//Luke 10:15; 12:5, 58).[103] "Anyone not abiding in me is like the branch cast away to wither; they're gathered, cast into the fire, and burned" (John 15:6). N. T. Wright summarized the obvious: "eternal punishment" comes "most clearly and unmistakably" from "the lips of Jesus Himself."[104] God's judgment thus unmistakably dispenses, along with eternal life, its negation.[105] To avoid this conclusion, universalists say *eternal* means something like *special*, which turns the two stated ultimates into really one ultimate,[106] or that Jesus engaged in a sort of pious fraud to frighten the faint-hearted into righteousness.[107]

The NT's epistles also establish that the ultimate consists of two opposites, including the undesirable one. While salvation comes to believers, its reverse comes to the unrighteous (Rom 1:16–18). So, in addition to "those being saved," there will be "those being annihilated [τοῖς ἀπολλυμένοις]" (2 Cor 2:15).[108] The saved are consistently distinguished from the annihilated (1 Cor 1:18; 2 Cor 4:3–4; Phil 1:27–30, 3:17–19; 2 Tim 2:10–13). The saved are repeatedly described as a human subset: "those loving God, those called by his purpose," "those he foreknew," "those he predestined," "those he called," "those he righted" (Rom 8:28–30). It is the rest of humanity that pays the "penalty" of "eternal destruction [ὄλεθρον]" (2 Thess 1:6–10) because election by its very nature discriminates, which is what results in those "being annihilated [ἀπολλυμένοις]" (2:10).[109] Those "following the way of Balaam" are "reserved for the dark of darkness," a "day of judgment and annihilation of irreverent men" (2 Pet 2:10–17; 3:7). Though believers have eternal life, those without the Son lack it (1 John 5:11–13). To universalists, these

---

103. Balthasar, *Dare We Hope*, 20–21; Marshall, "NT Does Not Teach Universalism," 57.

104. N. T. Wright, "Biblical View of Universalism," 55.

105. Balthasar, *Dare We Hope*, 30; Nickelsburg, *Resurrection, Immortality, and Eternal Life*, 238.

106. Ellul, *Apocalypse*, 276.

107. McClymond, *Devil's Redemption*, II: 961–62.

108. Guthrie, *2 Corinthians*, 174.

109. McClymond, *Devil's Redemption*, II: 861; S. Williams, *Election of Grace*, 201.

sentiments expressing the opposite of eternal life as eschatological annihilating reflect only a kind of dispensational annihilating that reboots the condemned such that they will love God before the promised annihilating becomes an actual one.[110] To treat *annihilating* this way, not only changes the concept's meaning, it reduces the two outcomes that are actually expressed to just the one good one, despite annihilation (ἀπώλεια) being *the* end (τὸ τέλος) for the ungodly (Phil 3:19).[111]

For a brief moment the back and forth between universalists and exclusivists seems on the verge of a clear resolution in Scripture because Jesus was asked directly at least once whether "those being saved [οἱ σῳζόμενοι]" are "few [ὀλίγοι]," but, unfortunately, Jesus answered with his usual allusiveness: "Contest to enter the narrow door, for I tell you all that many will try to enter but lack strength. Once the housemaster ever rises and shuts the door and you begin to stand outside, knock, and plead 'Lord, open to us,' he'll answer, 'I know not where you're from'" (Luke 13:23–25). If Christ's answer is, as it seems to be, responsive to the question, he is clearly implying that "many" will not be saved, certainly not everyone.[112] The Matthew parallel confirms that it is the "few" who find "the way leading to the life," while the "many are those entering" "the way leading to the destruction [ἀπώλειαν]" (7:13–14).[113] The take-away that Jesus himself expressed about his allusive answer seems consistent only with an exclusivity of salvation: God's reign is for those "doing my heavenly Father's will" and, so, "Not all [Οὐ πᾶς]" will enter it (7:21–23// Luke 13:26–27).

Thus, as Kierkegaard observed, while the salvation of everyone is a tempting position for any thoughtful person, the NT clearly resists that temptation and specifies that not everyone finds salvation.[114] At least according to Scripture, God's call to salvation is evidently not by itself irresistible.[115] Grenz summed up: "The New Testament writers repeatedly spoke of the fate of the unrighteous as exclusion, as eternal separation from community with God."[116] By portraying "a stark choice between

---

110. Talbott, "Reply to My Critics," 251.
111. McClymond, *Devil's Redemption*, II: 953; Thompson, "Philippians," 114–15.
112. Bock, *Luke 9:51—24:53*, 1234–36; Martin, *Will Many Be Saved?* 125–26.
113. Morris, *Matthew*, 174–75.
114. Kierkegaard, *Attack Upon "Christendom,"* 105.
115. Colijn, *Images of Salvation*, 232.
116. Grenz, *Theology for the Community*, 642.

two totally opposed orientations and their respective outcomes," R. T. France noted, Scripture takes for granted that not everyone will "find the way to life."[117] This, Balthasar concluded, excludes universalism's single all-good outcome.[118]

b. Themes

Scripture not only describes an inhabited negative ultimate, but it has two decisive themes that signal that there is an ultimate that opposes eternal life. Scripture's meta-theme might be God's saving mission to all creation,[119] and this entails reaching others.[120] Paul asks, how can people believe without being taught? (Rom 10:14), and the great commission answers, "disciple all nations" (Matt 28:18–20).[121] Universalism either must deny the palpable and claim that everyone has been evangelized or must deny that the evangelizing ultimately matters, but this is not what Scripture seemingly relates: "Amen, amen I tell you, except to the extent one is born above once, he can't see God's reign." That is, "Amen, amen I tell you, except to the extent one is born of water and Spirit, he can't enter God's reign" (John 3:3, 5). Indeed, it is difficult to believe that much of Scripture would have been written if not for the need to broadcast its message.[122] And, as scripturally portrayed, conversion is only one of the options we have, and the choice between them is consistently identified as determinative. "Amen I tell you, except to the extent you turn to become as little children, you'll never enter the heavens' reign" (Matt 18:3).[123] Because people have not been saved from merely being alive, missionaries grew Christianity among the living.[124]

The second exclusivist theme is the most blatant, and it is Scripture's recurring proclamation that salvation has a real obverse, which is

---

117. France, *Matthew*, 288.
118. Balthasar, *Theo-Drama*, V: 191.
119. C. Wright, *Mission of God*.
120. Marshall, "NT Does Not Teach Universalism," 63; R. Williams, *Christian Theology*, 31.
121. Osborne, "General Atonement View," 118.
122. Matera, *Romans*, 36–38.
123. Carson, "Matthew," 397; France, *Matthew*, 677–78; Morris, *Matthew*, 459.
124. Geisler, *ST*, 54; Mostert, *God and the Future*, 81; Piper, *Let the Nations Be Glad*, 111–54.

experienced as divine wrath (John 3:36; 1 Thess 5:9).[125] In the collision between God and humanity, only a human remnant emerges.[126] Universalism hardly seems realistic after reading: the Lord "destroys his hater," "will not consent to forgive him," and "blots out his name from under heaven" (Deut 7:9–10; 29:20). The Lord says, "No pity, sparing, or embracing will keep me from destroying them" (Jer 13:14). As the Lord "completed his wrath," "Women's compassionate hands cooked their own children" (Lam 4:10–11). Given this severity among his chosen for those who rebel, one can imagine how God treats those who are not his chosen, but no imagination is required: "an avenging day for vengeance on his foes. The sword will devour till satisfied, till it quenches its blood thirst, for the Lord of Forces will slaughter" (Jer 46:10). The Hebrew Scriptures fill with such divine wrath, and little else needs to be said to those who have read them.[127] To counter this obvious impression, universalists will sometimes reinterpret the remnant who survives God's wrath as really everyone.[128]

The primary universalist rationale for sidelining the divine wrath ubiquitously portrayed in the Hebrew Scriptures is that the "avenging God" (Ps 94:1; Nah 1:2), the "God of retribution" (Jer 51:56), is obviated with Christ's advent.[129] While this argument is as ancient as Marcion,[130] it ignores the continuing eschatological rigor in the NT, particularly the full version resisting his excisions.[131] Indeed, divine wrath is a popular NT topic, expressed thirty-six times,[132] which compares favorably to such important topics as the "cross" (σταυρός, twenty-seven times) or "baptism" (βάπτισμα, twenty-one times). Paul wrote, "God's wrath is . . . against all irreverence and unrighteousness" (Rom 1:18) and, citing Isaiah (10:22–23), reminded the church that, when God's word is "executed on the earth," only "the remnant will be saved" (Rom 9:27–28).[133] He added that God proceeds with "severity to the fallen" (11:22) and that God's wrath

---

125. Osborne, "General Atonement View," 122.

126. Balthasar, *Theo-Drama*, IV: 339; Bultmann, *Theology of the NT*, I: 32:1 (p. 288); Irenaeus, *Against Heresies*, 4:28,1 (p. 127).

127. Num 31:2; Deut 32:40–43; Ps 94:1–2; Jer 12:7–8; 13:13–14; 16:3–4; 19:3–6; Ezek 7:5–11; 8:17–18; Hos 9:12, 15–16; Nah 1:2–3; Zech 11:6, 9; 13:7.

128. McClymond, *Devil's Redemption*, II: 777–78.

129. Reitan, "Human Freedom," 127.

130. Rausch, *ST*, 55.

131. Lubac, *Catholicism*, 301.

132. Balthasar, *Theo-Drama*, IV: 340; Villiers, "Presence of God," 311.

133. Matera, *Romans*, 230.

is not diminished in the NT's ultimate but persists into it (Eph 2:2–3; 5:3–8; Col 3:5–8; 1 Thess 4:3–6).[134] Christ saves *from* the wrath; he does not disappear it (1:10).[135] Wrath continues to fall on the ungodly (Rom 5:9–10; 1 Thess 5:9–10).[136] A "certain terrifying expectation of judgment and zealous fire" awaits God's opponents (Heb 10:26–27, 29–31), and, for those succumbing to apostasy, "the end" is "burning" (6:4–8).

God's wrath is different from eternal life, but reflects one's exclusion from salvation because "whoever disobeys the Son will not see life, for God's wrath abides on him" (John 3:36; also Rom 11:22). The eschaton emphatically includes wrath for some, which is likened to Noah's flood and Sodom's brimstone (Luke 17:26–30//Matt 24:37–39),[137] and neither comparison ends well for the majority (Gen 7:21–23; 19:24–25). Each of these ancient stories is clearly not about a world free of divine wrath, but is "an example of suffering eternal fire's punishment" (Jude 7), foretelling "a day of judgment and annihilation of irreverent men" (2 Pet 3:7). That is, in the end, among humanity, "one will be taken and the other left" (Luke 17:27–35). When that happens, God's fury is envisioned to include human torture, 1,600 blood-filled stadiums, a blood-soaked avenging angel, vultures crying "gather for God's great supper, so you may eat . . . all fleshes," and a heavenly fire that "devoured [κατέφαγεν]" the rebels, and, at its peak, God will cast the ungodly into the fiery lake of the second death (Rev 14:9–11, 17–20; 16:5–6; 19:1–2, 11–21; 20:9–15; 21:6–8). If these eschatological images are to be taken seriously,[138] which some universalists cannot bring themselves to do,[139] universalists take what is being described as just a proper cleansing.[140] The argument satirizes itself.[141]

---

134. Dunning, *Grace, Faith, and Holiness*, 392.

135. Weima, *1–2 Thessalonians*, 112.

136. Augustine, *Enchiridion*, 29,112 (p. 133); Colijn, *Images of Salvation*, 180; Williamson, *Death and the Afterlife*, 178.

137. Stephens, *Annihilation or Renewal?* 216.

138. To take Scripture's eschatological (or millennial) literature seriously is to avoid two extremes, dismissing it as "mere hyperbole or 'poetry'" or treating it as "secret codes and ciphers for straightforward history . . ." Cook, *Ezekiel 38–48*, 79.

139. For David Hart, Revelation cannot contribute on the issue of salvation's extent because it is an "impenetrable puzzle." *That All Shall Be Saved*, 106–10.

140. Ellul, *Apocalypse*, 65, 213, 276; Talbott, "Pauline Interpretation," 42–43; "Reply to My Critics," 256–57.

141. McClymond, *Devil's Redemption*, II: 963, 1048.

3. Contradictions Reveal Fallacies

Given its record of overtly and repeatedly setting out both universalism and exclusivism, Scripture is definitely in contradiction either apparently or actually. An *apparent* contradiction, discussed further in chapter 5, is a paradox.[142] Scripture is full of paradoxes,[143] which are not contradictions.[144] Even a paradox is problematic, however, maybe especially so, because it demands what is difficult—dynamic thinking.[145] In contrast, an *actual* scriptural contradiction, at least one pertaining to such a thoroughly and topically addressed subject as salvation, would be a disaster for nearly all Christians.[146] This is because propositions that contradict actually (in the same way and at the same time) cannot be true.[147] This is recognized as the principle of noncontradiction. Without this principle, "it is equally possible either to affirm or deny anything of anything," Aristotle realized, "nothing truly exists."[148] It is this principle that distinguishes truth and falsehood.[149] Distinguishing between the two is not just handy, but our lives literally depend upon it.[150]

Truths that contradict are, if not trope, unintelligible.[151] While we often contradict ourselves, truth cannot contradict itself.[152] As if to prove the first half of that statement, the principle of noncontradiction has in postmodernity been disputed as merely a sort of cognitive bookkeeping,[153] but deniers are either wrong, right, or neither. 1) If wrong, the principle stands.

---

142. Netland, "Question of Criteria," 499.

143. Kierkegaard, *Concluding Unscientific Postscript*, I: 105; Lubac, *Catholicism*, 327.

144. Henry, *God, Revelation and Authority*, I: 233.

145. Heidegger, "Letter on Humanism," 242; Mazza, *Scholastics and the Jews*, 2.

146. F. Sanders, "Response to Matthew Levering," 101.

147. Geisler, *ST*, 60; Zalta, "In Defense of the Law," 418–36.

148. Aristotle, *Metaphysics: Books 1–9*, 1007b 19–27.

149. Henry, *God, Revelation and Authority*, I: 232–33; Wallenfang, *Human and Divine Being*, xxiv.

150. Blondel, *Action*, 429 [472]; Przywara, *Analogia Entis*, 207–8.

151. Aquinas, *ST*, Part II, Q. 1, art. 7, co; *De Potentia*, Q. 1, art. 3 (p. 11); Geisler, *ST*, 69; Perl, *Theophany*, 50.

152. Montaigne, "Essays," III,2 (p. 611)

153. See Priest, Beall, and Armour-Garb, eds., *Law of Noncontradiction*, 23–38, 197–313. Kierkegaard, despite his deserved reputation for praising *contradictions*, was actually praising, as the terms are used here, *paradoxes*; he affirmed the principle of noncontradiction. McCombs, *Paradoxical Rationality of Kierkegaard*, 13.

2) If right, given the denial, the deniers are also wrong; see 1. 3) If neither wrong nor right, the deniers are not denying; see 1 and 2. As the master of contradiction appreciated, to annul the principle of noncontradiction is to validate it because its annulling must use the principle.[154] When contradictions are taken as true, this amounts to, as Chesterton called out, an "ingenious defence of the indefensible," otherwise known as "lying."[155]

The noncontradiction principle, which says that both an affirmation and its negation cannot be true, differs from the related principle of the excluded middle, which says that either an affirmation or its negation must be true, *tertium non datur*. While the noncontradiction principle always works on actual contradictions, the excluded middle only works on the pellucid.[156] The principle of the excluded middle works where the abstractions are unambiguous, such as in mathematics where negating the negative yields the positive, in traveling where two reversals is again the original direction, in grammar where two negatives mean the affirmative, and in the cross where Christ's death cancels death and leads to resurrected life.[157] The excluded middle, though, is not so much a principle as a probability because, as a principle, it fails when words find equipoise,[158] and among the best violators of the principle of the excluded middle are paradoxes. Yet, this shortcoming of the excluded middle principle, which says *either* X or not-X *must* be true, does not shake the noncontradiction principle, which says *both* X and not-X *cannot* be true, because the former is using logic to discover truths while the latter is using logic to uncover falsehoods; and logic, well suited for ferreting out falsities, is notorious at finding truth on its own.[159] Truth is the narrower way (John 14:6; Matt 7:14//Luke 13:24).[160] The excluded middle thus claims too much.

Humans, who can find the in-between within truths, cannot long survive on contradicting truths.[161] While this is usually seen in

---

154. Kierkegaard, *Philosophical Fragments*, 108–9.
155. Chesterton, *Orthodoxy*, 3.
156. Copi, *Introduction to Logic*, 320.
157. Wallenfang, *Human and Divine Being*, 30.
158. Lemmon, *Beginning Logic*, 53.
159. Elster, *Sour Grapes*, 2, 16.
160. Jung, *Modern Man*, 46; Montaigne, "Essays," I,9 (p. 24).
161. Fabro, *God in Exile*, 19; Olson, *Mosaic of Christian Belief*, 68.

propositions,[162] it surfaces without language at all.[163] Those neglecting the principle of noncontradiction, even if prelinguistic, face extinction when such realities as *gravity, friend,* or *charging tiger* are as real as their repudiations. Faith too, as a realization of reality, is not immune to the noncontradiction principle.[164] To believe something is to know its meaning and its truth.[165] Bonhoeffer noted, "there can be no confession without saying, 'In the light of Christ, this is true and this is false.'"[166] Because Christianity, the cult of truth, identifies truth with God, incompatible truths are disallowed.[167] Scripture, accordingly, rejects "the falsely named knowledge" of "contradictions [ἀντιθέσεις]" (1 Tim 6:20). Our words are not to contradict (2 Cor 1:18), and even God honors this principle.[168] God's omnipotence, Thomas reminds us, "cannot cause an affirmation and a negation to be simultaneously true."[169] "You may attribute miracles to Him," C. S. Lewis added, "but not nonsense."[170]

The inescapability of the noncontradiction principle is what signals the crux of whether Scripture's accounts of salvation's extent are actually or apparently contradictory. If the accounts are *actually* contradicting, a substantial portion of Scripture is false, and, among Christians, only the most liberal can accept Scripture's falsity on such a critical issue as salvation. The theoretical option that might be hoped for—that Scripture's salvation-extent accounts are only *apparently* contradicting—looks to be practically unavailable because the accounts are expressed oxymoronically. That is, they explicitly state their simultaneity (*i.e.,* ultimately) and depend on no word's multivalency: *salvation* means the same in both accounts, as does *all*—everyone, no exceptions. The antimony of the salvation-extent accounts rests entirely on the one word that distinguishes

---

162. Harrison, "Logical Function of 'That,'" 67–96.

163. Geisler, *ST*, 77; Kierkegaard, *Two Ages*, 90.

164. Erickson, *Christian Theology*, 59; Pabst, *Metaphysics*, 71.

165. Luther, *Galatians*, 459 [WA 402,25 (5:5)]; A. Williams, *Architecture of Theology*, 222; B. Williams, *Problems of the Self*, 137.

166. Bonhoeffer, *Christ the Center*, 78.

167. A. Williams, *Architecture of Theology*, 31–32.

168. Krapiec, *I-Man*, 112; Przywara, *Analogia Entis*, 224; Shields and Pasnau, *Philosophy of Aquinas*, 156–57.

169. Aquinas, *De Potentia*, Q. 1, arts. 3, 5, Q. 5, art. 2 (pp. 10, 15, 137).

170. Lewis, *Problem of Pain*, 18.

them, which is "not," and even young children contextually understand the negative.[171]

The salvation paradox, therefore, is unlike most scriptural paradoxes, which typically involve conflicting concepts, not negating propositions. The propositions *Christ is God* and *Christ is man* form a paradox, while the propositions of *Christ is God* and *Christ is not God* would form a contradiction. Or so the words suggest. Yet, because *man is not God*, the logical relationship of the proposition pairs seem to correspond. Yet still, the salvation paradox—*everyone is saved* and *not everyone is saved*—seemingly affirms and negates the same fundamental idea, which is archetypically impossible.[172] Accordingly, faced with the principle of noncontradiction and what appear to be irreconcilable scriptural accounts on salvation's extent, Christians throughout the ages have demoted one scriptural account to only facially true so as to retain the other account's actual truth and thereby avoid the calamity of actual scriptural contradiction. That history is next.

---

171. Nordmeyer and Frank, "Role of Context," 25–39.

172. Aquinas, *De Potentia*, Q. 1, art. 3 (pp. 9–10); D. Hart, *That All Shall Be Saved*, 203; Plato, *Republic*, 437a.

4

The Responses

She said, "I would rather die."
"Oh," he said, "of course. That goes without saying. But we have to go on living."
—Greene, *The Power and the Glory*

After positive headway in the first two chapters towards discernment on what is involved in salvation as scripturally described, chapter 3 faced Scripture's seemingly contradicting accounts on the extent of that salvation, and this has interrupted the positive headway. The current chapter describes the church's responses to that contradiction, and, as it turns out, the interruption is prolonged. The church has of course correctly recognized the apparent contradiction of the scriptural accounts and sensibly recognized that to understand Scripture as actually contradicting on such a subject is to misunderstand it.[1] Even when cryptic or merely upsetting, Scripture is taken as euharmonic.[2] So, when Scripture is understood as actually contradictory, especially on a subject as central as salvation, the church understood that it was the understanding, not the Scripture, that had to change. Later, when modernity felt competent to

---

1. Blomberg, "Unity and Diversity," 64.
2. Kugel, *Traditions of the Bible*, 15–19.

master everything it put its mind to and the ancients came to be seen as quaintly naïve in this regard, scriptural harmony became optional,³ and this new-found appreciation for scriptural dissension offered a potential way forward for salvation's extent. At least in scriptural contexts that justified it, modernity allowed different authors to give different answers to the same question, such as the dissimilar gospel biographies or the divergent Genesis anthropogenies, and, even when seen as irreconcilable, these various portrayals reflected a freedom of expression, which the broad-minded auditor not only tolerated but valued.⁴

The contemporary tolerance for scriptural dissonance has, however, made little progress in dealing with Scripture's salvation paradox because the conflicting statements are too many and too varied.⁵ Paul's seven undisputed letters, to illustrate, express both accounts of salvation's extent.⁶ Just a single one of Paul's positively authentic letters seemingly takes both contrary positions.⁷ Therefore, from the church's beginning and even into our more forbearing age, tradition has been unable to accept wholly the contradicting accounts of salvation's extent as presented by Scripture and has remained committed to favoring one account over the other, but Christians, though agreeing that one has to be chosen, have disagreed over which one that should be.

1. Universalism Began Strong and Resurges

The church eventually determined that universalism was heretical, and that story is described in the next section. To show in this section that Christianity nevertheless features universalism, Christian universalists must be surveyed, which must be done mostly one by one. This citing of personages contrasts with the citing of creeds. Creeds reflect what groups believe, and the creeds do not favor universalism, which is again addressed in the next section. As a result, it is mainly through the labor of identifying those Christians who espouse universalism that establishes

---

3. Dunning, *Grace, Faith, and Holiness*, 45; R. Williams, *Christian Theology*, 16.

4. John Barton, "Source Criticism (OT)," 163; Blomberg, "Unity and Diversity," 64–65, 69–71; Brown, *Death of the Messiah*, I: 4–5, 22–23.

5. Robinson, *In the End, God . . .* , 94–95.

6. Boring, "Language of Universal Salvation," 269 & n.1.

7. Romans is both exclusivist (1:16–18, 8:28–30) and universalist (5:12, 15, 18–19, 21, 11:30–32, 33–36), as is 1 Corinthians (1:18 vs. 15:20–28).

to what extent Christianity is universalist, and this investment takes a bit, even with certain exclusions. The survey's primary exclusion is that those who are not Christians, such as Cabbalists and Muslims,[8] are omitted because non-Christians do not establish *Christian* universalism.[9] For a similar reason, the survey also largely excludes those who are unlikely to be reliable arbiters of the faith for Nicene Christians, who are the mainstream; so, as examples, mostly omitted are those generally tagged as "gnostics" or esoteric mystics (*e.g.*, Böhmists like Jane Lead).[10]

In spite of these exclusions, the survey remains long for three reasons. The first is that the universalism of the church's recognized thought leaders is often disputed by exclusivists.[11] This means that the universalism of any Christian has to be set out sufficiently so as to justify their inclusion in the survey. The length dedicated to any of them is not therefore primarily a function of how much universalist material is available, but depends on how influential the Christian is and how contested their universalism has been. Universalists also sometimes claim someone as one of theirs who is not a universalist. So, the survey must explain why they are excluded. The issue in each case is not what the Christian really thought, which can be inaccessible, especially before the time when preserving infamous thoughts was easy, but the issue in each case is what the Christian really wrote, which is, if not always determinable, almost always derivable.

The second reason the survey of universalists is long is that it cannot be a mere sample because this would leave the impression that the influence of universalism is less than it actually is, especially in contrast with exclusivism's prevalence. On the other hand, the survey cannot be so meticulous as to detract from its point of showing the magnitude of Christianity's universalism rather than what any particular Christian believed. Exhaustive studies are available (and are cited below), but they can be exhausting to absorb. Moreover, the work commitment they require tend to attract partisans, whether universalists or their opponents, and the universalists tend to fixate on the evidence for universalism no matter how slim while their opponents tend to highlight the universalist errors no matter how ad hoc. Even so, to be of a manageable length, the detailed

---

8. McClymond, *Devil's Redemption*, I: 5, 11, 158, 176–77.
9. Ludlow, *Universal Salvation*, 1.
10. McClymond, *Devil's Redemption*, I: 1, 7–10, 22–23, 126, 129, 155–58.
11. Harmon, "Subjection of All Things," 63.

studies must be temporally circumscribed or thematically selective. In contrast to these sorts of studies, this section covers extensively, if not thoroughly, two millennia of Christian universalism in a few thousand words with no incentive for tendentiousness.

The third and primary reason for the length of the universalist survey is that it must counterbalance the Christian meme that "it is clear" that exclusivism is "where the overwhelming consensus lies in the history of theology."[12]

a. To Origen

Though the authors of the NT were Christianity's first exclusivists,[13] they were its first universalists too.[14] So, of the first non-NT Christians trying to make sense of this scriptural conflict, some leaned universalist.[15] Ignatius (d. 110)[16] has been claimed as one,[17] having said, Christ "drew all men to himself for their eternal salvation,"[18] but he also said, "the corrupters of families will not inherit the Kingdom" and such "foul" people "will depart into unquenchable fire."[19] The first known true Christian universalist did not appear until late in the second century in the person of Clement of Alexandria (150–216), and, reflecting either universalism's novelty or its acceptability as of then, he was *not* condemned for it.[20] He observed that,

---

12. Walls, "Hell and Purgatory Response," 55. Accord Balthasar, *Dare We Hope*, 48.
13. Martin, *Will Many Be Saved?* 154.
14. Ramelli, *Christian Doctrine of Apokatastasis*, 11.
15. Ramelli, "Origen, Bardaisan, and Universalism," 135–68.
16. Most early dates are estimates.
17. Ramelli, *Christian Doctrine of Apokatastasis*, 62.
18. Ignatius, "Epistle to Smyrnaeans," 87.
19. Ignatius, "Letter to Ephesians," 18 [16, 1].
20. Balthasar, *Dare We Hope*, 63; Daley, *Hope of the Early Church*, 46–47; Ramelli, *Christian Doctrine of Apokatastasis*, 123–24. Michael McClymond argues that it "is not clear" whether Clement gave "a full-blown teaching on universal salvation." This might explain why Clement was never condemned for his universalism, but, if McClymond's assessment is intended to call into question whether Clement was actually a universalist, the stated observation imposes too high of a standard. *Full-blown* and *clear* evidence is an unrealistic requirement for any second-century writer's position and is certainly unrealistic for a position that became heretical before the printing press. McClymond concedes that Clement clearly took the position that divine punishment was restorative and that this clearly denotes universalism. *Devil's Redemption*, I: 243, 246, 259.

"all things are arranged with a view to the salvation of the universe by the Lord of the universe, both generally and particularly" because God will, by "necessary corrections . . . and by the perfect judgment, compel egregious sinners to repent." "God's punishments are saving and disciplinary, leading to conversion," which is "a universal movement."[21] God thus "saves all."[22] Clement's contemporary, Bardaisan of Edessa (154–223), a condemned gnostic, was a universalist too.[23] He argued human freewill faces "that Great and Holy Will," which is "kind and forbearing towards all beings" such that humanity's "propensity to inflict harm . . . shall be brought to end. . . . And at the establishment of that new world all evil commotions shall cease . . . and all deficiencies shall be filled up . . . ."[24]

Despite such second-century antecedents, Origen is unquestionably the leading universalist both because of his famous articulation of universalism in his masterpiece *First Principles* (225)[25] and because of his notorious condemnation as a heretic for universalism more than three centuries later, which is discussed in the next section.[26] Origen occasionally argued that unrepentant sinners would suffer everlasting damnation,[27] meaning his renown for universalism is more a product of the salvation-extent controversy rather than a synthesis of his corpus,[28] but Origen's reputation as a universalist was well earned. According to him, because Christ *subjected all* to himself (Phil 3:20–21),[29] this means everyone receives Christ's salvation.[30] Also, because Revelation says death ends, Origen argued that salvation's life must outlast damnation's death, leaving eternal life as the only outcome in the end.[31] He further

---

21. Clement, "Stromata," 6,6, 7,2 (pp. 490–91, 526).
22. Clement, "Fragments from Cassiodous," 1 John 2:2 (p. 575).
23. Ramelli, *Christian Doctrine of Apokatastasis*, 110, 113–15, 119, 800–801.
24. Bardaisan, "Book of the Laws," 733–34.
25. Butterworth, "Introduction," vii-viii.
26. Schwarz, *Eschatology*, 338–41.
27. Blosser, *Become Like the Angels*, 244–45, 256–57; Hennessey, "Place of Saints and Sinners," 311–12.
28. Crouzel, *Origen*, 264–65.
29. The passage, which says that God will make everything "subject [ὑποτάξαι]" to him, is not in universalism's scriptural basis because the verb means "cause to be in a submissive relationship" (*BDAG*, 1042), which expresses universal *dominion*, not universal salvation. Silva, *Philippians*, 185.
30. Origen, *On First Principles*, I,6,1 (pp. 52–53).
31. Origen, *Romans Books 1–5*, 5–9.

inferred from the Word being "in thy mouth and in thy heart" (Rom 10:8)[32] that "Christ is in the heart of all men." While, in God's judgment, "diversity of conduct is taken into account and each is treated according to" one's failures, everyone is ultimately saved. Perhaps most important to Origen was the obvious universalism in God's being "all in all" (1 Cor 15:28).[33] Origen did not leave unexplained the evident fact that God was not "all in all" now, but reasoned that, for God to be "all things in each individual person," this must be after the person is "purified," which is when each individual "will no longer be conscious of anything besides or other than God . . . ."[34] "There is a resurrection of the dead, and there is a punishment, but not everlasting. For when the body is punished the soul is gradually purified. . . . For all wicked men . . . punishment has an end, and . . . wicked men . . . shall be restored . . . ."[35] Such universal purifying, or purging, as chapter 8 will discuss, is how Origen (and subsequent universalists) handle God's wrath—that is, the wrath is frontloaded such that, after the purging it produces, God's wrath exhausts itself and everyone can then be ultimately saved.

b. To the Cappadocians

Several of Origen's speculative positions would be condemned, but universalism was not among them—that is, until much later.[36] Instead, universalism grew in the third century. The church father Methodius of Olympus (250–311), though an anti-Origenist, was a universalist.[37] The canonized Gregory of Neocaesarea (213–70) was one too, writing Christ is "the Savior of all," even "all those half-dead."[38] Anthony the Great (251–356) was a universalist, arguing that, although "each one of us has sold

---

32. This is not in universalism's scriptural basis because it mandates a human response, which is hardly universal (Rom 10:9–10). Schreiner, *Romans*, 555–61.

33. Ramelli, "Procus and Apokatastasis," 120.

34. Origen, *On First Principles*, I,3,6, 6,2, II,5,2, III,6,3 (pp. 35, 54, 102, 248) (internal quotations omitted).

35. Origen, *On First Principles*, II,10,8 (p. 146).

36. MacDonald, "Introduction," 5; Ramelli, *Christian Doctrine of Apokatastasis*, 257–73.

37. Methodius, "Banquet of the Ten Virgins," 318–19, 337–38, 348–49, 353.

38. Gregory of Neocaesarea, "Address of Thanksgiving," ch 17 (p. 200).

himself of his own free choice," "the bounty of God," "the Saviour of all the world," means that we cannot "bring about our own death."[39]

The fourth century produced several universalists. Church historian Eusebius (263–339) recorded that Christ was "the common Savior of all," "the very culmination of the salvation of us all," "sent . . . for the salvation of the human race"; "in the present age the promise comes to the worthy alone," but, "after the consummation," God will dwell in" "all human beings." "Thus . . . he will be 'all in all.'"[40] The "beneficent Savior of the universe" rescues "the souls of humanity," even the "godless," into "eternal life."[41] Trinitarian champion Athanasius (296–373) saw that, through Christ, "the salvation of all comes to pass"[42] such that "the human race is perfectly and wholly delivered . . . from the dead."[43] God "redeemed all of us, . . . the whole race of men," "the common salvation of us all" to "rescue all men generally to salvation."[44] Diodore of Tarsus (d. 390), orthodox bishop at Constantinople I, resolved that the "torment for sinners" was "not everlasting," but "in proportion to . . . their iniquity," and this results in everyone's "immortality" and "unending happiness."[45] The Origenist Didymus the Blind (313–98) agreed that ultimate salvation occurs in consecutive phases but, ultimately, is thorough—Christ first, believers second, and "all the other things" third, when death is destroyed.[46]

The Cappadocians were not of one mind on salvation's extent. Macrina (330–79), the eldest sister and an Origenist, taught universalism to her brothers.[47] For her, because "every knee will bow" to Jesus (Phil 2:10), everyone, even demons, will confess Christ's lordship, "expounding the

---

39. Anthony, *Letters*, Ltrs III, V, VI (pp. 10, 16, 22).

40. Eusebius, "Against Marcellus," 2,4,28 (p. 154); "On Ecclesiastical Theology," 1,7,2; 3,2,16, 2,21, 4,6, 16,1–2 (pp. 167, 281–82, 307, 327–28).

41. Eusebius, *Isaiah*, 25:1–8 (pp. 123–26).

42. Athanasius, "Against Arianism," 14,97, 17,33 (pp. 247, 280).

43. Athanasius, "Tomus Ad Antiochenos," ch 7 (p. 485).

44. Athanasius, "Letter X," 4, 10 (pp. 528–29, 531).

45. Solomon, *Book of the Bee*, 140 (quoting Diodore's no longer extant *Book of Dispensation*).

46. Didymus' comments are collected and translated in Croft, "Didymus the Blind," and the cited text is at pp. 8–9 (Greek, pp. 37, 39, 41). They are found within a ninth-/tenth-century manuscript at the Pantokratoros Monastery (Athos). Croft, "Didymus the Blind," 92.

47. Ramelli, *Christian Doctrine of Apokatastasis*, 372–73, 380–81; Silvas, *Asketikon of Basil*, 148.

agreement of the universe in the good."[48] Her younger brother Gregory was likeminded and is unique in the context of the church's dispute over salvation's extent—he is both well-known as a universalist theologian and nonetheless widely venerated without the taint of anathema.[49] He expressed his position succinctly in his essay on *First Corinthians* 15:28 (Migne PG 44.1304–26).[50] The divine "subjection" of all is the salvation of all. Evil "will be completely destroyed" "by refinement in fire," meaning "nothing made by God is excluded from his kingdom." "God will truly be in all things . . . ." Christ joins "all mankind . . . to the divinity," and, so, "the good begotten in human nature was bestowed upon every person as one entity . . . ."[51] Gregory concluded, "the final restoration [*apokatastasis*] . . . is expected to take place later in the kingdom of heaven of those who have suffered condemnation in Gehenna."[52] The catechism he prepared included universalism as a basic Christian belief.[53]

The other Cappadocians were exclusivists, though this is not always accepted.[54] Basil at times certainly wrote favorably of his brother's position: "Since the Father through the blood of His cross made peace with [all],[55] whether on earth or in heaven," "the peace from the Lord is co-extensive with the whole of eternity," and with "the cross He drew all to Himself," yielding "restoration [*apokatastasis*] of all."[56] In his "Rule" masterwork, however, Basil concluded that universalism's "end of punishment" is explicitly rejected "everywhere in the God-inspired Scripture." If perdition were in fact to end as universalists claim, he noted, "surely eternal life would also have an end. Now if we do not tolerate thinking like this about life, by what logic shall we assign an end to eternal punishment?"[57] Universalists argue that Basil's clear exclusivism here is interpolation or

---

48. Gregory of Nyssa, *Soul and Resurrection*, chs 4, 10 (pp. 64, 106).

49. Balthasar, *Dare We Hope*, 63; Ludlow, *Universal Salvation*, 30, 82; Zachhuber, *Human Nature*, 201.

50. Gregory, "In Illud: Tunc Et Ipse Filius." See Casimir, "When (the Father) Will Subject," 1 n.1, 12–25.

51. Casimir, "When (the Father) Will Subject," 16–19, 22, 24 (M.1312–13, 1316, 1320, 1324).

52. Gregory, *Life of Moses*, Bk II (p. 54).

53. Gregory, "Catechetical Oration," ch. 26 (p. 81).

54. Ramelli, *Christian Doctrine of Apokatastasis*, 348–59.

55. Implied.

56. Basil, *Isaiah*, 8,222, 9,226 (pp. 270, 276).

57. Basil, "Asketikon," SR 267 (pp. 418–19).

pious bluff, primarily because they find it so unpersuasive,[58] but the best evidence is that his *Rule* codifies his mature theology.[59]

Gregory of Nazianzus was an exclusivist too, claiming, for example, that Arians were among those specifically excluded from salvation.[60] It is sometimes claimed that he was an advocate for what is called discreet universalism—universalism is a sort of messianic secret where the church's public position is exclusivism so as to incentivize decorum among the bourgeois and proletariat, but the inner circle of Christians could be entrusted with the truth that salvation is covertly universal.[61] Along these lines, Gregory would at times write such notions as Christ's descent into hades was "to save everyone absolutely,"[62] "God will be all in all in the time of restitution" when he will have "cleansed the entire world" to "the ends of the earth,"[63] and "we were all without exception created anew," "saved by the heavenly Adam."[64] All things considered, however, given that Gregory's oeuvre plainly expresses exclusivism,[65] scholarship has generally concluded that sentiments like those quoted indicate that Gregory held that salvation was universally available, not universally received.[66]

c. To Anathema

After Origen's endorsement in the third century, universalism was decidedly viable within the church and remained so for the next two centuries, particularly in the East. Even John Chrysostom (347–407), though clearly a hell-and-damnation exclusivist,[67] noted how the extent of salva-

---

58. Ramelli, *Christian Doctrine of Apokatastasis*, 351–57.

59. Ludlow, *Universal Salvation*, 36; Silvas, *Asketikon of Basil*, 2–3, 17, 130, 143–45, 418 n.723.

60. Gregory, "Orations," 38.14.

61. Balthasar, *Dare We Hope*, 63; Ramelli, *Christian Doctrine of Apokatastasis*, 454–56.

62. Gregory, *Festal Orations*, Or. 45,24 (p. 185).

63. Gregory, *On God and Man*, poems 1.1.2, lns 75–76, 2.1, lns 162–69 (pp. 42, 94–95).

64. Gregory, "Orations," 30,6, 33,9 (pp. 312, 331).

65. *E.g.*, Gregory, "Orations," 2.28, 16.7, 16.9, 30.4, 30.21, 38.13, 38.18, 40.36.

66. Winslow, *Dynamics of Salvation*, 117–19, 129, 131, 154, 157–58, 166–67.

67. Balthasar, *Dare We Hope*, 50. See Chrysostom, *Homilies on Matthew*, 36,3–4; "Commentary on Galatians," 119 [2, 8]; "Homilies on Ephesians," 120 [1, 2].

tion seems unbounded: "the common Expiation of the world is . . . before us."[68] God "has given everyone the gift of immorality, everyone eternal life . . . ."[69] Homilies that tradition attributes to him are similar: Christ's sacrifice was "the salvation of mankind," "the salvation of the whole world," "the human race," "the whole earth."[70]

Other Easterners would argue for actual universal salvation. Cyril of Alexandria (378–444) wrote that Christ "is led to the slaughter for all, to drive away the sin of the world, . . . to abolish death by dying for all, . . . rescuing the entire flock on earth . . .—one for all," bringing "the whole world to its fitting consummation . . . , that is, salvation and life for all . . . ." Christ calls "even those who will not listen and who are hardened" so as to "restore" "the entire race," "belief" being "an inevitable necessity."[71] Cyril resolved that Satan is left alone in hell.[72] Theodoret (393–457), though Cyril's Three Chapters opponent, was likeminded on salvation's extent: Christ "led the whole human race back to life" and "achieves life for all people." "[T]he whole human race will follow Christ the Lord and share resurrection." "In the future life, when corruption comes to an end and immortality is conferred," "all human beings will share in the same resurrection"; "even if here and now we are not sharing in salvation, we shall not be deprived of it after departure from here." Though "unbelief is confined to this world," God imparts "in the next life" "the salvation of everyone."[73] Pseudo-Dionysius the Areopagite (fifth-sixth century) determined God is the destiny of "all things," "bring[ing] them to completion . . . in the one single, irrepressible, and supreme act."[74] Another pseudonymous book attributed to a different Syrian, *The Book of the Holy Hierotheos* (late fifth century), advocated universalism too.[75] Based on the critical 1 Corinthians passage, "Hells shall pass, and torments shall be done away"; so, "all is sanctified."[76]

---

68. Chrysostom, *Homilies on First Corinthians*, 41,8 (p. 254).

69. Chrysostom, "Homily 11 (on Ephesians)," 214E (p. 61).

70. Chrysostom, "Victory over Death," 3–4 (pp. 101, 103).

71. Cyril, *John*, I: 2 [intro., 170], 4,1 [488] (pp. 76, 217); II: 6,1 [217, 234], 9,1 [482], 11,10 [723–24], 12 [88] (pp. 60, 68, 186, 298–99, 346).

72. Cyril, "Festal Letter Seven," 135–36.

73. Theodoret, *Commentary on the Letters*, Rom 3:4,78, 5:14–18,101–3, 1 Cor 15:22–28,355–60, 2 Cor 4:4,400, 6:2,413 (pp. 60, 73–74, 227–31, 268, 274).

74. Pseudo-Dionysius, "Divine Names," 596C–597A (p. 56).

75. McClymond, *Devil's Redemption*, I: 345.

76. Sudhaile, *Book of the Holy Hierotheos*, 5.2 (p. 133).

Universalism was far less influential in the West as Christianity was established there and grew distinct.[77] The reason for this geographic distinction is unclear. It could be that universalism was associated with Origen and regionalism did the rest, both for and against. Two other plausible explanations for universalism's Eastern prevalence have been proposed. One is that Easterners may have been drawn to universalism because Greek philosophers were indicting Christianity for condemning other religions, which was unattractively undermining cultural solidarity, while Christian universalism would deprive the critics of this objection.[78] The other is that universalism's purity may have appealed to the Athenian predilection for abstraction, while its singularity was too divorced from the practicality of Roman ethics.[79] Another suggestion is less plausible, which is, after the Western church shifted in the third and fourth centuries to Latin,[80] only Easterners still appreciated the NT's Greek subtleties.[81] This does not, however, jive with the facts. First, as discussed in the next paragraph, Latinists had no trouble being universalists. Second, as discussed in the next section, numerous Greek-fluent theologians resisted whatever attraction Greek has for universalism.[82] Third, as also discussed in that section, universalism's anathematization came predominately out of the Greek-speaking East. Fourth, Greek proficiency has offered the East no noticeable protection from heresies generally, whether adoptionism, Apollinarism, Arianism, docetism, Marcionism, Montanism, Nestorianism, or Sabellianism.[83] Finally, if any language seems to correlate to universalism's acceptance throughout history, it is *not* Greek, but, as shown below, the late-to-theology and very Western one of English.

In any event, universalism did reach the Latin-speaking West. Hilary of Poitiers (310–65) reasoned that we all "have been lifted up again from the flesh to God" because Christ was "the body of the whole of humanity"

77. Ramelli, *Christian Doctrine of Apokatastasis*, 607–9.

78. Celsus, *On the True Doctrine*, 70, 79, 86; Simmons, *Universal Salvation*, 215–16, 225–26.

79. Sedgwick, *Life of Marcus Aurelius*, 28.

80. Chadwick, *Church in Ancient Society*, 132.

81. D. Hart, *New Testament*, 539–40.

82. McClymond, *Devil's Redemption*, I: 40–41.

83. Chadwick, *Early Church*, 37–41, 144–45, 202–5; Davies, *Early Christian Church*, 74–75, 176–81, 238–39; Kelly, *Early Christian Doctrines*, 23–28, 141–42, 226–31, 237–40, 310–17.

and "reproduced in all."[84] Hilary saw eternal life as the restoration to original perfection through evil's annihilation.[85] Ambrose (340–97) wrote that it was "The mystery of the Incarnation" that "is the salvation of the whole of creation."[86] Jerome too advocated for universalism, though by 390 (*after* he had gained fluency in Greek) he had become an exclusivist.[87] John Cassian (360–435) was a universalist based on God's nature.[88] He penned that "the purpose of God" for "man not to perish but to live for ever, stands immovable." God "draws men against their will to salvation."[89] Even the famously exclusivist Augustine, discussed in the next section, began his theological career as a universalist:[90] "the goodness of God does not permit" "corruption" or other "non-existence," but "orders *all things* . . . till in the order of their movements they return to that from which they fell away."[91] After adopting exclusivism (and becoming a bishop), he lithely claimed he did not really mean "all things" when he wrote that.[92]

Universalism was, therefore, unquestionably viable among the church fathers into the fifth century, although these sorts of citations to individuals must be the primary proof in the centuries before surveys were pioneered, before the printing press was common, and before the church officially decided the salvation-extent issue. A few additional facts that are less individualized can, however, confirm universalism's success in Christianity's first half-millennium. When Origenist monks were challenging the church's authority in 370–400, their universalism was *not* among their theological stances attacked (as it would be nearly two centuries later), which may suggest that universalism was not then incriminating.[93] Consistent with this, Augustine in about 420 (who was by then an exclusivist) was deploring universalists as being *immo quam plurimi*, "indeed

---

84. Hilary, *Tractatus Super Psalmos*, Pss 51:16–17, 54:9 (pp. 103–4, 146).
85. Ramelli, *Christian Doctrine of Apokatastasis*, 241.
86. Ambrose, "On the Christian Faith," 5,8,104 (p. 297).
87. Ramelli, *Christian Doctrine of Apokatastasis*, 631.
88. Ramelli, *Christian Doctrine of Apokatastasis*, 682–84.
89. Cassian, "Conferences," XIII, chs 7, 9, 11 (pp. 425–28).
90. Hilborn and Horrocks, "Universalistic Trends," 220; Ludlow, *Universal Salvation*, 1–2; MacDonald, "Between Heresy and Dogma," 9.
91. Augustine, "Morals of the Manichaeans," 7,9 (p. 71) (emphasis added).
92. Augustine, *Retractions*, 1,7,6.
93. Ramelli, *Christian Doctrine of Apokatastasis*, 577–98, 636–41, 823.

very many,"[94] suggesting something approaching a majority,[95] and Basil, a half century earlier, had assessed the number of universalists similarly.[96] Admittedly, exclusivists bemoaning universalism's success could just be catastrophizing. Regardless, trying to gauge universalism's popularity is probably about as meaningful as doing so for Arianism. Rather, the issue here is merely whether universalism was a Christian doctrine, and it is clear that for nearly five centuries after Christ, when those closest to the NT were interpreting it,[97] universalism was at least a well-established theologoumenon regardless of exact numbers.[98]

This period, however, represents Christian universalism's zenith because, as the next section sets out, the question of salvation's extent was called in the sixth century, and it was then that universalism was summarily defeated.[99] That universalism undermined the church's salvation monopoly did not help the cause.[100] If *"salus extra ecclesiam,"* Barth asked, "what becomes of the backbone of the Church?"[101] This too might explain why universalism was stronger in the East, where the empire continued. An emperor-imposed Christianity[102] would be homologous with a God-imposed salvation. That is, if a human emperor could successfully declare Christianity throughout his empire, it stood to reason that the Divine Emperor could do likewise for his empire. Irrespective of why universalism predominated in the East, it would after its anathematization, as will be discussed below, thin out everywhere, and by the Middle Ages nearly die out,[103] but, to anticipate the dis-

---

94. Augustine, "Enchiridion Ad Laurentium," § 112 (p. 245); "Enchiridion," ch 112 (p. 273).

95. Ramelli, *Christian Doctrine of Apokatastasis*, 673.

96. Basil, "Asketikon," 419; D. Hart, *That All Shall Be Saved*, 1–2.

97. D. Hart, *That All Shall Be Saved*, 2–3; Karkkainen, *Christology*, 62.

98. Balthasar, *Theo-Drama*, V: 316–17; Daley, *Hope of the Early Church*, 222; Ramelli, *Christian Doctrine of Apokatastasis*, 817–19, 823.

99. Crisp, "'I Do Teach It,'" 310; Gavrilyuk, "Judgment of Love," 284 n.22; Ludlow, "Universalism in History," 195.

100. Ludlow, *Universal Salvation*, 2.

101. Barth, *Romans*, 365 (9:30).

102. Brown, *Rise of Western Christendom*, 149.

103. Balthasar, *Dare We Hope*, 23; Grenz, *Theology for the Community*, 634; McClymond, *Devil's Redemption*, I: 77, 322, 390.

cussion slightly, universalism would resurface during the Reformation within the cracks in Rome's centralized authority.[104]

Though having been declared a heresy, universalism survived briefly in the East, attracting two seventh-century theologians—Maximus the Confessor (580–662) and Isaac of Nineveh (613–700). Maximus was never condemned by the church for his universalism,[105] but this could be because his universalism was discreet, treating it as a church secret, especially in light of its recent anathematization.[106] He gathered from the crucial 1 Corinthians account that "no existing thing will . . . be deprived of God's presence."[107] Christ will "transform the universe" "for the salvation of our souls and bodies . . . inasmuch as He is the pioneer of the salvation of all . . . ."[108] Christ "divinized all humanity" and "accomplished the complete salvation of humanity."[109] The hermit Isaac's universalism, in contrast, was not discreet. Anyone claiming that hell "is not full of love" is "full of blasphemy." Instead, hell is "a result of His eternal goodness" and involves God's "mercy," not "torment." Isaac argued God's decree of Adamic death, which has clearly afflicted everyone, was "the means of transporting us to that wonderful and glorious world" of Christ's redemption, which just as clearly is of no less equal extension.[110]

After its anathematization had set in, universalism was fleeting, and the exception literally proves it because Rome officially condemned that universalist exception, twice.[111] This exception was John Scotus Eriugena (810–77), "the greatest philosopher of the Dark Ages."[112] He wrote that the incarnation saves "the human race, without exception," returning the "whole of humanity . . . to its pristine state," obtaining "the perfection of all humanity as a whole and singly."[113] Except for this denounced maverick, universalism among medieval Christians hardly existed.[114]

---

104. MacDonald, "Between Heresy and Dogma," 10.

105. Balthasar, *Dare We Hope*, 63–64.

106. Andreopoulos, "Eschatology in Maximus," 325–33; Ramelli and Konstan, *Terms for Eternity*, 222.

107. Maximus, "Ambiguum 7," 1092C (p. 66).

108. Maximus, *Ambigua*, II: 42 [1332D, 1333A] (pp. 154–57).

109. Maximus, *Ambigua*, I: 4 [1044B-D] (pp. 26–27).

110. Isaac, *Second Part*, I: 39,4 & 22 (pp. 164, 172).

111. Bauckham, "Universalism: Historical Survey," 50.

112. Highet, *Man's Unconquerable Mind*, 31.

113. John, *Periphyseon*, Bk V, chs 23, 25, 36 (pp. 302–3, 312, 334–40).

114. Ramelli, *A Larger Hope?* I: 197; J. Sanders, *No Other Name*, 81.

One other arguable medieval exception might be certain women mystics who implored God to save everyone, which could be presumed to be effective,[115] though it seems more likely that any such hopeful supplications reflected the reality that not everyone is being saved.[116] A similar example is the near-death "showings" of Julian of Norwich (1342–1416), which had convinced her of universalism, though it contradicted the church's "lower" exclusivism. When she confronted God with the conflict that she saw in her visions as contrasted with the church's teachings, Jesus replied judiciously if not equivocally, "alle maner of thynge shalle be wele," even "alle that is lesse."[117] The Middle English version of "All shall be well" was her visions' refrain.[118] It must be acknowledged, however, that, on the issue of medieval visions about salvation's extent, the visions from others reflecting the reality of hell's eternal fires were more the norm.[119]

d. To Resurgence

After practically disappearing in the Middle Ages, universalism re-emerged during the Reformation.[120] Insubordinate ideas like universalism clearly had greater survivability in a Renaissance world where Luther could die of old age rather than a catholic world where the church was able to incinerate Jan Hus.[121] The primary reason for the reemergence of heterodoxies was likely the accelerating advance of the printing press, which meant that heresies could be produced and distributed faster than they could be found and destroyed.[122] Protestants, however, like their Catholic counterparts, were expected to identify who was saved and who was not,[123] and this continued to handicap universalism, whose decrees could not be personalized. In the event, all major Reformers rejected

---

115. Oakes, "Christ's Descent into Hell," 384.

116. Nemes, "Praying Confidently," 285–96.

117. Julian, *Book of Showings*, II: 404–5, 413, 487–89, 510–12. See Walsh, "Re-Imagining Redemption," 189–207.

118. Sweetman, "Sin Has Its Place," 78.

119. Gardiner, *Medieval Visions*; Thigpen, *Saints Who Saw Hell*.

120. J. Sanders, *No Other Name*, 81–82. Parry, *A Larger Hope?* II.

121. Bray, *God Has Spoken*, 792; Hillerbrand, *Division of Christendom*, 41, 58, 67–68, 89, 103, 109.

122. Ferguson, *Civilization*, 61–62.

123. Gockel, *Barth and Schleiermacher*, 146.

universalism,[124] and this included Luther.[125] Universalism reappeared on Protestantism's fringes, though.[126] Hans Denck (1495–1527), who was unconventional even for an Anabaptist, got himself imprisoned in Switzerland for espousing universalism.[127] Pietists and the Brethren, an Anabaptist offshoot, would also sometimes include universalism in their dissenting positions.[128]

Universalism obtained an early foothold only off continent, in the "demi-paradise" of that "happy breed of men."[129] English receptivity could have been because theology's ivory tower had already admitted the vernacular during the Middle Ages, which had broadened the discussion beyond the Latin educated.[130] Julian of Norwich was an example. Then, when the Reformation-era tectonics formed rifts in British ecclesiastical power, particularly when church discipline slipped during the interregnum, any expressed universalism faced less organized repression.[131] So, even during an era when killing was still an acceptable technique for winning religious arguments, British universalism seemed to be fatal to no one, but this was in part because its advocates were careful. Some Radical English Puritans were universalists,[132] which included Peter Sterry (1613–72) and Jeremiah White (1630–1707), Neoplatonic Cambridge chaplains under Oliver Cromwell, but their universalist tracts were published either anonymously or posthumously.[133] George Rust (d. 1670), Irish Anglican bishop, wrote that God's love produced an afterlife punishment that was so intolerable that it eventually convinced everyone, but his book too was originally produced anonymously.[134] George de Benneville (1703–93), a Huguenot turned London Pietist, publicly proclaimed the universalist vision he had while near death, and for this he was sentenced to death,

---

124. Ludlow, *Universal Salvation*, 2; MacDonald, "Between Heresy and Dogma," 10; Oakes, "Christ's Descent into Hell," 384.

125. Luther, *Genesis*, II: 56, 339 (25:7–11, 47:21–26).

126. Walter, *Eclipse of Eternity*, 19.

127. Hilborn and Horrocks, "Universalistic Trends," 221.

128. Bauckham, "Universalism: Historical Survey," 50; Hilborn and Horrocks, "Universalistic Trends," 222–25.

129. Shakespeare, "Richard II," 2.1.42–50.

130. Watson, "Visions of Incusion," 170.

131. McClymond, *Devil's Redemption*, I: 406.

132. Bauckham, "Universalism: Historical Survey," 50.

133. Hickman, "Love Is All," 95–113.

134. Ludlow, "Universalism in History," 201.

which was commuted (presumably not because of the irony).[135] James Relly (1722–78), Methodist London minister, distinguished between two salvations: one that believers had confidently and another that everyone else had suspensefully.[136]

In the rebellious English-speaking colonies, universalism had a similar existence—tentative but extant. Charles Chauncy (1705–87), Congregationalist pastor and Harvard College president, wrote *The Salvation of All Men*, but it was published under his name only after he died. A Baptist Boston preacher, Elhanan Winchester (1751–97), authored *The Universal Restoration* and was nearly forgotten, but his followers organized the Society of Universal Baptists.[137] They along with other Baptists, Quakers, revivalists, and dissenting Calvinists would later form the "Universalists," and, by the nineteenth century, this denomination would grow in the US and Britain to about 140,000 members, making it the sixth largest in the US.[138]

As the nineteenth century began, universalism was still as tangential as any attractive heresy,[139] but that century's spirit of inquiry encouraged freethinkers,[140] which included universalists.[141] That Scripture had for many people become less a source for truth and more an early draft may have contributed to the openness to universalism's philosophically attractive position.[142] The nineteenth century's quest for human perfection also favored universalism because humanity was thought to be perfecting itself anyway.[143] In this environment, criminal justice became reformatory, and, so, hell became that way too, which universalists had been urging all along. Finally, spiritualism was gaining followers, and paying customers were receiving reassuring universalistic reports from loved ones who had

---

135. MacDonald, "Between Heresy and Dogma," 15.

136. Clymer, "Union with Christ," 137–38.

137. McClymond, *Devil's Redemption*, I: 593. Parry, *A Larger Hope?* II: 111–20.

138. Cassara, ed., *Universalism in America*, 39; Noll, *History of Christianity*, 150–51, 220; Robinson, *Unitarians and Universalists*, 47–50, 54, 339–40.

139. Bauckham, "Universalism: Historical Survey," 48–49.

140. Bray, *God Has Spoken*, 23.

141. Horrocks, "Postmortem Education," 203; MacDonald, "Between Heresy and Dogma," 14; Oakes, "Christ's Descent into Hell," 384.

142. Shelley, *Church History*, 315–16, 396–401.

143. Bulgakov, "Heroism and Otherworldliness," 52; Walls, *Oxford Handbook of Eschatology*, 7–8.

passed over to the other side.[144] Theology too adjusted to the new era. The key turn was likely when liberal theologian Schleiermacher sanctioned universal salvation at the end of *The Christian Faith* (1821).[145] He argued Scripture contradicted itself on salvation's extent, and, so, the individualistic exclusivism had to yield to the all-embracing universalism; indeed, Calvinistic predestination as combined with God's salvific will meant that everyone was saved against their will.[146] Given such developments in the nineteenth century, universalism gained followers among the Orthodox, Anglicans, Methodists, Presbyterians, Baptists, Congregationalists, Evangelicals, and Quakers.[147]

Universalism nearly netted Kierkegaard (1813–55), who preached, "Christ came . . . with the purpose of saving the world,"[148] which he will "continue to complete unto the end of the world . . . ."[149] Though Kierkegaard often reasoned that "others were going to hell," he confided he did "not believe that; on the contrary, I believe that we will all be saved, I, too, and this awakens my deepest wonder,"[150] which universalists can quote as indicative of his privately held universalism.[151] He consistently maintained, however, that everyone had to fear for their salvation because God judged individually.[152] Because "the terms of salvation differ for every individual," Kierkegaard argued, the debate "about whether God intends the salvation of all or only of some" tended to be unproductive,[153] but salvation's particularized terms nevertheless justified exclusivism.[154] Scripture, he noted, certainly took that position.[155] Admittedly, God offers

---

144. McClymond, *Devil's Redemption*, I: 84, 96–98.

145. Bauckham, "Universalism: Historical Survey," 50–51; Gockel, *Barth and Schleiermacher*, 98, 198; Hans Schwarz, *Eschatology*, 341–42.

146. Schleiermacher, *Christian Faith*, II: §§ 119, 162–63 (pp. 778–85, 987–98).

147. Grenz, *Theology for the Community*, 634; Hilborn and Horrocks, "Universalistic Trends," 226–28; McClymond, *Devil's Redemption*, II: 1005; Schwarz, *Eschatology*, 341.

148. Kierkegaard, *Practice in Christianity*, 238. Accord *Works of Love*, 8.

149. Kierkegaard, *Training in Christianity*, 16, 151.

150. Kierkegaard, *JP*, VI: 557 (entry 6947).

151. D. Hart, *That All Shall Be Saved*, 198.

152. Kierkegaard, *JP*, III: ¶ 2551; *Upbuilding Discourses*, 260; *Christian Discourses*, 203–5; *Concluding Unscientific Postscript*, I: 275.

153. Kierkegaard, *JP*, IV: 530–31 (entries 4920, 4922).

154. Kierkegaard, *Fear and Trembling*, 66.

155. Kierkegaard, *Attack Upon "Christendom,"* 105.

"reconciliation ... for the salvation of humankind,"[156] but each individual must accept that offer.[157] "There is ... a danger ... called going astray," which is ultimately "perdition."[158] Scholarship's consensus, accordingly, is that Kierkegaard was an exclusivist.[159]

Silouan of Athos (1866–1938) has been claimed as a universalist too,[160] but his expressed expectations were more realistic: "help but a single soul to salvation." Human volition prevented more.[161] While he famously prayed for everyone's salvation, his apostle, who was responsible for conveying Silouan's thoughts in writing, explained that this prayer by implication "rule[s] out" universalism because praying for something to occur is saying that that something is not an occurrence. The prayer instead recognized that "There is a domain in human life ... where even love is not supreme. This domain is freedom." While "Christ's love hopes to draw all men to Him," some reject that love, "many or few, we do not know," though "not all will find salvation."[162]

The British Isles continued to produce universalists in the nineteenth century,[163] and they suffered even less then, though theology professor F. D. Maurice lost his job at King's College in 1853 for affirming universalism (based on eternal punishment being durationally limited).[164] Thomas Erskine argued in *The Doctrine of Election* (1837) that the unsaved were subject to punitive afterlife atonement "until the righteousness of God" achieves "the final salvation of the whole human race," and Andrew Jukes wrote the universalist *The Restitution of All Things* in 1867, which argued a person's death ushered in agelong redemption. Influential Victorian writer George MacDonald (1824–1905) was a universalist based on his

---

156. Kierkegaard, *Upbuilding Discourses*, 258.

157. Kierkegaard, *JP*, IV: ¶ 4950.

158. Kierkegaard, *Upbuilding Discourses*, 13.

159. Marks, "Kierkegaard's Understanding," 281–82; Mulder, "Must All Be Saved?" 1–24; Watkin, "Kierkegaard's View of Death," 74–75. Ellul, a Kierkegaardian who was a universalist, agreed that Kierkegaard was not also a universalist. Clendenin, "Freedom and Universal Salvation," 3.

160. D. Hart, *That All Shall Be Saved*, 16.

161. Silouan, "Writings," 336, 341.

162. Sophrony, "Staretz' Life and Teaching," 109, 222, 226, 230.

163. Wild, *Catholic Guide to Universalism*, 41.

164. Ludlow, "Universalism in History," 209; McClymond, *Devil's Redemption*, I: 31, 87–88.

view that hell destroys sin, which left everyone in eternal life.[165] Congregational minister P. T. Forsyth (1848–1921) wrote, "The certainty of revelation and faith is that in the universal Christ the world is chosen for salvation, and is saved in principle, and shall be saved in fact,"[166] and theologian John Baillie (1886–1960) concluded, because exclusivism meant that evil continued forever (in damnation), only universalism made sense of the all-good ending that God has planned.[167]

Universalism continued to grow as the twentieth century unfolded. It helped that the fascist and communist killing machines had exposed civilization as a fraud for perfecting humanity,[168] which had also dethroned the Enlightenment's Whiggish supposition of continuous human progression.[169] Universalism, as supernatural, thus became the only viable path to human perfection: No matter the extent of humanity's failings, only God could satisfy the longstanding desire for perfection and make everyone as they should be. Also, with Christianity's continued fall from influence during the twentieth century, universalism, by saving everyone, offered salvation for unchurched friends and family who were otherwise damned and once again numerous, and universalism could now do so without endangering a church monopoly on morality, which had clearly been lost.[170]

So, in the twentieth century, Christians began to feature universalism prominently in their credited works and remain prominent Christians. Christian universalists could often be more philosophical than scriptural. John Hick's universal salvation was, in his judgment, brought about by pantheistic reincarnations, where each person lived successively in mysterious otherworlds until they were eventually perfected.[171] Tillich's "correlation" of the positive and the negative addressed "the demonic cleavages," "the essential unity and the existential separation of finite man from his infinity." Ultimately, "God is everything for everything," "salvation in complete unity." In the "universal judgment," the good obtains eternal life

---

165. MacDonald, *Unspoken Sermons*, 30–32, 512–13, 516, 605, 618.
166. Forsyth, *Principle of Authority*, 357, 360.
167. Baillie, *And the Life Everlasting*, 245.
168. Bray, *God Has Spoken*, 1147; Fromm, "Modern Man," 20–21.
169. Butterfield, *Whig Interpretation of History*, passim.
170. Pannenberg, *Anthropology in Theological Perspective*, 13–14.
171. Hick, *Evil and the God of Love*, 381; *Death and Eternal Life*.

without life's "ambiguous mixture,"[172] and this universal purging saves all humanity.[173] Jacques Ellul based his universalism on God's love ultimately rejecting no one.[174] Any "distance existing between God and man . . . will be cancelled for all mankind at the time . . . of the new creation." "[E]very evil work of man is rooted out of him . . . , but that man himself . . . is saved," meaning exclusivism "is not theologically possible."[175]

Respected theologians more dependent on the scriptural record were also advocates for universal salvation in the twentieth century. Indeed, every major communion had at least one universalist with the notable exception of Catholicism.[176] Two twentieth-century Catholic theologians have, however, been suggested as universalists. Rahner purportedly said he was a universalist, but this was only in conversations, never in his writings.[177] Balthasar has been accused of universalism, but he denied it.[178] The published positions of these two theologians on salvation's extent are addressed in this chapter's third section.

Among the Eastern Orthodox, the most emphatic and influential universalist was Sergius Bulgakov, who reckoned that God's penultimate judgment "changes man's very being,"[179] a kind of universal purgatory that transports everyone to salvation,[180] which chapter 8 discusses further. Jesus "took upon Himself all humanity, . . . and all His works are . . . of universal value." With "salvation, life eternal in God," "He will raise up in the flesh all humanity."[181] "The God-man" is "universal resurrection" into eternal life for "all humanity without any exception . . . ."[182]

Nearly every reformed faith had a well-recognized twentieth-century universalist. Anglican John A. T. Robinson wrote *In the End, God . . .* in 1950: "In . . . Christ *all* are made alive" based "solely on the unconditional love of God. Consequently, *all* will be raised; and this despite the perennial tendency of the religious to assert—both within Scripture and outside

---

172. Tillich, *ST*, I: 49, 61, 66, 147; *ST*, III: 398–99.
173. Tillich, *ST*, II: 78, III: 400–401, 407–9, 415–18.
174. Ellul, *What I Believe*, 189–91; *Ethics of Freedom*, 79–80.
175. Ellul, *Apocalypse*, 118–19, 213, 219 (internal quotations omitted).
176. McClymond, *Devil's Redemption*, II: 867–935.
177. Ludlow, *Universal Salvation*, 143, 186.
178. Caldecott, *Radiance of Being*, 247.
179. Bulgakov, *Bride of the Lamb*, 455, 501.
180. Gavrilyuk, "Judgment of Love," 295.
181. Bulgakov, *Orthodox Church*, 106.
182. Bulgakov, *Bride of the Lamb*, 429, 436, 450.

it—that there can be resurrection only for the righteous." Instead, divine free love forces the decision for God in the next life.[183] Congregationalist Nels F. S. Ferré in *The Christian Understanding of God* (1951) suggested that Scripture, notwithstanding its irreconcilable positions on ultimate destinies, has a "total message" of "God's sovereign love."[184] Presbyterian William Barclay was a "convinced universalist" because "in the end all men" succumb to what Scripture describes as God's overpowering love.[185] Calvinist Jürgen Moltmann wrote extensively for universalism.[186] For him, the ultimate does not eternally condemn the unrighteous, but transforms everyone for eternal life. No one is lost.[187] God's will and power produce "universal salvation,"[188] "true Christian universalism."[189]

With the twentieth century supplying these sources for further growth, universalism's popularity surged in the twenty-first century. The theological acceptance that universalism had been receiving, along with the decline in personal responsibility growing out of the twentieth century's last decades,[190] confronted little resistance from the church, which had lost any real ecclesiastical discipline outside the conformity required in the now secularly disempowered Roman Church. So, the now uncontained salvation-extent debate grew such that universalism's acceptance rose to historic proportions, particularly among the avant-garde.[191] This included philosophers. Thomas Talbott in *The Inescapable Love of God* combined two orthodoxies to arrive at the heresy of universalism, namely that God wills everyone saved (per Arminianism) and that God is totally sovereign (per Calvinism), which unavoidably means that everyone will in fact be saved. The syllogism's usual escape—human freewill—he handles by observing that true freewill requires informed consent, and no one in their right mind rejects salvation.[192]

---

183. Robinson, *In the End, God . . .* , 73–74, 104–16.

184. Ferré, *Christian Understanding of God*, 228, 234–37, 242–49.

185. Barclay, *Spiritual Autobiography*, 65–67.

186. Moltmann, *Crucified God*, 194–95; *Theology of Hope*, 209; *Coming of God*, 255.

187. Moltmann, *Crucified God*, 176; *Coming of God*, 76, 106, 251, 271.

188. Moltmann, *Coming of God*, 244–45, 250.

189. Moltmann, *Crucified God*, 194.

190. McClymond, *Devil's Redemption*, I: 18, 30.

191. Parry, *A Larger Hope?* II: 277.

192. Talbott, "Towards a Better Understanding," 5–7.

Nearly every denomination has had in the twenty-first century a theologian in good standing who has bucked the orthodoxy of exclusivism. The Reformed David Congdon argues that everyone is co-crucified with Christ, who saves unbelievers "unconsciously."[193] The Methodist Tom Greggs advocates "particularistic universalism," where Christ saves everyone,[194] which, he acknowledged, is just universalism.[195] The universalism of the Eastern Orthodox David Hart is discussed in the next chapter. Once again the only confession not represented is Catholicism, whose maximum allowable extent of salvation seems still to be hoping for universalism,[196] a position discussed in this chapter's third section. Many more universalists in the relatively new twenty-first century could be listed (and the footnoted authorities cite many more), but any such list, no matter how thorough when written, would be outdated when read.[197]

The change that this century has witnessed has unquestionably been considerable. A twenty-first-century interdenominational organization has been ordaining universalist ministers since 2008.[198] As of 2011, 40 percent of Americans and even 25 percent of the self-described "born-again" accept universalism.[199] A 1996 book debating the top four primary damnation positions (*i.e.*, traditional hell along with nonliteral, purging, and annihilating hells) had to be updated in 2016 to credit universalism's ascension to one of the top four positions (replacing nonliteral hell).[200] In this century, books espousing universalism have become popular reading,[201] and books supporting exclusivism have been read as a defensive response to this positive trend.[202] The epithet *universalist* is clearly no longer an accusation, but has become an accolade.[203] Universalists in

---

193. Congdon, *God Who Saves*, 80, 90, 97–100, 215, 258–60, 268–74.

194. Greggs, *Barth, Origen, and Universalism*, 14, 119, 191, 195, 206.

195. Greggs, "Christian Universalist View," 197.

196. Bullivant, *Salvation of Atheists*, 1–12, 181–88.

197. Louth, "Eastern Orthodox Eschatology," 246; McClymond, *Devil's Redemption*, II: 938–39; Talbott, "Universalism," 458 n.1.

198. Christian Universalist Association, "History of the CUA."

199. Barna, "What Americans Believe."

200. Crockett, ed., *Four Views on Hell*; Sprinkle, ed., *Four Views on Hell*, 101.

201. In addition to those books that have already been cited (*e.g.*, Hart, *That All Shall Be Saved*; Parry and Partridge, eds., *Universal Salvation?*), see Bell, *Love Wins* and Pearson, *Gospel of Inclusion*.

202. Noval, "Divine Drama," 201, 210.

203. McClymond, *Devil's Redemption*, II: 751; Noval, "Divine Drama," 201–10.

the twenty-first century certainly do not have to hide their identities like their predecessors did.[204] Origen's reputation as a Christian theologian is being rehabilitated too, now more on par with Augustine but with the advantages of being speculative and fluent in Greek.[205] By all accounts, universalism is a more endorsed view now among Christians than at any time since before Origen's proscription.[206]

2. Exclusivism Is Orthodox

A corresponding resumé of exclusivists is impractical because it would be practically everyone else.[207] One compensation, therefore, for the length of the universalist survey is that it allows most every other historic figure not on it to be counted exclusivist *sub silentio*. Universalists will generally acknowledge that exclusivism has been, and remains even today, the Christian mainstream.[208] This exclusivist preponderance results partly from the latitude of its position. Universalism says that God saves every human, no exceptions, while exclusivism is simply every other extent of salvation.[209] Exclusivism is just not universalism, which is categorical. Exclusivists, who can differ a lot in their views on salvation degrees, can say that God nurtures everyone, judges everyone, graces everyone, and reveals to everyone.[210] Exclusivism is merely dualistic about the *ultimate* outcome; the godly live forever in eternal bliss and the ungodly do not, and, so, whatever the proportions or the reasons, some are not saved.[211]

---

204. McClymond, *Devil's Redemption*, II: 957.

205. Blosser, *Become Like the Angels*, 2–3.

206. Balthasar, *Theo-Drama*, V: 192; Grenz, *Theology for the Community*, 634; MacDonald, "Between Heresy and Dogma," 14, 17; Martin, *Will Many Be Saved?* 55; Ramelli, *Christian Doctrine of Apokatastasis*, 819–20.

207. Martin, *Will Many Be Saved?* 14; Wild, *Catholic Guide to Universalism*, 1.

208. Greggs, "Christian Universalist View," 198; D. Hart, *That All Shall Be Saved*, 4, 81.

209. Greggs, "Christian Universalist View," 198.

210. Lubac, *Catholicism*, 218–19.

211. Ludlow, *Universal Salvation*, 30. The primary varieties of exclusivism, such as whether the negative ultimate is *eternal torment* or *annihilation*, are not considered separately because they all agree that salvation's extent is not everyone. Ellis, "NT Teaching on Hell," 117–22.

a. Anathematizing Universalism

The most direct explanation for exclusivism's dominance within the church is the Second Council of Constantinople, which met in 553. The four previous ecumenical councils, which have come to define Christianity as the faith that worships the one God who is three Persons and whose Second Person has divine and human natures,[212] had not faced the issue of salvation's extent, and universalists can cite this as proof that universalism was for centuries an acceptable Christian understanding.[213] But in the decade before Constantinople II the dispute regarding the extent of salvation was coming to head. The spark was when the Jerusalem and Antioch patriarchs were quarreling with Origenists and complained to Justinian the Great, and it was now that the complaint included universalism.[214] In this dispute, the emperor sided with the patriarchs: "If anyone says . . . the punishment of . . . impious human beings is temporary . . . , let him be anathema."[215] Justinian was at the time engaged in the fight between the Nestorians and the monophysites about Christ's natures, and, so, when Constantinople II convened to address the Three Chapters controversy,[216] Justinian supplemented the council's agenda so that it would also address Origen's universalist "error" that "godless human beings will be with godly . . . men."[217] Canons specifically condemning Origenism were dutifully incorporated into the record of the council,[218] including, "If anyone says . . . all human beings . . . will be united to God . . . , let him be anathema," and the council's official list of heretics included "Origen," his "impious writings," and anyone "who . . . hold tenets like those of the aforesaid heretics."[219]

Some universalists and some defenders of Origen say it is unclear whether this Fifth Ecumenical Council condemned universalism or Origen (as opposed to certain Origenists), suggesting even that the council's

---

212. Fudge, *Fire That Consumes*, 276 & n.12.
213. Gavrilyuk, "Judgment of Love," 283–84; MacDonald, "Between Heresy and Dogma," 9.
214. Price, "General Introduction," 17; "Anti-Origenist Canons," 274, 277.
215. "Canons of 543," canon 9 (p. 281).
216. Price, "General Introduction," 22–23, 59.
217. "Letter of Justinian," 282–83.
218. Price, "Eighth Session," 104; "Anti-Origenist Canons," 271–72.
219. "Canons of 553," canon 12 (p. 286); "Proceedings," canon 11 (pp. 123–24).

records may have been doctored to reflect the emperor's position,[220] but the available evidence confirms the longstanding conviction that the council designated universalism as a heresy.[221] And that is the key point here. The anathematization of universalism occurred regardless of the extent of the council's deliberations, regardless of whether that decision made it into the minutes, or regardless of whether "Origen" referred to a sixth-century interpretation of him or the third-century theologian himself. That the council made universalism a heresy was certainly not doubted until recently,[222] including in sixth-century sources that recorded that it was one of the conciliar results.[223] Universalists, therefore, mostly "recognize that the doctrine of universal salvation was officially condemned" at Constantinople II, albeit without a proper deliberation.[224] So, independent of the questions about the propriety of this ecumenical decision, it was certainly made, and exclusivism then became the Christian norm.[225]

b. Subsequent Creeds and Confessions

While Balthasar overstates that "Every Christian creed can take no other position than" exclusivism,[226] each communion with an authoritative teaching on salvation's extent has done just that, and these Christian creeds best reflect exclusivism's continued dominance. Although the councilors of Constantinople II were predominantly Eastern,[227] the West fully endorsed the council's disavowal of universalism, as seen in their Athanasian Creed (technically, *Quicumque Vult*), which dated from the same timeframe.[228] While it mainly combated Arianism, the Athanasian

---

220. Crouzel, *Origen*, 178–79; Daley, *Hope of the Early Church*, 190; Oakes, "Christ's Descent into Hell," 383; Kimel, "Did the Fifth Ecumenical Council Condemn Universal Salvation?".

221. Price, "Anti-Origenist Canons," 270–72, 280.

222. Crisp, "'I Do Teach It,'" 310; Gavrilyuk, "Judgment of Love," 284 n.22; Ludlow, "Universalism in History," 195.

223. Price, "General Introduction," 100; "Eighth Session," 105; "Anti-Origenist Canons," 270–71.

224. Ramelli and Konstan, *Terms for Eternity*, 239.

225. Kelly, *Early Christian Doctrines*, 484.

226. Balthasar, *Dare We Hope*, 48.

227. McClymond, *Devil's Redemption*, I: 119.

228. Chadwick, *Church in Ancient Society*, 653–54.

Creed declared that "those who have done evil" will enter "eternal fire" and "cannot be saved."[229] Later, the Fourth Lateran Council (1215), canon 1, concluded: The evil have "everlasting punishment," and "no one at all" "outside the Church is saved."[230] Rome's latest authorities continue to teach exclusivism but in kinder tones. Vatican II noted that individuals were lost "more often [*saepius*]" than not,[231] and the current catechism "affirms . . . hell and its eternity" where sinners "suffer . . . 'eternal fire.'"[232] "[N]othing of the dreadful reality of Hell is denied," Ratzinger explained. "The doctrine of everlasting punishment preserves its real content."[233]

Protestants similarly affirm exclusivism in their catechisms and confessions,[234] including the Augsburg Confession by the Lutherans,[235] the Heidelberg Catechism and the Westminster Confession by the Reformed,[236] the Manual of the Nazarene Church by the Wesleyans,[237] the Dordrecht Confession by the Anabaptist/Mennonites,[238] the Philadelphia Confession of Faith by the Baptists,[239] and the Basis of Faith by the Evangelicals.[240]

The Eastern Orthodox has not felt the need to relitigate the Constantinople II decision, and, so, the East remains exclusivist, as universalists acknowledge.[241] Its Jerusalem Council of 1672, one of its more significant synods, outlined the traditional ultimates of joyful rest and "torment."[242] John Climacus, the universally revered eastern monk, denounced universalism as the "foul disease" "of the godless Origen,"[243] and Ecumenical Patriarch Gennadius II (George Scholarios), while appreciative of Origen

229. Denzinger and Rahner, eds., *Sources of Catholic Dogma*, 16 (39–40).
230. Denzinger and Rahner, eds., *Sources of Catholic Dogma*, 169 (429–30).
231. Vatican Council, "Dogmatic Constitution on the Church," 16.
232. Catholic Church, *Catechism*, 1035 (p. 292).
233. Ratzinger, *Eschatology*, 218.
234. Hebblethwaite, *Christian Hope*, 84.
235. Tappert, ed., *Book of Concord*, 38 (ch 17).
236. Presbyterian Church, "Book of Confessions," 4.020–22, 4.062–64, 6.177.
237. Dunning, *Grace, Faith, and Holiness*, 391.
238. Wenger, "Dordrecht Confession of Faith," 93 (art. 18).
239. George and George, eds., *Baptist Confessions*, 92 (ch 34).
240. Hilborn and Horrocks, "Universalistic Trends," 226; Horrocks, "Postmortem Education," 199.
241. Bulgakov, *Orthodox Church*, 185.
242. *Acts and Decrees*, Ch VI, Decree XVIII (pp. 150–52).
243. Climacus, *Ladder of Divine Ascent*, 131 (step 5).

generally, ranked his transitory hell among his errors and the "worst of all."[244] The Orthodox Church, however, mostly leaves authoritative theology to its liturgy and not proclamations beyond those settled at the first seven ecumenical councils (including Constantinople II),[245] but even its liturgy reflects exclusivism: Its mourning services mark the deceased's passage through an afterlife judgment that ends in either heaven or hell,[246] and, when the Orthodox expel catechumens and penitents before closing the church doors, this symbolizes the separation of the elect from the damned.[247] Because, however, rituals make for poor standards of enforcement and despite the doctrinal resolution of salvation's extent in the sixth century, universalists have gone undisciplined.[248]

One major Christian denomination is unaccounted for because Anglicanism lacks clarity on anything theological except for its Quadrilateral (Scripture is sufficient for salvation, the Apostles' and Nicene Creeds articulate the faith, the sacraments are baptism and communion, and succession is via the episcopacy).[249] As a result, the Church of England has not authoritatively settled salvation's extent.[250] Its founding Thirty-Nine Articles had distinguished the Church of England from Catholicism and affirmed certain basic Christian tenets, and the issue of salvation's extent was not a topic for either category. At one point, its Articles of Religion had numbered forty-two so as to also distinguish Anglicanism from radical Protestantism, and among the extra three articles was a condemnation of universalism.[251] The anti-universalist article (along with the other two) fell out at some point, but the reason why is now contested. Some universalists claim universalism was too obviously a Christian possibility to be denounceable, and exclusivists claim universalism was too obviously not Christian at all to be singled out as an exclusion.[252] Despite the absence of a foundational Anglican authority explicitly rejecting universalism, universalists generate opposition. When, for instance, the first Anglican bishop of Natal supported universalism (and tolerated polygamy), his

244. Chadwick, *Early Christian Thought*, 95.
245. Louth, "Eastern Orthodox Eschatology," 233.
246. Louth, "Eastern Orthodox Eschatology," 239–41.
247. Lossky, *Mystical Theology*, 190.
248. McClymond, *Devil's Redemption*, I: 39, 44.
249. Chapman, *Anglican Theology*, 4, 8, 70, 192–95.
250. Commission, "Doctrine in the Church of England," 25.
251. Hillerbrand, *Division of Christendom*, 254.
252. McClymond, *Devil's Redemption*, I: 80 & n.192.

archbishop adjudged him a heretic, but his excommunication, which nearly every bishop at the first international Anglican bishops conference (1867) favored, was avoided only because the archbishop of Canterbury tabled the uncongenial issue.[253] Similar stories recur of Anglicans tolerating but disapproving of universalists.[254]

The one denominational exception to exclusivism is the denomination mentioned above calling themselves the "Universalists," which made universalism credal: "one God . . . will finally restore the whole family of mankind to holiness and happiness."[255] Their leading theologian, Hosea Ballou, reasoned in *A Treatise on Atonement* that universalism resulted independently of the atonement and was achieved by a unitarian-style God.[256] The slide into unitarianism was thus inexorable, especially given the popularity of humanism in the nineteenth century, which had humanity saving itself anyway.[257] In the twentieth century, the Universalists officially merged into the Unitarians, dispensing with the complication of Christ as mediator, and, as a result, it disappeared as a Christian denomination.[258] No other Christian denomination before or since has adopted universalism.[259]

c. Exemplary Theologians

Given the consensus on salvation's extent as evidenced by Constantinople II, the denominational confessions, and historic practice, all of the faithful are presumptively exclusivist unless identifying explicitly as a universalist, which is what makes a survey of exclusivists unworkable.[260] To help further balance the presentation, however, a sampling of key

---

253. Chapman, *Anglican Theology*, 181–85; Ludlow, "Universalism in History," 210.

254. Rowell, *Hell and the Victorians*, 116–21.

255. Robinson, *Unitarians and Universalists*, 56 (1803 Winchester Profession).

256. Cassara, *Universalism in America*, 17, 21–23; Robinson, *Unitarians and Universalists*, 61–62.

257. Cassara, *Universalism in America*, 41–42.

258. Hughes, "Universalism, Universalists," 638–41; McClymond, *Devil's Redemption*, I: 16–17, 22, 86, 572–73, II: 1001, 1004, 1017–18, 1038–40; Robinson, *Unitarians and Universalists*, 171–73.

259. Ludlow, *Universal Salvation*, 170; McClymond, *Devil's Redemption*, I: 21–22.

260. McClymond, *Devil's Redemption*, I: xxi, II: 793.

theologians can represent the masses who say only some are saved.[261] One such sample can be of systematic theologians, and these are certainly the best representatives after the issue of salvation's extent was ecumenically decided in the sixth century because continuing to harp on the given answer became needless unless the theologian was being systematic. Of note, therefore, is that *the* most influential systematic theologian in each era of Western Christianity, Augustine in antiquity, Thomas in the Middle Ages, and Calvin in modernity, were all exclusivists.[262]

Augustine saw everyone damned, *massa perditionis*, until God grace rescues some. Faith, "the universal way" to salvation, is loving Christ more than anything, including family or life. Given this standard, "many more" receive "eternal punishment."[263] In "the universal judgment," one group "will live truly and happily in eternal life" and one "will exist unhappily in eternal death . . . , the condition of both will be without end."[264] Augustine faulted universalism for contradicting "the express words of God,"[265] arguing Scripture's salvation of *all* is just *some from all races*.[266]

Thomas found that, though Christ's power was sufficient to save everyone, some people reject him.[267] As a result, "mankind will be cleansed . . . by the separation of the wicked from the good . . . , so that all that is ugly and vile will be cast with the wicked into hell, and all that is beautiful and noble will be taken up above for the glory of the elect . . . ." That is, individuals "plunge into hell or soar to heaven" "in keeping with their reward or punishment." Universalism, therefore, "must be judged heretical" for violating the "truth . . . attested by the . . . the canonical Scriptures and the doctrine of the holy Fathers . . . ."[268]

Calvin, like Luther before him, was exclusivist, which he summarized in his *Institutes*' well-titled chapter, "Of the Eternal Election, by Which God Has Predestinated Some to Salvation, and Others to Destruction." Using "grace chooses a remnant" (Rom 11:5),[269] he concluded,

---

261. C. Taylor, *Secular Age*, 122; Trumbower, *Rescue for the Dead*, 41.

262. Erickson, *Christian Theology*, 63–64.

263. Augustine, *City of God*, X,32, XII,22–23, XIII,23, XIV,1, XXI,26 (pp. 420–26, 502–3, 540, 547, 1010–14).

264. Augustine, *Enchiridion*, 24,97–26,102, 29,111 (pp. 119–25, 132).

265. Augustine, *City of God*, XXI,12, 17 (pp. 989, 995–96).

266. Augustine, "On Rebuke and Grace," XIV,44.

267. O'Meara, *Thomas Aquinas Theologian*, 239–40.

268. Aquinas, *ST III (Suppl.)*, XX, Q. 69, art.2, co., Q. 74, art. 9, co (pp. 6, 116).

269. This is not in the exclusivist scriptural basis because the choosing of the

"many fall away and are lost, so that often a small portion only remains. ... The external invitation ... holds a kind of middle place between the rejection of the human race and the election of a small number of believers." "God ... determined once for all those whom it was his pleasure to admit to salvation, and those whom ... to doom to destruction...."[270]

The sample that is perhaps most telling about the influence that exclusivism had independent of its anathematization is, of course, patristic. As has been noted, many church fathers were universalists, but many others, if not most, were not.[271] The Didache, reflecting first-century tradition and perhaps the best extant indication of what the earliest non-canonical Christians believed, specified that there would be an eschatological "test" by fire where "many" "will be utterly destroyed [ἀπολοῦνται]."[272] Two other anonymous writers were exclusivists in the second century: The Letter to Diognetus concluded that the unfaithful "will be condemned to the everlasting fire,"[273] and pseudo-Clement noted that, unlike Christians who had "life everlasting" and were rescued "from eternal punishment," those denying Jesus "are punished with terrible torture in unquenchable fire...."[274]

The first theologians known by name were exclusivists too. Polycarp purportedly told his executioners they were "ignorant of the fire" "of eternal punishment" "reserved for the ungodly," which is not "extinguished."[275] Justin Martyr held that "everyone goes to eternal punishment or salvation in accordance with the character of his acts."[276] Athenagoras of Athens was persuaded that the godless will "in fire" "perish and be annihilated."[277] Theophilus of Antioch wrote, "For the unbelievers and for the contemptuous," etc., "there will be wrath and indignation, tribulation and anguish: and in the end, such men as these will be detained in everlasting fire."[278] As the second century ended, Irenaeus condemned

---

remnant that is referred to occurs ἐν τῷ νῦν καιρῷ, which means something like *in the now time* and, therefore, is clearly referring away from the ultimate. Cranfield, *Romans 9–16*, 547-48.

270. Calvin, *Institutes*, III,21 (pp. 606, 610, 612-13).
271. McClymond, *Devil's Redemption*, I: 40-41.
272. Milavec, ed., *Didache*, ix, 36-37 (16.5), 82.
273. "Letter to Diognetus," 42 [10, 7].
274. "So-Called Second Letter," 43 [5, 5; 6, 7; 17, 7].
275. Polycarp, "Martyrdom of Polycarp," XI (p. 41).
276. Justin, *First and Second Apologies*, I,12, 21, 52 (pp. 29, 38, 59).
277. Athenagoras, "Supplication for the Christians," 70 [31].
278. Theophilus, "To Autolycus," 74 [1, 14].

gnostics for saying that "all souls are saved,"[279] because the unfaithful are in fact "deprived of... life eternal" and sent "into everlasting fire" where "the anger of God will remain upon him."[280]

Exclusivism did not diminish after the second century. Hippolytus of Rome, the anti-pope celebrated in the East and the West, concluded that, while "everlasting enjoyment shall be given" to the good, the evil "shall be given eternal punishment," that of "the unquenchable and unending fire" and "a certain fiery worm which does not die."[281] Cyprian of Carthage was an exclusivist too,[282] as were the first Latin-writing theologians, Marcus Minucius Felix and Tertullian.[283]

After the third century, despite Origen's affirmation of universalism, exclusivists did not diminish and included, as noted above, Basil, Gregory of Nazianzus, Chrysostom, Jerome, and Augustine. They were joined by Cyril of Jerusalem,[284] Fabius Fulgentius of Ruspe,[285] and Gregory the Great.[286] There were more of course, but, conveniently for anyone trying to condense the patristic position on salvation's extent, the last of the Greek fathers, John Damascene, provided it in the eighth century: While believers have "eternal salvation," the rest have "chastisement and eternal punishment." "God has done everything for a man's salvation," but his foes are "given over to absolute perdition," "the most unspeakable and extremely wicked abyss" of "everlasting fire."[287]

3. Potentialism Hedges

Because of the enduring co-existence and obvious incompatibility of universalism and exclusivism, some twentieth-century theologians, Rahner among them, diagnosed the church as "bipolar" and concluded that

279. Irenaeus, "Against Heresies [1994]," 1.25.4 (p. 351).

280. Irenaeus, "Against Heresies [1970]," 1.10.1, 3.19.1, 4.37.5 (pp. 85, 93, 98).

281. Hippolytus, "Against the Greeks," 172 [3].

282. Cyprian, "Unity of the Catholic," 221 [6]; "To Demetrian," 223 [24]; "Letter to Thibar," 231 [58 (56), 10].

283. Felix, "Octavius," 110 [34, 9; 35, 3]; Tertullian, "Apology," 114, 117 [18, 3; 48, 12–13].

284. Cyril, "Catechetical Lectures," 359 [18, 18].

285. Fulgence, "Forgiveness of Sins," 292 [1, 19, 2]; "Rule of Faith," 296 [37].

286. Gregory I, "Moral Teachings," 318 [34, 19, 36].

287. John, "Fount of Knowledge," III,I,3, II,29, III,29, IV,13, IV,27 (pp. 168, 262, 334, 358, 406).

Scripture's obfuscation was what had bequeathed this psychosis.[288] Brunner, reaching the same conclusion, explained the pathology: Scripture's "lack of logic" on salvation's extent presented a "contradiction," which has forced the church to "ton[e] down" half of Scripture.[289] The cure these doctors of the faith have proposed for the manic-depressive disorder of alternating universalism and exclusivism is difficult to describe in a nonpartisan way other than that this third view is neither actual universalism nor abject exclusivism.[290] To describe succinctly the new position in the sense of what it is, rather than what it is not, is intractable unless it is that the position amounts to salvation's extent being *potentially* either universalist or exclusivist. Given this, its shorthand here is "potentialism."

Potentialism rejects universalism, which has recast Scripture's *wrath* as *therapeutic*, yet it tries also to avoid exclusivism, which has recast Scripture's *everyone* as *some*,[291] but, in trying to reject both, potentialism can seem to recast intelligibility as a vice.[292] What potentialism does is to piously excuse Scripture from being wholly true, and this compensates with a satisfying exegetical sophistication outside the exclusivism/universalism fray.[293] Thus potentialists have evolved beyond the first disciples and the church fathers, who believed "*the* Scripture [τῇ γραφῇ]" (John 2:22).[294] Instead, potentialists take Scripture dialectically—except that the thesis and the antithesis never meet.[295]

Because this boggle can befuddle those trying to understand what potentialism stands for, universalists may claim that potentialists are really universalists at heart,[296] and some exclusivists can agree with

---

288. Rahner, "Eschatology," 435.

289. Brunner, *Eternal Hope*, 180–81.

290. Molnar, "Thomas F. Torrance," 169–73.

291. Balthasar, *Dare We Hope*, 49–52, 62–64; Harmon, "Subjection of All Things," 61.

292. Ludlow, *Universal Salvation*, 241.

293. Bauckham, "Universalism: Historical Survey," 52; Erickson, *Christian Theology*, 252; Ludlow, *Universal Salvation*, 10, 241, 273.

294. Candler, *Theology, Rhetoric, Manuduction*, 83; Werner Jaeger, *Early Christianity*, 93; Jenson, *ST*, I: 85; Wiles, *Making of Christian Doctrine*, 47.

295. Boring, "Language of Universal Salvation," 278–82, 288, 289 n.62, 291–92 & n.70; D. Hart, *That All Shall Be Saved*, 66, 102–3; Ludlow, *Universal Salvation*, 186.

296. MacDonald, "Between Heresy and Dogma," 22.

them.[297] Yet, universalism is *actual* universal salvation,[298] while potentialism is definitely not that but only its possibility,[299] and it is this artifice that allows potentialism to avoid universalism's heresy.[300] Rather than being confused for universalism, potentialism appears effectively to be exclusivism at its most optimistic. Exclusivists have certainly included those who hope that salvation is universal.[301] Indeed, when so understood, potentialism could include any optimistic exclusivist, such as Kierkegaard.[302] Even the most orthodox can qualify as a potentialist if understood this way, such as Thomas.[303] Modern examples of exclusivists who can sound like potentialists, when potentialism is understood as maximally hopeful exclusivism, are Robert Jenson, Vladimir Lossky, Wolfhart Pannenberg, Hans Schwarz, and N. T. Wright.[304]

Exclusivists certainly include those who recognize that God's twofold will includes his antecedent will to save everyone.[305] A fifth-century church council even declared anyone a heretic who claimed God did not will that everyone be saved.[306] Conservative evangelist Norman Geisler recognized that "All persons are saved *potentially* . . . , but only some are saved *actually* . . . ."[307] Differently expressed, orthodoxy says Christ is *sufficient* for all, though *efficient* for the elect;[308] or salvation is objectively universal, though subjectively exclusive.[309] Reformed traditions have "hypothetical universalism," which is basically potentialism.[310] The Second

297. McClymond, *Devil's Redemption*, I: 33.

298. Bauckham, "Universalism: Historical Survey," 49; Crisp, "'I Do Teach It,'" 306–9 & n.4; Mason, "Universalism," 733.

299. D. Hart, *That All Shall Be Saved*, 66, 102–3.

300. Ludlow, "Universalism in History," 211; Wild, *Catholic Guide to Universalism*, xiii, 2.

301. Allen, *Extent of Atonement*, 398, 784; Cabasilas, *Life in Christ*, Bk I § 10 (p. 58); Ratzinger, *Eschatology*, 65, 215.

302. Ludlow, "Universalism in History," 208.

303. Trabbic, "Can Aquinas Hope?" 337–58.

304. Jensen, *ST*, II: 364–65; Lossky, *Mystical Theology*, 235; Pannenberg, "Constructive and Critical Functions," 136; Schwarz, *Human Being*, 382; N. T. Wright, *Surprised by Hope*, 177.

305. Gockel, *Barth and Schleiermacher*, 26; Martin, *Will Many Be Saved?* 172.

306. Holmes, *Origin and Development*, 404–5.

307. Geisler, *ST*, 863.

308. Lombard, *Sentences: Book 3*, 86.

309. Hammett, "Multiple-Intentions View," 162–63.

310. Bray, *God Has Spoken*, 905–7.

Helvetic Confession (1561), for example, "hopes well of all," "however many will be saved . . . ."[311] Only High Calvinists, believing in predetermined limited atonement, say that not everyone is potentially savable.[312] Hence, potentialism, when it reaches for an expressible position and when its clarity exceeds more than mere uncertainty about salvation's extent, appears to be the hopeful end of exclusivism, which puts potentialism at the middle of the theological spectrum for salvation's extent.[313]

Of those theologians purporting to reject both exclusivism and universalism, termed here potentialists, the leaders are almost certainly Barth, Balthasar, and Rahner. Barth may have been the first theologian to claim a salvation-extent position that rejected both universalism and exclusivism. His position, despite or perhaps because of his thorough expounding on the subject, has, however, been contested. Fellow theologians take his position, like potentialism generally, as either exclusivist,[314] agnostic,[315] universalist,[316] or confused.[317] Barth almost always described his position in terms that were literally universalist: God "is directed to the salvation of all men in intention, and sufficient for the salvation of all men in power;" "none is excluded." "[F]ellowship with God" exists for "the race as a whole, or the sum total of individuals." A person "cannot annul" "his election." It is "objectively impossible."[318] Salvation is "final and indestructible" with "all men," "all men and every man."[319] The faithful are saved "de facto," and "all men" are saved "de jure."[320]

Barth willingly acknowledged that these statements along with intellectual consistency would compel his acceptance of universalism, but he defied that designation.[321] His disavowal could have been a desire to

311. Presbyterian Church, "Book of Confessions," 5.048, 5.055–56, 5.077.

312. Allen, *Extent of Atonement*, xix–xx; Calvin, *Romans and Thessalonians*, 117–18; Martin, *Will Many Be Saved?* 172.

313. Sachs, "Apocatastasis in Patristic Theology," 253.

314. Bettis, "Was Barth a Universalist," 423, 426–27.

315. Tseng, "Condemnation and Universal Salvation," 324–38.

316. Gockel, *Barth and Schleiermacher*, 207–8; McClymond, *Devil's Redemption*, I: 33, II: 863; McCormack, "So That He May," 227.

317. Crisp, "'I Do Teach It,'" 305–6.

318. Barth, *CD II/2*, §§ 32.1, 32.3, 33.1–33.2, 34.1, 35.1–35.4, 39.2 (pp. 9, 13, 16, 19, 91–92, 118, 149, 195, 321, 346, 421–22, 450, 757).

319. Barth, *CD IV/1*, §§ 58.2, 61.4 (pp. 102, 631).

320. Barth, *CD IV/2*, § 66.2 (p. 511).

321. Barth, *CD IV/3.1*, § 70.3 (pp. 477–78).

avoid heresy,[322] but his stated reservation was that "we must not arrogate to ourselves that which can be given and received only as a free gift." So, despite everything else that he said about the universality of salvation's extent, Barth concluded that God can "acquiesce in the cheerless disintegration of man's existence."[323] Barth thus rejected both exclusivism and universalism and judged that the most that can be said about salvation's extent is that at least the latter is a "possibility."[324]

Balthasar reached the same non-answer in *Dare We Hope "That All Men Be Saved"?* as the question mark in his title forewarns. He disagrees with both universalism and exclusivism because Jesus expresses both, and, so, he argued that the scriptural accounts cannot be understood other than as a "hope for all men." Balthasar set out his position most succinctly when quoting his inspiration, von Speyr (discussed further in chapter 8), "The truth is not simply an either-or: either somebody is in hell or nobody is. Both are partial expressions of the whole truth."[325] Because God judges each individual, Christ's salvation entails the damned too. Balthasar explained:

> For the believer, hope remains where all speculative systems have failed: this is a hope that . . . "does not disappoint" (Rom 5:5). However, it has taken the whole modern movement against the dominance of the Augustinian tradition to liberate this hope with regard to our fellow men . . . from the restrictions and reservations that are still latent in Thomas.
>
> If we look back from this vantage point to the judgment that awaits every sinful human being, the appropriate attitude will be a hope that is not without a certain fear. . . . [A] man is somehow both to the right and to the left of the Judge.[326]

So, for Balthasar, universal salvation is a possibility.[327]

Rahner's renown on who all is saved comes from his position that "anonymous" Christians, namely the non-churched, can be saved.[328] On the specific issue of salvation's extent, though his position is not as

322. Gockel, *Barth and Schleiermacher*, 208.

323. Barth, *CD IV/3.1*, § 70.3 (pp. 473, 477).

324. Barth, *CD II/2*, § 35.3 (pp. 415, 417–18, 421–23); *CD IV/3.1*, § 70.3 (pp. 477–78).

325. Balthasar, *Dare We Hope*, 20–22, 29, 69, 111–13; "Short Discourse on Hell," 177, 181, 186–87.

326. Balthasar, *Theo-Drama*, V: 321.

327. Balthasar, *Dare We Hope*, 85.

328. Ludlow, *Universal Salvation*, 176–78.

well-known as that of Barth or Balthasar, Rahner too was a potentialist, but he leads a different perspective on this middle approach. Instead of hoping for universal salvation while acknowledging the ultimate threat for the damned, Rahner surrendered to the scriptural contradiction. He has been called a universalist, but this has been based on his statements in reported but unrecorded conversations.[329] In writing, he was perfectly circumspect: "damnation is a real genuine and inevitable possibility,"[330] though "not on the same plane" as salvation.[331] Because the contradicting accounts in Scripture cannot be reconciled, he reasoned, Christians have no certainty about salvation's extent.[332] According to Rahner and the other potentialists who are not just hopeful exclusivists, this means Scripture is "not true in every respect," its paradox is not "coherent," and the scriptural propositions are "ultimately irreducible."[333]

In sum, theologians dissatisfied with universalism and exclusivism have articulated in the last century a compromise for the salvation paradox—potential universalism.[334] Theirs is only possibly a third position because exclusivism has always included those hoping for everyone's salvation.[335] When potentialism is treated not as an exclusivist subset of hopefuls, but as a position distinct from exclusivism like its proponents claim it is, potentialism reads Scripture as an unanswerable contradiction. That is, potentialism either says that it is somehow potentially the case that everyone is saved and also potentially the case that not everyone is saved or says that universalism and exclusivism are contradictory and yet are still somehow both true. In short, on the question of salvation's extent, potentialists take Scripture either as exclusivist with a hope for universalism or as without hope of an answer.

※

The church, from all sides, has treated the salvation paradox as a contradiction. To resolve it, the church mostly opts for exclusivism because universalism is too dependent on scriptural snippets and on a God too

---

329. Ludlow, *Universal Salvation*, 143, 186.
330. Rahner, "Hermeneutics of Eschatological Assertions," 338–39.
331. Rahner, "Eschatology," 245.
332. Rahner, *Foundations*, 103, 443.
333. Ludlow, *Universal Salvation*, 246–48.
334. McClymond, *Devil's Redemption*, I: 20.
335. Lubac, *Catholicism*, 218–19; Ratzinger, *Eschatology*, 65, 215.

purified of temperament, but many within the church find universalism too clearly stated in those snippets and too pleasing an understanding to not be preferred. Potentialists, after recognizing that the accounts clearly contradict, find universalism a fine idea, but, with the majority, lack conviction in it given the inescapability of the exclusivist account. What remains is to evaluate these responses and to begin the labor of preserving Scripture's paradox of salvation's extent.

5

Unconvincing Treatments

We are all humiliated by the sudden discovery of a fact which has existed very comfortably and perhaps been staring at us in private while we have been making up our world entirely without it.

—George Eliot, *Middlemarch*

THE PROBLEM HAS BEEN presented, which is that Scripture has two accounts of salvation's extent—everyone is saved *and* not everyone is saved—and that tradition has the same two accounts but with one key difference—everyone is saved *or* not everyone is saved. That is, though Scripture has expressed salvation's extent paradoxically, tradition has reformed this into a contradiction and resolved it in mutually exclusive ways.[1] This chapter marks the discourse's turning point because the problem that has been presented is now to be worked.

Each competing tradition on salvation's extent has reconstructed Scripture with a three-step method as old as Tertullian: 1) quote the problematic text, 2) recite its various meanings, and 3) adopt a meaning that is opposite its most common.[2] *All* and *world* are pliant for exclusiv-

---

1. Bulgakov, *Orthodox Church*, 185; Daley, *Hope of the Early Church*, 221.
2. Fudge, *Fire That Consumes*, 156.

ists, as is *perishing* and *wrath* for universalists, while potentialists read *potentially* into each scriptural account. Problem solved. Though the reconstructions unwind the paradox, unanswered is why Scripture is so poorly expressed that it needs the reconstructions. More programmatically, Scripture's paradoxes do not call for *Scripture* to be reconstructed, but calls for *us* to be reconstructed.[3]

1. Tradition Lacks Consensus

Despite exclusivism's coup at Constantinople II, tradition has failed at consensus.[4] That 500 years of intramural back and forth before then had not settled the salvation-extent question is disturbing because we expect those passing on God's revelations to have agreed on at least the basics of what they were passing on.[5] That the eventual resolution came about without a recorded debate and without stated reasons add to the dismay, and the passage of time has of late only made the resolution more insecure. The Vincentian Canon that orthodoxy is what is eventually taught "everywhere, always, by all" helps the salvation paradox not at all, and even the fallback standard of ascertaining "the consentient belief" of the "masters" of the church hardly helps either.[6] As the last chapter established, the masters have given two incompatible answers to salvation's extent,[7] and their disagreement has merely confirmed the central point: Scripture seems to disagree with itself. The twentieth-century position of potentialism verifies that neither exclusivism nor universalism has a sure hold, but, when not genteel exclusivism, potentialism must adopt Orwell's "labyrinthine world of doublethink," where they claim "to hold simultaneously two opinions which canceled out, knowing them to be contradictory and believing in both . . . ."[8] Given such a state of affairs, a sage observed, "Maybe a humble agnosticism is the wisest option."[9]

---

3. Stephens, *Annihilation or Renewal?* 8.
4. Dunning, *Grace, Faith, and Holiness*, 82.
5. Bulgakov, *Orthodox Church*, 12–13; Walls, *Hell*, 53.
6. Vincent, "A Commonitory," chs II, III, XXVII [6, 8, 70] (pp. 132, 152).
7. Balthasar, *Theo-Drama*, V: 192, 269.
8. Orwell, *1984*, 35.
9. Marshall, "Divine and Human Punishment," 227.

2. Each Response Is Problematic

Though no controversy has generated more heat at times than salvation's extent,[10] theologians have not much advanced the understanding of salvation's extent after 2,000 years. The eventual resolution, which disfavored universalism, was from governance, not forensics, and the resolution that was a half millennium in coming has eroded. Now, what had been a decisive resolution has again become almost an open question. The issue drifted originally and does so again today because each disjunctive, whether universalism, exclusivism, or potentialism, is on its own questionable.

Perhaps the instability is the obvious consequence of each side mistreating the other's scriptural account. In debating salvation's extent, theologians have resorted to anointing one account rather than the other mostly by choosing the account that says a few are saved, often by choosing the account that says everyone is saved, and occasionally by giving up on the choosing,[11] but no one has intelligibly taken the position that both scriptural accounts are entirely true. The following is intended to show, not how everyone is wrong, but how, like reading Scripture itself, everyone is right until saying everyone else is wrong. That is, error happens when universalism rejects exclusivism, when exclusivism rejects universalism, and when potentialism, if different, rejects both.

a. Universalism

Universalism is often accused of being unbiblical because its basis seems less dependent on Scripture, which is clearly messy, and more dependent on a philosophy that is pat.[12] Though unfair, the accusation that universalism is unbiblical persists because an entirely happy ending is hardly the sense with which Scripture leaves the sincere reader.[13] Scripture bristles with eschatological calamity.[14] In imagery as in life, the end is both bitter and sweet (Rev 10:10). Universalists mostly acknowledge this, and, so, to accommodate their more civilized perspective where not a single person

---

10. Moltmann, *Coming of God*, 237; Oakes, "Christ's Descent into Hell," 382–83.
11. Parry and Partridge, eds., *Universal Salvation?* xix–xx.
12. Beougher, "Are All Doomed to Be Saved?" 98–100; Schwarz, *Eschatology*, 338.
13. Louth, "Response to Tom Greggs," 218; Schwarz, *Eschatology*, 346; Scott, *Journey Back to God*, 163.
14. Goddard, "Totality of Condemnation," 348–49; T. Hart, "In the End, God," 364.

is damned,[15] they argue that Scripture's unfiltered witness is too primitive for their exacting position.[16] They must purify Scripture of its harshness in the ultimate[17] and refashion its divine wrath into a divine therapy.[18] Universalists forget that, while the *threat* of divine wrath can produce repentance (Jonah 3:5–9), *actual* divine wrath tends not to (Rev 9:20–21, 16:9, 11). God definitely allows impenitence: "Let the unrighteous be unrighteous still, and the vile be vile still" (22:11). Yet, say the universalists, the God who risks rejection everywhere we look must ultimately relent and remake everything as he had wanted in the first place,[19] but Scripture defends God's consistency over time (Num 23:19; Ps 55:18–19; Mal 3:6; Jas 1:17), particularly in the end (Heb 1:12; 6:18; 13:8).[20] Thus, universalists, by proclaiming all is well despite God's afflicting judgment, echo not Scripture but the lying prophets (Isa 30:10; Jer 6:13–14; 8:11; 14:13–14; 23:14–17; Ezek 13:10–16). A God worthy of love but not fear, Buber recognized, is a creation of the self, not Scripture.[21]

The latest apology, Hart's *That All Shall Be Saved*, showcases universalism's scriptural avoidance. Scripture's exclusivism is depreciated as "three or four deeply ambiguous verses that seem . . . to threaten eternal torments for the wicked"—namely Matthew 25:46 ("These will go away into eternal castigation") and "a couple of verses from Revelation." "True, Jesus speaks of a final judgment, and uses many metaphors to describe the unhappy lot of the condemned," such as "the annihilation of chaff . . . in ovens, or the final death of body and soul." Yet, "Every good New Testament scholar" knows that these exclusivist images are not "literal" or even "instruct[ive]," but "dissolve into evocation, atmosphere, and poetry."[22] Even Scripture's universalism, which is apparently more prosaic, does not best Scripture's poetic exclusivism, Hart argues; rather, it is the rectitude

---

15. Driver, *Images of the Church*, 22.

16. Congdon, *God Who Saves*, 19 n.29; Gulley and Mulholland, *If Grace Is True*, 36, 49, 51; Moltmann, *Coming of God*, 241.

17. Ellul, *What I Believe*, 188; Rae, "Salvation in Community," 183; Robinson, *In the End, God . . .*, 95, 113–15.

18. MacDonald, "Between Heresy and Dogma," 19–20; Marshall, "NT Does Not Teach Universalism," 73.

19. J. Sanders, "Freewill Theist's Response," 175.

20. Aquinas, *ST, Part I*, I, Q. 9, art. 1, co; Barth, *CD II/1*, §§ 31.2-3 (pp. 490-678); Kierkegaard, *The Moment*, 286–87.

21. Buber, "Religion and Philosophy," 36–37.

22. D. Hart, *That All Shall Be Saved*, 86, 93–94, 111–12, 115–20.

of God's nature that simplifies the answer—God, who created everything, is entirely good, and, so, ultimately, everything created is entirely good too and is thus saved, no exceptions. That is, because God is all being and all good, all being is ultimately all good, though God is obviously and inexplicably accommodative of our being not all that good until then.[23] Hart acknowledges that God can allow what amount to semi-hells in this life and even afterwards if needed, but any such hell is temporary because ultimately everyone will be obliged to be the heavenly self that the good Father necessarily ordains.[24] As a result, the God who is said to be "able to save and to annihilate" (Jas 4:12) is apparently only able to do the first. Hart acknowledges that this argument has been around since at least Origen,[25] but he willingly adds what most would consider its obvious but necessary absurdity: If God is as the orthodox understand him, God is wicked.[26]

In favoring the clear-eyed philosophical position that God's nature necessitates universal salvation over the baffling record in Scripture that also expresses salvation's exclusivity,[27] universalism must treat Scripture's imperatives as indicatives, at least in the ultimate.[28] So, everything that Scripture commands only concerns salvation sooner rather than later. Whatever the unforgivable sin is, it cannot actually be anything (Matt 12:31–32//Mark 3:29//Luke 12:10).[29] Nor can apostates "end" in "burning" (Heb 6:4–8; also 10:26–31). Nor can "sin unto death" mean much (1 John 5:16). And the lesson taught by Christ in cursing the fruitless fig tree to destruction gets lost (Mark 11:12–14, 20–26//Matt 21:18–22). Indeed, when Jesus was asked "What must we do to gain eternal life?" He missed the opportunity to say simply, "*Exist*" (Matt 19:16–22//Mark 10:17–22//Luke 18:18–23; 10:25–28).

Accordingly, to universalists, salvation is never absent; it is always evident or latent. God's creation just amounts to God's salvation, but on a long, drawn-out fuse. When Scripture literally describes the saved and the not-saved, universalists see literally the saved and the not-yet-saved.

---

23. D. Hart, *That All Shall Be Saved*, 13, 27–28, 47–53, 58, 61–62, 65, 69–70, 78, 81–86, 90–91, 93, 95–109, 133–38, 166–67, 202–3, 208.

24. D. Hart, *That All Shall Be Saved*, 27, 44–45, 54, 62, 84–85, 103–4, 129, 168–70.

25. Ramelli, "Procus and Apokatastasis," 101.

26. D. Hart, *That All Shall Be Saved*, 4–5, 28, 43, 59–60, 62, 86–87, 90–91, 103–4, 129, 202.

27. Brant, *John*, 197.

28. Bultmann, *Theology of the NT*, II: 59.1 (pp. 203–4).

29. Beavis, *Mark*, 70–71; Caird and Hurst, *New Testament Theology*, 116.

Salvation itself therefore becomes the Omnipresent One.[30] As a result, little distinguishes Christian universalism from Unitarian universalism because, if salvation necessarily follows from God's nature or the like, such revelations as Christ's life, death, and resurrection become as inconsequential to salvation as the revelations of salvation's extent and perishing.[31] As Nietzsche observed, God shrinks as God's kingdom enlarges.[32]

Scripture's mandate for evangelism (John 5:24; Rom 10:14–15) must be treated as ultimately optional too because salvation occurs regardless.[33] The "conviction that salvation is in Christ alone," Ratzinger saw, "drove the great missionaries" so as to spare others damnation,[34] but, with universalism, the outcome is fixed.[35] Universalism not only discourages the missionaries, but its message disincentivizes the target audience: *Accept God or else eternal life comes anyway.* Pascal's wager[36] is, not only unconvincing,[37] but apparently rigged. Ludwig Wittgenstein complained, with universalism, "all seriousness of life is done away with,"[38] whether scripturally depicted or commonly observed,[39] and many concur with this assessment.[40]

Universalism must be similarly dismissive of human freewill,[41] a Christian fundamental.[42] Origen's exaggeration that Scripture has "ten thousand passages which with the utmost clearness prove the existence of free will"[43] is apt,[44] and it was this clear scriptural premise that drew

---

30. F. Sanders, "Response to Tom Greggs," 238.
31. Gregor, *Philosophical Anthropology*, 186–87.
32. Nietzsche, "Anti-Christ," 17 (p. 15).
33. Lubac, *Catholicism*, 220–21; Martin, *Will Many Be Saved?* 5, 13–14, 197.
34. Ratzinger, *Theological Highlights*, 172.
35. Caldecott, *Radiance of Being*, 248; Olson, *Mosaic of Christian Belief*, 276.
36. Pascal, *Pensees*, 233 (pp. 66–69).
37. Fraassen, *Empirical Stance*, 95–101, 245 & n.45.
38. Drury, "Conversations with Wittgenstein," 175.
39. Bavinck, *Last Things*, 152.
40. Balthasar, *Theo-Drama*, V: 269; Beougher, "Are All Doomed to Be Saved?" 96; Gavrilyuk, "Judgment of Love," 301; Ludlow, *Universal Salvation*, 157; McClymond, *Devil's Redemption*, II: 1031.
41. Lewis, *Problem of Pain*, 119; Scott, *Journey Back to God*, 163.
42. Bray, *God Has Spoken*, 510.
43. Origen, *On First Principles*, III,1,6 (p. 166).
44. Balthasar, *Theo-Drama*, II: 213–15, 273; Carson, *Divine Sovereignty*, 18–23, 206, 212.

Origen to exclusivism.⁴⁵ In Scripture, we *choose* (*bāḥărū*) to follow God or not (Josh 24:15). What matters if whether one *wills* (θέλῃ) to do God's *will* (θέλημα, John 7:17). Christ has called us to *freedom* (ἐλευθερίᾳ) that has *freed* (ἠλευθέρωσεν) us (Gal 5:1, 13). In imagery, Christ stands at the door beckoning us to him, not busting it down to reach us (Matt 7:7–8// Luke 11:9–10; Matt 11:28; Rev 3:20).⁴⁶ The anti-Pelagian Augustine noted that God gives "the power of free choice" between good or evil, God or flesh.⁴⁷ We are not God's automatons.⁴⁸ Even Luther, who "completely den[ied] free choice [*liberum arbitrium*]," held that God's words and works "are presented to the human will so that it may apply itself to them or turn away from them."⁴⁹ In short, God's commands are willable or wasted.⁵⁰ Indeed, every denial of freewill is squandered on us if we lack it.⁵¹

Notwithstanding the denials,⁵² we experience freewill.⁵³ It is the old saw: I chose to have freewill or I have been forced to. As Ingolf Dalferth recognized, "The paths of our lives evolve as a series of contingent decisions within a realm of contingent decisions in which only one thing is constant: not only can we choose; we must choose. And while in most cases we could have chosen differently, we could never not have chosen."⁵⁴ We are as conscious of freedom in our will as we are of its absence in our feelings.⁵⁵ Christians, like most humans, know that freewill is what deeply distinguishes persons.⁵⁶ Freewill undergirds ethics

---

45. Crouzel, *Origen*, 264–65.

46. Sutton, *Heaven Opens*, 132.

47. Augustine, *City of God*, XII,1, 3, 6–9, XIV,1, 4, 9, 13, 28, XIX,4, XX,6, XXII,1 (pp. 471, 474, 478–82, 547, 553, 566, 572, 593–94, 852, 904, 1022).

48. Pinnock, "Annihilationism," 472.

49. Luther, "De Servo Arbitrio," 172, 181, 291.

50. Augustine, "Grace and Free Will," 2.4 (p. 253); Cabasilas, *Life in Christ*, Bk VI § 1 (p. 160); Origen, *On First Principles*, III,1,19 (p. 200).

51. Badham, *Christian Beliefs*, 129; Balthasar, *Theo-Logic*, I: 80; Guardini, *Freedom, Grace, and Destiny*, 61; Krapiec, *I-Man*, 185.

52. Haggard, "Do We Have Conscious Free Will," 192–93; Murphy, *Bodies and Souls*, 105–9; Schindler, *Perfection of Freedom*, 74–75, 90, 374.

53. Arendt, "Willing," 140; Hartshorne, *Logic of Perfection*, 162; Schwarz, *Human Being*, 133.

54. Dalferth, *Creatures of Possibility*, 170–71.

55. Finney, *ST*, 15, 19.

56. Balthasar, *Theo-Drama*, II: 215; Harrison, *God's Many-Splendored Image*, 9–27; Irenaeus, *Against Heresies*, 4:37,2–5 (pp. 146–47).

and laws,[57] and without it our life would be just mechanisms or random generators,[58] "Without which we are pictures or mere beasts," says the Bard.[59] While never absolute and always frangible,[60] our freewill at least involves the question of what kind of person we want to be or for whom we want to be so.[61] If we lack free-will, we have free-won't.[62] We are, Balthasar remarked, not "congealed," but we "choose one's own highest value."[63] Buber realized, it "is the basic view that man, while created by God, was established by Him in an independence which has since remained undiminished."[64]

And some of us freely reject God.[65] Atheists admit they would ultimately reject God, if he existed, because eternally living with the Person responsible for misery is "a perfect definition of hell," and any afterlife glorification does not change the conclusion but would "only intensify the nightmare."[66] Nietzsche explained, "we certainly do not want to enter into the kingdom of heaven: we have become men, *so we want the kingdom of earth*."[67] "Heaven for sparrows and Christians, earth for us," the Nazis purportedly declared.[68] Even Christians, if they are universalists, can find God literally insufferable if he is as tradition says, exclusivist.[69] And the human rejections of God will endure after this life because those not won over by his grace in this life are not plausibly won over by its absence in perdition or, if then accessible, just more of the same.[70]

Universalists such as Hart reason that refusing God is ultimately not an actual option because true freewill consists of pure good, and, though

---

57. Arendt, "Willing," 4–5.
58. Schiller, "On the Sublime," 147.
59. Shakespeare, "Hamlet," 4.5.68.
60. Kierkegaard, *JP*, III: ¶ 3281.
61. Demarest, *Cross and Salvation*, 271; Gregory of Nyssa, *Life of Moses*, Bk II (p. 51); Rahner, *Foundations*, 38.
62. McGilchrist, *Master and His Emissary*, 198.
63. Balthasar, *Dare We Hope*, 145.
64. Buber, "Religion and Ethics," 105.
65. Geisler, *ST*, 818.
66. Meillassoux, "Immanence of the World Beyond," 454–55. Accord McCombs, *Paradoxical Rationality*, 177.
67. Nietzsche, *Thus Spoke Zarathustra*, Pt IV, "The ass festival",2 (p. 325).
68. Käsemann, *Jesus Means Freedom*, 134.
69. D. Hart, *That All Shall Be Saved*, 208–9.
70. Geisler, *ST*, 1276.

we can in this life "gravitate . . . toward nothingness," God cannot allow anyone actually to stay this way.[71] To reach this understanding, universalists have to reinterpret a free-will as a good-will,[72] though a free-will is what allows an ill-will.[73] When the early Christians sang, *If (εἰ) we are to deny Christ, he will deny us* (2 Tim 2:12), they prevaricated because he won't. In arguing that God is too noble to allow people to actually perish because of their disobedience, God is to the universalist as the serpent insinuated (Gen 3:1–4).[74] Our choices are therefore ultimately unthreatening, which of course begs the question of why God allows wrong choices if perfection is by divine fiat anyway. If universalism is true, our life is burdened with the realization that its miseries are futilities, and our faith is burdened with a God who created a world whose miseries are irrelevant to the outcome.

Yet, Bonhoeffer noted, "Force and love are opposites."[75] Because love is given freely or not at all, it is commonly understood that people reject God by willing this.[76] Therefore, to the extent that God's unforced love has not worked in this life, some form of force is needed. For universalists, accordingly, anyone who has not consented to God's rejectable overtures in this life suffer in the afterlife the offer that cannot be refused, a sort of salvation by divine rape.[77] Everyone is to be seduced like a Lolita: "What I had madly possessed was not she, but my own creation," "more real than Lolita; . . . having no will, . . . indeed, no life of her own."[78] Resistance is futile, and everyone is assimilated, even Satan.[79] This irrecusable salvation is brought about by God's ontological superiority coercing the freewill,[80] but coercion is what displaces freewill.[81] So, under universal-

71. D. Hart, *That All Shall Be Saved*, 33–43, 57–58, 79–80, 171–95.

72. Gavrilyuk, "Judgment of Love," 300 & n.99; Ludlow, *Universal Salvation*, 95–97, 101–2, 142; Talbott, "Universalism," 455.

73. Cabasilas, *Life in Christ*, Bk II § 11 (p. 85); Gilson, *Spirit of Mediaeval Philosophy*, 317–18; Hamann, "Philological Ideas," 115.

74. Gregor, *Philosophical Anthropology*, 66.

75. Bonhoeffer, *Ethics*, 240 [239].

76. Come, *Kierkegaard as Theologian*, 140, 245.

77. Davies, *Thomas on God and Evil*, 109–10.

78. Nabokov, *Lolita*, 65.

79. Levering, "Response to Professor Greggs," 225.

80. Congdon, *God Who Saves*, 16–17.

81. Arendt, "Willing," 26; Lewis, *Mere Christianity*, 37; Walls, "Philosophical Critique," 111–17.

ism, God is a Rousseauist forcing us to be free,[82] the afterlife is a reeducation camp where subversives learn to think rightly,[83] and salvation is a Clausewitzian war "to compel the other to submit,"[84] though, luckily, we are undone by Huxleyan conditioning, not kinetic brutality.[85] Regardless, morally responsible agents making meaningful choices become ultimately meaningless,[86] as universalists will admit.[87]

b. Exclusivism

Exclusivism's central vulnerability is the same as universalism's—a shifting scriptural exegesis. Scripture is straightforward when the faithful are saved, but the reading must go between the lines when Scripture says that everyone is saved. The exclusivist favorite is to reinterpret *all* as *some* whenever Scripture speaks the word in the context of salvation, which naturally divests every universalist declaration of any real contribution.[88] An exclusivist like evangelist Bruce Demarest can recognize that various places in Scripture "at first blush, appear to contravene" exclusivism by "suggesting... the salvation of all creatures," but this scriptural impression just has to be misleading.[89] Balthasar summarized the exclusivist situation: When Christ says he saves all humanity, he is told, "Unfortunately, only half of it, despite your efforts, Lord," and, when Scripture persists in claiming universal salvation, "All just pious exaggeration."[90]

Exclusivists not only diminish what Scripture says when it expresses too much universalism, but they diminish either God's love or his power.[91] Either the rebellious will of a mere human overcomes the

---

82. Rousseau, "Social Contract," I,vii (p. 58).

83. Hartshorne, *Logic of Perfection*, 19; Schaff, *Marxism and the Human*, 8, 36–37, 208, 213; Sutton, *Heaven Opens*, 132.

84. Clausewitz, *On War*, I,I,1.

85. Huxley, *Brave New World*, 50.

86. Ludlow, *Universal Salvation*, 102, 110–11.

87. Ansell, "Annihilation of Hell," 424; Origen, *On First Principles*, III,5,8 (p. 244); Robinson, *In the End, God...*, 104–5.

88. Allen, *Extent of Atonement*, 718; Balthasar, "Short Discourse on Hell," 166; Horton, "Traditional Reformed View," 131–32.

89. Demarest, *Cross and Salvation*, 142–43.

90. Balthasar, "Short Discourse on Hell," 184, 186.

91. Walls, *Hell*, 3. Most philosophical objections to exclusivism pertain to its eternal torment variety. Marshall, "Divine and Human Punishment," 218–19. Because

Almighty's expressed will for salvation, which means that the Almighty is not almighty in the way we think, or that God actually wills who is to be damned independent of anything else about the human, which is an arbitrary God.[92] Exclusivists likewise have trouble with those barely damned having the same fate as those thoroughly so. The same outcome for the entire human spectrum of the godless is, if not inequitable, bizarre.[93] The frequent recourse of easing eschatological sufferings on a sliding scale is "a groping" failure, Balthasar perceived, "an idea that links up with Scholastic speculations."[94] So, without this resort, exclusivists have used two tactics to squeeze humanity into the two ultimates. The easiest is simply to affect willful blindness by ignoring the reality that humanity blankets the godliness spectrum or by assuming counterfactually that humans spontaneously fall into just the two primary types so as to correspond to the two ultimates.[95]

The second exclusivist tactic for dealing with non-binary humanity is to postulate that an extrabiblical threshold acts to segregate humanity into the two required eschatological groups.[96] In Judaism, the threshold for determining the group bound for eternal life depended on the rabbi espousing it, ranging from 100 percent godly (Shammai), 51 percent godly (Hillel), or anything in excess of 0 percent godly (Aqiba).[97] Christian exclusivists would be apostates if they specified an eternal-life threshold too strict to save anyone and would be universalists if they specified a threshold too lenient to reject anyone. A middling threshold is, therefore, always fashioned, but, because nearly everyone lives between the two extremes as will be examined in the next chapter,[98] any eternal-life threshold must be autocratic, if not quirky, to be effective in distinguishing anyone beyond the odd paragon.[99]

---

exclusivism also includes annihilation as the negative ultimate, the torment objections are omitted, though answers are available. Holten, "Hell and the Goodness of God," 37–55.

92. Ludlow, *Universal Salvation*, 169.

93. Crosby, *Selfhood of the Human*, 183–84; Nichols, *Death and Afterlife*, 188–89; Scott, *Journey Back to God*, 9.

94. Balthasar, "Short Discourse on Hell," 218.

95. Ludlow, *Universal Salvation*, 14; Tillich, *ST*, III: 408.

96. Kvanvig, "Hell," 422; Marshall, "Divine and Human Punishment," 222.

97. Bruce, *Galatians*, 159, 230.

98. James, *Varieties of Religious Experience*, 234.

99. Bates, *Salvation by Allegiance Alone*, 124.

So, to fashion a realistic threshold, exclusivists posit an aggregating faith that says the individual is basically of the right sort such that God can discern, usually at death, who is and who is not, more or less, hell-bound.[100] This opportunistic solution is usually based on the idea that the chosen "cannot be joined to Him in some ways, and yet be separated from Him in others," as Cabasilas claimed.[101] The scriptural warrant for saying that everyone is either entirely godly or entirely ungodly is that Christ's death completes his redemptive work,[102] but this confuses Christ's decisiveness with our indefiniteness. The next chapter presents the fuller response, but, to anticipate, humans prove daily that each of us serves incompletely two masters.[103] Any "barcode"[104] for identifying the saved from the rest of us tends to reflect, not Scripture, but the human concocting it.[105] Plus, any proposed threshold for ultimate salvation inevitably cheapens this life. If salvation is based on election, faith professions, or baptism/penance, the remainder of this life hardly seems worth the trouble.[106] If the moment of death or any other select moment is decisive, the rest is ultimately vacuous.[107] And if, as some exclusivists argue, God just arbitrarily spares the saved,[108] the entirety of this life is that way.

c. Potentialism

Potentialism, when it is intelligible, does not seem to be separate from exclusivism, though potentialism is mostly treated here as a separate position because its advocates claim that it is one. If potentialism is not a subset of exclusivism and therefore not subject to the same problems as

---

100. Balthasar, "Short Discourse on Hell," 172–73; Hebblethwaite, *Christian Hope*, 212; Nichols, *Death and Afterlife*, 187.

101. Cabasilas, *Life in Christ*, Bk VI § 1, Bk VII § 1 (pp. 161, 197).

102. Balthasar, *Mysterium Paschale*, 13.

103. Bulgakov, *Orthodox Church*, 96. This alludes to the principle that no one can *simultaneously* serve two conflicting masters (Matt 6:24//Luke 16:13). Bock, *Luke 9:51—24:53*, 1336–67.

104. Willard, *Divine Conspiracy*, 36–37.

105. Balthasar, "Short Discourse on Hell," 191.

106. Robinson, *In the End, God . . .* , 110.

107. Kierkegaard, *Eighteen Upbuilding Discourses*, 258.

108. Calvin, *Institutes*, II,3, III,13 (pp. 176–89, 498–501); Wallenfang, *Human and Divine Being*, 197.

exclusivism, potentialism's basis is unclear.[109] By disavowing both universalism and exclusivism, potentialists are, Hart observed, "tentatively and timidly groping" for "some anxious, uncertain, fragile hope" based on "something like a dialectical oscillation between two kinds of absolute statements, both indissoluble in themselves and each seemingly irreconcilable with the other." Potentialism is thereby trying to signal the same "tenderheartedness" as universalism without committing to its simplicity, which amounts to an "intellectual timidity" that displays "a little too much post-Hegelian dialectical disenchantment" and "a touch of disingenuous obscurantism."[110]

As a matter of logic, however, potentialism can be and has been justified in three ways, each of which is "typed" for later discussion:

Type I: *Change both scriptural propositions*. The primary potentialist position is that Scripture's conflicting accounts on salvation's extent are each potentially true, and, thus, potentialists implicitly add "potentially" wherever Scripture addresses salvation's extent. Even if such scriptural editing were permissible, saying it is potentially true that everyone is saved and potentially true that not everyone is saved does not, as intended, suspend the truth within the antinomy's middle.[111] It just suspends the truth generally. While such word alchemy eliminates the conflict, it does so only by neutering both scriptural accounts, which is a Faustian strategy rarely tolerated.[112] Potentialism so understood, though purporting to respect each account, fails doubly by defying the accord that sees at least one account in Scripture unadulterated.[113] Potentialism of this variety is the typical philosopher recourse for inadequate schemes, which is to hope that fusing them together works.[114] The salvation paradox, however, does not call for negating both accounts partially, but, like all paradoxes, calls for affirming both entirely.[115]

Type II: *Suspend the principle of noncontradiction*. A few potentialists take the scriptural accounts as they appear to be—that is, actually contradictory—but also take the conflicting accounts as still somehow

---

109. Phan, "Roman Catholic Theology," 224.

110. D. Hart, *That All Shall Be Saved*, 66, 102–3.

111. Kierkegaard, *Eighteen Upbuilding Discourses*, 216–17.

112. Martin, *Will Many Be Saved?* 134; Robinson, *In the End, God . . .* , 96. See Goethe, *Faust*, lns 1250–64.

113. Robinson, *In the End, God . . .* , 112–13.

114. Whitehead, *Process and Reality*, viii.

115. Robinson, *In the End, God . . .* , 113.

true. Rahner, as noted, is of this type. Brunner concurs: Each scriptural account "logically excludes the other," "juxtaposed in their harsh incompatibility," but "both" are "ultimately valid."[116] This way of facing a paradox, chapter 3 explained, is elegant wordsmithing but poor sense.[117] These potentialists can claim to be like Lewis Carroll's Red Queen and believe in six impossible things before breakfast, but taking an actual contradiction as true is not even impossible, it is just meaningless.[118] Attenuating a paradox to a contradiction and then accepting its truth can admittedly seem pious by appearing to leave our knowledge of salvation's extent on God's altar, but the equivocation sacrifices nothing but our understanding of the faith.[119] Such aphasia can of course be justified when trying to understand what is out of our reach, such as God's immanence, but taking contradicting accounts as true when trying to understand the salvation we affirm is inexcusable, at least for theologians.[120]

Type III: *Not explain the position.* Potentialists, when they do not license themselves to amend Scripture or to rescind the principle of non-contradiction, avoid settling on a rationale for the uncertainty in salvation's extent.[121] The failure to take a position on salvation's extent is not their problem because potentialism *is* a position, but the problem is that potentialists who give no explanation for their position are infringing the Principle of Sufficient Reason—every true statement has a sufficient explanation for its truth.[122] Confessing ignorance is allowable of course, but "a learned demonstration of it," Hamann noticed, reveals "a powerful resistance to the truth."[123] Kierkegaard added, "anyone who wants to end with the inexplicable" "would really do best to begin with it and say nothing else . . . ."[124] If we are to speak of what we know (John 3:11), which includes salvation, not knowing is out,[125] and, since we know, not

---

116. Brunner, *Eternal Hope*, 183.

117. D. Hart, *That All Shall Be Saved*, 103.

118. Dunning, *Grace, Faith, and Holiness*, 42–43; Trueman, "Definite Atonement View," 73.

119. Pannenberg, "Task of Christian Eschatology," 3.

120. Levering, "Response to Andrew Louth," 45.

121. Gockel, *Barth and Schleiermacher*, 208.

122. D. Hart, *Experience of God*, 146.

123. Hamann, "Socratic Memorabilia," NII,73,15–20 (p. 391).

124. Kierkegaard, *Stages*, 35.

125. Polkinghorne, *God of Hope*, 138.

answering is a failure of nerve.[126] Such incomprehension is positively untheological.[127] Mysteries are fine, but unenlightening ones belong to the Beast (Rev 17:5–7).[128] So, Christians definitely believe in definite beliefs,[129] even when they are paradoxical.[130] To their credit, these potentialists leave the salvation paradox in a holding pattern, but, contrary to their intent, holding patterns cannot last because assertions of truth have more gravity than confessions of ignorance[131] and the contradiction eventually lands in confusion.[132]

3. The Responses Undervalue Paradox

Scriptural paradoxes thus deserve better than the write-offs offered by universalism, exclusivism, or potentialism,[133] but distinguishing what that something better could be requires distinguishing a paradox from its kin. Paradoxes are not actual *contradictions*, but are *apparent* ones.[134] An actual contradiction, as chapter 3 explained, has at least two propositions such that both cannot be true.[135] A contradiction's *raison d'être* is identifying the falsehood among the propositions. Contradictions are not mere incongruities, but even those who think so put *actual* contradictions "near the top of any list of nonsense."[136] To deflect this weaker meaning, "actual," i.e., formal or logical, can sometimes here preface "contradiction." A paradox is also no *dialectic*, which synthesizes two contraries to advance on a truth.[137] A dialectic's *raison d'être* is the synthesis that results, a sort of pendulum towards a new insight between the original contraries. A

126. Dunning, *Grace, Faith, and Holiness*, 37; D. Hart, *That All Shall Be Saved*, 102–3.
127. Tillich, *ST*, III: 396, 404.
128. Rahner, "Mystery," 1000–1004.
129. Congdon, *God Who Saves*, 2; Finney, *ST*, 47.
130. Kierkegaard, *Christian Discourses*, 244.
131. Erickson, *Christian Theology*, 148; Lonergan, *Insight*, 4.
132. Feuerbach, *Essence of Christianity*, I.II (p. 39); Hamann, "Golgotha and Sheblimini!," 180.
133. Whitehead, *Process and Reality*, 403.
134. Walsh, *Living Christianly*, 66.
135. *OED*, s.v. "contradiction."
136. Westphal, *Becoming a Self*, 165–66, 182.
137. Connell, "Georg Wilhelm Friedrich Hegel," 35; Fuyarchuk, *Gadamer's Path to Plato*, 126.

paradox, in contrast to both of these concepts, consists of truths that are in apparent (not actual) contradiction.[138] A paradox's *raison d'être* is to conceptualize the truthful relationship of all its conflicting components.

Paradoxes, which animate Christianity,[139] deserve one response—understand their truth.[140] This is not to compromise the paradox's opposites, but to work them.[141] Regrettably, modern reasoning is "most of all unable to stomach" paradoxes, Milbank observed.[142] Under this mindset, paradoxes are taken as contradictions that must be tidied up by identifying which proposition is actually false.[143] Postmodern thinking has the contrary bias, but, all the same, treats paradoxes as contradictions too because, so understood, contradictions née paradoxes justify despair.[144] Irony is no longer dramatic contradiction, but is how we are to face the cosmos.[145] Neither response preserves the paradox, as W. H. Auden realized: "The either-ors" "see only one side of the paradox," and "the mongrel halves" are "too woolly-minded to recognize a paradox when he meets one . . . ."[146] Contemporary philosophy is often no antidote because, in imposing definiteness, it can impose rigidity in thinking, and paradoxes require elasticity.[147] And this elasticity can make the thinking uncomfortable until the understanding is reached, and then it gets worse. Nietzsche explained, we no longer esteem the "prurient taste for whatever is . . . painfully paradoxical."[148]

So, throughout human thought, paradoxes have incited these three responses. The response prevailing since *modernity* has been to disarm any paradox so that it becomes a more manageable contradiction, which

---

138. OED, s.v. "paradox." Avoided here are the other definitions of paradox, each of which render the word merely a fine synonym for some other perfectly adequate word. Thus, paradox is not used here as a euphemism for "absurdity," a gloss for "mystery," or grandiloquence for "surprise." The last is what παράδοξος means in the NT. Doble, *Paradox of Salvation*, 31, 33, 238–40.

139. Kierkegaard, *Concluding Unscientific Postscript*, I: 105; Lubac, *Catholicism*, 327.

140. Scott, *Journey Back to God*, 5.

141. McCombs, *Paradoxical Rationality*, 64.

142. Milbank, *Beyond Secular Order*, 5.

143. James, *Varieties of Religious Experience*, 423.

144. McGowan, *Postmodernism and Its Critics*, 49–50.

145. Glicksberg, *Ironic Vision*, 11.

146. Auden, *Double Man*, 115 (note to ln 821).

147. Husserl, "Author's Preface," 20.

148. Nietzsche, "Genealogy of Morals," 1st,I (p. 158).

means treating the paradox as illusory and then privileging one proposition.[149] That is, the contradiction is actualized, and the exercise becomes determining which of its propositions is actually true and which only facially so. The response that *postmodernism* has preferred also reduces any paradox to a contradiction, but, because postmodernism is starved for affirmation of negation, it then cherishes the contradiction's impenetrability. That is, the paradox is suspended as nonsense, violating what is officially the principle of noncontradiction but is really just part of the thought process.[150] The third response, which has thrived since before modernity, preserves the paradox. This *classical* response accepts that the truths in the paradox seemingly contradict, but only seemingly. This is unlike, but can be confused with, the first response where the paradox is illusory. A contradiction has a proposition that is not actually true, while a paradox (an apparent contradiction) has true propositions that are not actually contradicting. In sum, the modern response takes at least one proposition as not actually true, which changes the paradox into a contradiction; the postmodern response leaves the paradox as an inexplicable contradiction, which changes nothing; and the classical response retains the paradox's dynamic truths, which changes the listener's understanding.[151]

A simple paradox can illustrate the difference: I have won every chess game *and* have lost fifty of them. Without more information, both cannot be true. So, the modern converts the least favored proposition into what it must "really" mean: I actually lost fifty games as one proposition states, but, since losses instruct, they must be counted as "wins"; or, because I actually won every game as one proposition states, I must have played poorly in fifty of them, which means they can count as "losses." The postmodern, in contrast, needs to do nothing (no irony there) because the contradiction wonderfully exposes how winning and losing are mere constructs in this woe-is-me world. The classical response, however, which takes both propositions as true, will discover a way for this to be the case so that the apparent contradiction is not reduced to an actual one. Perhaps the answer is that I played myself in fifty games, thereby both winning and losing each of them. Such riddle paradoxes are, of

---

149. Kierkegaard, *Concluding Unscientific Postscript*, I: 218–19.
150. Dilthey, *Introduction to Human Sciences*, 312 (II.4.4); Geisler, *ST*, 69.
151. Milbank, "Double Glory," 116.

course, unlike genuine paradoxes,[152] but they do exercise the skill that genuine paradoxes require—thinking more than one thought at once.[153]

Christianity's definitive paradoxes expose the three varieties in responding to paradoxes in the real world.[154] Faced with the apparent contradiction that both God is one and God is three, heresies demoted a truth, but the church refused to compromise part of Scripture and, so, offered the Trinity.[155] The key, de Lubac described, was "to set oneself free from those habits of thought that contemplation of material things develops."[156] Scripture similarly yielded the apparent contradiction that the Son, while not *two* Persons, is both a divine *one plus* a human *one*.[157] Heresies, justified by a scriptural proposition, jettisoned a different scriptural proposition, but the church offered the hypostatic union to preserve the scriptural paradox,[158] facing two complete entities as a unity nevertheless.[159] A human's divinity and the God's humanity, Bonhoeffer concluded, had "to be held together at the risk of destroying the rationality of the exposition."[160]

For these classic theological debates, it is the universalist and exclusivist arguments that echo in the heresies: Because God is one, he is not literally three; because God is three, his oneness must be poetic; when Christ is described as human, he only seems to be; when Christ is described as God, it means only he is nearly God. This, after all, "is the best way to turn a doctrine into a heresy," Henri Crouzel noted, "the heresy in effect suppresses the tension of the antitheses that express Christian doctrine, it rejects one aspect and makes the other absolute."[161] That is, in these first critical disputations, heretics employed the first response to the scriptural paradoxes

---

152. Tillich, *ST*, I: 109.

153. Wallenfang, *Human and Divine Being*, 28.

154. The paragraph grossly summarizes Ayres, *Nicaea and Its Legacy*; Chadwick, *Church in Ancient Society*; Davies, *Early Christian Church*; Kelly, *Early Christian Doctrines*, 83–162, 223–343.

155. Grenz, *Theology for the Community*, 60; Lossky, *Mystical Theology*, 46, 50–66.

156. Lubac, *Catholicism*, 329.

157 Gabelman, *Theology of Nonsense*, 58–64, 165.

158. Behr, *Mystery of Christ*, 38; Cooper, *Naturally Human, Supernaturally God*, 41, 44, 48; Riches, *Ecce Homo*, 38–41.

159. Kelly, *Early Christian Doctrines*, 296.

160. Bonhoeffer, *Christ the Center*, 88.

161. Crouzel, *Origen*, 176.

and reformulated one proposition to dissolve the contradiction.[162] Not even heretics dared try the second response; at least none reportedly argued that God is *potentially* one or that Christ is *potentially* divine. In each case, orthodoxy took the third response—embrace both halves of the scriptural paradox by modeling the contradiction as apparent.[163]

Application of the three paradox responses to the salvation paradox should now be plain. Exclusivism and universalism have taken the first response and favored one scriptural account, and they differ only on which account to prefer. Potentialism, if a distinctive position, has tried the second response and purported to accept both scriptural accounts as contradictory and true. The third paradox response, though as a rule the orthodox approach, has yet to be tried on the paradox of salvation's extent, but this has been excusable because the salvation paradox affirms and negates the same idea; the salvation of *everyone* and the salvation of *not everyone* are too clearly opposites of each other to not be a contradiction.

Given this predicament, the church, having grasped the paradoxes of who the Son was and what he had done, had not settled on the paradox of his efficacy by the mid-fifth century.[164] At around that time, the church's environment was tipping from pagan to Christian, and, so, universalism was no longer needed to save those outside the church and in fact disincentivized the few holdouts. Accordingly, exclusivism ascended in the church with little inspiration added to the resolution. J. N. D. Kelly assessed the post-Chalcedon era: "so far as the central stream of Christendom was concerned, the brilliant upsurge of fresh ideas which had distinguished the earlier centuries had spent itself."[165] Also, the church, fatigued from its centuries of infighting, feared traversing additional and ever more nebulous doctrinal frontlines that might erode the church's hegemony,[166] and this left the disputants echoing the same centuries-old arguments in the same centuries-old standoff in which to make an overdue decision.[167] With only universalism and exclusivism to choose from and obliged to choose one of them, the church chose exclusivism, but the

---

162. Gabelman, *Theology of Nonsense*, 88.
163. A. Williams, *Architecture of Theology*, 24–25, 27.
164. Bray, *God Has Spoken*, 399.
165. Kelly, *Early Christian Doctrines*, 3.
166. Chadwick, *Church in Ancient Society*, 437.
167. Hick, *Death and Eternal Life*, 242.

debate is, if it not incessant, continuing. Perhaps today ancient insights can be revitalized for lost answers.[168]

⁂

Preserving a scriptural paradox is orthodox, at least if the church's first doctrinal decisions are indicative. Though Scripture says salvation's extent is paradoxically both universal and exclusive, the church in this case says different. Its response has thus far been to adopt the usual conceit of heresies: Treat the paradox as a contradiction and, so as to avoid the resulting disaster of partial falsehood, compromise part of Scripture. Thus, regardless of the side taken, each existing position says Scripture is on its face in contradiction and must, as a result, treat the other side's scriptural account as superficially true or as figures of speech or prefer one account over the other based on some overarching judgment. Not yet taken is retaining the import and truthfulness of both scriptural accounts.

We are almost to that point. To explain the model that preserves the salvation paradox, the *individual* and its divisibility must be understood, which is the subject of the next chapter.

---

168. Oliver, "Radical Orthodoxy," 428–29.

6

Divisibility's Coherence

As twos swim the dead,
as twos, in wine flowing.
Into wine, that's over you pouring,
swim as twos the dead.

—CELAN, "ZU ZWEIEN"[1]

CHRISTIANITY HAS A PROBLEM. In spite of the consensus on much of what salvation entails (chapter 2), Christians have lacked a consensus on the seminal issue of its extent (chapters 3–4). This is partly because each propounded position on salvation's extent has philosophical troubles, but is mostly because each side must refashion what Scripture says so as to settle on the preferred half of the paradox (chapter 5). Certainly no position that has been adopted has accepted the scriptural presentation of salvation's extent as a true paradox. Rather, each side, justified by one scriptural account and its confliction with the other, has depleted the disfavored account using extraordinary exegesis or thematic absorption; and philosophical reasoning, which is naturally drawn to purity, has

---

1. This is my rendering of *"Zu zweien schwimmen die Toten, / zu zweien, umflossen von Wein. / In Weim, den sie über dich gossen, / schwimmen die Toten zu zwein."*

favored one well-defined all-inclusive account, not the two clashing ones that Scripture seemingly favors. This discourse seeks as an alternative an opening into the clash on salvation's extent without discounting either scriptural account, and, to do this, the proposal requires a model of the individual that deviates from the one we use reflexively (chapter 1). This chapter presents that model.

The next chapter will advance the thesis for salvation's extent, but this chapter presents the critical element of that thesis—the divisibility of the individual. Such divisibility galls Westerners because they tend to bind identity and person.[2] This tendency is unlikely to be just Western because the human body encourages this view. The functional body's immune response, for instance, differentiates the particular self from other selves at the biochemical level.[3] To deal with this bias in favor of the individual's *in*divisibility, this chapter must be lengthy, and this is despite the fact that the body, as we generally intuit, is inadequate to establish personal unity. The typical individual has already had several bodies—the body of an embryo, a fetus, a newborn, an infant, a toddler, a child, an adolescent, an adult, and, for some of us, a dotage.[4] And medical science frequently demonstrates the individual's corporeal divisibility by amputating, transplanting, or transfusing.[5] In the case of conjoined twins, medical science has actually bifurcated the body.[6] Furthermore, each earthly body without exception thoroughly divides eventually in "time's gullet," Tertullian's expression.[7] In death, "one after another, as it were the sepulchral inscriptions of all peoples and times," Walter Pater observed, we are "dissolved again into their dust."[8] With death, therefore, the earthly body becomes even less of a unifier. The body manifestly discontinues then because the body's discontinuance is what we mean by death, but death is not the end of our experiences, at least as Christianity understands what happens then.

As is to be discussed below, the individual's first-person awareness in this life is continuable after biological death, but mere awareness is not

---

2. Jenson, *ST*, I: 120.
3. Gallup, Anderson, and Platek, "Self-Recognition," 81.
4. Merricks, "Resurrection of the Dead," 267.
5. Hacking, "Our Neo-Cartesian Bodies in Parts," 78–105.
6. Spitz, "Conjoined Twins," 1028–30.
7. Tertullian, "Resurrection of the Flesh," ch IV (p. 548, trans. modified).
8. Pater, *Marius the Epicurean*, 149.

the individual at issue because awareness alone is just a personal void with a center. Anyone without memories, beliefs, preferences, attitudes is no one. Instead, if the self is to continue, whether in this life or the next, what continues must include a core suite of personality features, which is typically called the character, and this is the terminology adopted here. The personal character is inexorably lived as divided in this life. This division can be stark in the pathological (*e.g.*, multiple personalities), but even the healthy debate themselves, struggle with themselves, and dislike themselves for liking themselves too much. So, a truly divided individual, though never encountered in this life, is conceivable in the next because we are nearly divisible now. At least that is what this chapter strives to show. To make the showing, this chapter's citations come furiously so as to cross-check with the interdisciplinary sages on whether a divisible individual is only as weird as it sounds.

1. The Individual Takes Personal Identity and Character

Individual, from all viewpoints that has recognized the concept, is profound, multilateral, and transformable.[9] Though it is a specific reference, the individual has always been a chameleon worked out contextually.[10] "In the dark night of thought dwells a glimmering of Being," says a phenomenologist,[11] and this Being we barely detect in ourselves.[12] Oscar Wilde knew, "to recognize that the soul of a man is unknowable is the ultimate achievement of Wisdom. The final mystery is oneself."[13] While the individual as the *I* is incomprehensible, it is as the *you* that it is even more so.[14] "[I]n broad daylight my neighbor is dark and impenetrable, separated from me by his apparent resemblances," noted Jean-Paul Sartre.[15] This is "not because the alter ego is an alter," Michel Henry clarified, but "because the other is an ego."[16] And such is

---

9. Harrison, *God's Many-Splendored Image*, 194; Kallistos (Ware), "Unity of the Human," 67–76.

10. Lee, "Standing Accused," 11; McConville, *Being Human*, 61, 79; Ziegler, *Militant Grace*, 188.

11. Merleau-Ponty, *Signs*, 15.

12. Highet, *Man's Unconquerable Mind*, 35.

13. Wilde, *De Profundis*, 87.

14. Grenz, *Theology for the Community*, 84; Proust, *In Search of Lost Time*, III: 57.

15. Sartre, *Between Existentialism and Marxism*, 155.

16. Henry, *Material Phenomenology*, 112–13.

the inscrutability of *individual* in this life, but the concept rarefies only further afterwards.[17] Fortunately, the individual in whatever context, while incomprehensible practically, is lived practically.[18]

Every individual we have come to know plainly correlates to a natural body,[19] but, as we also know, we must each be more than an "ingenious machine for turning, with infinite artfulness, the red wine of Shiraz into urine," Karen Blixen recognized.[20] "Is not the soul more than meat?" Wilde asks.[21] "I," Walt Whitman answers, "am not contain'd between my hat and boots . . . ."[22] Certainly, if we are to experience anything after death, which most cultures, especially Christian ones, have concluded is at least a possibility, we must be more than our bodies, which have so far clearly remained lifeless after actual biological death, with hardly an exception, and the bodies themselves attest to their afterlife inadequacy as they disintegrate around us at the speeds appropriate to the environments in which we have left them.[23] "We have this treasure in clay vessels" (2 Cor 4:7).

Since it is not the body that best specifies this self that we all encounter in life through the body and which we all see depart in death from the body, the self that Sartre called "the adventure that I am"[24] is who Wollheim, glossing Kierkegaard, identified as *the life that is led*.[25] This describes what each of us senses about ourselves without intruding upon the incessant debate about anthropological substances.[26] As Barth realized, an individual "does not exist abstractly but concretely, *i.e.*, in experiences, in determinations of his existence by objects, by things outside him and distinct from him."[27]

---

17. Berkouwer, *Man: Image of God*, 264.
18. Balthasar, *Theo-Logic*, I: 249.
19. Moore, *Where Are the Dead?* 7, 21, 34, 49.
20. Dinesen, "Dreamers," 344.
21. Wilde, *De Profundis*, 83 (rendering Matt 6:25c).
22. Whitman, "Song of Myself," 7 (p. 41).
23. Bynum, *Resurrection of the Body*, 8; Fitzpatrick, *Aquinas on Bodily Identity*, 62, 145.
24. Sartre, *Between Existentialism and Marxism*, 166.
25. Wollheim, *Thread of Life*, 1–2.
26. Caputo, *Radical Hermeneutics*, 29.
27. Barth, *CD I/1*, § 6.3 (p. 198).

The led life might be ontological,[28] but is certainly revelatory.[29] "So Life," as Henry saw, is "the principle of every thing" and "always founds what we call 'being' rather than the contrary."[30] The led life is, of course, not merely being alive, like the lives of plankton, but it is what distinguishes who each of the current participants in this dialogue are from other organisms.[31] From leading this life, we understand what that led life is,[32] and the led life is what forms the individual's beliefs, values, attitudes, preferences, emotions, thoughts.[33] Here, "personal character" is the term labeling these features, particularly the enduring ones,[34] and "personal identity" is what labels the experiencing of them.[35] That is, the personal character is the self itself, the actual individual, while the personal identity is the self's self, the individual's center.[36] In short, personal character is the life led, and personal identity is its awareness.[37]

2. Most Any Metaphysic Works

"We can no more think than we can will, without being conscious of our self," as Hamann understood.[38] Kierkegaard concurred, "The inner being announces itself and craves an explanation."[39] Theology, science, philosophy, almost every discipline, has quested for the self, knowing beforehand that it is there somehow.[40] *Who am I?* or, simplified, *what*

---

28. Zizioulas, *Being as Communion*, 16–17.
29. Henry, *Essence of Manifestation*, 285, 443.
30. Henry, *Material Phenomenology*, 3.
31. Hamann, "Philological Ideas," 114; Jaeger, "Biochemical Perspective," 27; Wollheim, *Thread of Life*, 1, 31.
32. Dalferth, *Creatures of Possibility*, 169; Dilthey, *Introduction to the Human Sciences*, 169 (II.2.1); Hamann, "Cloverleaf," 53.
33. Henry, *Incarnation*, 19; Schechtman, *Staying Alive*, 111, 118; Wilkes, *Real People*, 163.
34. See the synonyms note at *AHD*, s.v. "disposition."
35. Cooper, *Naturally Human, Supernaturally God*, 47; C. Taylor, *Sources of the Self*, 49.
36. Deikman, "'I' = Awareness," 424.
37. Lowe, *Subjects of Experience*, 182; Sorabji, *Self*, 21.
38. Hamann, "Fragments," I (p. 162).
39. Kierkegaard, *Eighteen Upbuilding Discourses*, 87.
40. Grenz, *Theology for the Community*, 10; Heidegger, "Being and Time," 59–60.

am I? is the quintessential human question.[41] Despite the question's ubiquity and the effort given to answering it, a generally accepted definitive answer remains elusive.[42] Kant, though identifying the question and feeling competent to handle the most profound, never tried this one.[43] As Highet found, "The cave we inhabit is our own mind; and consciousness is like a tiny torch, flickering and flaring, which can at best show us only a few outlines . . . ."[44] Nor need we pursue a definitive answer much beyond recognizing the significance of asking the question. As novelists know, "you can assert the existence of something—Being—having not the slightest notion of what it is,"[45] as do reflective philosophers, "we can never entirely reduce to ideas what is given in the totality of our being."[46]

Given the enigma that is *individual*, the thesis proposed in this book relies explicitly on no particular metaphysic, but, to express what is the minimum required within this obscurity, the thesis relies on factual experiences.[47] That is, the thesis accepts the realization that factual experiences suggest a meta- to the -physic, but, like the factual experiences themselves, the thesis is coy about what that metaphysic is. And, among our factual experiences, perhaps the most rudimentary is the individual.[48] "It has no name but I," a neuroscientist recognized.[49] We naturally equate our *seeming* to think, will, and act with our *really* doing them.[50] As a result, "our knowledge of the human world is better than that of the natural world," Milbank observed.[51] "There is one thing," C. S. Lewis explained, "in the whole universe which we know more about than we could learn from external observation. That one thing is Man. We do not merely observe men, we *are* men. In this case, we have, so to speak, inside information; we are in the know."[52] Because we understand the individual

---

41. Bonhoeffer, *Christ the Center*, 30; Jobes, "Remember These Things," 189; Zizioulas, "On Being a Person," 44.

42. Bobonich, *Plato's Utopia Recast*, 282.

43. Buber, *Between Man and Man*, 118–21.

44. Highet, *Man's Unconquerable Mind*, 36.

45. Robinson, *Gilead*, 178.

46. Dilthey, *Introduction to Human Sciences*, 315 (II.4.4).

47. Fraassen, *Empirical Stance*, 3–4; Pater, *Marius the Epicurean*, 61, 115.

48. Guardini, *Freedom, Grace, and Destiny*, 17, 63.

49. Tononi, *Phi*, 8.

50. Blondel, "Letter on Apologetics," 156–57.

51. Milbank, *Theology and Social Theory*, 272.

52. Lewis, *Mere Christianity*, 18–19.

through our sense, affectivity, and desire, we search there for who lives.[53] In brief, *individual* is understood through the observations, intuitions, and conclusions made by individuals.[54] Briefer still, we look to our life to understand our life.[55]

Therefore, unanswered here is whether we constitute anything like bodies, souls, or their combinations or emergents, and also unanswered is whether any of them sufficiently identify any of us. By staying at the experiential, the discourse has the obvious benefit of skirting the perennial battles over what individuals consist of or what brings them into existence.[56] Wittgenstein noted "a great variety of criteria for the *'identity'* of a person," but "which of them leads me to say *I* am in pain? None."[57] In agreement with this observation, the thetic understanding of the individual takes no ontological position, just a necessary stance,[58] which is that phenomena reflect truth.[59] This is similar to Thomas' recognition that humans can never comprehend the essential, only learn of its accidents.[60] As Romano Guardini reminds, "we are not concerned with the astronomical but with the existential world, whose center is always the person who inquires about it."[61]

The approach here, however, is *not* phenomenology, which is what allows phenomena, but is rather the phenomena themselves.[62] "The object of phenomenology," Henry distinguished, "is not the things but their how," not what appears but "appearing itself."[63] Phenomenology "move[s] in the field of pure phenomena," Edmond Husserl explained, and "existence" "has no bearing on the matter."[64] In contrast, the thesis depends on

53. Cooper, *Holy Eros*, 10.
54. McConville, *Being Human*, 4; Tillich, *ST*, I: 110–11.
55. Richardson, *Christian Apologetics*, 50, 94.
56. Baker, "Persons and Metaphysics," 333; Buckareff and Wagenen, "Surviving Resurrection," 126; Turner, "No Explanation of Persons," 298; Gassar and Stefan, eds., *Personal Identity*, 2–17.
57. Wittgenstein, *Philosophische Untersuchungen*, § 404.
58. Fraassen, *Empirical Stance*, 47.
59. Krapiec, *I-Man*, 129, 143; Proust, *In Search of Lost Time*, IV: 188; Shields and Pasnau, *Philosophy of Aquinas*, 101.
60. Cunningham, *Genealogy of Nihilism*, 220.
61. Guardini, *World and the Person*, 55.
62. Henry, "Phenomenology of Life," 241–42.
63. Henry, *Material Phenomenology*, 64–65.
64. Husserl, *Idea of Phenomenology*, 36, 50.

the things, not their how, *what appears*, not appearing itself, and *existence*, not the purified phenomena.⁶⁵ While, as John Caputo observed, phenomenology "unpack[s]" experience so as to find the "truth-event," to be "always 'more' than it factually is,"⁶⁶ the approach here is less adventuresome. What is applied here is the actuality, not the essence.⁶⁷ It is satisfied with the demonstrable, not reaching for the *Dasein*.⁶⁸

Modeling only the phenomena offers the advantage of suspending the riddle of reality's connection to appearance,⁶⁹ and the empiricist-realist battle can wage on outside the thesis.⁷⁰ Focusing on the fathomable stops short of ontology or ontology-replacing reductions.⁷¹ Instead, this discourse satiates itself on the existing without tasting the existential.⁷² Except when venturing into the insights that only Scripture can expose, the discourse truly stays—that is, intentionally stays—on this side of Lucretius' "tight-barred gates of Nature," which allows the discourse to avoid his (and his successors') unsubstantiated supposition of nothing beyond what has been merely detected.⁷³ Because "*Physis* loves to hide," Caputo's maxim,⁷⁴ the thesis is content to take appearances as what they appear to be.⁷⁵ The thesis is willing to retreat from comprehension to advance on understanding.⁷⁶ We need here only the sort of knowledge that keeps us from bumping into walls (Prov 3:23).⁷⁷ That is enough.

This basic approach helps particularly on the issue of *individual* because it is, as Socrates appreciated, the "sort of thing" whose "lengthy explanation" is "beyond human power," whereas "what it is *like*" "is within human capability, and briefer."⁷⁸ Like Paul's downright *indi-*

65. Milbank, *Word Made Strange*, 125.
66. Caputo, *Radical Hermeneutics*, 39, 53, 69, 115.
67. Rosenzweig, "New Thinking," 190–92.
68. Heidegger, "End of Philosophy," 391.
69. Fraassen, *Scientific Representation*, 168, 270.
70. Dilworth, *Metaphysics of Science*, 9, 19–20, 49.
71. Krapiec, *I-Man*, 331; Lee, "Standing Accused," 86.
72. Guignon, "Heidegger and Kierkegaard," 186–88, 200–201.
73. Lucretius, *Nature of Things*, I,71–73, 445–46.
74. Caputo, *Radical Hermeneutics*, 63.
75. Balthasar, *Theo-Logic*, II: 249.
76. Cunningham, *Genealogy of Nihilism*, 221–22.
77. Kierkegaard, *Stages*, 476; Locke, *Essay Concerning Human Understanding*, IV,XI,10, XIV,1.
78. Plato, *Phaedrus* (2000), 246a.

vidual (more below),[79] we stay here in Kierkegaard's subjective, where the individual faces the universal.[80] Lacking "virtuosity in playing with categories," we grasp life's meaning as best we can.[81] I "must be content with existing" "because I am only a poor existing human being who neither eternally nor divinely nor theocentrically is able to observe the eternal."[82] Following this lead, the thesis leaves undetermined what carries the individual's essence,[83] but it instead uses what every functional person lives: You are, I am, and others like us are each a unique package of personal stuff experienced through an irreducible awareness, whether ontological or delusional.[84]

The context of the thesis should alone justify this focus on the led life. Because the topic concerns the afterlife, a purely material individual is a non sequitur. Epictetus' "little soul, carrying around a corpse"[85] can be denied, but, if we are merely the physical, we cease with dying[86] and, when we are being honest, a lifetime before that.[87] As cultures throughout history have testified to, afterlives oppose pure materialism and entail continuing consciousness.[88] Christians need not decide what survives to know that something may,[89] and they commonly hold that whatever happens after this life necessitates continuity of the individual if salvation is to have any significance to this life.[90] As the corpse unravels, something else can experience,[91] something like spirit,[92] and, to understand

---

79. Arendt, "Willing," 57.

80. Kierkegaard, *Concluding Unscientific Postscript*, I: 129-32, 207-51. See McCombs, *Paradoxical Rationality*, 38-44.

81. Kierkegaard, *Either/Or*, II: 190.

82. Kierkegaard, *Concluding Unscientific Postscript*, I: 212.

83. Goetz, "Substance Dualism," 37.

84. Baker, *Persons and Bodies*, 146; Wilkes, *Real People*, 157.

85. Epictetus, "Fragments," 26 (p. 471).

86. Merricks, "How to Live Forever," 183-84.

87. Cunningham, "Is There Life?" 120-51.

88. Moore, *Where Are the Dead?* 30; Pieper, *Death and Immortality*, 94; Sherman, *Partakers of the Divine*, 20-21.

89. Jenson, *ST*, II: 104; Murphy, *Bodies and Souls*, 3, 21-22, 37-39.

90. Berkouwer, *Man: Image of God*, 251-53; J. Cooper, *Body, Soul, and Life*, 3, 9, 59, 75, 171; Rankin, *Early Church*, 1.

91. Bray, *God Has Spoken*, 81; Gundry, *Soma in Biblical Theology*, 159; Harding, *Paul's Eschatological Anthropology*, 334-35.

92. Davis, "Physicalism and Resurrection," 238; Olson, "Compound of Two Substances," 81; Ratzinger, *Eschatology*, 267.

this, we do not need to know *what* the individual's continuity is, only *that* it can be.[93] The led life, as we know from leading one, intersects body *and* consciousness,[94] and, because the body discontinues and because any afterlife entails consciousness of some manner of experience, the afterlife must at least involve that consciousness from this life. That is, given that with death (as in life) something may continue (with or without an interruption) and that something must discontinue, what is relevant is a qualitative dual*ity*, without necessarily being a substantive dual*ism*.[95]

Dividing an individual, as is to be proposed, obviously challenges the body's wholeness. Our nervous system's singularity, for instance, gives a clear sense of undivided existence,[96] but death dichotomizes any unity that the earthly body provides.[97] Death is what ends the body's role as our interface with the world generally.[98] Given this, we agree to donate upon death our previously cherished organs because they are no longer useful to us, even if there continues to be an us.[99] Secularists and Christians both assess the dead body similarly by erasing it through intent, such as cremation, or through default, such as burial.[100] Even when preservation of the body is the objective, whether mummified or embalmed, corpses are hardly more fleshy than wax figures, and, if a corpse is truly preserved as flesh, it is not because the flesh is important—the hundreds of corpses in Mount Everest's permafrost are classed as garbage.[101]

Even before death, corporeal indicators can lose out to the autobiographical self, such as when an identical twin must correct a misidentification based on corporeal appearances, and the next life, if it is to be us and not someone else, desperately needs the same sort of led-life identity.[102] A life afterwards, Bulgakov remarked, clearly "supposes a con-

---

93. Dilthey, *Introduction to Human Sciences*, 298 (II.4.2).

94. Stein, *Potency and Act*, 102, 118, 124–26, 223.

95. Berkouwer, *Man: Image of God*, 213–14; J. Cooper, "Biblical Anthropology," 228; Yates, *Between Death and Resurrection*, 35–37, 58–59.

96. Dilthey, *Introduction to Human Sciences*, 85 (I.3).

97. J. Cooper, *Body, Soul, and Life*, 214; Leget, "Eschatology," 367; Schumacher, *Death and Mortality*, 48.

98. Arendt, *Love and Augustine*, 78; Krapiec, *I-Man*, 351; Vidal, "Brains, Bodies, Selves, and Science," 938.

99. Perkins, *First Corinthians*, 193.

100. Novakovic, *Resurrection*, 164–65; Walter, *Eclipse of Eternity*, 91–116.

101. Mazzolini, "Food, Waste, and Judgment," 2, 14.

102. Moore, *Where Are the Dead?* 200.

tinuous identity and unity of life."[103] This fuller self consists of thinking, consciousness, and other personhood affairs,[104] which is what forms the personal drama of the inner, indispensable *I*.[105] That is how we know we are who we are. Only other people use our fingerprints or the like to identify ourself. Thus, for Christians at least, the earthly body, though this is how we currently find selves, is not the self that is saved or that continues.[106] In Christianity, what continues in any intermediate state is a discarnate essence, and what continues in the resurrection is that essence with a radically new body.[107]

Recognizing that an individual is more than an earthly body means disallowing anthropological nihilism, which is just to recognize the physical body, not anything extra.[108] The thesis therefore safely accepts that we are more than Dennett's "organic robots"[109] or Hollywood's electrified Frankenstein cadavers.[110] Naturalism might not require this something more, but Christianity does,[111] whether the individual's something more is substantively a spirit, a memory held by God,[112] or some sort of biological software. Hence, irrelevancies here include whether reality is as perceived, whether being is predicate,[113] and the entire mind-body problem.[114] Relevant, rather, is something like Anthony's "invisible substance which does not pass away with the body,"[115] or this "strange, enigmatic,

---

103. Bulgakov, *Bride of the Lamb*, 354.

104. Fraassen, *Empirical Stance*, 191; Grenz, *Theology for the Community*, 596; Wallenfang, *Human and Divine Being*, 36.

105. Blondel, "Letter on Apologetics," 161–62.

106. Badham, *Christian Beliefs*, 64, 86–87; Bovon, "Soul's Comeback," 406; Bynum, *Resurrection of the Body*, 9; Grenz, *Theology for the Community*, 586–87; Hebblethwaite, *Christian Hope*, 174; International Commission, "Some Current Questions on Eschatology," 5.4; Johnston, *Surviving Death*, 125; Novakovic, *Resurrection*, 68, 71; Pannenberg, "Task of Christian Eschatology," 7–8.

107. J. Cooper, *Body, Soul, and Life*, 117, 176, 179, 181–82, 189, 209; Dahl, *Resurrection of the Body*, 18, 37–39, 46, 94; Yates, *Between Death and Resurrection*, 7.

108. Jenson, *ST*, II: 57–58.

109. Dennett, *Elbow Room*, 186.

110. Mary Shelley had the good sense to leave life's source unsaid. *Frankenstein*, I,3, III,7 (pp. 31, 146).

111. Geisler, *ST*, 721.

112. Unamuno, *Tragic Sense of Life*, 149.

113. Milbank, *Beyond Secular Order*, 53–55.

114. Montero, "Post-Physicalism," 61–80.

115. Anthony, *Letters*, Ltr VI (p. 21).

personal essence," in Pater's words,[116] which can, for the model, transcend matter or be mental substance, ectoplasm, or photons.[117] This personal something more is traditionally termed *soul*, *spirit*, or *form*,[118] but, to acknowledge here that the self's ontology is left unanswered, terms specifying personal attributes are deployed instead: *personal identity* is the individual's first-person perspective on life, and *personal character* is the set of features that are the individual's life that is led.[119]

3. Anthropology Historically and Currently Reflects the Essential *I*

The act of thinking is an undeniable reality as acts like the forming of this sentence and its understanding reveal, even if the thinking is feeble or wrong, and any thinking without a thinker is, frankly, unthinkable.[120] Therefore, the nearest, most immediate thinker, which has in various cultures throughout history mostly been called the *I*, is ineliminable.[121] The *I* is involuntarily primordial,[122] more overt even than God.[123] It exists unmistakably because only what exists can be mistaken,[124] and it must be real because it is what judges what is real.[125] If the existence of the *I* is ever doubted, "It is a doubt with no reason or reply" except Hamann's "Bah!"[126] "Through acts of immediate intuition we intuit a 'self,'" Husserl reminded.[127] Everything that is observed carries this sense,[128] and this sense of *I* is powerful. As anyone who has dreamed vividly or seen

---

116. Pater, *Marius the Epicurean*, 107.
117. Fraassen, *Empirical Stance*, 190–92.
118. J. Cooper, "Whose Interpretation? Which Anthropology?" 241; Ratzinger, *Eschatology*, 146–49, 154–55.
119. Pannenberg, *Anthropology in Theological Perspective*, 61, 65.
120. Foster, "Brief Defense," 17; Husserl, *Ideas*, 46 (p. 130).
121. Baker, *Persons and Bodies*, 67.
122. Balthasar, *Theo-Logic*, I: 166; C. Taylor, *Hegel*, 141.
123. Locke, *Essay Concerning Human Understanding*, IV,IX,3; Rosenzweig, *Star of Redemption*, 49.
124. Augustine, *City of God*, XI,26 (pp. 459–60); Henry, *Material Phenomenology*, 130.
125. Husserl, *Ideas*, 135 (p. 348).
126. Jacobi, *Werke Vol. 4, Pt. 3*, 34 (Hamann 22 Jan. 1785 letter).
127. Husserl, *Ideas*, 43 (p. 123).
128. Henry, *Incarnation*, 172.

something not there can verify, the sights inside the head are more immediate than those from outside it.[129]

Self-awareness has been chronic for humanity, perhaps arriving as early as when humans first walked upright with a purpose.[130] Human reasoning, though antedating this self-awareness,[131] quickly recognized the self who was doing the reasoning. This first moment of recognition certainly occurred before the Common Era because it was by then that Eurasians from end to end were recording consciousness of consciousness.[132] In the West at least, what advanced this understanding was the idea behind the ancient maxim that Socrates inherited from an unknown proverbialist, "Know thyself."[133] "Socrates' infinite merit," Kierkegaard reminded, "is precisely that of being an *existing* thinker, not a speculative thinker who forgets what it means to exist,"[134] and Socrates taught, using the metaphors available to him, that the individual lives like a single chariot team, consisting of a chariot powered by two horses, one good, one bad, driven by a charioteer.[135]

Socrates' successors, though disagreeing on a great deal, agreed with the fundamental insight that the single individual was a multiple.[136] For Plato, the individual was a unitizing soul of competing interior parts,[137] living as the one who is two.[138] According to some interpreters, Plato at times partitioned a person's soul into distinct agents with different characters, one that was base and one that was better, and only later did he treat these inner conflicts as aspects of a unified entity.[139] For Aristotle, the individual was matter of the same essence distinctively formed; the

---

129. Henry, *Essence of Manifestation*, 465–66, 682–83; Schroeder, *Hidden Face of God*, 5, 9.

130. Burdett, "Transcendence and Human Enhancement," 26.

131. J. Betz, *After Enlightenment*, 326.

132. Arendt, "Karl Jaspers," 88–89; Pannenberg, *Anthropology in Theological Perspective*, 166.

133. Bergson, *Two Sources*, 61; Vanhoozer, "Human Being," 158.

134. Kierkegaard, *Concluding Unscientific Postscript*, I: 172.

135. Plato, "Phaedrus" (2017), 246a-b, 253c-e.

136. Barresi and Martin, "History as Prologue," 34–35.

137. Plato, *Republic*, 431a, 435c, 436a-b, 437c, 439d-440a, 440e-442b, 443d, 444b, 486b-e, 495e, 505d, 544e, 590c, 609d-612c. See generally Gerson, *Knowing Persons*.

138. Stang, *Our Divine Double*, 22.

139. Bobonich, *Plato's Utopia Recast*, 217, 259, 336; Hendrik, *Brute Within*, 14, 21–22, 35, 63.

body materialized the soul, and the soul actualized the body.[140] According to Plotinus, the individual was a unified soul dominating what was divisible.[141] As a result, the Neoplatonist idea was that the individual's consciousness held together a double inner self.[142]

These Socratic views lasted. Plato's dualistic influence is seen in the Creed of Chalcedon, which described Christ's humanity as a "rational soul and body."[143] Aristotle's embodied subjectivity developed through such thinkers as Hegel.[144] Medieval Islamic philosophers borrowed indistinguishably from all three Socratic branches,[145] and Christian theologians like Augustine and Thomas deepened ensoulment and embodiment,[146] culminating in the Thomist fusion of Platonic duality and Aristotelian holism.[147] The body was understood as the soul's matter and the soul as the body's form.[148] Thus, by the Middle Ages, the individual was a soul that fits the body, not like the hand in the glove, but like the life in the hand.[149]

This rush through the history of *individual* is of course necessary to avoid being a book onto itself,[150] but is also warranted because the trajectory of *individual* inverted in late modernity from its Socratic paths and this is the mindset in which we now converse.[151] Moderns, in freeing themselves universally, freed themselves from themselves as well. To such skeptics, "Know thyself" was empty of content and concocted entirely by

---

140. Gilson, *Being and Some Philosophers*, 42–50, 74; Martin, *Corinthian Body*, 7–8; Pabst, *Metaphysics*, 21. See particularly Aristotle, *De Anima*, 412a-415a.

141. Plotinus, *Ennead* IV.2.1–2 (p. 140).

142. Stang, *Our Divine Double*, 187, 196–201.

143. Kelly, *Early Christian Doctrines*, 339.

144. C. Taylor, *Hegel*, 87, 332, 570–71.

145. MacDonald, *History of the Concept*, 161–77.

146. Clarke, *Person and Being*, 27–53; Pabst, *Metaphysics*, 90–91, 95–103, 202–8, 246–51, 266–67; Vaught, *Access to God*, 43–44.

147. Aquinas, *Quaestiones De Anima*, Q. 6, ad. 13, Q. 14, ad. 11, Q. 15, s.c. (pp. 98, 179, 185–86); *ST*, 1a, XI, Q. 75, arts. 3–4 (pp. 13–21). See J. Cooper, *Body, Soul, and Life*, 80; Pannenberg, *ST*, II: 184.

148. Bynum, *Resurrection of the Body*, 257; Clark, "Inquiry into Personhood," 23; Fitzpatrick, *Aquinas on Bodily Identity*, 27–30, 42, 49–51, 80, 96–97.

149. Leftow, "Souls Dipped in Dust," 120–38; Leget, "Eschatology," 366; Pieper, *Death and Immortality*, 30.

150. E.g., MacDonald, *History of the Concept*.

151. MacDonald, *History of the Concept*, 350–51; Turner, *Theology, Psychology and Plural Self*, 2.

our ego, which itself is also apparently a fiction.[152] Science, once it figured out how to trigger physiologically our senses of love, morality, spirit, and transcendence and after it merged with skepticism, figured that our inner life is only physiological.[153] No one under this worldview's influence troubled to realize that science can trigger our sense of heat too, of which no one denies its real-world existence.

The incestuous bedfellows of science and skepticism thus gave birth to the dogma of materialism,[154] which takes persons as pure physicality.[155] Philosophers succumbed to physicalism too,[156] directing "a radical critique against the philosophy of the subject and the ego-subject," Henry reported, producing "its own self-destructing."[157] Various Romantic existentialisms, after combing through the facts leftover after scientific confirmation, have tried to find a substitute *individual* that somehow retains an affirmation of human life or is "nothing but" something blatant like gene-reproducing atoms.[158] The response has been, Conor Cunningham observed, "an almost fanatical effort . . . to reduce consciousness to nothing, at least nothing significant—yet still maintain that this pre-conscious essence of consciousness *provides* consciousness."[159] Of late, therefore, persons suffer an identity crisis.[160] "We are witnessing the process of dehumanization in all phases of culture and social life," Nikolai Berdyaev recapped. "Man has ceased to be the supreme value; he has ceased to have any value at all."[161]

Abridging in five paragraphs the history of *individual* from premodernity to now, not only omits the fits and starts that got us here, but avoids the scholarly dispute of who is responsible for the latest answer. Proposals for patient zero in the loss of the self have included Plotinus through Hegel for abstracting away existential layers,[162] Thomas for

---

152. Sloterdijk, *Critique of Cynical Reason*, 537.
153. Carter and Frith, *Mapping the Mind*, 13.
154. Brower, *Aquinas's Ontology*, 265.
155. Schwobel, "Introduction," 4.
156. Bourget and Chalmers, "What Do Philosophers Believe?" 476, 496.
157. Henry, *Material Phenomenology*, 123.
158. Lee, "Standing Accused," 10.
159. Cunningham, *Genealogy of Nihilism*, xiv.
160. Vanhoozer, "Human Being," 158.
161. Berdyaev, *Fate of Man*, 25.
162. Cunningham, *Genealogy of Nihilism*, 3–125.

basing Christian revelation on speculative reason,[163] Descartes for banking on subjectivity,[164] Darwin for leaving us mere animals, or Freud for assigning our innermost sensibilities to myth.[165] The terminology may have changed first. *Soul* became *mind* with Descartes' cogito,[166] and *mind* became *self* with Hume's empiricism.[167] When the jargon could retreat no further and the newly christened *self* remained unreachable, skepticism turned to science, whose microscopes found only the microscopic.[168] The myth then became that superstition had given way to theology, which had given way to metaphysics, which has given way to science,[169] which gives way to nothing, literally.

The discourse does not choose among these theories of why the modern conclusions about the individual have become unrealistic. The discourse willingly suffers from Nietzsche's "democratic prejudice" against genealogies.[170] The discourse instead recognizes that truths can be highborn or low-, as can lies. By accepting this reality, the discourse avoids the genetic fallacy, which is to suppose that an idea's descent indicates its truth.[171] Genealogies may matter to rationality, but not to truth (Titus 3:9)[172] and not to the thesis. So, for the obvious reasons, the thesis rejects the self-is-nothing conclusion without trying to explain why anyone would stumble upon that error and then accept it as anything more than a brain-twister.

Unlike the genealogy of the *individual's* demise, the role of science in determining what the individual is cannot be so quickly put aside. Science rightfully earns our appreciation when conducting its discipline, such as when it eradicates small pox or provides artificial light.[173] The

---

163. Dunning, *Grace, Faith, and Holiness*, 143; Henry, *God, Revelation and Authority*, I: 36–37, 185, 203.

164. Krapiec, *I-Man*, 24.

165. Henry, *God, Revelation and Authority*, I: 152.

166. Moore, *Where Are the Dead?* 183.

167. Krapiec, *I-Man*, 71.

168. Barresi and Martin, "History as Prologue," 51, 55; Hooke, *Micrographia*, 19–22 (pref.); Jenson, *ST*, I: 120–21.

169. Bulgakov, "Vladimir Solovyov," 42–43; Krell, "General Introduction," 6.

170. Nietzsche, "Genealogy of Morals," I: 4 (p. 162).

171. Engel and Soldan, *Study of Philosophy*, 141–42.

172. Elster, *Sour Grapes*, 140.

173. Heidegger, "Modern Science," 3, 12–13; Pinker, *Enlightenment Now*, 253–54, 386.

diminishment of science on the subject of the self is partly because of what science has become. Until relatively recently, science had been "a collection of true facts about the world," but has now, a biologist concluded, become what "scientists say about the world."[174] This unfortunate transformation occurred about when the world was taken to be mechanistic, which was about when those who had been "natural philosophers" stopped being philosophers altogether[175] and started calling themselves "scientists" (coined in 1833).[176] Science, which had been the endless appreciation of truth,[177] became, Henry realized, "systematized information gained by the observational method."[178]

Science is, therefore, ill-equipped to find the individual. While science awakens our interiority,[179] scientism excludes it.[180] As a result, scientists can submit to Montaigne's "fateful presumption" of disdaining what is not comprehended.[181] The world of course fills with singular judgments—John is hungry, Jane is upset—but science excludes these judgments as unobjective, which they are.[182] Science impersonalizes, again literally.[183] Its trademark of isolating the repeatable, therefore, necessarily obscures individualities.[184] The objective sciences confront a subject who knows it is living even before its physical is taken,[185] and no self ever sits still for the required controlled experiment,[186] except in lifeless facsimiles or cadavers.[187] Van Fraassen noticed, "no objectifying

---

174. Lewontin, *Biology as Ideology*, 103.

175. Heidegger, "Modern Science," 247.

176. Snyder, "William Whewell."

177. Hartshorne, *Logic of Perfection*, 129.

178. Henry, *God, Revelation and Authority*, I: 202.

179. C. Taylor, *Hegel*, 82.

180. Edwards, *After Death?* 57; Pfuetze, *Self, Society, Existence*, 149; Wallenfang, *Human and Divine Being*, 62.

181. Montaigne, "Essays," I,27 (p. 134).

182. Henry, *Incarnation*, 74.

183. Highet, *Man's Unconquerable Mind*, 34–35.

184. Milbank, *Theology and Social Theory*, 259.

185. Henry, *I Am the Truth*, 38; Husserl, *Crisis of European Sciences*, 6; Rochat, "What Is It Like?" 57.

186. Bultmann, "Theology as Science," 46; Richardson, *Christian Apologetics*, 34, 40.

187. Arendt, "Thinking," 40, 56; Bishop, "On Medical Corpses," 166; Carter and Frith, *Mapping the Mind*, 26–27.

inquiry can reveal what persons are or who the persons are among things in the world."[188]

Modern science in its pure form is thus the wrong endeavor for understanding the self. Whichever field of science that has been tried has failed. Science has tried biology, psychology, and sociology,[189] but "Biologists no longer study life," only life's structures,[190] "Modern psychology is psychology without the *psyche*,"[191] and sociology involves, not *self* and *identity*, but things like *self-image* and *sexual identity*.[192] To a zoologist, it is no longer death but life itself that has become "the great puzzle of human existence."[193] Certainly science has found no *you* or *me* among the quarks,[194] nor has it found any quarks that enjoy good music.[195] Likewise, philosophy, the science of science, when not nihilistic,[196] honors here its founder's admonition to "beware of the wish to be edifying."[197] Dalferth noted, "Where once we saw a 'child of God,' we now see an animal, without the quotation marks."[198] Accordingly, *you* and *I* are no longer obvious to everyone,[199] and the doubters cannot possibly accept *our* protests because they are just more folk-metaphysics.[200] The led life is therefore beyond science,[201] which, when objective, finds that the led life lacks meaning.[202] The same deconstruction that eviscerated God has eviscerated the self.[203]

188. Fraassen, *Empirical Stance*, 191.
189. Barresi and Martin, "History as Prologue," 49.
190. Jacob, *Logic of Life*, 299.
191. Tillich, *ST*, III: 24.
192. Barresi and Martin, "History as Prologue," 51.
193. Portmann, *Essays in Philosophical Zoology*, 258.
194. Goetz, "Substance Dualism," 48–50; Lockwood, "Consciousness and the Quantum," 447; Metzinger, "No-Self Alternative," 279, 285.
195. Hasker, "Do My Quarks Enjoy," 13–40.
196. Cunningham, *Genealogy of Nihilism*, 3–179, 238–60.
197. Hegel, *Phenomenology of Spirit*, ¶ 9 (p. 6). Marx concurred, "Philosophy is to investigation of the real world what masturbation is to sexual love." Schaff, *Marxism and the Human*, 77.
198. Dalferth, *Creatures of Possibility*, 178.
199. Gallagher, "Introduction," 27.
200. Metzinger, "No-Self Alternative," 279.
201. Dilworth, *Metaphysics of Science*, 265–67; Lewontin, *Biology as Ideology*, 12–13.
202. Harari, *Sapiens*, 391.
203. Barresi and Martin, "History as Prologue," 43; Fromm, "Modern Man," 27; Hemming, "Heidegger and Grounds of Redemption," 99.

When science thinks it is on the trail of the self, it is merely following the physical bit, namely the body or a part of it, such as the brain.[204] This is because scientific fundamentalism accepts the physic but no meta.[205] According to a Nobel-laureate physiologist, "'You,' your joys and your sorrows, your memories and your ambitions, your sense of personal identity and free will, are in fact no more than the behavior of a vast assembly of nerve cells and their associated molecules," and, paraphrasing Lewis Carroll's wonderland, "You are nothing but a pack of neurons."[206] The corporeal is philosophy's dominant view too,[207] making it, in Milbank's words, "radically incompetent with relation to reality."[208] However, while the material body offers the space-time coordinates for the individual and is therefore our first line of defense in preserving identity,[209] this cannot sustain the individual's continuity.[210] The continuing self is obviously beyond the everchanging particles we use from day to day.[211] Science is thus mostly noncontributing to who leads this life and continues afterwards.[212] The "mysterious reality, contradicting all rationalist explanation and yet impossible to gainsay," Guardini recognized, is that "man, though he is part of the general pattern of Nature, represents in addition a genuine starting point . . . ."[213]

The scientific fixation on the body is explicable, however, because ethereals like the mind, unlike the measurable body, resist fixation.[214] And trying to scientifically determine the reality of what has *not* been measured (and may never be) based on what has already been measured bakes in error, especially since science will course-correct even on the

204. Grenz, *Theology for the Community*, 588; LeDoux, *Synaptic Self*, 13; McGilchrist, *Master and His Emissary*, 135.

205. Haeckel, *Riddle of the Universe*, 182; Milbank, "Mystery of Reason," 72.

206. Crick, *Astonishing Hypothesis*, 3, 7, 203. Accord LeDoux, *Synaptic Self*, 2, 324.

207. Dalferth, *Creatures of Possibility*, 20–21; Eastman, *Paul and the Person*, 70, 85, 93; Hudson, "Morphing Block," 237; B. Williams, *Problems of the Self*, 10.

208. Milbank, *Theology and Social Theory*, 211.

209. Davies, *Aquinas on God and Evil*, 48–49; Mitchell, *Being and Participation*, I: 379.

210. Ratzinger, *Eschatology*, 158.

211. Hartshorne, *Logic of Perfection*, 168; Küng, *Eternal Life?* 18–19, 111; Song, *Covenant and Calling*, 56.

212. Henry, *Incarnation*, 3, 18, 86, 108; Lowe, *Subjects of Experience*, 43; Pinker, *Enlightenment Now*, 426–28.

213. Guardini, *Freedom, Grace, and Destiny*, 28.

214. Dilworth, *Metaphysics of Science*, 187.

measured after several generations—recall that the physical was at one time pre-Aristotelian, pre-Copernican, pre-Galilean, pre-Newtonian, pre-Einsteinian, and pre-Copenhagen.[215] Modern science is still incapable of differentiating the magical and the spiritual[216] or of identifying the proof that it needs to find the self.[217] Science, despite the certainty of our consciousness, must in its quest for human nature resort to subhuman nature.[218] While the instruments of science are being used by the actual inner life, this means that they can never detect it.[219] Scientific cluelessness in this area is, accordingly, no gap to be closed.[220] The perceiver cannot be perceived and remain the perceiver,[221] and, so, method and problem pass each other by.[222] "All science is a science of experience," Wilhelm Dilthey explained, "but all experience" occurs in "our consciousness," "which logically sees the impossibility of going beyond these conditions, which would be like seeing without an eye . . . ."[223]

Besides, science has human prejudices,[224] and this includes the desire to neutralize the fear of death, which a life limited to the body delightfully does.[225] If the self is never anything, its death is not so much tragic as matter being reorganized.[226] The death of a human means only that the human is in a physical condition that deteriorates faster. As Nietzsche argued, "Let us beware of saying that death is opposed to life. The living is only a form of what is dead . . . ."[227]

---

215. Arendt, "Thinking," 54; Balthasar, *Theo-Logic*, I: 84; Fraassen, *Empirical Stance*, 78–82.

216. Dilworth, *Metaphysics of Science*, 267.

217. Lowe, *Subjects of Experience*, 43.

218. Spaemann, *Essays in Anthropology*, 23; Wilson, *Statement and Inference*, II: 857; Yu, *Being and Relation*, 53.

219. Wallenfang, *Human and Divine Being*, 38, 95; Wittgenstein, *Philosophische Untersuchungen*, ¶ 430.

220. Blondel, *Action*, 77, 89, 92 [68, 82, 85]; Tillich, *ST*, I: 6.

221. Balthasar, *Theo-Drama*, I: 483; Maritain, *Existence and the Existent*, 69–72.

222. Crick, *Astonishing Hypothesis*, 259; Wittgenstein, "Philosophie Der Psychologie," ¶ 371.

223. Dilthey, *Introduction to Human Sciences*, 72–73 (Pref.).

224. Lewontin, *Biology as Ideology*, 41.

225. Krapiec, *I-Man*, 343; Ratzinger, *Eschatology*, 70–71.

226. Epicurus, "Letter to Menoeceus," 180; Levering, *Proofs of God*, 209; Moore, *Where Are the Dead?* 139.

227. Nietzsche, *Gay Science*, 109 (p. 110).

Pure science thus sees consciousness as pure illusion,[228] despite the commonsense givenness of consciousness.[229] As one mind philosopher found, identity's ontology "has by and large been abandoned" by "most empirical researchers."[230] Thomas Metzinger reports, "no such things as selves exist in the world: Nobody ever *was* or *had* a self."[231] Instead, *self* is seen as a culturally created fiction.[232] It is surmised that the self was only taken as real because we mistook reflexive pronouns for reality[233] and presumably because we mistook our actual reflections this way too. Today's emperor not only has no clothes on, but there is no person underneath. Hans Christian's fellow Dane anticipated this: With "breathless busyness or worldly desire or abstract thinking or whatever the distraction might be," a person now ignores "his own *I* and the pulse beat and heart beat of his own self."[234] The "existing individual," who had directed "all his attention to his existing," travels the only other available path: "do everything he can to forget that he is existing and thereby manage to become comic."[235] Blondel summarized, "How far removed we are now from the simplicity of conscience. . . . It is no longer a simple accidental doubling of the personality; it is a complete frittering of it, the decomposition of death in life itself. Isn't that what we wanted: . . . a complete liquidation, a huge burst of laughter, a mournful joke, a mystification and, that's the word, a hoax, nothing, that is what a man and his destiny have become."[236]

However, "To think that the individual is being liquidated without trace is over-optimistic," Theodor Adorno conceded.[237] What is left in most places, Nietzsche saw, was a "falsity towards oneself," whether called "nature," "Darwinism," or "fatalism," and these unscientific vestiges of the self "we owe Christianity."[238] Christianity has therefore in most places been

---

228. Crick, *Astonishing Hypothesis*, 33.

229. Milbank, *Beyond Secular Order*, 93.

230. Zahavi, "Unity of Consciousness," 324–25.

231. Metzinger, *Being No One*, 1. Accord Johnston, *Surviving Death*, 306.

232. Barresi and Martin, "History as Prologue," 51; Henry, *I Am the Truth*, 262–63.

233. Kenny, *Legacy of Wittgenstein*, 81.

234. Kierkegaard, *Book on Adler*, 103.

235. Kierkegaard, *Concluding Unscientific Postscript*, I: 120 [VII 99].

236. Blondel, *Action*, 24 [10].

237. Adorno, *Minima Moralia*, 135 [ch 88].

238. Nietzsche, *Writings from the Late Notebooks*, 174 (NB 10, entry 7); *Will to Power*, 268–70, 285–86, 294.

the preservative of the meta-scientific *individual*, wherever it persists.[239] This is in part because, despite methodological detours, Christian tradition returns to actuality.[240] And the self is that. "The first part then of Christianity is," Luther recognized, "the knowledge of ourselves."[241] John Zizioulas agreed, "historically as well as existentially the concept of the person is indissolubly bound up with theology,"[242] as did Richard Niebuhr, "The only word in our vocabulary which does justice to the knowledge of persons or selves is 'revelation.'"[243] So, theologians, at least those not gripped by contemporary notions hostile to the *I*,[244] understand that the individual is as beyond mere material as the state of death is beyond mere biology.[245] "To be spirit," Kierkegaard concluded, "is the human being's invisible glory."[246]

While theologians can sometimes privilege the earthly body,[247] this is often from over-exegeting Paul[248] or from de-Hellenizing him.[249] Privileging the body can also be from forgetting how Christianity upset the ancient dogma of physiognomy, which had said the corporeal connoted the intrinsic, such as how physical disfigurement meant inner depravity.[250] Regardless, the Christian debate about the importance of the *earthly* body is irrelevant to ultimate salvation because that body blatantly discontinues.[251] "We are indeed flesh and blood," van Fraassen saw, but this is only how "we persons manifest ourselves *in the first instance*," because "What counts as thinking counts as consciousness, and what

239. Bultmann, "New Testament and Mythology," 25; Dalferth, *Creatures of Possibility*, 158; Henry, *I Am the Truth*, 35.

240. Rosenzweig, "New Thinking," 130.

241. Luther, *Galatians*, 131 [WA 401,221 (2:16)].

242. Zizioulas, *Being as Communion*, 27.

243. Niebuhr, *Meaning of Revelation*, 76.

244. Eastman, *Paul and the Person*, 166–67.

245. Cooper, *Holy Eros*, 20; Olson, *Mosaic of Christian Belief*, 201; Schwarz, *Human Being*, 171.

246. Kierkegaard, *Upbuilding Discourses*, 193.

247. Behr, *Mystery of Christ*, 146–58; White, *Life Beyond Death*, 49.

248. *E.g.*, Harding, *Paul's Eschatological Anthropology*, 171: In the hands of an exegete, Paul's "I punish my body" (1 Cor 9:27) can expand into "I, who am one interrelated aspect of the indivisible entity called the σῶμα, recognize my identity with this totality—it is an aspect of me, and I am an aspect of it."

249. Kooton, "St Paul on Soul," 25–44.

250. Parsons, *Body and Character*, 15–17, 64–65, 144–45.

251. Davis, *Risen Indeed*, 90.

counts as conscious counts as a person, with the rights of person—that is the crucial point."[252] In other words, the afterlife continuity of a person has to be something like spirit (Jas 2:26) or, in inclusive non-substantive vocabulary, personal identity and personal character.[253] What continues, as Christian philosopher Stephen T. Davis lists them, are "experiences, beliefs, wishes, knowledge, memory, inner (rather than bodily) feelings, thoughts, language (assuming memory of earthly existence)—in short, much of what makes up what we call personality."[254]

4. We Each Live through an Indivisible Personal Identity

As has been seen, *individual* must be more than what objective science or its philosophy has offered and, possibly, may be able to offer.[255] Scientists can of course be forgiven for knowing not what they do because science exists for humans, not humans for science. The scientific agnosy is not only forgivable but entirely tolerable for most of us because we know that the finest authorities on *individual* have not been professionals fashioning theories, but ordinary people, including the professional ones, experiencing life.[256] While scientists have been examining such things as molecules, neurotransmitters, and amino acids, the individual has been bearing such things as suffering and joy, desires and choices, hopes and fetishes.[257]

The same people who are grateful to science for its contributions to life and its conveniences and who welcome its related contributions to our understanding of the human body know that, though they experience this life through the scientifically studied body, it is the experience itself that is the life. Hamann observed, "Between an idea in our soul and a sound produced by the lips lies the distance between spirit and body";[258] so, "our philosophy must begin from heaven and not from the *theatrum anatomicum* and the dissection of a cadaver."[259] Apart from "the

---

252. Fraassen, *Empirical Stance*, 191–92 (emphasis added).

253. D. Hart, *That All Shall Be Saved*, 152; Taliaferro, "Human Nature," 534; Volf, *End of Memory*, 24, 192.

254. Davis, *Risen Indeed*, 90–91.

255. D. Hart, *Experience of God*, 161, 181, 204, 210, 213–15, 227; Hasker, "Persons as Emergent Substances," 114; McCombs, *Paradoxical Rationality*, 128, 134–36.

256. Reddy, *How Infants Know Minds*, 5; Wollheim, *Thread of Life*, 30.

257. Gschwandtner, "Fully Alive?" 59–60; Merleau-Ponty, *Signs*, 71.

258. Hamann, "Letter to Lindner," 67.

259. O'Flaherty, *Unity and Language*, 89.

visible" "body," Henry noted, we are "the invisible" "human being itself," "his or her true reality."[260] While the self works through the body,[261] this working relationship derives from the body's servantship (1 Cor 9:27).[262] Our optic systems do not see; *we* see through them.[263] Hamann again: "The veiled figure of the body" is "the visible schema in which we move along; yet in truth" is "nothing but a finger pointing to the hidden man within us."[264] Even a committed materialist like Lynne Baker recognizes that "bodily continuity seems neither sufficient nor necessary for personal identity."[265] The body is thus not all the individual is,[266] and, with death, this body becomes less so as it so clearly discontinues then.[267] The individual, Cunningham recapped, is "only contingently related to this body."[268] *Individual* becomes therefore an eschatological specialty, where earthly bodies become obsolete.[269]

Unlike the individual's body, the individual's interiority is unsharable.[270] Not only is your awareness outside mine, but my awareness is outside mine—it *is* my awareness. Balthasar noticed, "we can never get it within our sights, for it itself holds the rifle."[271] We nonetheless sense our own experiences converging,[272] which is an immediate access to the awareness of the *I*.[273] It is hard reality.[274] It is not volitional,[275] but primal

---

260. Henry, *Words of Christ*, 17.

261. Mooney, "Critiques of Pairing," 453.

262. Goetz, "Substance Dualism," 39; Henry, *Incarnation*, 4; Pannenberg, *ST*, II: 181.

263. McGilchrist, *Master and His Emissary*, 372–73.

264. Hamann, "Aesthetica in Nuce," 64.

265. Baker, *Persons and Bodies*, 119.

266. Rankin, *Early Church*, 52–53.

267. Grenz, *Theology for the Community*, 645–46.

268. Cunningham, "Is There Life?" 130.

269. Gunton, "Trinity, Ontology and Anthropology," 60; Harding, *Paul's Eschatological Anthropology*, 6.

270. Caldecott, *Radiance of Being*, 104; Henry, *Words of Christ*, 107.

271. Balthasar, *Theo-Drama*, I: 484.

272. Guardini, *Freedom, Grace, and Destiny*, 42.

273. Crosby, *Selfhood of the Human*, 87; Husserl, "Author's Preface," 11; Krapiec, *I-Man*, 95.

274. Goetz, "Substance Dualist Response," 140–41; Henry, *I Am the Truth*, 39; *Barbarism*, 10.

275. Parnas and Sass, "Structure of Self-Consciousness," 529.

like the principle of noncontradiction.[276] Just as nothing makes anything identical and it just is,[277] the personal identity just is.[278] Though personal identity is not identity per se, which involves thinghood or the relation between a thing and itself,[279] it does involve personhood,[280] and this is like any identity and entirely passive.[281] Without our doing anything, our personal identity is just there.[282] This internal observer is known to us, not by our observing it, but by us observing everything else.[283] "Even in those moments when we are most disinterested spectators," Marcel Proust mused, "every impression is double and the one half which is sheathed in the object is prolonged in ourselves by another half which we alone can know...."[284]

This discrete first-person identity is unqualifiedly singular and indivisible.[285] Every awareness, including awareness of awareness, awareness of that, and on and on until induction is satisfied, attaches to that awareness.[286] This awareness, which is personal identity, is thus unified consciousness.[287] Even schizophrenics sense this enough to realize that they are the ones thinking the thoughts that they think are not theirs.[288] Likewise, those with surgically disconnected cerebral hemispheres, which allows each hemisphere to act with full autonomy, still experience life as

---

276. Przywara, *Analogia Entis*, 199.

277. Noonan, *Personal Identity*, 87; Perry, *Identity*, 68; Schindler, *Perfection of Freedom*, 210.

278. Merricks, "How to Live Forever," 191–92.

279. Baker, *Persons and Bodies*, 40–41; Cunningham, *Genealogy of Nihilism*, 226; Henry, *Essence of Manifestation*, 25, 33–42, 45.

280. Macquarrie, *Principles of Christian Theology*, 65–66.

281. Henry, *Incarnation*, 168–71; *Words of Christ*, 73, 95; *Essence of Manifestation*, 474.

282. Balthasar, *Theo-Drama*, II: 58; Henry, *Words of Christ*, 96.

283. Deikman, "'I' = Awareness," 426; Henry, *I Am the Truth*, 107.

284. Proust, *In Search of Lost Time*, VI: 470.

285. Gallagher, "Diversity of Selves," 20; D. Hart, *Experience of God*, 156, 171, 197; Sorabji, *Self*, 260–61.

286. Henry, *Words of Christ*, 12; Vogeley and Gallagher, "Self in the Brain," 118–19, 129.

287. Barresi and Martin, "History as Prologue," 34–47; Murphy, "Nonreductive Physicalist Response," 67.

288. Perry, "On Knowing One's Self," 388.

a unity.[289] Our interiority intuits its unified distinctiveness,[290] even in infancy.[291] Though disorders can degrade its appreciation,[292] the psyche regulates the life-sustaining equilibrium.[293] The personal identity's unity thereby resists actual disruption.[294]

Each personal identity as our perspective on everything, including that identity itself, normally correlates to a particular body, which is from where we have that perspective.[295] "The human body," Wittgenstein saw, "is the best picture of the human soul."[296] The earthly body seals this unity of our individuality,[297] but death breaks that seal (1 Cor 15:50). A dead body is a nobody. In the afterlife, to the extent an intermediate state exists, an operative body is effectively absent,[298] and the body in the resurrected life is a revolutionary one.[299] In the latter, the "soul-based" "corruptible" body of this life "will be changed out [ἀλλαγησόμεθα]"[300] for the "spirit-based" "incorruptible" body (15:42–53). The "earthly house, the frame, is dismantled [καταλυθῇ]" and replaced with "a building from God, a house made with no hands, eternal in the heavens" (2 Cor 5:1). "Though what is buried cannot inhabit the eternal heavenly regions," Pheme Perkins explained, "what is raised has the attributes appropriate to eternal bodies."[301]

The incorruptible body is clearly not the body we have now nor the result of salvaging this chassis, but is from God's intervention.[302] In

289. Panksepp, *Affective Neuroscience*, 307.

290. Balthasar, *Theo-Drama*, II: 285–86; Vogeley and Gallagher, "Self in the Brain," 125.

291. Rochat, "What Is It Like?" 69–71; Stern, *Interpersonal World*, 10.

292. Parnas and Sass, "Structure of Self-Consciousness," 532–40.

293. Jung, *Modern Man*, 17

294. D. Hart, *Experience of God*, 198–200; Hasker, *Emergent Self*, 128; Strawson, "Minimal Subject," 253–55.

295. Henry, *I Am the Truth*, 123; Wippel, *Metaphysical Thought of Thomas*, 367–75.

296. Wittgenstein, "Philosophie Der Psychologie," ¶ 25.

297. Barth, *Romans*, 199 (6:6); Henry, *Incarnation*, 179; Legrand, "Phenomenological Dimensions," 217.

298. Nichols, *Death and Afterlife*, 46–75.

299. Demarest, *Cross and Salvation*, 475–76; Yates, *Between Death and Resurrection*, 209–10.

300. This verb, from the adjective *another* (ἄλλος), means changing form without changing identity. BDAG, 45–47; Thiselton, *First Corinthians*, 1295 & n.187.

301. Perkins, *First Corinthians*, 187.

302. Bynum, "Material Continuity," 51–85; Dalferth, *Creatures of Possibility*, xviii.

Thomastic terms, the resurrection is "supernatural,"³⁰³ entirely different prime matter,³⁰⁴ or, in modern terms, "transphysical."³⁰⁵ Thus, no matter how similar the terrestrial and resurrected bodies turn out to be, they are discontinuous, separated by the eon and the glories.³⁰⁶ As Ernst Käsemann concluded, death does not "change" the body but "breach[es] . . . the old and the new. Only miracle can bridge the two."³⁰⁷ The terrestrial body, to the extent it is a unifying package in this life,³⁰⁸ therefore cannot preclude division in the next. Only the personal identity can do that.

5. We Each Live as a Multilateral Personal Character

The personal identity, despite its centrality to us, is not us.³⁰⁹ It experiences the life we are leading, but is not who is leading that life.³¹⁰ The personal identity underlies, but is not, the inner life.³¹¹ As psychiatry bears witness, identity lacks form.³¹² While identity centers the psychological contents of this life, it is not the contents of this life,³¹³ and without the contents we are bare stare.³¹⁴ Instead, the *I* who lives and is formed in life is the personal character.³¹⁵ Each individual life is this character.³¹⁶ "Character is the fixed individual form of a human," Carl Jung perceived.³¹⁷ This personal character is the bundle of self-things, the things that matter to us and drive

---

303. Dahl, *Resurrection of the Body*, 49.

304. Brower, *Aquinas's Ontology*, 202–3.

305. N. T. Wright, *Resurrection*, 477.

306. Harding, *Paul's Eschatological Anthropology*, 405; Kooton, *Paul's Anthropology in Context*, 305.

307. Käsemann, *Perspectives on Paul*, 8–9.

308. Fitzpatrick, *Aquinas on Bodily Identity*, 124.

309. Parnas and Sass, "Structure of Self-Consciousness," 528; Rosenzweig, *Star of Redemption*, 76–79; C. Taylor, *Sources of the Self*, 27.

310. Baker, *Persons and Bodies*, 59, 69, 92; Gillman, *Death of Death*, 266; Pannenberg, *ST*, III: 561–62.

311. D. Hart, *Experience of God*, 198–99.

312. Deikman, "'I' = Awareness," 422.

313. Tillich, *ST*, III: 27–28.

314. Whitehead, *Process and Reality*, 194.

315. Balthasar, *Theo-Drama*, I: 485; Bergson, *Time and Free Will*, 172; Cooper, *Holy Eros*, 12.

316. Guardini, *World and the Person*, 112–13, 119.

317. Jung, *Modern Man*, 74.

us.[318] The "self worth wanting," Kathy Wilkes observed, is "something with a character; where emotions, decisions, actions, and reactions spring from a reasonably coherent cluster of beliefs and values."[319] Charles Taylor concurred, "What I am as a self . . . is essentially defined by the way things have significance for me."[320]

Humanity has repeatedly found that each of us, centered on a personal identity, is a personal character, though different terminologies have been applied in expressing this finding.[321] To label the individual essence as the *personal character* is to label the same phenomena that is traditionally labeled the *soul* but without the suggestion of the latter's contested substantiality.[322] Origen understood the soul as the willed personality guided both by the spirit (the higher element) and by the flesh (the carnal element), or, as Crouzel explained Origen's position, "The soul is torn between the spirit and the attraction of the earthly body, the flesh. . . . In itself, by reason of the two elements or tendencies that divide it, the soul is in league with both sides."[323] The Hegelian *I* is similarly viewed as the "individual personality" with "its self-identity."[324] The "I," Hegel noted, has "a *content* which it *differentiates* from itself" and through this is "the dividing of itself." "This content is, in its difference, itself the 'I' . . . ."[325] Rahner describes the "categorical experience" built on the "irreducible datum of existence."[326] The term that Jennifer Radden uses for "the attributes comprising individuals' own unique self-concepts," including the "beliefs, values, desires, and other psychological features," is the "characterization identity."[327] Other scholars see the personal character and the personal identity as the narrative self, constituting our experiences and

---

318. Henry, *Material Phenomenology*, 6, 132; Highet, *Man's Unconquerable Mind*, 8; Perry, *Identity*, 234.

319. Wilkes, "Know Thyself," 29.

320. C. Taylor, *Sources of the Self*, 74.

321. Horst, *Cognitive Pluralism*, 324; Johnston, *Surviving Death*, 261–63, 316–17; Krapiec, *I-Man*, 90–91.

322. Edwards, *After Death?* 81–82; Karkkainen, "Multidimensional Monism," 219; O'Laughlin, "Anthropology of Evagrius Ponticus," 359.

323. Crouzel, *Origen*, 88–89, 92.

324. C. Taylor, *Hegel*, 298.

325. Hegel, *Phenomenology of Spirit*, ¶ 799 (p. 486).

326. Rahner, *Foundations*, 26–35.

327. Radden, "Multiple Selves," 550–51.

dispositions, built upon the subjective person.[328] Or each of us can be the self-as-object and the self-as-subject.[329]

One reviewer concluded that, after the soul lost the uncontestedness of its existence, "Contemporary human identity has become a cauldron of conflicting and relativised ego-expressions jostling for a safe anchor amidst the chaos of pluriformity."[330] The unending word combinations vindicate in other contexts the philosophical serviceability of numerical identity and qualitative identity;[331] the former has one instance, which is like the personal identity, and the latter tracks its changes, which is like the personal character.[332] Despite the many labels and once the mysteries of existence, awareness, and substance are conceded,[333] the various scholarly formulations all see the individual as a package of inner features centered on the unitary identity.[334] For convenience, if not accuracy, this is called here the *personal character* on which is centered the *personal identity*. This, not coincidentally, is also the everyday sense of the individual.[335]

This exploration therefore concentrates on the *essential* self, not the Christian Neoplatonist idea of essentially *relating* to Creator and creations.[336] This direction is taken for three reasons. First, as has been explained, the elemental *I* is the more common understanding,[337] which means the proposed model should work broadly. Second, given the personal identity's unity as described in the last section, the essential *I* is more sensible at least when we are being sensible, which means the proposed model can be sensibly applied. Third, the essential *I* only taxes the thesis more because the essential *I* implies indivisibility; if the individual merely exists in relation to something such as God,[338] nothing precludes

---

328. Parnas and Sass, "Structure of Self-Consciousness," 525; Vogeley and Gallagher, "Self in the Brain," 118–19, 129.

329. Legrand, "Phenomenological Dimensions," 205.

330. McFarlane, "Strange News," 110.

331. Parfit, *Reasons and Persons*, 201–2.

332. Gallagher, "Diversity of Selves," 15–16.

333. Lopez, *Gift and Unity*, 1.

334. Kierkegaard, *Two Ages*, 73.

335. Strawson, "The Self," 3.

336. Pabst, *Metaphysics*, 248–51, 270, 286, 300, 383, 442.

337. Baker, *Persons and Bodies*, 125; Yu, *Being and Relation*, 61, 67.

338. Balthasar, *Theo-Drama*, III: 204–7; Guardini, *World and the Person*, 21, 31, 141; Volf, *After Our Likeness*, 182.

its division. God can relate to a bifurcated entity as easily as a unified one. If God is *the* constant for the individual, then any indivisibility of the individual is not a constant.[339] As Francis of Assisi recognized, "what a man is in the sight of God, so much he is, and no more."[340] This means that the proposed model should work at least as well with any other understanding of the *I* as it does with the indivisible essential *I*.

Indeed, if relationships are what essentially comprise the individual, division is eventually the individual's fate.[341] Composites naturally divide.[342] That is, an individual based exclusively on relationships has, as a proponent of this view observed, "no essential, stable, autonomous self," but "is continuously reconstituted by the complex interactions." "Insofar as the self is always a self-in-relationship, when it is embedded in a new relational matrix it becomes a new self."[343] So, if the individual is composed entirely of relationships, the individual is unavoidably divisible as relationships come and go.[344] In contrast, it is the essential *I* that resists division.

In any event, the in-itself individual can co-exist with the relational model if that is normative, but limiting the examination here to the in-itself model is less presumptive about to what extent the relational model contributes. In other words, even if the individual is exclusively based on relationships, a relationship still entails at least two related things, and a personal relationship entails at least two related persons; so, where there is a personal relationship, there are necessarily persons, and each is an *I*, regardless of whether the relationship is the chicken or egg. Accordingly, the *I* exists no matter how focused we are on relationships and can be called almost anything, but, independent of labels, humanity has learned that the *I* is at a minimum the accretion of the led life, which is called here the personal character, along with the inherently unifying first-person perspective, called here the personal identity.

---

339. Speyr, *Gates of Eternal Life*, 17.

340. Francis, "Words of Admonition," 20.

341. Kierkegaard, *Sickness Unto Death*, 13; Reddy, *How Infants Know Minds*, 122.

342. Gregory of Nyssa, *Life of Moses*, Bk II (p. 101); John, "Fount of Knowledge," III,I,8 (p. 185); Mullin, "Selves, Diverse and Divided," 6–8.

343. Eastman, *Paul and the Person*, 146, 160, 167.

344. James, *Principles of Psychology*, I: 294; Turner, *Theology, Psychology and Plural Self*, 46, 52–53, 82–83.

6. The Personal Character Is Divided

Despite the individual's practical singularity in the earthly body as has been noticed everywhere and the individual's inherent unity in the personal identity as has been noticed by nearly everyone, the individual as a personal character is widely known to be a multiplicity.[345] Any misunderstanding of this is a misunderstanding of life.[346] "Every man lives in the twofold *I*," resolved Buber.[347] Poets know this, whether Auden's "Double Man," whose "bones cannot help reassembling themselves," T. S. Eliot's "Both one and many," "a familiar compound ghost," "So I assumed a double part," Emily Dickinson's "cleavage in my mind" unable to "make them fit," Whitman's "I contradict myself," "I contain multitudes," William Wordsworth's "often do I seem / Two consciousnesses," Goethe's "Two souls live in me, alas, / Forever warring with each other," or Alexander Pope's "This light and darkness in our chaos join'd, / What shall divide? The God within the mind."[348] Before the Common Era, Valerius Catullus could elegize, "I love, I hate. / You ask why do this. / I know not, yet feel this. / And it can excruciate."[349]

Wordsworth's "the crowded solitude"[350] is therefore our shared experience,[351] and it is why aloneness is not always loneliness.[352] A person's life always has Dilthey's "double aspect."[353] As each of us asks ourself *What to do?* we posit two *I*'s, the internal asker and the internal listener.[354]

---

345. Gerson, *Knowing Persons*, 277; James, *Varieties of Religious Experience*, 168; Krapiec, *I-Man*, 100, 107, 198, 202; Lawlor, "Postmodern Self," 705; Lowe, *Subjects of Experience*, 30–31.

346. Kierkegaard, *Eighteen Upbuilding Discourses*, 99.

347. Buber, *I and Thou*, 65.

348. Auden, *Double Man*, 12 (prol.); Dickinson, "Life," CVI (p. 57); Eliot, *Four Quartets*, Little Gidding,II,94–97 (p. 53); Goethe, *Faust*, lns 1136–41; Pope, "Essay on Man," 204–5 (II,IV, VI); Whitman, "Song of Myself," 51 (p. 113); Wordsworth, *The Prelude*, II,31–33.

349. This is my rendering of Catullus, "Poem 85": *Odi et amo. / Quare id faciam fortasse requiris. / Nescio, sed fieri sentio / et excrucior.*

350. Wordsmith, *The Prelude*, IX,29.

351. Gallagher, "Diversity of Selves," 21; Küng, *Eternal Life?* 137–38; Wilkes, *Real People*, 102, 130.

352. Arendt, "Thinking," 185; Kierkegaard, *Stages*, 333–34; Montaigne, "Essays," I,39 (p. 177).

353. Dilthey, *Introduction to Human Sciences*, 160 (II.1.3).

354. Kierkegaard, *Concept of Anxiety*, 313.

"With their mixed minds," Radden observed, "normal people are far from simple unities" "and rarely entirely 'single-minded' in its goals and attributes"; "variations among normal people in respect to self-unity" are "a valuable part of human nature."[355] The individual internally moves among opposing voices as if multiple characters in a single story.[356] The singular individual is thus legion[357] and consists of competing personalities of divine and beast.[358] Plato, for this reason, analogized a single self to a city with many residents.[359] Hannah Arendt saw each mind as both "willing and nilling."[360] Wherever *is* and *ought* exist, bifurcation exists.[361] Each human heart is recognizably of two hearts.[362] This is because "different persons," Proust realized, "compose our personality."[363]

The subjective sciences too accept that we each are complex characters on unified platforms.[364] Psychologists treat patients as singular identities anchoring empirical pluralities.[365] Jung saw that, "What drives people to war with themselves is the intuition or the knowledge that they consist of two persons in opposition to one another."[366] James perceived that we are not "ideal abstractions," but "concrete human beings" of "intermediate varieties and mixtures."[367] Extreme cases highlight in the general population this multiplicity of the personal character. The most recognizable case of divisibility is the multiple personality (nka dissociative identity disorder), where memory buffers become pathological.[368]

355. Radden, "Multiple Selves," 547, 561.
356. Hermans, "Dialogical Self," 660.
357. D. Hart, *Experience of God*, 201; Mooney, "Pseudonyms and 'Style,'" 198.
358. Rist, "Plato Says," 103–4, 116.
359. Plato, *Republic*, 368e-369b, 435b-c.
360. Arendt, "Willing," 94, 109.
361. M. Taylor, *Journeys to Selfhood*, 48.
362. Blondel, *Action*, 115, 167 [110, 169].
363. Proust, *In Search of Lost Time*, V: 4.
364. Henry, *I Am the Truth*, 150.
365. James, *Principles of Psychology*, I: 224–25, 338, 344–46, 371–73, 400–401; Turner, *Theology, Psychology and Plural Self*, 76, 119–20, 180–81.
366. Jung, *Modern Man*, 236–37.
367. James, *Varieties of Religious Experience*, 164.
368. Carter and Frith, *Mapping the Mind*, 175–76; Radden, "Multiple Selves," 552–60, 564–67. The *Diagnostic and Statistical Manual of Mental Disorders* (DSM-5) defines a dissociative identity disorder as "two or more distinct personality states" of "marked discontinuity in sense of self" with "[r]ecurrent gaps in the recall . . . inconsistent with ordinary forgetting" that "cause clinically significant distress or impairment in . . . functioning."

Such a plurality of personalities does not become pathological when plural, which is normal, but when the plurality becomes dysfunctional.[369] We all have subpersonalities, but professionals are called in to treat alternate personalities.[370] Another odd case of real-world divisibility involves commissurotomy patients whose brain halves act, instead of semi-independently as is normal, but actually independently, as if two people shared one body; for them, one person simultaneously both senses and does not sense the same object and both registers and does not register the same idea.[371] Such abnormals do more than illustrate that one individual *can* be divisible, but magnify normal selfhood to reveal that it starts out as nearly divided just before the unified selfhood metastasizes. Each of us, to illustrate, has two cerebral hemispheres that have autonomously different orientations—the right half that perceives and intuits holistically, and the left half that analyzes and knows sequentially.[372]

Though in this life the personal character is obviously divided as in conflicted, it is just as obviously not normally divided as in separable, but this is because the previously described personal *identity* unifies experience for self-preservation.[373] This personal identity is what centers the *I*'s of our multiple desires and activities.[374] That is, the first-person experience singularizes the divisible life.[375] While this centering *I* resists division, the lived *I*, which is the personal character, constantly divides with denial, dissociation, self-deception, and repression.[376] Each self, therefore, is a unity that is in either harmony or disharmony, and either one of these implies a unity or else there would be no synchronicity and both imply multiples because even harmony takes two.[377] Kierkegaard summarizes, "there is not one single living human being... who does not

---

369. Hermans, "Dialogical Self," 662; B. Williams, *Problems of the Self*, 17.

370. Turner, *Theology, Psychology and Plural Self*, 90, 101, 179.

371. Wilkes, *Real People*, 141.

372. McGilchrist, *Master and His Emissary*, 1–3, 11, 19, 27–28, 40–44, 52, 220, 226, 330, 352–53, 428.

373. Frankfurt, "Freedom of the Will," 18; James, *Varieties of Religious Experience*, 167; Wilkes, *Real People*, 142–43.

374. Deikman, "'I' = Awareness," 421.

375. Strawson, "The Self," 13.

376. Cavell, "The Self," 601.

377. Arendt, "Thinking," 183, 186; "Willing," 64; McGilchrist, *Master and His Emissary*, 128.

secretly harbor . . . an inner strife, a disharmony . . . ."[378] Hegel reached a similar conclusion: "I am not one of these two taking part in the strife, but I am both the combatants, and am the strife itself."[379]

As individuals have reflected on individuals throughout history, *individual* has had this one constant—each of them is both one and many. The parable is ancient that says each person has two dogs internally warring and is dominated by whichever one the owner chooses to feed.[380] In Jewish tradition, each of us is choosing between two opposing impulses.[381] The *Rule of the Community*, as an example, explains that we each have a spirit of darkness and a spirit of light until the dark spirit is ripped out on judgment day.[382] The church fathers believed that each of us has both a personal angel and a personal demon between which we are constantly preferring.[383] Origen wrote, "To every man there are two attending angels, the one of justice and the other of wickedness. The first speaks to us good thoughts," but, if "the thoughts of our heart be turned to evil, an angel of the devil is speaking to us."[384] "Between these two," Gregory of Nyssa added, "in the middle is man."[385] Such concretizations of the one person's two inner orientations have been recorded since antiquity.[386] Even moderns who believe the self is merely billions of neurons explain that those neurons coalesce into competing orientations like how citizens in a single republic coalesce into factional parties.[387] No matter the approach, after differences in idioms are shelved and once nihilism is flushed out, the consensus of thought follows the common observation that the personal character (centered on the personal identity) is divided.[388] In this life, therefore, each one of us is two selves[389] or, as persons

---

378. Kierkegaard, *Sickness Unto Death*, 136.

379. Hegel, *Lectures on Philosophy of Religion*, I: 64.

380. Graham, *Holy Spirit*, 89–90.

381. Gammie, "Spatial and Ethical Dualism," 357–58; McKnight, *James*, 92, 119.

382. Kooton, *Paul's Anthropology in Context*, 18–20, 24, 92.

383. Gregory of Nyssa, *Life of Moses*, Bk II (p. 43); Eckhart, "Book of 'Benedictus,'" 240.

384. Origen, "Homilies on Luke," 201 [Hom. 12].

385. Gregory of Nyssa, "Life of Moses," 45 [2: *Jaeger*, pp. 45–46].

386. Balthasar, *Theo-Logic*, III: 387–88.

387. Hofstadter, *Metamagical Themas*, 782–90.

388. Grenz, *Theology for the Community*, 181; McGilchrist, *Master and His Emissary*, 243, 461–62.

389. Koehn, *Nature of Evil*, 239; Montaigne, "Essays," II,16 (p. 469).

are normally counted, is the one divided self.[390] "[W]e are, I know not how," Montaigne saw, "double in ourselves."[391] Socrates was right: One individual is two inner selves.[392]

7. Scripture Reflects Personal Identity Centering Divided Character

Christian anthropology, like the reality it comes from, reflects that we are a divided personal character centered on a unified personal identity, and this is primarily because Christian anthropology is realistic rather than speculative.[393] Scriptural terminology is likewise realistic, omitting philosophical terms like ipseity, form, or Me*,[394] while employing such lyricist terms as soul, spirit, or heart.[395] Scripture also uses definite descriptions or indexicals for the individual. Jesus' declaration "I Am" (Matt 14:27// Mark 6:50//John 6:20) is an example. Scripture's principal designations, however, are like those in life—names.[396] Names define, separate, and signal being,[397] such as the Father, the Son, the Spirit,[398] or the emphatically first-person singular Tetragrammaton (Exod 3:13–15).[399] God's name is God's self (Isa 52:6; Col 3:17; Rev 19:12),[400] and salvation is in no other name (Acts 4:12). Names designate even in tough cases like the raised dead, such as Lazarus before and after death (John 11:17–44).[401] And names identify eternal destiny (Rev 13:8).

Perhaps more relevantly to the afterlife topic, Scripture's postmortem designations entail unified identities. Neither the spirit-mistress of

---

390. James, *Varieties of Religious Experience*, 498–99.

391. Montaigne, *Complete Works*, 315.

392. Plato, *Republic*, 439b-e, 443d-e, 580d, 603c-d, 604b.

393. Berkouwer, *Man: Image of God*, 30 n.37, 194–95; Richardson, *Christian Apologetics*, 224.

394. This is Galen Strawson's terminology. "The Self," 16.

395. Brown, "Spirit," 689–708; Harder, "Soul," 676–86; Sorg, "Heart," 180–84.

396. Gracia, *Individuality*, 201–2; Pannenberg, *Anthropology in Theological Perspective*, 294.

397. Montaigne, "Essays," II,16 (p. 468).

398. Basil, "Letters," 210.4 (p. 250).

399. Erickson, *Christian Theology*, 295; Zizioulas, "On Being a Person," 33.

400. Beale, *Colossians and Philemon*, 307; Tonstad, *Revelation*, 277.

401. See also 1 Kgs 17:17–23; 2 Kgs 4:20–35; 13:21; Matt 9:23–25//Mark 5:35–42// Luke 8:49–55; 7:12–15; Acts 9:37–41; 20:9–12.

Endor nor Saul nor even Samuel had difficulty with Samuel's identity in death once he was revealed (1 Sam 28:3–15).[402] When the transfigured Jesus met the deceased Moses and Elijah, their names identified (Matt 17:3//Mark 9:4//Luke 9:30, 33). Identities in the Lazarus parable were likewise seamless into death (16:19–31). Finally, the Jesus who is resurrected has full identity with the Jesus who was crucified.[403]

Unlike personal designations in Scripture, which are consistent, personal integrity in Scripture is not.[404] Identities blur, for instance, when the Son comes from God, the Spirit comes from the Father, the Son and Father are of one, and the Father is in the Son and vice-versa (John 8:42; 10:30, 38; 14:11; 15:26). Despite the nearly seamless distinctions, the church took each Divine as a personal identity (ὑπόστασις), and God was not a fourth.[405] Another scriptural identity challenge is when God makes "accommodation within" each beloved, the Father abiding within us through the Spirit, we being in Christ and he in us, each in God's image (Gen 1:26–27; 5:1–3; John 14:16–20, 23–24; 17:20–24; 1 John 2:6, 24; 3:23–24; 4:12–16).[406] This relation between God and believer, despite being unbounded, does not endanger the existence of either,[407] but the relationship exposes unity without lost identity.[408] Your identity does not cease although you are "not your own" (1 Cor 6:19).[409] Rather, the individual, when uniting with the other, retains identity.[410] Salvation involves participating individually in God's personal existence,[411] and this includes identifying with Christ.[412]

---

402. J. Cooper, *Body, Soul, and Life*, 65.

403. Jenson, *ST*, I: 174, 198–200; Karkkainen, *Christology*, 151; Moltmann, *Theology of Hope*, 187.

404. Jenson, *ST*, I: 119.

405. Ayres, *Augustine and the Trinity*, 108, 325–26; Jenson, *ST*, I: 118–19, 152; Monk, *Christianity and Non-Dualism*, 20.

406. Demarest, *Cross and Salvation*, 330–33.

407. Guardini, *World and the Person*, 145; Kruse, *Letters of John*, 81, 143, 165.

408. Marshall, *Epistles of John*, 202; Volf, *After Our Likeness*, 187.

409. Christensen, "Problem, Promise, and Process," 28–29; Cyril, *John*, II: Bk 11, ch 11 [734] (p. 303).

410. Henry, *God, Revelation and Authority*, I: 73; Lubac, *Catholicism*, 330; *Theological Fragments*, 60–61.

411. Cooper, *Naturally Human, Supernaturally God*, 41; A. Williams, *Architecture of Theology*, 219; Zizioulas, *Being as Communion*, 49–50.

412. Charlton, *Non-Dualism*, 15.

In Scripture, the earthly *body*, while it is the substrate for the single psychophysical entity,[413] is not the personal *whole*, but is the personal *physicality*.[414] Said from the noncorporeal side, the person, though unquestionably a spirit-body,[415] is spirit-based (1 Cor 12:12–16, 24–26; 2 Cor 5:1–2).[416] And, at death, the unity of the spirit-body as described in Scripture undeniably breaks,[417] for "the body without spirit is death" (Jas 2:26). "The Spirit gives life; the flesh profits nothing" (John 6:63). At home in the body is exiled from the Lord (2 Cor 5:6–8).[418] Even the Hebrew Scriptures, which are insulated from Greek philosophical influence and its soul-body dualism, "repeatedly call attention to cognitive and affective aspects of human nature," philosopher of the mind Paul MacDonald concluded, and these "indicate an inner, personal dimension, something which is hidden from others but open to one's own awareness."[419] Scripture often conceptualizes the individual's interiority with such Hebraic terms as the *conflicted soul* (Pss 42:5, 11; 43:5), the *heart and heart* (12:2), the *core* (51:5–6, 64:6)[420] or, in Greek, the *belly* (John 7:38).[421] Unlike the earthly body, this inner life can live eternally[422] and includes, as philosopher of science Nancey Murphy lists, "memory, moral character, interpersonal relations, and, especially, relationship with God."[423]

Scripture reveals that this frequently referred-to inner life for each of us is a duality.[424] Otherwise, the imperative "Let your left hand not know what your right does" (Matt 6:3) is literally nonsense.[425] The James epistle notes, though it "should not be" the case, somehow "From the same mouth comes blessing and cursing" (3:10). Scripture shows, as Bornkamm

---

413. Murphy, *Bodies and Souls*, 22, 141.
414. Gundry, *Soma in Biblical Theology*, 79, 84, 112–13, 154–55, 212.
415. Hughes, "Is the Soul Immortal?" 188.
416. Gundry, *Soma in Biblical Theology*, 175.
417. Erickson, *Christian Theology*, 555.
418. Harding, *Paul's Eschatological Anthropology*, 356.
419. MacDonald, *History of the Concept*, 2–3, 12.
420. "Midst [*qereb*]" in the construct to *person* means the "inward part of man," as in the "seat" "of thought and emotion." *BDB*, 899.
421. Bultmann, *Theology of the NT*, I: 20.1 (pp. 221–22); J. Cooper, "Biblical Anthropology," 219–20, 227; Geisler, *ST*, 721–22.
422. Ratzinger, *Eschatology*, 159.
423. Murphy, *Bodies and Souls*, 132, 138.
424. Blosser, *Become Like the Angels*, 36.
425. Lenski, *Matthew*, 257–58; Nolland, *Matthew*, 276.

found, that "Man's discord is part of his human nature. He himself is the contradiction. This is the 'I' of [Paul's] cry 'Wretched man that I am!'"[426] This dualistic understanding of the individual is, however, best recognized in Scripture's portrayal of our two orientations, the next topic.

8. Each Individual Is Oriented Both Towards and Away from God

While pagan anthropology relies on a dualism of substances like body and soul,[427] Christian anthropology relies on a duality of lifeways understood chiefly as for and against God,[428] but also understood as Spirit and Sin,[429] morality and immorality,[430] faith and unfaith,[431] towards eternity and towards death,[432] or love oriented outwardly and inwardly (Augustine's *caritas* and *cupiditas*).[433] Regardless of the precise terminology used for the primary orientations, the images of God, namely each self,[434] choose in primordial sinfulness between for God and for self.[435] From this Hebrew inheritance, the NT "laid the foundations of the structure," Guardini discerned, which is "a division," "a separation of two 'worlds.'"[436] That is, the life that the NT describes, which is expressed independent of "ontological structure," Bultmann realized, "offers the possibility of choosing one's goal, of deciding for good or evil, for or against God."[437]

---

426. Bornkamm, *Paulus*, 127.

427. Brookins, "Greco-Roman Perspectives," 44–45.

428. Dunning, *Grace, Faith, and Holiness*, 158–59; Gunton, *Father, Son and Holy Spirit*, 161; Jenson, *ST*, II: 137; Pannenberg, *Anthropology in Theological Perspective*, 21; Ratzinger, *Eschatology*, 63–64, 156; C. Taylor, *Secular Age*, 276.

429. Harding, *Paul's Eschatological Anthropology*, 4, 87.

430. Kierkegaard, *Two Ages*, 73.

431. Dalferth, *Creatures of Possibility*, 26–27, 197–98.

432. White, *Life Beyond Death*, 26.

433. Arendt, *Love and Augustine*, 17–19, 23, 27, 30, 34, 77–78, 90–91, 94–95.

434. Barth, *CD III* §43–44, 43.2 (pp. 26, 43 [029, 047]); Pannenberg, *Human Nature*, 13.

435. Guardini, *World and the Person*, 42–43; Watkin, "Kierkegaard—Dying," 106–7.

436. Guardini, *World and the Person*, 93.

437. Bultmann, *Theology of the NT*, I: 18.4 (p. 209).

Which orientation is natural to us need not be decided here; we each clearly have both, and each of us jostle the positive and the negative.[438] The individual is thus split in this way, noted Augustine,[439] and on this split pivots ethical life,[440] worshipping God or self.[441] "[W]hatever is done or devised among men is," Luther saw, "either righteousness or sin before God."[442] Even if postlapsarian humans are in essence totally depraved, they are in reality dually oriented,[443] God's child and God's enemy.[444] We are godly in essence and ungodly in practice[445] or, in postmodern terms, essentially good and existentially estranged.[446] The designations mostly used in this discourse are the encompassing ones of godly and ungodly, but, regardless of what labels the dualistic sides, each of us is both.[447]

Living with temptation, which we all experience, is itself an internal clash of orientations,[448] and we each choose Adam's assertion of the self *and* Jesus' obedience of the divine.[449] Balthasar speaks for each of us, who is to glorify God wholly:[450] "the powers of evil are not simply alien and external to him," but "a shaft in him that reaches down to the deepest abysses. Thus, he stands in a baffling solidarity with the powers and superior forces of negativity . . . , while at the same time he is fighting off these same powers as far as he can."[451] While no one entirely opts for evil because something intrinsic longs for God,[452] "For the most part, men are by nature," even the humanist prince had to accept, "prone to

---

438. Balthasar, *Theo-Drama*, IV: 188; Guardini, *Freedom, Grace, and Destiny*, 34; Kempis, *Imitation of Christ*, II,IX,7.

439. Augustine, *Confessions*, VIII,v,11, ix,21–23 (pp. 140, 147–49).

440. Evans and Roberts, "Ethics," 224–25, 228.

441. Grenz, *Theology for the Community*, 188.

442. Luther, "De Servo Arbitrio," 308.

443. Berkouwer, *Man: Image of God*, 38, 65, 140–41, 146–55.

444. Greggs, *Barth, Origen, and Universalism*, 207; Luther, *Galatians*, 226 [WA 401,367 (3:6)].

445. Olson, *Mosaic of Christian Belief*, 204, 208.

446. Dunning, *Grace, Faith, and Holiness*, 160.

447. Freud, *Future of an Illusion*, VII.F (p. 659).

448. Baker, *Persons and Bodies*, 157; Kempis, *Imitation of Christ*, I,XIII,3.

449. Rosner, "Son of God," 234.

450. Gunton, *Father, Son and Holy Spirit*, 9.

451. Balthasar, *Theo-Drama*, IV: 137.

452. Aquinas, *Compendium*, § 174 (p. 135); Perl, *Theophany*, 55–56; Tillich, *ST*, II: 167.

unbelief, inclined to evil. . . ."[453] Paul agreed, "All have sinned" (Rom 3:23). Christ, therefore, indicts everyone at least to an extent with, "you being evil" (Luke 11:13//Matt 7:11).[454] We cannot occupy the other extreme either.[455] Only One is entirely good (Matt 19:17//Mark 10:18//Luke 18:19) and thereby lacks division.[456] Apart from this exception, everyone or nearly everyone is not wholly holy,[457] though the healthy among us live life whole, leaning good or evil in any given moment.[458] Each of us is oriented both godly and ungodly[459] or, in superficially secular terms, both good and evil.[460] Whenever anyone takes life not as both but as either-or, Kierkegaard understood, this is "tragic proof of how flabby your soul is."[461] No one "is so lowly that he can do no wrong," nor is anyone "too lowly to carry the image of God."[462] We are each an "Edenic echo" *and* a "side of deep depravity."[463] The image of God is certainly godly and more or less godless.[464] While the extraordinary could at least theoretically be entirely consumed with hatred or utterly permeated by God, neither is realistic.[465]

Because so much turns on these dueling personal orientations, Scripture stresses them.[466] "You're from the below; I am from the above. You're of this world; of this world I am not" (John 8:23).[467] We are either

---

453. Erasmus, "De Libero Arbitrio," 41.

454. Henry, *Words of Christ*, 22.

455. Gregory of Nyssa, *Life of Moses*, Bk I,Prol. (pp. 4–5).

456. Gilson, *Spirit of Mediaeval Philosophy*, 92.

457. Balthasar, "Epilogue: Apokatastasis," 242–43; Barth, *CD II/2*, § 39.2 (p. 746); Cabasilas, *Life in Christ*, Bk II § 7 (p. 77).

458. Milbank, *Theology and Social Theory*, 415.

459. Charlton, *Non-Dualism*, 53.

460. Fromm, "Modern Man," 27.

461. Kierkegaard, *Either/Or*, II: 145.

462. Kierkegaard, *Upbuilding Discourses*, 210.

463. Kierkegaard, *Eighteen Upbuilding Discourses*, 126–27; *For Self-Examination*, 20.

464. "[T]he human race [*Slægt*] is certainly related [*i Slægt*] to the divine, but it is also more or less degenerate [*vanslægtet*]." Kierkegaard, *Upbuilding Discourses*, 231.

465. Benedict XVI, *Spe Salvi*, 45–46; Dalferth, *Creatures of Possibility*, 78; Marsilius, *Defensor Pacis*, II: I,XI,6 (p. 42).

466. Balthasar, *Theo-Drama*, IV: 184; Richardson, *Christian Apologetics*, 131.

467. Schwarz, *Human Being*, 19.

toward or against God (8:44, 47),⁴⁶⁸ and humanity began this way. To the image of God, who is endowed with godly wisdom and love connecting us to God,⁴⁶⁹ it was the partaking of good and evil's knowledge that offered godlikeness, though it also meant God's condemnation (Gen 2:9, 17; 3:5–6, 22). In striving to be godlike, the human worships the self, the personal god, which is the opposite of godlikeness. Thus, God's image, even when unspoiled, was torn between enjoying God's glory and having God-like glory, and that image choose disobediently and achieved separation from God.⁴⁷⁰ On this primordial anthropology, Christianity has built (Gen 9:6; 1 Cor 11:7; 2 Cor 3:18).⁴⁷¹ That is, despite the human rebellion, we each remain his image to a degree, even the unbelieving, even if infinitesimally,⁴⁷² and the divine pedigree is indestructible.⁴⁷³ Humanity's "divine likeness," de Lubac noted, "may be dimmed, veiled, disfigured, but it is always there."⁴⁷⁴

The image of God, though all around us, is unequally distributed among us—the best heroically holy, the worst not wholly lacking.⁴⁷⁵ For all of us, our life choices are scripturally described as the two ways, which God presented to his chosen as "blessing and curse," "life and good, death and evil, for I command you today to love the Lord your God, walk in his ways, . . . so you may live . . . , but, if your heart turns and you disobey, . . . you will perish in perishing" (Deut 11:26; 30:15–20). And we have chosen both ways (Jer 21:8; Jas 3:5–12).⁴⁷⁶ Following this scriptural approach for expressing the individual's dualistic choices, early Christian training taught that humanity faced the two ways of life and of death.⁴⁷⁷ Since we chronically choose against God, Scripture tells us to *turn back* (šûb) or to *change the mind* (μετανοέω), often translated in each case as *repent*,

---

468. C. Taylor, "Humanity," 321–23.

469. Harrison, *God's Many-Splendored Image*, 15, 187.

470. Mostert, *God and the Future*, 206.

471. Berkouwer, *Man: Image of God*, 44; McConville, *Being Human*, 28, 43; Schwobel, "Human Being as Relational," 149.

472. Geisler, *ST*, 57; Ludlow, *Universal Salvation*, 45; Rae, "Salvation in Community," 190.

473. Lossky, *Mystical Theology*, 124.

474. Lubac, *Catholicism*, 283.

475. Harrison, *God's Many-Splendored Image*, 35; Spaemann, *Essays in Anthropology*, 60–61.

476. Luther, "De Servo Arbitrio," 316; Martin, *Will Many Be Saved?* 91.

477. Milavec, *Didache*, 3 (1:1), 44.

which is calling for us to orient away from the wrath and toward the life (*e.g.*, Acts 26:17–18; 2 Cor 3:16; 12:21; 1 Thess 1:9; Jas 5:20; 1 Pet 2:25).[478] But we don't, not always. "To each by his deeds he will give: eternal life to those who by enduring in doing good, seek glory, honor, and incorruption, but wrath and fury to those partisans who, while disobeying the truth, obey unrighteousness" (Rom 2:6–8).[479]

The NT often expresses these orientations of for-self and for-God as two forces—the flesh of *I* and the Spirit in *me*.[480] Our problem is not living in the flesh, which is what this life is, but is our life being oriented by the flesh, which is what spiritual death is.[481] "Love not the world nor things in the world," "for all in the world—the flesh's craving, the eyes' craving, and the living's arrogance—is from not the Father but the world. The world with its cravings is passing, but anyone doing God's will abides into the age" (1 John 2:15–17). The priority is "the removal of the body of flesh" (Col 2:11). The pathology described is not the carnal, but the carnality. "The flesh's mindset is death, but the spirit's mindset is life and peace, for the flesh's mindset is hostile to God"; "while the body is death through sin, the spirit is life through righteousness" (Rom 8:6–7, 10–11). We live out these opposing mindsets of flesh and spirit.[482] "While I live no more, in me lives Christ. As now I live in flesh, I live in faith" (Gal 2:20). But we resist the call: "the flesh craves against the spirit, and the spirit against the flesh" (5:17), and we are the battleground.[483] Among less certain points, the scriptural call is for a "transformed identity," Susan Eastman noted, and the battle "suggest[s] two contrasting yet concurrent realms of existence in which 'I live.' The first is characterized as 'the flesh' and the second is characterized as 'the faith.'"[484]

The source of the dual orientations is outside the thesis, which is intentional because the source of one of them, ungodliness, is controverted. It is sufficient here to accept that we are earth-spirit composites

---

478. Demarest, *Cross and Salvation*, 250–51.

479. Boer, *Defeat of Death*, 154.

480. J. Cooper, *Body, Soul, and Life*, 109–10; Nickelsburg, *Resurrection, Immortality, and Eternal Life*, 232–34; Watkin, "Kierkegaard—Dying," 105.

481. Bultmann, *Theology of the NT*, I: 23.1 (pp. 239–40); Mouw, "Relevance of Biblical Eschatology," 65.

482. Eastman, *Paul and the Person*, 91.

483. Oakes, *Galatians*, 167.

484. Eastman, *Paul and the Person*, 156.

(Gen 2:7; 3:17–19; Ps 104:29–30)[485] that each consist of the infirm and the willing (Matt 26:41//Mark 14:38; 14:33).[486] The foolishly best explanation of humanity's fall need not be endorsed.[487] "To want to give a logical explanation of the coming of sin into the world is a stupidity that can occur only to people who are comically worried about finding an explanation," Kierkegaard disapproved.[488] Only the flagrant must be acknowledged on this point—each mere human, or nearly all of them, is a mixture of both orientations.[489]

So, both are true: "To the extent we say 'we have no sin,' we mislead ourselves," and "All abiding in him are not sinning" (1 John 1:8, 3:6). In close order the same author says believers necessarily sin and necessarily do not, and the text hardly bears the traditional escape: The first statement, by using the noun "sin" with the present indicative "have," is taken as *occasional* sinning, and the second, by using the verb "sin" itself in the present indicative, is taken as *habitual* sinning.[490] Rather than straining at grammatical distinctions for an unstated sinning frequency, which will vary in any case, the stated positions are clearly paradoxical, and the orientations are the paradox.[491] When sinning, we refuse God, and, when godly, we do not. Each individual is demonic and divine.[492]

Faith, understood as either believing or not, might seem to be an exception and actually be either-or, but here too we resist extremes.[493] Scripture repeatedly states the obvious: The faith of believers can range from strong to weak (Rom 14:1—15:13).[494] They can have *great* faith, *much* faith, or *little* faith (Matt 8:26; 14:31; 15:28; 16:8; 17:20; 8:10//Luke 7:9; Matt 6:30//Luke 12:28).[495] As a result, the apostles sought more faith

485. Dunning, *Grace, Faith, and Holiness*, 65.

486. Brown, *Death of the Messiah*, I: 199–200; Gundry, *Soma in Biblical Theology*, 110–11.

487. Dahl, *Resurrection of the Body*, 69, 82; Pascal, *Pensees*, 445 (p. 124).

488. Kierkegaard, *Concept of Anxiety*, 320–22.

489. Come, *Kierkegaard as Theologian*, 132–33; Torrance, *Atonement*, 314. Christ is no exception to a statement about a *mere* human. Guardini, *Freedom, Grace, and Destiny*, 195–96.

490. Kruse, *Letters of John*, 126–32.

491. Parsenios, *First . . . John*, 62, 73–74, 93.

492. Tillich, *ST*, III: 231.

493. Barth, *CD II/2*, § 35.2 (p. 348).

494. Matera, *Romans*, 142.

495. Carson, "Matthew," 202, 215–16.

and were thankful when their faith increased (17:5; 2 Cor 10:15; 1 Thess 3:10; 2 Thess 1:3). We are therefore to seek our faith's completion or maturation (Col 1:28—2:2). For this reason, we are called to love God with our *whole* being (Deut 6:5; Matt 22:37//Mark 12:30//Luke 10:27; 1 Thess 5:23), which of course is recognizing that partial is where we are.[496] Even when worshiping the risen Christ, the disciples were *two-minded* (ἐδίστασαν,[497] Matt 28:17).

James, to describe these divided orientations, blended *two* and *soul* to coin *dual-souled* (δίψυχος, 1:8, 4:8).[498] This term likely reflects the Platonic divided self.[499] The neologism resurfaced in *The Shepherd of Hermas* where its multiple uses (fifty-five times) confirm that δίψυχος refers to a person divided between two spirits, one good and one evil.[500] We all are divided in this way unless our innermost being wills exclusively the good.[501] Although doubt displaces faith,[502] both ordinarily go together in us,[503] which is no contradiction but again the coexisting orientations.[504] Each of us has "as God has distributed faith's measure" (Rom 12:3), and "the Son of God's true knowledge" is what is "completing a fellow into the measure of Christ's fullness" (Eph 4:13). Some scholars are not "prepared" to accept that these statements reveal that faith varies until completion,[505] but prepared scholars recognize that faith in this life comes in degrees.[506] Invariably understood, therefore, is the cry, "I believe; help my unbelief" (Mark 9:24).[507]

---

496. Dahl, *Resurrection of the Body*, 59; France, *Matthew*, 846; Hartshorne, *Logic of Perfection*, 40.

497. This blends δίς, the adverb for "two," and στάσις, which means "place," so as to mean uncertainty about one's position. BDAG, 252.

498. Davids, *James*, 74–75; Johnson, *James*, 287.

499. Kooton, "Two Inclinations," 143–58

500. Osiek, *Shepherd of Hermas*, 20, 30.

501. Kierkegaard, *Upbuilding Discourses*, 25, 30, 67.

502. Kierkegaard, *Book on Adler*, 184; *Eighteen Upbuilding Discourses*, 27.

503. Calvin, *Institutes*, III,2,37 (p. 379); Demarest, *Cross and Salvation*, 273–75; Nicholas, "Learned Ignorance," 153 [III,12,254].

504. Ludlow, *Universal Salvation*, 187.

505. Moo, *Romans*, 778–80.

506. Aquinas, *Compendium*, § 215 (p. 169); Basil, "De Spiritu Sancto," 9.22; Dunn, *Romans 9–16*, 721–22; Origen, *On First Principles*, I,3,4, 3,6, IV,4,2 (pp. 32, 34–35, 316); Schreiner, *Romans*, 652–53.

507. Donahue and Harrington, *Mark*, II: 279, France, *Mark*, 368.

Paul analogized a single person's two orientations to two persons: "disrobe the old man with its practices and put on the new [man], the renewing into true knowledge after his Creator's icon" (Col 3:9–10).[508] "Walk no more as the nations walk, in their mind's emptiness, darkened in their reasoning, alienated from God's life." "Put aside from your former living the worn-out man, corrupted by its wily cravings," so as to be "renewing your mind's spirit," "and to put on the new man created by God in truth's righteousness" (Eph 4:17–18, 22–24). Andrew Lincoln perceived, "As opposed to the new person who is in a process of renewal" in God-like righteousness "the old person is in a process of moral corruption" "under the dominion of this present age."[509] Synonymously,[510] Paul described the orientations as a worldly "outer man" and a godly "inner one" (2 Cor 4:16).[511] Because the referenced "inner one" is in other contexts a literal second person, such as someone inside a citadel, Paul was manifestly adopting the image of two persons in each person.[512] Exegetes can interpret the two persons as sequential, not synchronic,[513] but the orientations clearly remain viable throughout life. Hamann discerned, "The mystery of the marriage between natures so opposed as the outer and the inner man . . . is great," but these cohabiting oppositions comprise "a comprehensive concept of the fullness within the unity of our human essence. . . ."[514] Paul's two persons in each of us are obviously *not* two distinct beings, but are as obviously two distinct ways of being.[515]

Paul expressed this famously in Romans, offering himself as the object lesson:

> I know not what I am working out, for I am doing not what I am willing for, but doing what I hate. . . . I know nothing good lives . . . in my flesh, for the willing reclines beside me, but the working out the noble, never. For I am not doing the good I am willing for, but am doing the evil I am not willing for. If what I

---

508. Demarest, *Cross and Salvation*, 410.

509. Lincoln, *Ephesians*, 285–88.

510. Kooton, *Paul's Anthropology in Context*, 358.

511. Barnett, *Second Corinthians*, 250–51; Garland, *2 Corinthians*, 240; Martin, *2 Corinthians*, 91–92.

512. Kooton, *Paul's Anthropology in Context*, 358–59.

513. Bruce, *Colossians, Philemon, and Ephesians*, 146–48, 358–59; Hoehner, *Ephesians*, 598–613; N. T. Wright, *Colossians and Philemon*, 138–39.

514. Hamann, "Philological Ideas," 118.

515. Harris, *Second Corinthians*, 360.

am not willing for I am doing, no more am I the one working it out but sin alive in me. The law I then find in me: the one willing to do the noble reclines beside the evil, for, in the inner man, I subscribe to God's law, but I see another law in my appendages, warring against my mind's law and imprisoning me in sin's law. ... I, wretched man! (7:15, 18–24)

Paul used thirty-five first-person singular Greek words in just eight verses, making his description explicitly autobiographical.[516] Some interpreters disagree, but cannot agree on whether he is describing Christians or degenerates.[517] Regardless, if this is not "a dualistic way of looking at things," Käsemann asks, "What else can an understanding of existence be called if it sees man as being in conflict with himself?"[518] Paul's *I*'s and *me*'s (and his present tense verbs) answer: The universal human condition is that each of us is two of us.[519] The duality of the human condition was "Paul's discovery," acknowledged a more recent popularizer of the human condition, which is that the individual is "two-in-one" with the characters "in constant struggle with each other."[520]

Many other self-reflective writers have shared this self-discovery.[521] For instance, Augustine's *civitas dei* and *civitas terrena* reflect the human will's opposing orientations.[522] He confessed, "I turned from unity in" God "to be lost in multiplicity." "Who can untie this extremely twisted and tangled knot"? "I have become a question [*quaestio*] to myself."[523] To Eckhart, "what is very evident" is that "man has in himself a twofold nature," "the earthly man" who is "hostile" to God and "a heavenly man."[524] Luther too realized, "we have against us even the one half of ourselves,"

---

516. Augustine, *Retractions*, 1.22.2 (p. 97); Bray, *God Has Spoken*, 974; Schreiner, *Romans*, 371, 379.

517. Moo, *Romans*, 480–89.

518. Käsemann, *Perspectives on Paul*, 16.

519. Cranfield, *Romans 1–8*, 341–47; Guardini, *Freedom, Grace, and Destiny*, 66; Oakes, *Theology of Grace*, 60; Origen, "Dialogue with Heraclides," 11,28–12,7, 16,13 (pp. 66, 70).

520. Arendt, "Willing," 64.

521. *E.g.*, Arendt, "Thinking," 214; Buber, "Religion and Philosophy," 44; "God and Spirit of Man," 127; Graham, *Holy Spirit*, 90, 95, 131; Merton, *Seven Storey Mountain*, 3; Teresa, *Come Be My Light*, 169, 210.

522. Pannenberg, *Anthropology in Theological Perspective*, 89 n.22.

523. Augustine, *Confessions*, I,v,5, II,i,1, x,18, IV,iv,9, X,xxx,50 (pp. 5, 24, 34, 57, 208, translation modified).

524. Eckhart, "Book of 'Benedictus,'" 240–41.

"a double life. The first is mine, which is natural or animal; the second is the life of another, that is to say, the life of Christ in me."[525] Kierkegaard's introspections perhaps most resemble Paul's:

> A person in despair despairingly wills to be himself. But if he despairingly wills to be himself, he certainly does not want to be rid of himself. Well, so it seems, but upon closer examination it is clear that the contradiction is the same. The self that he despairingly wants to be is a self that he is not . . . , that is, he wants to tear his self away from the power that established it. In spite of all his despair, however, he cannot manage to do it; . . . that power is the stronger and forces him to be the self he does not want to be. But this is his way of willing to get rid of himself, to rid himself of the self that he is in order to be the self that he has dreamed up.[526]
>
> Whether he, the weak one, despairs over not being able to tear himself loose from the evil or he, the presumptuous one, despairs over not being able to tear himself completely loose from the good—they are both double-minded, they both have two wills . . . .[527]

"Man's 'I' is no longer what was named by God," Bonhoeffer concluded, which yields this reflection: "I am separated from the 'I' that I should be by a boundary which I am unable to cross. This boundary lies between me and myself, between the old 'I' and the new 'I.'"[528]

9. Life Forms Personal Character, Which Forms Life

A personal character only forms with a succession of lived events, and events take time. The individual's "eternal dignity," Kierkegaard observed, "lies precisely in this, that he can gain a history."[529] Thus, leading a life is what shapes character, which is in turn what shapes the life led.[530] Plato

---

525. Luther, *Galatians*, 76, 171 [WA 401,128, 287 (1:11, 2:20)].
526. Kierkegaard, *Sickness Unto Death*, 20.
527. Kierkegaard, *Upbuilding Discourses*, 139.
528. Bonhoeffer, *Christ the Center*, 54, 61.
529. Kierkegaard, *Either/Or*, II: 224.
530. Barth, *CD* I/2, § 15.3 (p. 195); Basil, "Asketikon," LR 6 ¶ 1 (p. 178); Swinburne, "Future of the Totally Corrupt," 236.

and his predecessors knew this,[531] as do those since.[532] "The soul," John Climacus concluded, "is molded by the doings of the body, conforming to and taking shape from what it does."[533] Wilde recognized, "every little action of the common day makes or unmakes character."[534] Individuals in this life, Kathryn Tanner saw, "cultivate or discourage those natural drives and tendencies" "from the uses to which they put themselves," and this "adds to the plastic, shape-shifting character of human nature."[535]

Scripture too reflects that how we live changes us.[536] In life, we press on to the end (Phil 3:11–16), where "affliction works out endurance; endurance, attestation; attestation, hope; and hope will not shame" (Rom 5:3–4). Also, "underwrite in the faith your virtue; in the virtue, the knowledge; in the knowledge, the self-control; in the self-control, the endurance; in the endurance, the reverence; in the reverence, the brotherliness; and in the brotherliness, the love" (2 Pet 1:5–7). Wrongdoing makes us wrong, justifying "the ancient parable, From the evil comes evil" (1 Sam 24:13). "[E]ach is tried by his own craving, hooked and baited. The craving conceived then births sin, while the matured sin births death" (Jas 1:14–16). "Know you not, when you present yourselves as slaves into obedience, you are slaves to what you obey, whether sin into death, or obedience into righteousness?" (Rom 6:16).[537]

We become what our actions intend,[538] for and against God,[539] and all of this is particularly true of Christian life.[540] Acts as broadly defined influence character as broadly defined.[541] So, as God invests in us,[542] we

531. Heraclitus, *Fragments*, 82–83, 97 (Fragment 121); Plato, *Republic*, 444c-d; Shaw, *Theurgy and the Soul*, 6.

532. Krapiec, *I-Man*, 98–99, 185, 203, 221; Schindler, *Perfection of Freedom*, 290–93; Wallenfang, *Human and Divine Being*, 194.

533. Climacus, *Ladder*, 227 (step 25).

534. Wilde, *De Profundis*, 58.

535. Tanner, *Christ the Key*, 44–47.

536. McConville, *Being Human*, 201.

537. Boer, *Defeat of Death*, 170–72.

538. Garff, "Formation and the Critique," 253; Healy, *Eschatology of Balthasar*, 121; Kierkegaard, *Concept of Anxiety*, 48.

539. Harrison, *God's Many-Splendored Image*, 186; Lewis, *Problem of Pain*, 106–7; Russell, *Doctrine of Deification*, 318.

540. A. Cooper, *Holy Eros*, 20–22; Henry, *I Am the Truth*, 171; Speyr, *Gates of Eternal Life*, 15.

541. Guardini, *Freedom, Grace, and Destiny*, 157.

542. Lubac, *Catholicism*, 266.

are invented. Loving God grows godliness,[543] while sin both infects us and arises in us.[544] "[T]he totality of those acts" of a "personal life process," Tillich discerned, "never comes to an end."[545] This relationship between who we are and what we do sustains punishment.[546] Sins make sinners, and sinners make sins.[547] So, God "disciplines his beloved and punishes every son he receives. Into discipline persevere," which "yields the peaceful fruit of righteousness for those it trained" (Heb 12:6–7, 11).

Science, attesting to the intuition that earlier properties lead to later ones,[548] confirms that what we do affects who we are and vice-versa.[549] Our actions, to illustrate, anatomically shape our brains, and of course our brains shape our actions.[550] Even before birth, we are experiencing, learning, and changing as we interact with our world,[551] not only with the world outside the womb but the chemical one inside it.[552] Ever onward, experiences change the brain and conversely.[553] Psychoanalysis understands that each incident imprints us, even if subconsciously.[554] Even our memories, which form us, are in turn formed by us.[555] We are how we have lived.[556] "The present moment is the sepulchre of all that went before it," Schilling composed.[557]

So, the led life is a feedback loop between the experiences of life and the character fashioned by that life, and this loop is usually a positive one

---

543. Aquinas, *ST, 1a*, XIII, Q. 93, art. 4 (pp. 59–61).

544. Grenz, *Theology for the Community*, 184–85; Ziegler, *Militant Grace*, 59.

545. Tillich, *ST*, III: 38.

546. Cole, "Justice: Retributive or Reformative," 5–12.

547. Pannenberg, *Anthropology in Theological Perspective*, 119–20.

548. Campbell, "Personal Identity," 340.

549. Gallagher, "Diversity of Selves," 17, 22; Pacherie, "Self-Agency," 442; Schroeder, *Hidden Face of God*, 182.

550. Alvaro et al., "Plastic Human Brain Cortex," 377–401; Carter and Frith, *Mapping the Mind*, 19; Corcoran and Sharpe, "Neuroscience and the Human," 127.

551. Rochat, "What Is It Like?" 62–63.

552. LeDoux, *Synaptic Self*, 66–67, 92.

553. LeDoux, *Synaptic Self*, 8–9; Mountcastle, "Brain Science," 7.

554. Horne, "Person as Confession," 70.

555. Volf, *End of Memory*, 25, 52.

556. Blondel, *Action*, 215, 277 [223, 296]; Brunner, *Eternal Hope*, 48; Welz, *Humanity in God's Image*, 73.

557. Schiller, "Philosophical Letters," 384 (Ltr II).

where a change produces further change in the same direction.[558] We live as we have done and do as we have lived because what is once done stays done to that extent.[559] Our faith and our conduct form our character, which forms our faith and our conduct.[560] Like the tree and its fruit, so the individual and its life (Matt 7:16–20; 15:17–20; 12:33–37//Luke 6:43–45), "for His workmanship we are, created in Christ Jesus for good works" (Eph 2:10). Our decisions shape us, define us, feed our divided orientations, and reflect our eternal destiny.[561] Thus, our experiences deliver what endures in us, "an eternal weight of glory" (2 Cor 4:17). As a result of this relationship between our life and our character, this life has been called "the road to our personality" by Rosenzweig[562] and "the trial by existence" by Frost.[563] Therefore, contrary to the obvious, we are living not in a vale of tears (*cf.* Ps 84:6), at least not only that, but we are living in John Keats' "vale of Soul-making."[564] And it is this living that yields the personal character, which is who enters the next life for transformation.[565]

10. Evil Exists

Because this discourse has recognized the two primary character orientations in each of us, nominally godly and ungodly, and because the proposed model will employ both of them, two problems could be a concern. The easiest to address is any objection that the model, like Manichaeism, supposes two souls for each individual.[566] Nothing like that is supposed at all, however, because the model supposes nothing about substances. While the model admittedly uses an individual's internal two-ness, this two-ness is from the realization that each individual has two orientations or, if preferred, one conflicted character or will, not the supposition that

---

558. Graham, *Holy Spirit*, 258; Henry, *Essence of Manifestation*, 459; McCombs, *Paradoxical Rationality*, 105–8, 192–93.

559. Balthasar, *Theo-Logic*, I: 198; Welz, *Humanity in God's Image*, 98; Wollheim, *Thread of Life*, 31.

560. Milbank, *Theology and Social Theory*, 139; Welz, *Humanity in God's Image*, 132.

561. Tillich, *ST*, III: 413.

562. Rosenzweig, "Life," 81 (18 Aug. 1918 letter).

563. Frost, "Trial by Existence," 19.

564. Keats, *Selected Letters*, 109.

565. M. Taylor, *Journeys to Selfhood*, 138.

566. Blosser, *Become Like the Angels*, 62.

each individual is two souls (and certainly not two identities) or even two wills.[567] Hence, the model is not like Christ's special case of one united individual with two wills.[568] The recognition that the thesis models two orientations, and not two substances, and employs the individual's singularity despite its confliction must be retained in the next chapter when the character is in the afterlife divided into two as the identity remains whole. As should be evident and will be discussed in the next section, only that which actually begins as one can, when split, be two.

The second potential pitfall from a model that recognizes both orientations of godly and ungodly, which can be termed good and evil, is that this gives heft to evil, which can seemingly transgress theologians who via Aristotle[569] say evil is nonbeing.[570] The Aristotelians argue that, when evil is present, this does not merely *mean* that good is absent but that evil's presence *is* actually the absence of good. This is much like how physicists say cold is nothing but heat's absence. While I fully accept what the physicists say until I grab ice, I cannot follow the theologians as I listen to myself, who is as substantive as anything I know.[571] Evil does not strike like a void, but like a demon, or me. "I am no philosopher," the philosopher Montaigne confessed, but "Evils crush me according to their weight . . . ."[572] According to the ancient wisdom, evil is not nil, but attacks.[573] Many theologians, such as Barth, Vladimir Lossky, Kierkegaard, and Luther, agree that evil is a negativity in being, not a negation of being.[574] Hans Schwarz explained: Evil is no "deficiency of being." "When something is good and a little evil is added to it, say 5 percent, one could not for this reason reduce its existence to 95 percent."[575] Henry concurred, "Evil is no less real than Good . . . ."[576] Some like Buber even

---

567. Connolly, *Living without Why*, 42–85.

568. Blowers, *Maximus the Confessor*, 135–65.

569. Bray, *God Has Spoken*, 998.

570. Davies, *Aquinas on God and Evil*, 32–36, 71; Perl, *Theophany*, 53, 60; Schwarz, *Evil*, 163–68.

571. Balthasar, *Theo-Drama*, V: 314; Bulgakov, *Bride of the Lamb*, 153; Purkiser, Taylor, and Taylor, *God, Man, and Salvation*, 120.

572. Montaigne, "Essays," III,9 (p. 725).

573. Koehn, *Nature of Evil*, 31.

574. Barth, *Romans*, 199 (6:6); Kierkegaard, *Sickness Unto Death*, 96; Lossky, *Mystical Theology*, 128; Luther, "De Servo Arbitrio," 232.

575. Schwarz, *Human Being*, 146.

576. Henry, *Essence of Manifestation*, 451.

claim that evil is, not only not nothing, but that evil must be something for good also to be something.[577] Regardless, in Christianity, if not mere life, evil is less an absence like darkness or silence and is more a presence like cancer or pain.[578] C. S. Lewis concurred: "real Christianity" is not a pantheism likening God to all that has being, but is nearly a "dualism" involving a civil war between God and "a Dark Power" and we are "in a part of the universe occupied by the rebel."[579]

Scripture shares this view. It describes evil as being or, to permit an anachronism, as anti-being, not as nonbeing.[580] God primordially actuated the distinction between good and evil[581] and can be said to have himself *created* and *formed* evil (Isa 45:7; Jer 18:11).[582] Our inner nature has certainly produced evil, and it then defiles us (Mark 7:20–23//Matt 15:18–20). Evil spoils and corrupts, which God destroys (Gen 6:12; Exod 32:7–8; Ps 145:20). Sin quasi-autonomously reigns and enslaves us, seduces and kills us (Rom 6:12, 16; 7:11).[583] We are to loathe evil, which can overcome us and from which we need rescue (12:9, 21; 2 Tim 4:18). Evil makes demands, which we are to refuse (Gen 4:7; Rom 6:14; Eph 6:12). Accordingly, Jesus portrayed evil, not as a void, but as a person (Matt 6:13; Luke 22:53; John 17:15), and only in Revelation's final scene does the good and evil dualism finally cease.[584]

The proposed model of divisibility can work for even Aristotelians, however, because the philosophical dispute about evil's being is about what is *being* (that which is) and not about what is *evil* (that which is wicked), and the model concerns the latter. So, in the model, evil does not need to *be* being; it need only be *in* being. And this should be uncontroversial. Evil, if not a noun or a nature, is an adjective or a condition.[585] Evil's es-

---

577. Buber, *Ten Rungs*, 89–90.

578. Ludlow, *Universal Salvation*, 238.

579. Lewis, *Mere Christianity*, 36.

580. Bray, *God Has Spoken*, 86.

581. Theodoret, *Letters of Paul*, I: Rom 47 (p. 43).

582. Hamann, "Fragments," IV (p. 167). The first verb (*bârâ'*) always refers to divine creation, and the second (*yâtsar*) describes what a potter does to clay. BDB, 135, 427.

583. Boyd, "Christus Victor View," 29; Matera, *Romans*, 3, 137.

584. Gooder, *Heaven*, 67; Stephens, *Annihilation or Renewal?* 233–34; Tonstad, *Revelation*, 29.

585. Koehn, *Nature of Evil*, 5, 240; Lossky, *Mystical Theology*, 128.

sentialness is thus inessential to the model, which uses evil things, not evil as a thing.[586] In this world, evil is clearly present, even if not a presence.

So, even if Aristotle is correct that evil is substantively good's absence, the model still functions because such predicates as evil are unquestionably part of being without necessarily being being itself.[587] As Hamann discerned, "everything is divine, and the question of the origin of evil amounts in the end to word-play and scholastic prattle."[588] Regardless therefore of whether the negative orientation is good's perversion or anti-good, the individual in the model is, as in reality, the two orientations,[589] and these orientations are what distance us from God or what pleases him.[590] In short, because the model uses evil's separability, not its substantiality, the dispute about whether being includes evil is immaterial, so to speak.

11. Dividing an Individual in the Afterlife Is Realizable

The individual's manifest dividedness in this life manifestly differs from its actual divisibility afterwards,[591] but now forearmed with the former we should be able to mentally transition our understanding to the latter. Plato clearly could do so given that he could take the inner individual's conflict in this life as reflective of an actually partitive inner life, a soul with separately motivated parts,[592] and, if Plato can do so, that means, not that it is true, but that it is conceivable. Further, as is more normally the case when the one individual is understood as indivisible in this life, the transitioning of the individual's obvious confliction in this life to an actually divisible one in the next is manageable because it is similar to how we easily accept that a country can be one country despite its internal conflicts but can become two countries if a civil war divides it.[593]

---

586. Krapiec, *I-Man*, 235–36.
587. Feuerbach, *Essence of Christianity*, I.2 (p. 14).
588. Hamann, "Last Will," 99.
589. Balthasar, *Theo-Logic*, II: 350; *Theo-Drama*, III: 482–86, IV: 369, 479.
590. Crosby, *Selfhood of the Human*, 228–29; Lewis, "Weight of Glory," 36–37.
591. Chesterton, *St Thomas Aquinas*, 17–18.
592. Bobonich, *Plato's Utopia Recast*, 217, 259, 336; Hendrik, *Brute Within*, 14, 21–22, 24–25, 35, 63.
593. Wippel, *Metaphysical Thought of Aquinas*, 356.

As has been seen, though the individual experiences this life as a psychophysical unity, the individual's potential for division is multifarious in this life. Our mere thinking suggests an internal division because it involves an inner dialogue,[594] and this thinking self has divisive orientations.[595] The thinker also divides what reflects from what is reflected upon.[596] More essentially, anything "in being related to God is divided from itself," Cunningham discerned.[597] All of this allows, perhaps too easily, the modeling of the individual as divisible as is to be proposed here.[598] This potential for division, while there is no practical division, is like how a water molecule's thoroughly united atoms of hydrogen and oxygen imply, once those elements are called out, their divisibility if the molecule was ever to encounter the right circumstance.[599]

The individual's two orientations in this life, now that they have been called out, should suggest divisibility too, at least as a plausibility. Some individuals can display this more obviously by having pathologically, not just metaphorically, divided minds, but everyone else experiences the self as not yet actually divided.[600] A person "ordinarily experiences the dimension of self-awareness in unity," Tillich recognized. "The psychological and the personal self are united in him. Only in such special situations as dream, intoxication, half-sleep, and so on, does a partial separation occur, and this separation is never so complete that a sharply distinct description of the psychological is possible."[601] But Kierkegaard understood, "The view which sees life's doubleness or duality is higher and deeper than that which seeks unity."[602]

Husserl found that "*all real unities are 'unities of meaning.'*"[603] Only the dimensionless point seems to be truly indivisible, and that is so

---

594. Plato, *Sophist*, 263e; *Theaetetus*, 189e-190a.

595. Lowe, *Subjects of Experience*, 36, 40.

596. Henry, *Essence of Manifestation*, 690–91.

597. Cunningham, *Genealogy of Nihilism*, 226.

598. Hume, *Treatise of Human Nature*, I.I.3 (p. 7); Krapiec, *I-Man*, 347–49; Schiller, "Letters on the Aesthetical," 115 (Ltr XXVI).

599. Williamson, *Death and the Afterlife*, 36.

600. Horst, *Cognitive Pluralism*, 322; Radden, "Pathologically Divided Minds," 356.

601. Tillich, *ST*, III: 37.

602. Kierkegaard, *JP*, I: ¶ 704.

603. Husserl, *Ideas*, 55 (p. 152).

definitionally.[604] Even things that are invariant, such as a line, can be divided, as can prime numbers notwithstanding the fractional messes that result.[605] The perforated life should be as splitable, if it is ever required to be, as these abstractions clearly are.[606] Personal orientations and personal identity are admittedly not parts of the person,[607] nor does the proposed division require that they be, any more than the left side of the line is separate from the right side or than the hydrogen atoms in a water molecule are separate from the oxygen atom. Rather, individual divisibility is similar to how Benjamin Blosser described Origen's anthropology, which is "not from an ontological partition into distinct metaphysical units, but rather from a moral crisis."[608] Modeling the orientations' divisibility does not materialize the orientations, but it does re-model what has inveterately been modeled as indivisible.[609] The individual has "two natures in his created hypostasis," Lossky observed, "on the one side there is the divine and deifying will" and "on the other side there is the human will . . . ."[610] Though disturbing to the ego, each individual is a confluence, and only God's gift—or, in common terms, this life—is what coheres the individual.[611]

The *corporeal* cohesion in this life does not foreclose the possibility of division afterwards. The model willingly accepts in this life that the natural body enables character and anchors identity, but, even in this life, matter by itself is a weak identifier, fluxing like river water through an individual, whose form also changes as much as a river's form shifts throughout its geological life.[612] More significantly, the terrestrial body disintegrates in death, which necessarily denies it this unifying function altogether after this life.[613] Christians have known this since the

604. Euclid, *Elements*, I.1 (p. 2).

605. Brower, *Aquinas's Ontology*, 118; Lowe, *Subjects of Experience*, 36; Whitehead, *Process and Reality*, 77.

606. Luther, *Galatians*, 472 [WA 402,45 (5:9)].

607. Wojtyla, *Acting Person*, 189–219.

608. Blosser, *Become Like the Angels*, 18.

609. Spaemann, *Essays in Anthropology*, 38.

610. Lossky, *Mystical Theology*, 126–27.

611. Bell, "Corrupt Mind," 215; Gundry, *Soma in Biblical Theology*, 201–2.

612. Bynum, *Resurrection of the Body*, 112; J. Cooper, *Body, Soul, and Life*, 189; Wallenfang, *Human and Divine Being*, 156. The comparison is ancient. Heraclitus, *Fragments*, 81 (pp. 50–51).

613. Krapiec, *I-Man*, 358.

beginning. Ignatius prayed for his corpse to be entirely consumed in his martyrdom so as to fulfill, not contravene, his resurrection.[614] Similarly, the Roman Empire, according to the epistle from Lyons in 177, tried to deter further Christian martyrs by having the remains of their predecessors eaten by dogs, burned to ash, and then thrown in the Rhone river, which flushes out to the sea, but the policy of obliterating the martyrs' bodies to preclude their resurrection failed.[615] The incorporeal can find eternity.[616] Even if the corpse were to somehow persist as an identifier in death, it becomes divisible then particularly, as Christians (and others) prove whenever they divide a corpse into relics to venerate in dispersed locations the single life that it once had.[617]

As for our body's disjunction between this life and the next, Christ's body is no counterexample. Christ's terrestrial body most definitely differed from his resurrected body too.[618] In his resurrected body, he recurrently vanishes and appears, walking into locked rooms, and can travel via clouds while not being easy to recognize.[619] More importantly, Christ's resurrection is not our timing (1 Cor 15:20–23),[620] and, thus, it does not reflect our afterlife continuity. He was resurrected on the third day and suffered no decay (Acts 2:27, 31–32), which has happened exactly once.[621] Even his naturally unifying body did not unify him in death because, after yielding his spirit to the Father (Matt 27:50//John 19:30//Luke 23:46), his body was in the tomb as he was to experience paradise (23:42–43).[622] Therefore, even the united Son was divided in death between body and spirit,[623] which makes sense because the body's cessation is what death is precisely, and that is what all Nicene Christians say Christ suffered, even if more is experienced afterwards.[624]

614. Ignatius, "Epistle to the Romans," ch IV (p. 75).

615. Musurillo, *Acts of the Christian Martyrs*, xx-xxii, 80–83.

616. Augustine, *City of God*, I,12 (pp. 21–22); Behr, "Life and Death," 82; Bynum, *Resurrection of the Body*, 49.

617. Moore, *Where Are the Dead?* 148.

618. Ward, "Displaced Body," 173.

619. Davis, *Risen Indeed*, 57; N. T. Wright, *Resurrection*, 478.

620. Yates, *Between Death and Resurrection*, 22.

621. Bock, *Acts*, 124–25, 129; Novakovic, *Resurrection*, 172; Riches, *Ecce Homo*, 194–95, 206–7.

622. Brown, *Death of the Messiah*, II: 1005–13.

623. Bock, *Luke 9:51—24:53*, 1857; Brown, *Death of the Messiah*, II: 1010; Riches, *Ecce Homo*, 197–208.

624. J. Cooper, *Body, Soul, and Life*, 214; Leget, "Eschatology," 367; Schumacher,

Divisibility's Coherence

Because an individual is no mere body, but includes thoughts, experiences, feelings, beliefs,[625] this thick self, which this life forms and which eternal life requires, includes the character that transitions to the next life,[626] and it is on this that the proposed model works. Though the personal identity, which is unitary by necessity, also necessarily transitions, the personal character, which is normally lived as conflicted, can be divisible because nothing about the afterlife requires that the orientations remain together or that any personal identity experience both. The argument now is not that any divisibility occurs in the afterlife because that derives from the paradox of salvation's extent. Instead, this chapter's burden is limited to showing that a division of an individual in the afterlife is a coherent idea, not that it is part of reality.

The coherency of dividing what is experienced everyday as indivisible is paralleled in theology's two essential Christian paradoxes—the Trinity and the hypostatic union. The Triune God is three identities of one nature, and the Christ is two natures of one identity.[627] These paradoxes, as Gregory of Nyssa saw, involve being "at once conjoined and separated," offering "a new and strange kind of conjoined separation and separated conjunction."[628] His confederate Gregory added that the Persons of the Divine "are divided without division" and "united in division."[629] These notions, despite being so divergent from everyday reality where each healthy person and just about everything else we know of has only one identity and only one nature, were accepted only because of the scriptural paradoxes. That too is what justifies dividing the individual after this life. While this understanding is extraordinary, paradoxes require that from us, or they are not really paradoxes.

The reason that the divisibility of the individual seems absurd, or at least to the extent that it does, is the venerable idea of the essential *I*,[630]

Death and Mortality, 48.

625. Welz, *Humanity in God's Image*, 126.

626. Harrison, *God's Many-Splendored Image*, 49.

627. Riches, *Ecce Homo*, 82–83, 97; Vishnevskaya, "Divinization as Perichoretic Embrace," 132.

628. Gregory, "Letter 35," ¶ 4 (p. 255). Tradition preserved this as Basil's Letter No. 38 ("Letters," 139), but modern scholarship has determined that the letter is Gregory's. Benedetto et al., "Puzzle of Basil's Epistula 38," 267–87; Silvas, *Gregory of Nyssa*, 247.

629. Gregory of Nazianzus, "Orations," 39.11.

630. Feuerbach, *Essence of Christianity*, I.II (p. 42); Heidegger, "Modern Science," 274, 280–81; Olson, "Compound of Two Substances," 84.

which Descartes educed.[631] Most everyone in the West, if not everywhere, is effectively an anthropological Cartesian in this regard, including those who explicitly deny the Cartesian dualism, even those who pre-date him (most famously, Aristotle[632] and Augustine[633]). This is because, in recognizing a self in the life that we lead, if not in the theory that we publish, we all recognize an elemental *I*.[634] This Cartesianesque *I* results from merely appreciating the obvious, which begins with step one: There is awareness. This step is proven whenever any sentence such as step one is truly read, regardless of whether it is followed by agreement, disagreement, or confusion. This is followed by step two: Awareness means something is aware. By a convention in every language, this something is known, among other identifiers, as the *I*.[635] The unanimous reality, therefore, is the Descartes formula but modified: *sum, ergo ego sum*.[636] Now, if this understanding of the essential *I* could ever be successfully overturned, this would not deny the desired result of the proposed model, individual divisibility. Instead, individual divisibility would become easier because, without the essential *I*, the individual would then be an incongruous dipolar mass that is all too easily disunited.[637] Selfhood, if understood without an essential *I*, could naturally rupture between its towards-self and its towards-God.[638]

But we all have weathered the Cartesian Enlightenment, and, so, we moderns find individual division troubling. We therefore underappreciate the challenge the early church faced in retaining the unity of Christ's self despite the difference in his two natures. How the church faced that issue is telling here. It worried that Christ's personal division would follow if his two natures were fully recognized,[639] and, therefore, the church had to positively affirm that the difference in his natures did

---

631. MacDonald, *History of the Concept*, 279–91; Riches, *Ecce Homo*, 11, 63.

632. Aristotle, "Ethica Nicomachea," 1170a29–1170b1.

633. Augustine, *City of God*, XI,26 (p. 460).

634. McGilchrist, *Master and His Emissary*, 20; Reddy, *How Infants Know Minds*, 11, 23, 29–30; Tononi and Koch, "Consciousness," 2, 5; Turner, *Theology, Psychology and Plural Self*, 35.

635. Goddard, "Natural Semantic Metalanguage Approach," 462; MacDonald, *History of the Concept*, 279.

636. Panksepp, *Affective Neuroscience*, 311–12, 420, n.34.

637. Westphal, *Becoming a Self*, 180.

638. Garff, "Formation and the Critique," 264.

639. Riches, *Ecce Homo*, 30–33.

not mean the division of his person.[640] The church knew that individuals could divide[641] and knew that Christ could too,[642] although he was singly oriented.[643] Like the splitting of the proto-individual, when God took the androgyne's "side"[644] for "flesh of my flesh" (Gen 2:7, 15–25), the church had no trouble with God dividing one individual into two individuals.[645] Divinely dividing individuals actually seems to have been commonplace in antiquity.[646] Plato, as an example, tells of humanity's legendary origin where everyone had eight limbs and two faces until Zeus split each person into a male person and a female person.[647] Dividing Christ into two persons was therefore an attraction that the church had to affirmatively resist,[648] particularly because his two distinct natures uniquely intimated his division.[649] So, the Son's natures were resolved to be "without division," "not parted or divided into two *prosopa* [persons]."[650] What unified was his personhood.[651] The obvious need for the credal contention that the Son was in truth indivisible thus implies that an individual could potentially be divided if that were ever called for.[652]

Unlike the early church, all of us who have recognized the essential *I*, both before and after Descartes, can have difficulty with what it would mean to disunite the individual, but, just as the divine and human can be one person (Christ) as well as two separate persons (the Father and me),[653] an individual's godliness and godlessness can be separated under the right circumstance. Cartesianesque anthropology has in fact concealed how real dividing an individual is already: Bodies are bisected (*e.g.*, conjoined twins), personalities are split (*e.g.*, dissociative identity

---

640. Blowers, *Maximus the Confessor*, 176.
641. John, "Fount of Knowledge," I,11, 43 (pp. 41, 68).
642. Maximus, "Opusculum 6," PG 91:65C-68D (pp. 174–76); Stang, "Two 'I's of Christ," 529–47; Wallenfang, *Human and Divine Being*, 92 & n.87.
643. Lossky, *Mystical Theology*, 146–47.
644. *BDB*, 854; Fabry, "Ṣēlā," 400–402.
645. Kierkegaard, *Concept of Anxiety*, 317–18.
646. Doniger, *Splitting the Difference*, 1.
647. Plato, "Symposium," 189d–193a.
648. Erickson, *Christian Theology*, 739–41.
649. Mateiescu, "Counting Natures and Hypostases," 64–65, 76.
650. Kelly, *Early Christian Doctrines*, 339–40.
651. Ratzinger, *Behold the Pierced One*, 39.
652. Olson, *Mosaic of Christian Belief*, 226–27.
653. Riches, *Ecce Homo*, 4, 176; Vanhoozer, "Origin of Paul's Soteriology," 198.

disorder), and brains are halved (*e.g.*, commissurotomy patients). For the Cartesian, however, the difficulty comes, not from dividing such individuals, but from dividing the typical individual, who is unitary. "There is nothing comic in half an apple," Kierkegaard said in mocking this kind of thinking, "the comic would become apparent only if a whole apple were half an apple."[654] Dividing a water molecule, returning to that metaphor, does *not* yield two water molecules, but two elements that are very much unlike water. Solomon's gambit was similar; he depended on the parties knowing that splitting the one disputed baby would not mean two babies, but zero babies. Dividing a person is therefore unlike the civil war metaphor where one country becomes two countries. Instead, we moderns find the metaphor of the water molecule more applicable to individual division—splitting the water molecule destroys that molecule, making it no longer water. This is true although selfhood scholarship never uses the water metaphor to explain the self, while it often uses the country metaphor. A statue, however, is a common metaphor for identity, and, under this metaphor, division destroys. Dividing the essential *I* is like dividing the statue, we tend to think. While a lump of bronze can be divided into two lumps without destroying the bronze, a bronze statue will be destroyed if it is divided.

Dividing an individual in the afterlife is not similarly destructive, though, even to a Cartesian for two reasons. First, as has been explained, the *I*, regardless of substance, entails personal identity *and* personal character, and the model divides the latter, the dually oriented led life. The essential *I* nonetheless retains its indivisibility to the extent of the personal identity, and this should satisfy the Cartesian and everyone else expecting a continuation of an essential *I*. Second, as chapter 2 noted, the afterlife already includes in tradition an extremely potent culling and an amazingly thorough completion. So, adding division to the afterlife process is unlike dividing the ordinary statue. If in the metaphor the original bronze statue was to be remade entirely out of just its copper, then adding statuary division to that remaking so as to also make a tin statue would hardly be more than a different remaking of the original statue. Metamorphosis plus division is just a different metamorphosis.[655] No problem. The best metaphor for the individual in the afterlife might, therefore, not be the typical bronze statue. Rather, the afterlife division of the individual could

---

654. Kierkegaard, *Stages*, 43.
655. Maimonides, *Guide for the Perplexed*, Pt II, prop. VII (p. 146).

be analogized to a ray of sunlight, which, as the Nyssen appreciated, is one color until it becomes a rainbow,[656] and we have known since Newton that a colorless prism can divide an indivisible white light into various streams of red, yellow, and blue.[657]

12. A Divided Individual Can Be Modeled

Although our personal character is almost divided in this life, only in our imagination now can we actually divide one individual into two.[658] This is because conceptual separability is dramatically different from real separability.[659] To bridge this difference, fictionalized characters have helped.[660] Jane Eyre, for instance, dramatized the one person's typical inner conflict as two persons:

> I wrestled with my own resolution: I wanted to be weak that I might avoid the awful passage of further suffering I saw laid out for me; and conscience, turned tyrant, held passion by the throat, told her tauntingly, she had yet but dipped her dainty foot in the slough, and swore that with that arm of iron, he would thrust her down to unsounded depths of agony.
>
> "Let me be torn away, then!" I cried. "Let another help me!"
>
> "No; you shall tear yourself away, none shall help you: you shall, yourself, pluck out your right eye: yourself cut off your right hand: your heart shall be the victim; and you, the priest, to transfix it."[661]

Dr. Jekyll infamously suffered in this way but to an extreme because of "even a deeper trench than the majority of men," which "severed in me those provinces of good and ill which divide and compound man's dual nature," and, from this, he concluded "that man is not truly one, but truly two."[662] An author's pseudonymous writings where the pen names expose alternative characters within the underlying author also expose

---

656. Gregory of Nyssa, "Letter 35," ¶ 5 (pp. 255-57).
657. Colic and Smailhodzic, "Study of Light," 849.
658. Wiener, *Human Use of Human Beings*, 95.
659. MacDonald, *History of the Concept*, 358.
660. Doniger, *Splitting the Difference*, 79-87; Kierkegaard, "Repetition," 23-24 [30].
661. Brontë, *Jane Eyre*, II: 76 (ch XXVII).
662. Stevenson, *Strange Case*, 42-43.

the internal conflict.[663] Kierkegaard went so far as to have his pseudonymous publisher ponder whether his two pseudonymous authors might be one person.[664] "[W]ithout my knowing it," he complained, "I really have been used."[665] Autobiographical characters more commonly reflect the author's split into multiple persons.[666] As Samuel Butler observed, "whether I like it or no I am portraying myself more surely than I am portraying any of the characters whom I set before the reader."[667] Even regardless of the fictional portrayals, each littérateur is a plus one, the one who lives plus the one who writes: "It would be an exaggeration to say that our relationship is hostile," Borges wrote, "I allow myself to live, so that Borges can spin out his literature."[668] Like Dostoevsky, we each know, "the trouble is that I have two tales, and only one life story."[669]

The less artistic among us must use thought experiments to perceive ideas like individual divisibility, but thought experiments depend on intuitions in imagined scenarios so as to expose features of reality that we have supposedly not realized until we imagine them.[670] Because our intuitions exist only because reality has informed them either through our experiences or that of our predecessors, thought experiments reverse this time-tested process by asking intuitions to inform reality, and, as a result, they tend to evoke truths unreliably.[671] Word pictures, however, are similar to thought experiments in that they require less creativity than literature, but, unlike thought experiments, word pictures do not purport to discover what has gone undiscovered in reality, just what is coherent.[672] Hence, word pictures cannot misrepresent what is real because they only purport to represent what is conceivable. In the event, a word picture, if successful, should be able to portray individual division as a coherent idea without making any pretense that it can actually happen.[673] It is worth a reminder that what actually happens regarding individual divisibility is the product

---

663. Stang, *Apophasis and Pseudonymity*, 204–5.
664. Kierkegaard, *Either/Or*, I: 13.
665. Kierkegaard, *JP*, VI: 231–32 (entry 6505).
666. Hermans, "Dialogical Self," 59.
667. Butler, *Way of All Flesh*, 85.
668. Borges, "Borges and I," 324.
669. Dostoevsky, *Brothers Karamazov*, 2.
670. Wasserman, "Personal Identity, Indeterminacy and Obligation," 64.
671. Gendler, "Exceptional Persons," 459; Wilkes, *Real People*, 1–48.
672. Morrison, *Reconstructing Reality*, 92; Volf, *End of Memory*, 142 n.34.
673. Gallagher, "Diversity of Selves," 5.

of the salvation paradox, not this or any other word picture, and this final step will be taken in the next chapter.

In selfhood scholarship, where scientific advances can occur without much work, dividing an individual so as to produce two identical individuals is a familiar scenario.[674] Like the word picture to be proposed, scholarship's thought experiment involves one person being divided into two through duplication (not one person being divided into two half-persons). Such individual duplication is often from appropriating the teleportation that science fiction invented and then commercialized into an incredibly efficient form of transportation. With this fictional technology, an identical individual is materialized at a distant location while the original individual is usually dematerialized, though sometimes the original individual remains, which, because this defeats the purpose of the teleportation, is often just to create a selfhood puzzle of what is to be done with the two identical people.[675]

The proposed word picture is similar to this teletransportation-with-a-glitch scenario.[676] When the original person remains at the original location after also being teleported to the distant location, the person has been doubled,[677] and this exact doubling of substances accommodates our natural bias that the individual is based on material substances.[678] The thought is, if the two duplicated persons are the exact same stuff in the exact same arrangement, there is no evident difference between them. We all recognize this when we do not change who we are when we move from one chair to another, and this seems to be the only difference between the duplicated individuals—the individual has moved to another chair but also remained in the original chair. Even if we are not strict materialists, we live in a material world, and, so, as Gregory of Nazianzus accepted, "it is no more possible for those who are in the body to be conversant with objects of thought apart from bodily objects than it is for a man to step over his own shadow, be he ever so quick."[679]

Suppose, therefore, that the ultimate 4D printer is like the familiar teleporter that suffers the duplication glitch, and this device duplicates

---

674. Barresi and Martin, "History as Prologue," 41.
675. Parfit, "Unimportance of Identity," 419.
676. Kierkegaard, Attack Upon "Christendom," 162.
677. Sloterdijk, Critique of Cynical Reason, 199.
678. Gregor, Philosophical Anthropology, 54.
679. Gregory of Nazianzus, "Second Theological Oration," 30 [28, 12].

an individual in every way imaginable by supplying and arranging every micro particle of an individual exactly as the original, while intentionally leaving the original exactly as it is.[680] The word picture can avoid an obvious original and give a more direct sense of dividing the individual by having the device, in addition to exactly duplicating the original's array of subatomic particles, equally redistribute one by one the original particles and the duplicated particles between the two identical individuals. Each of the duplicates would then have an undifferentiated claim to originality, but this subatomic dissolution of the original might hazard the continuity of the original's identity (just as it always does with classic teleportation).[681] Regardless, either version of the word picture entails *one* individual being divided into *two* through the duplication of that individual. Suppose also the device will not duplicate (or redistribute) a certain noncontagious but incurably lethal virus as it duplicates the person, which means the device will effectively cure the duplicated individual of that virus, and suppose *you* secretly submit to the duplication because you have that virus.

With that as the setting, the word picture begins with you waking up after the duplication lying next to someone who is indistinguishable from you, who is also waking up. You feel like the original who is looking at a duplicate, but you realize the other "you" must be feeling that too. From your first words together, you find that your memories—what is recalled, forgotten, and falsely remembered—are identical.[682] You both, therefore, remember having the virus and choosing to be duplicated so as to be virus-free. You both feel like you have lived the span of your remembered life, yet you each know that only one of you has done so up to this point. Though you both therefore feel like the original, you both want to be the duplicate who is virus-free. You two are, except for the virus, by all accounts and by every observer entirely identical apart from being in slightly different places.[683] You are as identical as two things can be and still be two things.[684]

---

680. Hick, *Death and Eternal Life*, 280–94.
681. Edwards, *Works*, I: cclxiv; Merricks, "How to Live Forever," 193.
682. Volf, *End of Memory*, 194–95, 197.
683. Badham, *Christian Beliefs*, 72–73.
684. Hick, *Death and Eternal Life*, 282–85; Hill, *Rethinking Identity and Metaphysics*, 43–45.

Interrelating with this other you, who is fully independent of you but otherwise is you, is disorienting.[685] It is not like watching a film or reflection of yourself, though you two share everything—appearances, mannerisms, memories, attitudes. The disorientation is from this other you, which your senses are telling you is you, being independent of you. When asked separately for an entirely new password, you each give the same one, though you both thought you were choosing it at random; in buffet lines, you take the same foods in the same quantities; and, in your first sleep, you dream identically, among the most personal activities.[686] You do not literally think the other's thoughts, but correctly surmise them because you are thinking them too.[687] Apart from testing differently for the virus, nothing distinguishes you two; even you cannot find a difference except that you are the one seeing the other you.[688] Differences emerge, however. Your blinking, breathing, and heart rates were initially synchronized, but they cease to be after a short while. The small differentials increase over time, but none of them indicates who is the original. Until you find out which of you has the virus, this is how things stand.

This duplication need never be technologically achievable. It is probably unattainable in spite of teleportation's popularity because it depends on us being entirely made of physical bits, which seems to be, as has been explained, inadequate.[689] Even if the merely physical were wholly sufficient, exactly duplicating a person's subatomic particles would mean determining the position and momentum of each particle of the original person so as to duplicate them exactly, but the Heisenberg principle would seemingly disallow this determination.[690] Irrespective of feasibility, however, the scenario is metaphysically possible.[691] Similar thought experiments have been offered in selfhood scholarship,[692] and literature offers full-length treatments.[693] We understand such depictions

---

685. Mooney, "Critiques of Pairing," 491.

686. Freud, *Future of an Illusion*, I.B, VII.B, E, F (pp. 54, 578, 630, 647, 652); Jung, *Modern Man*, 16.

687. Merleau-Ponty, *Signs*, 170–72.

688. D. Hart, *Experience of God*, 158–59.

689. Henry, *I Am the Truth*, 103–4; *Words of Christ*, 84.

690. Lowe, *Subjects of Experience*, 46 n.49.

691. Baker, *Persons and Bodies*, 127.

692. Corcoran, "Persons and Bodies," 335; Zimmerman, "Compatibility of Materialism and Survival," 205–7.

693. *E.g.*, Priest, *The Prestige*.

as we read them. The real world even has psychotics who suffer autoscopic delusion or subjective doubles syndrome, where they imagine that a double of them exists or they imagine that someone is their double, and we understand their reports as we deny their reality.[694] We sometimes nearly find our double when we discover a heartfelt note that we composed long ago but have completely forgotten and confront this other author who is us, yet who is not us.[695]

Regardless of how successful these other anomalies are in exposing the coherency of individual division, the word picture offered here, no matter how impracticable, can be visualized, which is the point: Two 'you's exist, with one having your personal identity.[696] Indeed, the critical difference of personal identity in the word picture is no difference at all for such philosophers as Darek Parfit who say that personal identity is literally nothing but a concept that we use as a stand-in for our identity judgment about personal characteristics.[697] Regardless of the question of the other you's personal identity, neither of you in the word picture knows who is original without testing for the virus. Division has doubled life.[698] Worth repeating is that you feel like the original, but, until tested for the virus, you have no way of knowing whether you are the original because everything pre-duplication has been duplicated. All that you can discern in this regard is that two qualitatively identical individuals live in the first moment and that you are one of them.[699]

Just as nothing can truly repeat exactly or it would just be the original,[700] nothing is literally identical with anything else in the sense of being exactly the same thing because *two* things cannot be only *one* of those things.[701] Two things, no matter how identical, are still different things. In the case of the word picture, the two of you have been in slightly different locations. Despite this difference, things can be identical in the sense that one thing has exactly everything that the other has and has

---

694. Carter and Frith, *Mapping the Mind*, 127–28; Klein and Hirachan, "Masks of Identities," 370.

695. Goethe, *Wilhelm Meister's Apprenticeship*, 44 (II,2).

696. Wiener, *Human Use of Human Beings*, 96, 102.

697. Parfit, *Reasons and Persons*, 253, 264, 271; Zimmerman, "Materialism, Dualism, and 'Simple,'" 206.

698. Parfit, *Reasons and Persons*, 253, 262.

699. Davis, *Risen Indeed*, 137.

700. Caputo, *Radical Hermeneutics*, 142.

701. Eckhart, "John," 146; Nicholas, "Learned Ignorance," 69 [I,17,49], 88 [II,1,92].

Divisibility's Coherence

exactly nothing that the other one lacks. They are indistinguishable one from the other, but are distinguishable in that there is one and there is the other. This sense of identicality is the sense used in the word picture. The two 'you's are the most perfectly identical of twins or clones, except for the presence of the virus and the difference in first-person perspective.

Even with these two differences, one intentional from the process and one inherent to personal identity, and despite the impossibility of two different things being the exact same thing, a person can still identify with a different person, even when not sharing everything, and this identifying is a cognitive act.[702] Using the word picture, you naturally identify with the other you, whether the other you is the original who was sick or the duplicated who is to live on.[703] That is, before the duplication, you were just *you*, with no other descriptor, and, after the duplication, you have become *you-sick* and *you-healthy*.[704] Often the point of a thought experiment involving a duplicated individual is how you would regard the other you,[705] but this is not the point of the word picture. It is trying to portray what is happening and is not trying to determine what should happen as a result. Presumably, though, you-sick wants you-healthy to live on, while you-healthy wants you-sick to make the best of the life that has been shortened.[706]

Even when identity is not a given, identifying can still occur. I do not have my neighbor's identity, but I can identify with her. Yet, such identifying is mostly experienced, not chosen, because identity and identification correspond, not just grammatically, but meaningfully.[707] So, in the word picture, given everything that the two 'you's share and given that there is no zero-sum conflict between you, you each cannot help but identify with the other. The absence of a zero-sum conflict may be necessary for this identifying. If only one of you, for instance, could live or live happily, a competitive conflict could overpower any sense of identifying. This of course is irrelevant to the identifying in the first place. If I had to choose one of my legs to lose, I could do that, but that I can choose one over the other does not mean I do not identify with both. Stories can

---

702. Lowe, "Probable Simplicity," 139.
703. Baker, *Persons and Bodies*, 136–37, 141.
704. Perry, *Identity*, 42–61, 82, 131–32, 160–61.
705. Parfit, "Unimportance of Identity," 421.
706. Parfit, *Reasons and Persons*, 264.
707. Perry, *Identity*, 153–56.

toy with this sort of clashing identification. Two sympathetic characters in conflict—*e.g.*, a suave jewel thief and a police detective—can create identification tension. I choicelessly identify with the detective. In WWII stories, I identify with the Allies no matter how sympathetic the Axis characters are. I, a Southerner, internally root in Civil War stories for the South, though losers in two senses. Identifying, like identity itself, is a product of or part of life, not entirely a choice. So, in the word picture, unless suffering from self-hatred so perverse as to be literally self-destructive (in which case the virus is not your biggest problem), the you who experiences through your personal identity also identifies with the you who does not.[708]

None of this changes which you it is through which you experience life. Identity is a fact in the word picture and in life.[709] Moving around your personal identity is thus unavailable; subjectivity is inalienable.[710] In each moment, a person has one's perceptions and no one else's with no other explanation at hand.[711] While you may prefer in the word picture to be the duplicate who is free of the virus, it is irrelevant to whether you are. "Life, thrown into itself, has always already thrown us into ourselves, into this Self that is similar to none other, that at no moment ever chose to be this Self that he is," Henry concluded.[712] Nor is personal identity duplicated in the word picture or ever.[713] This is because, as noted previously, personal identity inherently integrates.[714] Your personal identity in two bodies is conceivable if you could somehow control and receive inputs from both bodies, but, if this happened, you would in time integrate the two corporeal experiences just as we have done in real life with our two eyes, our two hands, and our two cerebrums.[715] This sort of duplication would not be *individual* duplication, but be *body* duplication.

Because your personal identity can never be doubled in the true sense of being the same and being two, the other you's personal identity

---

708. Welz, *Humanity in God's Image*, 54.

709. Grenz, *Theology for the Community*, 140; Kind, *Persons and Personal Identity*, 103.

710. Wallenfang, *Human and Divine Being*, 164.

711. Henry, *Incarnation*, 36.

712. Henry, *I Am the Truth*, 227–28.

713. Baker, *Persons and Bodies*, 108, 133; Jüngel, *God as the Mystery*, 182.

714. Strawson, "The Self," 12; Swinburne, "How to Determine Which," 108; Wippel, *Metaphysical Thought of Aquinas*, 363.

715. Zahavi, "Unity of Consciousness," 316.

in the word picture is an open issue, though the other you's personal identity is presumed to exist just as it is for every other person you meet.[716] The other you's personal character can be detected through observation and interrogation, but the other's identity cannot really be detected at all. The other you naturally seems to have a personal identity because the other you seems to have the same caliber of awareness as you do,[717] but only the other you is truly aware of its own awareness. If the other's personal identity does exist as it is presumed to, the reason for its existence is entirely unknown, as it always is, even yours. As to how the second personal identity happened, almost anything is possible. The duplicator may have added it, it may have naturally emerged when the brain was duplicated, the Creator may have given a special assist, or something entirely unknown may have been at work. It is of course also entirely possible that the personal identity is not a substance in need of creation at all, but is just the unity through which we experience our personal character. Since this is a word picture, not reality, the how-this-happened question needs no answer. Regardless of any duplication or division, the personal identity just is (or is not).

While the imperceptible personal identity necessarily distinguishes the two you's, this is *not* what makes you you. If "you" had emerged from the duplication without your memories, feelings, beliefs, and preferences, it could not in any meaningful sense be you.[718] If your memories, not to say the rest, are lacking, the so-called "duplicator" has failed.[719] Not only are your memories gone, but memories themselves form love, happiness,[720] faith,[721] and thankfulness,[722] which means that all of these of yours would be gone too. Further, your expectations need memories,[723] so your expectations would be gone as well, and, because your humor depends on expectations, this too would disappear. Indeed, all thinking involves connecting one thought to another, which requires a

---

716. Fichte, *Vocation of Man*, 108–9.

717. Bergson, *Time and Free Will*, 186.

718. Barresi and Martin, "History as Prologue," 42; Carter and Frith, *Mapping the Mind*, 169; Shoemaker, "On What We Are," 359, 362.

719. Moore, *Where Are the Dead?* 202.

720. Candler, *Theology, Rhetoric, Manuduction*, 62; Cavell, "The Self," 604–5.

721. Volf, *End of Memory*, 97.

722. Dalferth, *Creatures of Possibility*, 104.

723. Arendt, *Love and Augustine*, 56.

first thought to be applied to a second;[724] so, since none of your thoughts have survived, your thinking is no more. And without memories, you do not even know that "you" have lost anything because that "you" is gone. Thus, one need not be a Lockean—your memories are sufficient to be you—to realize that your memories are necessary to be you.[725]

The criticality of memory to being "you" is confirmed by the worst actual memory deprivation that has been reported, at least the worst by a patient who could bear witness. A hippocampus virus had destroyed the patient's ability to retain explicit memories beyond a few minutes old (while retaining implicit memories like language), and even this incomplete memory loss was to its sufferer "like being dead."[726] It is easy enough to understand, even without suffering a hippocampus virus, that, as Kierkegaard recognized, if all memories, all preferences, indeed all character, were lost, you are no one.[727] Characterless identity is a blank stare,[728] an empty clone.[729] It is memory, Augustine realized, that wards off "disintegration."[730] Proust aptly asked what is "the meaning of that immortality of the soul" if "The being that I shall be after death has no more reason to remember the man I have been since my birth than the latter to remember what I was before it."[731] The "resurrection of the soul after death," he answered, is "a phenomenon of memory."[732] No wonder Scripture demands remembrances.[733]

✼

A divided individual is understandable because this life's divided character is divisible, not in the world we know obviously, at least not utterly, but conceptually and sometimes pathologically. If, however, individual

---

724. Arendt, "Thinking," 78; "Willing," 37; McGilchrist, *Master and His Emissary*, 164.

725. Augustine, *Confessions*, X,xvii,26 (p. 194); Carter and Frith, *Mapping the Mind*, 177; Volf, *End of Memory*, 24, 147.

726. Corcoran and Sharpe, "Neuroscience and the Human," 123–25 & n.4.

727. Kierkegaard, *Either/Or*, II: 168.

728. Henry, *Material Phenomenology*, 45–48, 51, 66, 72; McCombs, *Paradoxical Rationality*, 151; Perry, *Identity*, 161.

729. Horne, "Person as Confession," 71; Whitehead, *Process and Reality*, 283.

730. Augustine, *Confessions*, II,i,1 (p. 24).

731. Proust, *In Search of Lost Time*, IV: 365.

732. Proust, *In Search of Lost Time*, III: 77.

733. Jobes, "Remember These Things," 192–93.

division were to happen, imaginatively now or actually in the afterlife, such that an individual was divided truly as well as recompleted into two individuals, we would know what has happened. The reason for demonstrating the coherency of individual divisibility in this way is that applying this notion to the afterlife preserves the paradox of salvation's extent, the next chapter's topic.

# 7

Preserving the Paradox

I have no other way out. One of us is stupid. Well, and you know one can never say that about oneself.

—Tolstoy, *Anna Karenina*

The thesis can be considered now that the extensive work of examining and, it is hoped, explaining the prerequisites has been provided. Prior chapters have shown that Scripture expresses about as well as it can that both everyone is ultimately saved and not everyone is, that the church's greats have through the centuries confirmed that Scripture sufficiently expresses each account, and that those articulating what Christianity means have, in order to avoid the obvious contradiction between the two accounts, been obliged to devalue one account so as to advocate for the other. As an alternative, so as to depreciate neither scriptural account and retain Scripture's full sense, the thesis is proposing a model that joins a divisible individual to the salvation paradox, which model allows both scriptural accounts to be as they purport to be—true. After the last chapter, this model should appear, if not evident, at least meaningful.

Christians can be in denial about a scriptural problem by assuming tradition has handled it,[1] but, for the paradox of salvation's extent, tradition has not handled it. The problem is not the Scripture, however, but the handling. "May I," Hamann asks, "venture a conjecture that strikes me as at least ingenious?"[2] Rather than subjecting Scripture's salvation paradox to an interpretation that is contrary to what it seems to be trying to say,[3] what is offered here is preserving the scriptural paradox, full stop. To do that, what is proposed is the divisibility of the individual, which is outwardly similar to tradition's afterlife purging, but no variety of purging does anything for the paradox of salvation's extent. Universalists purge everyone in order that no one is damned, and exclusivists purge only the saved in order that they enjoy eternal life. The proposed individual divisibility, in contrast, is applicable to everyone to allow for the saved *and* the damned in order that salvation's extent be paradoxical.

1. After This Life, Godly Is Divided from Ungodly

If the proposed model succeeds in preserving the salvation paradox by dividing the individual, *individual* would not be the first word to defy its etymology. The Greek variant of the Latinized *individual*, which is "atom," also meant like its Latin counterpart non-splittable, and the atom mostly was until the Manhattan Project proved otherwise.[4] Whether God will ultimately prove that the individual can likewise suffer divisibility (and do so without the hellish landscape) depends on Scripture's paradox of salvation's extent, and it is this chapter's special burden to deal with how individual divisibility preserves that paradox.

For individual divisibility to happen, that concept must be at least conceivable, which the last chapter has presumably addressed fully. The current chapter's exploration of what individual divisibility means in the afterlife also begins with the minimalist but manifest conception of the individual that was charted in the last chapter:

- An individual, according to appearances and independent of any constitutional elements, lives as a terrestrial body, a personal identity, and a personal character.

1. D. Hart, *That All Shall Be Saved*, 203.
2. Hamann, "Aesthetica in Nuce," 65.
3. Parry, "Universalist View," 103.
4. Fromm, "Modern Man," 21.

- Of those three, the personal identity and the personal character must be in the afterlife if there is to be such a life because otherwise there would be no us in it.
- Of those two, the personal character has in this life divided orientations, godly and ungodly.

With this understanding and again regardless of what substantively carries these personal features, the thesis is: For each individual, the dually oriented personal character is divisible between godly and ungodly after this life with the godly being saved and the ungodly not being saved, though the unifying personal identity experiences one or the other.

a. Divisible Individual (Personal Character)

As has been acknowledged, the proposal has taken no position on anthropological dualism, which is traditionally the body and the soul, nor any mediating hierarchy of essence.[5] On the subject of the individual's substances, Christianity, as well as philosophy generally, has ranged from a monism (or holism) where the individual is a unified substance such as just a body (or a spirited body), a dualism where the individual is the physical body with something beyond the physical like the soul, and a trichotomism where the individual is the physical body along with the life-force of the soul and the transcendent spirit.[6] Paul was likely a trichotomist (1 Thess 5:23),[7] as were most coeval theorists, such as Plato, Philo, Justin, Plutarch, Aurelius, Clement of Alexandria, Plotinus, and Didymus.[8] The model here can be agnostic on this ancient and ongoing dispute because a proposed division of the individual does not require knowing the substance of what is divided; instead, what must be known is what distinguishes what is to be divided. Darnel, as an illustration, is differentiated so as to be divided from wheat without any substantive differentiation of either, and, by analogy, godliness can be similarly differentiated from its negation so as to be divided irrespective of substance (Matt 13:26, 38).[9]

---

5. Martin, *Corinthian Body*, 15.
6. Lanzillotta, "One Human Being," 418–43; "Spirit, Soul and Body," 15–39.
7. Kooton, *Paul's Anthropology in Context*, 294, 296.
8. O'Laughlin, "Anthropology of Evagrius Ponticus," 363.
9. Nolland, *Matthew*, 545.

The internal life "correspond[s] to different and distinguishable aspects, but not to separable bits," Wollheim noted.[10]

The proposed model, while it bypasses the question of the individual's primary substances, including any dual*isms*, nonetheless uses personal dual*ities*, and it uses the two that have been explained and that tradition necessarily supplies. The first traditional duality that is used pertains to what is discontinuous and what is continuous from this life to the next. For the next life to not be this one, there must be discontinuity, and, for it is to be us from this life in the next, there must be continuity.[11] Traditionally, this division is something like spirit from body,[12] and that is not the divisibility proposed here, though this view can co-exist with the model. The model takes whatever continues, whether understood substantively as a soul, a mind, or a blueprint of the individual, and recognizes that the continuity must at least carry the personal identity and the personal character. To this doctrinal minimum regarding the first duality, the thesis adds divisibility to whatever its personal continuation is, and this divisibility is the result of the second traditional duality of the individual—our orientations.[13] That is, tradition's second duality is applied to the continuity of tradition's first duality, which Kevin Vanhoozer felicitously describes: The "fault-line that threatens to rip a human being apart is not that of body and soul, nor finitude or infinity, but rather the tension between what men and women were originally created and destined to be, on the one hand, and what they have actually become, on the other."[14] Recognizing that *individual* is divisible along these lines should preserve the salvation paradox—everyone who is damned is also saved, which means that everyone is saved and also that not everyone is, just as Scripture says.

As noted in chapter 6, the model rejects those anthropologies that are nihilistic, such as our being nothing but organic robots, but, given that the individual lives as a conflicted character, as also justified in chapter 6, the model must also discount anthropologies like those of revival perfectionist Charles Finney, who says godliness and ungodliness cannot "by

---

10. Wollheim, *Thread of Life*, 71.

11. Aquinas, *De Potentia*, Q.3, art. 2 (pp. 39–40); Polkinghorne, *God of Hope*, xxiii, 77, 149; Williamson, *Death and the Afterlife*, 87.

12. Balthasar, *Theo-Drama*, IV: 223; Brunner, *Eternal Hope*, 94; Ratzinger, *Eschatology*, 73–75, 104–5.

13. J. Cooper, *Body, Soul, and Life*, 49–50, 77, 101.

14. Vanhoozer, "Human Being," 162.

any possibility, co-exist in the same mind."[15] Cabasilas, as noted above, argued similarly,[16] and Luther expressed the same sentiment: "if God is in us, Satan is absent, and only a good will is present; if God is absent, Satan is present, and only an evil will is in us."[17] This position, found in such diverse traditions, is difficult to resist but for its lack of self-awareness, at least mine. Admittedly, if this position about being pure godly or pure ungodly is taken as merely a useful approximation of our condition or as an exhortation for what we should aspire to be, it is unobjectionable. It can even be accepted as descriptive of reality if it is taken to mean something like "*to the extent* God is in us, Satan is absent." The literal implication, however, that any of us in this life are only godly would be wonderful if true or that any of us are only ungodly would certainly make discernment simpler, but life and Scripture disabuse us of these fantasies, at least for nearly all of us.[18] Chapter 6 was intended to be convincing at least on that point.

Even the truism that we cannot be godly and ungodly at the same time in the same way still reflects that we live both, and, no matter how much the one predominates, the other remains potent.[19] Recognizing this means that entirely eliminating evil means eliminating, not just the evil that surfaces, but the source bringing it to the surface.[20] Using Luther's terms, both God and Satan are in each of us. While God could no doubt eliminate our fiendishness, that would entail eliminating us.[21] Speaking for myself, removing my evil means removing not just the evil that is mine but also the me that is me. This, fortunately, is not God's promised manner. God makes all things new, not all new things (2 Cor 5:17; Rev 21:5).[22]

The individual divisibility that is proposed, therefore, matches the distinctive of Christ reconciling an individual to God without destroying the individual.[23] He insists on each of us from each of us.[24] In becoming

---

15. Finney, *ST*, 38, 50.
16. Cabasilas, *Life in Christ*, Bk VI § 1, Bk VII § 1 (pp. 161, 197).
17. Luther, "De Servo Arbitrio," 180.
18. Come, *Kierkegaard as Theologian*, 133.
19. Harding, *Paul's Eschatological Anthropology*, 214, 218, 274.
20. Geisler, *ST*, 790.
21. H. Betz, *Galatians*, 272; Come, *Kierkegaard as Theologian*, 271; Guardini, *World and the Person*, 95.
22. Tonstad, *Revelation*, 309; Williamson, *Death and the Afterlife*, 181.
23. Pannenberg, *Human Nature*, 13.
24. Milbank, *Beyond Secular Order*, 127.

godly, we join God, not become God, and, when God faces us, he draws us in, away from what has charmed us.[25] If we face away from God, we face what is not God, which is ultimately tormenting or annihilating.[26] We are either becoming the self that God intends or spiraling into something like self-centeredness.[27] It is the difference between confronting our ungodliness and abiding in it.[28] "The light shines in the darkness, and no darkness grasped it," and those "doing evil" avoid the light, "but whoever does the truth comes toward the light" (John 1:5; 3:20–21). We might not identify with both light and darkness, but we live both.[29] The light and the darkness, though concurrent in this life, do not cohabitate in the ultimate (Rev. 22:5)—hence, the division.

In summary, apart from the naturally unifying terrestrial body (discussed repeatedly) and the inherently unifying personal identity (discussed further below), the next life's continuity includes the personal character, and the personal character's previously discussed dividedness in this life is divisible in the next.

b. Not Purging

In the afterlife, divisibility and purging, though similar, should not be confused. While both address how in the afterlife the ungodliness of a person discontinues as the saved person continues, the concepts of purging and divisibility differ essentially in the context of salvation's extent. Within Christian tradition, purging never applies to the damned, but applies only to persons on the eternal life trajectory.[30] For exclusivists, purging prepares the saved for eternal life, while the damned are not purged but perished, whether tormented or annihilated. For universalists, purging conveys everyone, particularly the laggards, into eternal life such that nothing is left but what survives the purging. That is, with exclusivism, purging saves no one because purging is for the saved, and,

---

25. Henry, *Words of Christ*, 31; Krapiec, *I-Man*, 356.
26. Balthasar, *Dare We Hope*, 129; Lewis, "Weight of Glory," 38; Pannenberg, *Anthropology in Theological Perspective*, 89.
27. Welz, *Humanity in God's Image*, 265.
28. Gregor, *Philosophical Anthropology*, 97; Lewis, *Mere Christianity*, 137–39, 161, 173–75.
29. Gregory of Nyssa, *Life of Moses*, Bk II (p. 53).
30. Schwarz, *Eschatology*, 337.

with universalism, purging damns no one because purging is what avoids damnation. Therefore, regardless of whichever conventional answer is given to salvation's extent, purging has no effect on the salvation paradox. Divisibility, on the other hand, is what models that paradox.

The reason that tradition does not apply purging to the damned is that the concept is unfit for that purpose. The perspective that purging necessarily entails is that of the preferred component. Purging silver, for instance, means removing impurities from the silver. Yet, from the impurities' perspective, the silver is removed from them. Because we generally prefer the silver over the rest, we call the process purging silver. From the ore's perspective, however, which is the total perspective, the silver and the non-silver are separated from each other—the ore is *divided* between the silver and the rest. It is the holistic perspective that calls the process divisibility and not purging. Like the perspective of the ore, divisibility treats both godliness and ungodliness as the individual, which they in fact are, whereas purging, like the perspective of the silver, removes ungodliness from the godly individual, which is the desirable bit.

Thomas demonstrated this distinction when he described this sort of eschatological process for the world (division) and for humans (purgation). For the world, "there will be a separation [*separatio*] of the elements, whatever is pure and noble remaining above for the glory of the blessed, and whatever is ignoble and sordid being cast down for the punishment of the damned." But, for humans, "it behooves . . . those things to be removed [*removeri*] which are opposed to glory. There are two, namely the corruption and stain of sin."[31] That is, for the world, the desired and undesired elements are separated from each other—they are divided—while, for humans, the undesired is removed from the desired—they are purged. Yet, regardless of whether it is the world or the person that is being made suitable for the end, the holistic perspective is that of division, good separated from bad.

This all-encompassing view is of course the divine view. God sees all of all, both godly and ungodly, though his relationship to each of them obviously differs.[32] If love endures all (1 Cor 13:7), God's love endures no less. As Barth understood, while we cannot literally "adopt the point of view of God," "we are exhorted" to "bear it in mind, consider it from

---

31. Aquinas, *ST III (Suppl.)*, XX, Q. 74, art. 1, co. (p. 95); *ST, Part III (Suppl.)*, XXI, Q. 97, art. 1, co. (p. 169); *Tertia Pars ST a Quaestione 60–90*.

32. Bultmann, "Theology as Science," 50; Jobes, "Remember These Things," 202.

all sides, and then live within its gravity."[33] Theology too, Adam Cooper recognized, should "embrace all things with a sensitivity and judgement shaped by the perspective of eternity."[34] This difference in perspective matters to that which is undergoing the process. Purging inherently disunites what is alien to each other, while division inherently disunites what is allied with each other.

In the context of the individual, unlike divisibility and contrary to fact, purging takes *self*ishness as foreign to the *self*.[35] Speaking for at least one of those selves, I am not who God wants me to be plus something apart from me, despite purging's implication; rather, I am both who God desires for me and who God does not. I want to be God's object *me*, but the subject *I* is too lazy and too attached to self-gratifying. As Barth encapsulated the situation, "the pronoun 'I' spells judgement."[36] This is probably a universal experience because humans acquire their ability to say things like "I" about the same age as they acquire their sense of *I*.[37] "The word 'I' remains the shibboleth of mankind," Buber noted.[38]

If God has chosen me for eternal life and even if I have done whatever is required of me, my glorification involves more than removing impurities, but involves saying farewell to the all of me that I have come to know. I have not died to myself in this life, not entirely, though I will to do so, mainly. On how rotten I am, my assessment can be off, and yet I can still be attached to nearly all of me because I remain my fallen universe's center. As Vittorio Montemaggi discerns, it is possible that there are "some who are able to live in total, loving surrender of self. I am not. . . . [I]t . . . has to do with . . . pride . . . I hope the reader will be able to forgive this, and to forgive also the impression of false modesty that this request is likely to give."[39] Removing the selfish me is not purging what is *not* me, but is, rather, dividing what *is* me.[40] Evil is of course alien to God, but he is not the one being transformed, whether purged or divided.

---

33. Barth, *Romans*, 516 (14:13).
34. A. Cooper, *Holy Eros*, 3.
35. Gundry, *Soma in Biblical Theology*, 213; Kierkegaard, *For Self-Examination*, 90.
36. Barth, *Romans*, 85 (3:9).
37. Carter and Frith, *Mapping the Mind*, 156.
38. Buber, *I and Thou*, 69.
39. Montemaggi, *Reading Dante's Commedia*, 39.
40. Gracia, *Individuality*, 30.

In contrast, for a biped, amputating a leg, no matter how necessary the surgery is to the patient's life, is still a subtraction, not a cleanse.

Afterlife purging is therefore decidedly different from afterlife divisibility, notwithstanding that both concepts understand humans as conflicted in this life and needing transformation afterwards. Because divisibility is, with the proposal, to be applied in the afterlife along with purging to deal with what is ungodly, the proposed divisibility can relieve the extent of purging traditionally called for or vice versa, and this issue is taken up in chapter 9. At hand, however, is the vital contrast between purging and divisibility. Purging removes what is unworthy for eternal life from the saved, but divisibility is regardless of destiny and does not presume which part of us is desired by us or ignore that the part that is removed is us—the us that we should not be, but the us that we are all the same. Thus, purging applies only to the saved, while divisibility applies to the damned too. As a consequence, purging, unlike divisibility, does nothing for Scripture's paradox of salvation's extent.

c. Undivided Personal Identity

The proposed model has not specified what substantively constitutes the individual, nor does the model require this sort of specificity to be workable. Instead, being the individual before and after death, regardless of any precise ontology, requires the individual's personal character, which is what differentiates the individual from all the other individual's in creation as well as from every other potential individual that the individual could have lived to be.[41] If any individual were to lose in bulk that individual's actual feelings, dispositions, and memories (whether real, corrupted, or imagined), that individual has been lost, and, if the individual were to lose any of them to any significant (*i.e.*, unnatural) extent, that individual is now a different individual. What is personally experiencing this loss, though, is the individual's personal identity.[42] No matter how radical the changes to the individual's personal character, they are changes to the *I*, and, if the changes are total, the *I* has been replaced. So long as it is the individual who experiences the loss, however, the individual's personal identity remains, which is, as Proust described, "the persevering and unalterable servant of our successive personalities; hidden away in

---

41. B. Williams, *Moral Luck*, 15.
42. McFarland, "Upward Call," 226, 228.

the shadow, . . . with no thought for the variability of the self. . . . It is as invariable as the intelligence and the sensibility are fickle, but since it is silent, gives no account of its actions, it seems almost non-existent. . . ."[43]

This bare personal identity bears on the person's ultimate destiny.[44] We may hope that we can identify with the blessed even when it is us, but, as polymath Stratford Caldecott explained, even those of us who are the hell-bound will not "regret their choice, since they are now completely identified (if not 'happy') with it. They have what they want."[45] Being possessed by God or being not so possessed is what is decisive here.[46] The more immersed in sin we are, the more sin is missed and the more painful the attraction to God.[47] Our orientations naturally appeal to us or we would not have them, and we thereby identify with them. My godliness, as an example, is drawn to God, and my ungodliness is drawn away; yet, if I identify with the ungodly, that is my identity, and vice-versa.[48]

The personal identity properly understood in this way highlights three features of how the proposed model works theologically. First, the model is intentionally ambivalent on whether the personal identity is entirely given or partially chosen, and this tolerates either of the conceptions of identity previously described—either the personal identi*ty* that is given or the person's identi*fying* that is partly chosen. The first conception, the purely given personal identi*ty*, is entirely based on our experienced perspective, which is just present or not, and the second, the person's identi*fying*, which is partly chosen, is something that we do but that is nevertheless strongly constrained, such as the way we identify with characters in a story. This latter sense of a more active identifying is admittedly beyond mere awareness, but is a sort of empathy resulting from life's experiences;[49] and this sort of identifying requires at least a trace of the personal character that a led life renders, but this is no problem for the model because personal identity accompanies personal character in any event. As Fromm saw, this kind of identity for a person "is nothing but the expression of his character."[50]

43. Proust, *In Search of Lost Time*, II: 425–26.
44. Welz, *Humanity in God's Image*, 153.
45. Caldecott, *Radiance of Being*, 243.
46. Speyr, *The Word*, 112.
47. Ramelli, *Christian Doctrine of Apokatastasis*, 379.
48. Clarke, *Person and Being*, 98–99; Ludlow, *Universal Salvation*, 60.
49. Lowe, "Probable Simplicity," 139.
50. Fromm, *Man for Himself*, 233.

The particular theological implication of this range of understanding, from the experienc*ing* identi*ty* to the experienc*ed* identi*fying*, is that the model is thereby agnostic on the issue of atonement's extent and the tension between predestination and freewill. That is, the model can manage the Christian pole of Wesleyanism, Arminianism, and Molinism, where a person responsively chooses to identify as godly (or not), as well as the Christian pole of five-point Calvinism, where God alone chooses a person's identity as godly (or not), and any of the more common intermediate Christian combinations of divine grace and human response.[51] Thus, the modeled personal identity can be any blend of the given and the formed.

The second theological implication of the modeled personal identity is that, while the *pre*mortem personal identity is part of the model, the model does not entirely account for the *post*mortem personal identity because, as chapter 6 explained, the personal identity cannot be divided into two and remain that person's identity. Even saying "two awarenesses (sic)" is ungrammatical. If any awareness were ever to be in the plural, it would either literally refer to different persons or nonliterally refer to personalities sharing one person's body or to one person whose one (literal) awareness was in a sort of stereo, such as the way the brain hemispheres of one person have different outlooks. Factually, as well as grammatically, each awareness is unitary. The personal identity's inherent unity, which entails its indivisibility, therefore raises the question of what happens postmortem to the personal identity when the personal character is divided postmortem.

The model gives no answer to that question, which is consistent with the model not addressing what all is included postmortem generally. The model accepts that our life has a personal identity and that the saved has eternal life, which means the premortem personal identity may generally continue postmortem, but, because the personal character of one person can suffer the two ultimates and because no identity can be divided into two and be that one person's identity, how the postmortem transformation handles the personal identity is left open. That is, after the individual division, one of two personal characters can experience postmortem through the premortem personal identity, but the model says nothing about the existence, nature, or source of the personal identity, if any, for the other personal character.

---

51. Johnson, ed., *Five Views on Extent of Atonement*.

While the thesis does not model what happens postmortem regarding the personal identity beyond the premortem one, answers are available for those requiring one. If the negative ultimate is oblivion rather than torment, the personal identity of the damned is ultimately a nonissue because no second personal identity is required for what is annihilated. Another mitigation would be if the saved were purged as tradition already provides; then the saved would also not require division at all because, after purging, nothing is left to be divided and, thus, no extra personal identity is required. Regardless of these extenuations, the personal identity question can remain, and its answer turns on whether the personal character, once it is divided into two, requires a second personal identity.

If each personal character after its division does require a personal identity, any postmortem transformation must include a new one to pair with the characters that are divided into two. This doubling of the personal identity is presumably what happened in chapter 6's word picture, though even in that scenario when the two you's confronted each other, the other's personal identity was as foreign to you as anyone else's. A second personal identity presumably manifested then just as it does with each fictional teleportation. This supposed second personal identity could of course just be the natural consequence of a personal character experiencing rather than any additional *thing* being present.

On the other hand, if a personal identity is *not* required for each postmortem personal character, which seems likely, then no personal identity needs to be added postmortem under any circumstance. While it has been insisted that every personal character in this life has a personal identity, and the one that we are most intimately aware of certainly has one, nothing but that familiarity precludes its absence later. As has been noted, some theorists of the self, like Parfit, hold that no one has a personal identity at all beyond the (fully duplicatable) personal character.[52] This position is not based on common experience, at least not mine, but is based on rhetorical questions following thought experiments,[53] which are hardly ever convincing,[54] and this was controverted in chapter 6 when dealing with the personal identity. The Parfitian holding, however, entails the more limited and more commonsensical point that a personal character does not *need* a personal identity. While the main Parfitian

---

52. Parfit, *Reasons and Persons*, 253, 264, 271; Zimmerman, "Materialism, Dualism, and 'Simple,'" 206.

53. Baker, *Persons and Bodies*, 134 n.28.

54. Gendler, "Exceptional Persons," 459; Wilkes, *Real People*, 1–48.

holding depends on thought experiments convincing us of a reality that we do not recognize outside of science fiction, its more limited point takes the thought experiments as word pictures, which need only convey what is possible, not what is real. That is, Christian theorists can reject the main Parfitian holding because they know that the personal identity is real,[55] but they can agree with the more limited Parfitian point that the personal identity is not required because they also know that such identity is largely a matter of God's will.[56] So, the personal character can conceivably lack a personal identity, and, therefore, any character in the afterlife can exist without one.

In any event—that is, regardless of whether an additional personal identity is needed or not in the afterlife—the personal identity's indivisibility is no obstacle for the model. Either an extra one is mysteriously present when needed in the same way the original one is mysteriously present now, or an extra one is not needed at all. The issue of what happens postmortem is uncertain because the *post*mortem experience is not modeled here other than what happens postmortem to the *pre*mortem personal identity and character, which is all the salvation paradox contemplates. Admittedly, the fact that the model raises at all the prospect of a new personal identity validates the initial reaction that individual divisibility is strange, but this is to be expected from modeling paradoxes. Christians are familiar with the feeling. Modeling a man as God means he had a mother[57] and genitalia.[58] Very strange. And modeling life as eternal means that to die is to live (Matt 10:39; John 12:25; Gal 2:20).[59] No less strange.

The third noteworthy theological feature of how personal identity works in the proposed model is that it reinforces the difference with universalism. While the model recognizes that anyone can be both saved and damned, which preserves Scripture's salvation paradox, the model leaves in play the personal identity, which as a unity cannot be both saved and damned. The two "ways of life meet not only in the personal form for which he is responsible before God," von Speyr explained, but the individual "has himself become a point of convergence"; "whatever

---

55. Baker, *Persons and Bodies*, 134 n.28.

56. Davis, *Risen Indeed*, 116–22.

57. Gonzalez, *Story of Christianity*, 299–302, 304–5; Kelly, *Early Christian Doctrines*, 343, 498.

58. Cunningham, *Genealogy of Nihilism*, 259.

59. Colijn, *Images of Salvation*, 87.

in our offer of ourselves may seem to have a . . . relative character," "we can always live at the center, the axis, of God's choice."[60] If we knew only God, universalism would make perfect sense, but we know ourselves too. And as students of history, we know others as well.[61] Marx's "The more man puts into God, the less he retains in himself"[62] can be felt despite its fallaciousness.

Therefore, my personal identity's destiny, which follows from with whom I identify, is not unquestionably the God-oriented me. Desiring one orientation does not eliminate the other.[63] The me that is self-oriented draws me away.[64] God "is waiting and watching" for what in each of us "even He cannot produce," C. S. Lewis remarked, and it is for what we "freely give Him or freely refuse Him."[65] "It would not truly be salvation if it were given to someone who did not want it," the Ambrosiaster observed.[66] Because the personal identity by its nature integrates even when, if not especially when, the personal character is conflicted, we identify, at least predominantly, with the character that is oriented toward God or we do not identify with it, and, so, our personal identity has to be one or the other. It cannot be both because, if personal identity is two, it is not personal identity any more than a bachelor who is married is a bachelor. In a manner of speaking, our personal character can be universalist to an extent, but our personal identity is exclusivist to its only extent.

☙❧

The thesis is that whatever the individual is that continues from this life into the next is divisible. That which continues, as has been noted repeatedly, is manifestly not the earthly body, which in death eventually suffers its own thoroughly disassembling division. Rather, what continues beyond this life, regardless of how it subsists and of whatever it becomes, includes the personal character that has lived and the personal identity that has experienced that life. Of the two, the personal identity, your awareness, is intrinsically indivisible, but the personal character, the

---

60. Speyr, *Christian State of Life*, 93, 109.
61. Pannenberg, *Anthropology in Theological Perspective*, 485.
62. Marx, "Economic and Philosophical Manuscripts," 79.
63. Wollheim, *Thread of Life*, 183.
64. Lubac, *Catholicism*, 342.
65. Lewis, *Mere Christianity*, 164–65.
66. Ambrosiaster, "Commentaries on Pauline Epistles," 179 [1 Tim 2:4].

actual lived you, is nearly divided normally and, therefore, can be divided actually. The next section revisits the justification for modeling the divisibility of the personal character after this life.

2. Individual Afterlife Divisibility Allows the Salvation Paradox

Though Scripture says both that everyone is saved and that not everyone is, no interpreter has yet entirely tolerated that position. An exclusivist majority says Scripture only *seems* to declare that everyone is saved, a universalist dissent says Scripture only *seems* to declare that some are damned, and potentialists, when they are not hopeful exclusivists, say Scripture only *seems* lucid in declaring both. Taking either scriptural account as not meaning what it says can ring false, and taking Scripture as effectively unmeaningful can ring not at all. As an alternative to these traditional answers, the thesis here offers the model of an individual who is divisible after this life. Incorporating all the scriptural data, however, comes, as it almost always does, at a high price. In this case, the cost is to eviscerate the common presumption that the individual is indivisible, but the payoff is that the proposal takes both scriptural accounts as they are presented—true and meaningful. Incorporating all the data is, after all, the measure of a theory's worth.[67]

To make plain the difference among the various positions on salvation's extent, the responses that theologians have given to the salvation paradox can be compared in simple tabular form based on each position's fidelity to the scriptural accounts of salvation's extent and each position's sufferance of the principle of noncontradiction. The table separately treats the two potentialist rationales that were previously typed (Type III having no rationale) and, like the other positions, the thesis is given a handle, "paradoxism":

---

67. Rawls, *Theory of Justice*, 52.

Preserving the Paradox

	Universalism	Exclusivism	Potentialism I	Potentialism II	Paradoxism
Everyone is ultimately saved	True	*False*	*Maybe*	True	True
Not everyone is ultimately saved	*False*	True	*Maybe*	True	True
Truths cannot (actually) contradict	True	True	True	*False*	True

Universalism is true in that everyone is saved; exclusivism is true in that only some are; and potentialism, when not just optimistic exclusivism, is true in not choosing between the two accounts. Each position, however, denies a truth (italicized), and they do so when rejecting what is evident and agreed on by the others. Universalism denies that Scripture says some are not ultimately saved, when it patently does say so at times. Exclusivism denies that Scripture says everyone is ultimately saved, when it patently does say so at times. Potentialism either (I) denies both accounts by adding *potentially* every time or (II) denies reality by believing in an actual contradiction. Each position, true in the positive, strays in the denial.

In short, when embracing Scripture, each position is true; when refraining, each is deficient. "For it is . . . by negation rather than positively," adopting Pater's description, "that such theories fail to satisfy us permanently, and what they really need for their correction, is the complementary influence of some greater system . . . in which they may find their due place."[68] Paradoxism, in contrast to the traditional answers, is scripturally all in, and, despite taking the scriptural accounts as-is, it still takes the principle of noncontradiction as indispensable. That is, universalism is true, exclusivism is true, and, when distinct, potentialism is right; but only paradoxism treats the salvation paradox as truths in apparent contradiction. In terms of the noncontradiction principle, paradoxism models the scriptural accounts such that they are not contradicting *in the same way*.

Paradoxism, as has been admitted, comes with a cost. That cost comes from exploiting the resiliency of "one" as expressed in words like

---

68. Pater, *Marius the Epicurean*, 183.

"every*one*" and as implied in words like "all," but this cost is taken to be worth it because it is Scripture's paradox of salvation's extent that exposes this resiliency. Of those who are not saved, they are also saved by being divided between their orientations, which means that what Scripture says about salvation's extent is all true, everyone is saved and not everyone is. This particular cost for the model of the salvation paradox may be no coincidence since the models of both the Trinity and the hypostatic union, each exposing a full scriptural truth, have already traveled a similar path, each taking advantage of the resilience of "one" in those paradoxes. Just as the Trinity models how the *one* God can be three and just as the hypostatic union models how the *one* Son can be both the Divine and the human, the divisible individual models how the *one* person can be both saved and not. With this understanding of the divisibility of life, the salvation paradox can rejoin the other Christian paradoxes and be taken in its entirety.[69] That is, paradoxism fully retains both scriptural accounts without changing what they mean or, which is the same thing, changing what the same word in each account means.

Scriptural necessity divides the individual in order to preserve the salvation paradox, and, if the maxim is true, *necessity can break iron*,[70] necessity can break the individual. Paradoxism, however, seemingly violates a different maxim, *a part cannot exceed its whole*,[71] because, under the proposed model, dividing one individual counterintuitively results in more than that, which is two individuals and not two fractional individuals as a division would ordinarily entail. Yet, this too is no problem because this maxim is frequently disproven, even in this life, whenever division produces doubling. As examples, identical doubles occur when the first two cells of a fertilized sea-urchin egg are separated or when flatworms are split.[72] More commonly, division doubles each time a cell reproduces via mitosis.[73] In this life, therefore, a doubling is possible whenever there is a division *plus* energy, and there is no reason to suspect that eternal life's division is any less dynamic since its "plus" transcends mere energy. This notion of an individual divisibility that doubles reveals, instead of scriptural cul-de-sacs for salvation's extent, one universalist,

---

69. Wallenfang, *Human and Divine Being*, 28–29.

70. Feuerbach, *Essence of Christianity*, I,XV (p .146).

71. Marsilius, *Defensor Pacis*, II: I,XIII,2 (p. 51).

72. Crick, *Astonishing Hypothesis*, 6; Neuhof, Levin, and Rechavi, "Vertically- and Horizontally-Transmitted Memories," 1177–88.

73. McIntosh and Koonce, "Mitosis," 622.

one exclusivist, formed by an inviolate individual, the truth of both scriptural accounts as reconnected through the divisible individual. Hesiod knew that it was only "fools" who "do not know how much more the half is than the whole . . . ."[74]

3. The Divisible Individual Transitions into the Afterlife

The proposed model can now be exercised within the nonparadoxical features of ultimate salvation that chapter 2 identified and that have since been worked within. These, to summarize, involve roughly three explanatory moments:

- Death: This life ends.
- Separation: The godly are separated from the ungodly for eternal life.
- Completion: The eternally living are completed.

Paradoxism, as part of the separation moment, applies after the first moment and leads to the third. The first of the three moments, biological death, which ushers in the afterlife moments of separation and completion, is temporally before the latter two at least in their ultimate form, but the subsequent pair need not be sequential with respect to each other. Because the accomplishments of each of these last two moments are different, however, their occurrence can be addressed separately, but their sequencing is not required.

Paradoxism, like the salvation paradox itself, has no effect on the temporally and causatively prior first moment. While "death marks an end for the whole person," Rahner observed, "the reality of man . . . is not abolished in death, but rather is transposed into another mode of existence . . . ."[75] This transposition is unaffected by, but well timed for, paradoxism. To whatever extent we believe in an afterlife, we appreciate its radical divergence from this one. As for the second moment, when paradoxism *is* applied to the salvation paradox, the effect of the proposed model is circumscribed here too. Paradoxism changes the separation from that of the traditional one of between godly individuals *and* ungodly individuals to that of between the godly and ungodly *as to* each individual. Otherwise, it remains the case that the godly have eternal

---

74. Hesiod, "Works and Days," 41 (pp. 88–91).
75. Rahner, *Foundations*, 437–38.

life, the ungodly do not, and individuals have both; and eternity still somehow conserves and completes this life.[76] As for the third moment of completion, which is the result of the salvation paradox, it too involves a transformation[77] and is also untouched by paradoxism because whatever completion that occurs in the afterlife still occurs with paradoxism.[78] Paradoxism, as part of the separation moment, enables the completion moment, but does not change it. That which bears no fruit is cut off, and all that bears fruit is cut clean to be completed (John 15:2).[79]

As applied between the transitioning moment of death and the transforming moment of completion, paradoxism is at home in ultimate salvation's broad understanding. Each of us is oriented godly and selfish, the first orientation because that was the design and the second because, as C. S. Lewis observed, "The moment you have a self at all, there is a possibility of putting yourself first—wanting to be the centre—wanting to be God, in fact."[80] The doomed worship the self, and death gives them their ambition,[81] vindicating the Hasidic aphorism, "There is no room for God in him who is full of himself."[82] That is, both those seeking God and those seeking any other god obtain their desire.[83] Individuals who are unprepared to live with God leave authentic existence, usually by claiming godhood.[84] Ratzinger explained, "man wishes to be God." "Yet man pursues it in the style of a Prometheus, hunting the prey which is equality with God, taking it by violence. But man is not God. By making himself like unto God he sets himself over against truth, and so the adventure ends in that nothingness where truth is not."[85] Because identity and identification are coupled,[86] if we identify *with* God, we are with him, and, if we identify *as* God, either directly or through a surrogate, we are with someone less. In God's realm, we are living glorified; in any other realm,

---

76. White, *Life Beyond Death*, 68.

77. Behr, *Mystery of Christ*, 105, 143; Blowers, *Maximus the Confessor*, 229, 236, 247.

78. Edwards, "Miscellanies," 1099; Rahner, *Foundations*, 441.

79. Keener, *John*, II: 993–98.

80. Lewis, *Mere Christianity*, 38.

81. Lewis, *Problem of Pain*, 124–25.

82. Buber, *Ten Rungs*, 102.

83. Lewis, *Great Divorce*, 75.

84. Guardini, *Freedom, Grace, and Destiny*, 80.

85. Ratzinger, *Eschatology*, 64–65.

86. B. Williams, *Problems of the Self*, 41.

we are living nowhere, or worse.[87] Paradoxism highlights all this. Despite its radicality, people still experience eternal life and perishing, including resurrection, judgment, and completion, and this existence still relates to Father-glorifying, Son-following, and Spirit-filling. The only change that individual divisibility offers is the preservation of the salvation paradox.

※

The chapters before this one established independently the thesis' two elaborate but fundamental requisites that are seemingly disconnected: The church has not preserved the scriptural paradox of salvation's extent, and the individual is notionally divisible. This chapter has taken the by-now fully anticipated, almost inevitable, step of connecting these two observations, and that step is to preserve the paradox by dividing the individual. To reach this point, the issue has not been what are salvation's binary outcomes, but the extent to which non-binary individuals have them. And the answer is that, with division, an individual can have both outcomes to an extent. It is a Dickensian tale, not of two kinds of persons, not even of two cities except as metaphor, but of one person in two kinds, and the tale begins, "we were all going direct to Heaven, we were all going direct the other way . . . ."[88]

In sum, paradoxism is literally and specifically: That which is godly has eternal life, and that which is ungodly has perishing. While the church has thus far preferred to destroy the salvation paradox so as to preserve the individual, whether purged or not, by saying that an individual is either saved or unsaved, paradoxism prefers the paradox even if to hell with the individual. This reading of Scripture is as it should be. Its "most unvarying fate," Luther pointed out, is "to have the world in a state of tumult . . . ."[89] Though this dividing of an individual is perhaps ironic given the positive focus here on the individual, whatever distress the individual is found to suffer as exposed by paradoxism confirms the intuition that something can only be transformed by attending to it.

If dividing the individual seems too costly to preserve the scriptural paradox, the following chapters might help the reader to appreciate that cost. The next chapter detects substantiation for the individual's afterlife

---

87. Henry, *Words of Christ*, 83; Kempis, *Imitation of Christ*, III,IX,1; Pieper, *Death and Immortality*, 59.

88. Dickens, *Tale of Two Cities*, 1.

89. Luther, "De Servo Arbitrio," 129.

division within Scripture and its theological tradition, and the ensuing chapter deals with how paradoxism can otherwise suit Christian doctrine.

8

Christianity's Divisible Individual

> *Understanding clearly then for the first time that for every man and for himself nothing lay ahead but suffering, death, and eternal oblivion, he decided that . . . he had either to explain his life so that it did not look like the wicked mockery of some devil, or shoot himself.*
>
> —Tolstoy, *Anna Karenina*

As chapter 1 committed to concerning the data sources to be exploited, Scripture has seeded the discourse throughout and formed the paradox from which the individual's afterlife divisibility has emerged, but the discourse has to this point not examined Scripture for what, if anything, it says about the afterlife divisibility of the individual outside of the salvation paradox's intimation of it and the concept of the individual's dividedness generally. This chapter adds that examination. Scripture, no surprise to anyone familiar with it, never says the individual is actually divisible, but what is surprising is that, once paradoxism is allowed to compete for our understanding, scriptural oddities if taken at face value can point in that direction. The chapter's second half considers those working with Scripture who, without preserving the salvation paradox, approach paradoxism's strangest feature. That is, several theologians, in explaining the incongruity of nonbinary individuals entering the binary of eternal life, have offered such graphic descriptions of afterlife purging that they nearly substantiate paradoxism's claim that the individual is divisible after this life.

1. Scriptural Hints of Afterlife Divisibility Are Ignored

Scripture could theoretically have repudiated afterlife individual divisibility, but, even to the casual reader, it is obvious that it does not deal with this topic at all. Scripture, of course, is not obliged to reject every craziness. Indeed, the specifics of any life beyond this one is almost in any regard an unexplored topic,[1] as exemplified by the scriptural quiet concerning Holy Saturday (Mark 16:1) and by Paul's account of his heavenly trip "in or out of the body, I know not, God knows" (2 Cor 12:2–3). Scripture's seeming disinterest in any life beyond this one cannot be compensated for by other data on this question because non-scriptural afterlife data is inherently subjective—each reported experience is, and is bound to be, a personal one.[2] So, no evidence is available that disproves the individual's divisibility in the afterlife, but this absence of evidence is obviously no evidence of the absence.

While the absence of evidence is generally no evidence, the very absence does become evidential when it is weighed against the evidence for divisibility because the latter, to be offered below, will necessarily preponderate. Further, evidentiary silence, like Sherlock's unbarking dog, can be evidentiary if affirmative evidence should exist but does not.[3] Scripture, as noted, frequently employs concepts involving the individual and relies acutely on the individual's orientations to answer the question of *who we are*.[4] "The Bible focuses relentlessly on the human being," Gordon McConville summarized, and "it identifies the nature of humanity as belonging centrally to the subject matter of biblical portrayal . . . ."[5] Scripture, despite this extended treatment of who the individual is, not

---

1. Ratzinger, *Eschatology*, 128; Rowland, "Eschatology of the NT Church," 59.
2. Nichols, *Death and Afterlife*, 91–112; White, *Life Beyond Death*, 61–62; Zaleski, "Near-Death Experiences," 614–28.
3. Frost, "Death of Josiah," 369; Lange, "Argument from Silence," 288–301.
4. Crisp and Sanders, eds., *Christian Doctrine of Humanity*, 15; Pannenberg, *Anthropology in Theological Perspective*, 395; Rosner, "Son of God," 224.
5. McConville, *Being Human*, 7, 9.

once indicates that that individual can never be divisible.[6] This contrasts with the intimations about individual divisibility to be discussed now.

The meaning of Scripture is inexhaustible, which explains why novel lessons have properly been learned as circumstances have warranted them.[7] "There is something to be gained from the obscurity of the inspired discourses of Scripture," Augustine understood.[8] Indeed, sources like Scripture that put demands on their auditors tend to answer only the questions that are put to them,[9] and this requires that the proper questions be put. In the case at hand, Scripture, if it is interrogated without assuming that the individual is always indivisible, hints at divisibility in at least five ways. First, Scripture relates descriptions of the afterlife that are so violent that they tend to be written off as gratuitously so, but, if read plainly, they suggest individual divisibility then. Second, Scripture says not infrequently that eternal life pertains to *what*, not *who*, experiences it and these grammatical anomalies may point to ultimate salvation pertaining to individual predicates, not individuals *in toto*. Third, Scripture adds that eternal life and perishing, despite being binaries, can be experienced to an extent, which must be taken as nonliteral to preserve the integrity of the binaries, but individual divisibility literally accounts for these expressions. Fourth, to relate how binary outcomes can be scalably experienced, the NT uses extensively a small Greek word that contributes additional contingency to the already contingent "if," whose combination should mean "to the extent," a relationship common in English but is otherwise unexpressed in the NT. Finally, Scripture describes everyone in the eschaton experiencing eternal life, oddly including those who also perish then, which is taken as muddled on a literal level, but actually describes the unsaved person experiencing both ultimates, for which a divided person allows.

These five readings run exegetically upstream, but follow to a fault that which is written. These scriptural oddities ordinarily suffer the exegetical stratagem that the reader has repeatedly encountered already. It is the technique that exclusivists and universalists have launched at those passages inconveniencing their own position: Scripture is figurative whenever its more obvious meaning infringes the interpreter's preconception.

---

6. Berkouwer, *Man: Image of God*, 264.
7. Blowers, *Maximus the Confessor*, 137.
8. Augustine, *City of God*, XI,19 (p. 450).
9. Zizioulas, *Being as Communion*, 215.

In contrast, the readings proposed here are almost Kierkegaardian: "What is needed above all is to get the huge libraries and scribblings and the eighteen hundred years out of the way in order to gain the view."[10] "Would it ever occur to a lover to read a letter from his beloved with a commentary!" After translation, "Every commentary detracts."[11] While, as the discipline requires, the experts are still consulted here and the readings have benefited from the consultation, the fuller explanation for their inclusion may only reflect a timidity that Kierkegaard did not share.

The readings offered are admittedly inventive and hence precarious, but this does not threaten the thesis even if the readings later prove to be more original than correct because they are *not* what establish paradoxism. Its model derives its justification entirely from Scripture's paradox of salvation's extent, and this is what the prior chapters have addressed. The exegesis here is not even secondary support for paradoxism. That honor belongs to the scriptural insistence that the ultimates are binary extremes while humans run the gamut between the extremes, of which paradoxism, like purging, makes sense. Instead, the readings that appear below, which purport to find paradoxism within Scripture, are similar to how the church found Scripture expressing Trinitarianism. The church did not first see the Trinity expressed in Scripture, but, after finding Scripture in paradox, arrived at the Trinity and only then found Scripture expressing it.[12] This is the preferred approach for advancing the human understanding of reality's difficulties,[13] and it has become the scientific method: Develop a model to explain the unintelligible and *then* proceed to the facts for validation or invalidation.[14]

a. Unheeded Descriptions

Scripture, as has been seen, frequently portrays the individual as conflicted in this life, but it also occasionally, as will be shown in what follows, suggests more, which is divisibility afterwards. Scripture is not read this

---

10. Kierkegaard, *Book on Adler*, 43.

11. Kierkegaard, *JP*, I: 85 (entry 210).

12. Dunning, *Grace, Faith, and Holiness*, 177; Wiles, *Making of Christian Doctrine*, 53; Wolinski, "Trinity: Theological History," 1606–7.

13. Al-Ghazali, "Deliverance from Error," 25; Kant, "Preface to Second Edition," 20 (B xiii).

14. Caputo, *Radical Hermeneutics*, 215–16; Northrop, "Introduction," 3–4.

way, however, because of the innocent assumption that the individual is *in*divisible, and, given this assumption, Scripture must be reinterpreted to protect itself from the outlandishness of the opposing idea. The outlandish of afterlife divisibility is found in two sorts of statements credited to Jesus, both literally expressing the severing of the individual in the context of eschatological judgment.

In a series of parables about God's coming judgment, Jesus warns that he has come to give the earth *division* (διαμερισμόν, Luke 12:5, 36–38, 45–46, 51//Matt 10:28, 34; 24:51). Tradition politely takes the warned-of division as the usual one of people being eschatologically sorted into two different groups, one saved and one not, but Jesus betrays this reading by saying that the God-figure *will cut in two* (διχοτομήσει) the unworthy servant and assign *part* (μέρος) of him to the unbelievers. Sensing that Jesus could say nothing so grisly as that people will be divinely cleaved in two and with little choice outside of quitclaiming the gospels altogether, some exegetes blame the gospel writers in this case for mistranslating Christ's unrecorded Aramaic, which would naturally have been less savage.[15] This theory is pure conjecture, of course.[16] So, the usual recourse for any uncomfortable scriptural idea is adopted instead—it is figurative! Specifically, Christ's twisted phrasing is excused as a particularly flashy image of a severe beating.[17] Yet, no exemplars support this hypothesis either, which leaves Jesus expressing διχοτομήσει with its literal meaning of *cut in two*.[18] Josephus, for instance, contemporaneously uses the word in his Greek account of the key article in Solomon's split-the-baby decision.[19]

So, on its surface, this parable is referring to an individual's eschatological division based on the presence and absence of that person's faith.[20] Further endorsing διχοτομήσει's literal "cut in two" meaning is its use with μέρος, which uncontroversially denotes "part, in contrast to the whole" or derivatively "body parts."[21] Parts are what obviously result from something being divided.[22] The literal meaning of the *cutting in two* of a

15. Hagner, *Matthew 14–28*, 724–25.
16. Nolland, *Luke 9:21—18:34*, 704.
17. Bock, *Luke 9:51—24:53*, 1182; Carson, "Matthew," 511; Morris, *Matthew*, 617–18.
18. BDAG, 253; Plummer, *Luke*, 332–33.
19. Spicq, *Theological Lexicon*, I:351.
20. Bovon, *Luke 9:51—19:27*, 240.
21. BDAG, 633–34; Nebe, "Μέρος," 409–10.
22. Stein, *Luke*, 362.

person also serves the parable's point that the unworthy servant is leading a "double" life of faithfulness and faithlessness.[23] The parable certainly has in view the notion that a person variably experiences afterlife judgment given that Jesus contemporaneously refers to a range of individualized eschatological floggings (Luke 12:47–48).[24] Why would this parable describe a person's bisection based on faith if that is not what it meant? Admittedly, the parable could be an inexplicable anomaly, but, if so, it is one that the authors of both Luke and Matthew, each with a demonstrated willingness to edit,[25] separately choose to retain. If as seems more likely the wording is intentional, the parable indicates that the individual is divisible in the afterlife.[26]

This afterlife parable of a person being cut in two is not even Jesus' most gruesome depiction of the divisive consequences to come. He twice commends to audiences that lack anesthetics self-amputation so as to avoid hell. "If your right eye scandalizes you, extract it and cast it away, for one appendage perishing, and not your whole body cast into hell, secures you," and, in case that were not clear enough, he repeats the amputation point for the right hand (Matt 5:29–30). When Christ revisits the subject, he is ebullient:

> To the extent your hand scandalizes you, cut it off; you're better off entering life maimed than having two hands entering hell, the unquenchable fire. To the extent your foot scandalizes you, cut it off; you're better off entering life lame than having two feet cast into hell. To the extent your eye scandalizes you, cast it out; you're better off entering God's reign one eyed than having two eyes cast into hell, where their worm dies not and the fire quenches not .... (Mark 9:43–49//Matt 18:8–9)

Because these passages would seem to be literally insane (*i.e.*, apotemnophilia, the compulsion to amputate one's own limbs), they too must be interpreted nonliterally and this time as a figure of speech for how seriously sin should be taken.[27] Using here this device, however, thoroughly dulls the point of Christ's vivid images.[28] He is supposedly offering these

---

23. Fitzmyer, *Luke*, II: 986.
24. Bock, *Luke 9:51—24:53*, 1184–86.
25. Carson, "Matthew," 16–17; Stein, *Luke*, 59.
26. Origen, *On First Principles*, II,10,7 (pp. 144–45).
27. Blomberg, *Matthew*, 109, 275; Carson, "Matthew," 151; Edwards, *Mark*, 293–96; Lane, *Mark*, 347–50.
28. Czachesz, "Why Body Matters," 406; Morris, *Matthew*, 119; Stein, *Mark*, 449.

"shocking" words to say that sin should be taken very seriously, but, if they are "exaggerations," they should obviously not be taken as seriously as all that.[29]

These expressions truly shock, however, if the individual is, no exaggeration, divisible.[30] The initial audiences presumably understood, as do we, that the ultimate, which is binary, does not correspond well to humanity, which is nonbinary,[31] and, therefore, something in our understanding must yield so as to allow the as-observed nonbinary nature of humanity to reach the as-stated binary nature of the ultimate. Jesus is here explaining what that something is. When he says eternal life is better partly than not at all and says parting with a damned part is better than damnation entirely, only exegetical predispositions make them hyperbole.[32] Paradoxism, in contrast, understands Christ's words as neither surgical recommendations nor wild exaggerations, but as wild truths nonetheless. Salvation, C. S. Lewis reminded, is not "like the development from seed to flower," but "Our Lord speaks of eyes being plucked out and hands lopped off—a frankly Procrustean method of adaptation."[33]

b. Separating the Godly Predicate

The well-recognized principle of parsimony as applied to the two scripturally specified ultimates implies that humanity also falls into two groups to match those ultimates, and Scripture can reinforce that implication. In the Lazarus parable, only a chasm exists between the parable's protagonist, who is comforted by the angels, and the parable's foil, who is tormented in hades' flames, with no one of middling character laying between them (Luke 16:19–31). Likewise, the sheep and goats parable has no mongrels of mixed righteousness in the middle; on the right hand is only sheep who are exclusively righteous, and on the left hand is only goats who are exclusively unrighteous (Matt 25:31–46).[34] In spite of the fact that such parables seemingly portray humanity as if it lived in only the two extremes, which would nicely match the two ultimates, the audience could be expected to

---

29. France, *Matthew*, 205, 683.
30. Gavrilyuk, "Judgment of Love," 296.
31. Bulgakov, *Bride of the Lamb*, 465.
32. Berkouwer, *Man: Image of God*, 245; Hagner, *Matthew 1–13*, 121.
33. Lewis, "Membership," 174.
34. France, *Matthew*, 961 n.86; Morris, *Matthew*, 633–35.

recall that humanity generally lives outside the utter extremes.[35] Universalists certainly understand the parables in this way. Macrina took Lazarus and Dives as representing the two orientations in each of us,[36] and Bulgakov took the sheep-goats parable similarly:

> the separation into sheep and goat is accomplished (of course to different degrees) within every individual, and his right and left sides are bared in this separation. To a certain extent all are condemned and all are justified.... Thus, the *judgment* and its sentence introduce into the life of every person an antinomic separation that consists in participating in glory and incorruptibility and, at the same time, in burning in the fire of divine rejection. The difference between the two states can here be only a quantitative one.[37]

The human condition might justify these loose interpretations, but elsewhere Scripture's irregular wording is what justifies the position that salvation is not per individual, at least not always. John's gospel does this particularly. It uses, for example, neuter nouns, not personal ones, to distinguish the saved: "All [Πᾶν] the Father gives me will come to me; whoever comes to me I'll never ever cast out." "And this is my sender's will: I may annihilate none of all [πᾶν] he has given me, but raise it [αὐτὸ] up on the last day, for my Father wills that all [πᾶς] who note and believe in the Son have eternal life, and me, I'll raise him [αὐτὸν] up on the last day" (6:37, 39–40). Though his topic is expressly people, Jesus is using neuter nouns (πᾶν and αὐτὸ) to refer to the saved, and these neuter nouns, unlike masculine ones, stress qualities, not persons.[38] Exegetes nonetheless take these singular neuters as representing plural persons, and the usual assumption that persons come in binary salvation groups necessitates this move.[39] If an individual were divisible, however, the reference expresses what its quality-expressing grammar suggests—the salvation division is within, not between, individuals.

John offers further examples: The Son was "granted liberty over all flesh so he might give all [πᾶν] that you [the Father] have given him eternal life" (17:2). While the gospel is saying that Christ has authority over

---

35. Nichols, *Death and Afterlife*, 164.

36. Gregory of Nyssa, *Soul and Resurrection*, ch. 6 (pp. 75–76).

37. Bulgakov, *Bride of the Lamb*, 462.

38. BDF, § 138 (p. 76); Klink, *John*, 332; Porter, *Idioms*, 101; Turner, *Grammar*, III: 21.

39. Carson, *John*, 290; Kostenberger, *John*, 211 n.61; Morris, *John*, 325.

the grammatically feminine "all flesh," it is the neuter "all" that is said to have eternal life.⁴⁰ The expectation is either the feminine *all*, which would refer back to "flesh," or the masculine *all*, which would be the grammatical way to refer to people, but the gospel text has the neuter *all*, which unexpectedly emphasizes a quality, presumably of a human; yet, convention still takes it as humans anyway.⁴¹ Personifying is an understandable strategy for explaining a difficult concept to persons, such as how we personify death to help persons understand it,⁴² but de-personifying, which is what referring to saved people as an abstraction does, is an affectation in search of a purpose. On the other hand, if John's author deserves his reputation for craftsmanship,⁴³ his choice of neuter is informative—the quality of godliness is what eternally lives.

John's third odd usage of this kind is, "Father, my will is that what [ὅ] you've given me be where I am and be with me" (17:24). In this case, the first word in the Greek after the vocative *Father* is the out-of-place *what*, and this priority placement of the neuter emphasizes that it is not the expected masculine *who*, which would refer to the persons given to Christ.⁴⁴ This prominence thereby highlights that the division is not between persons—those who follow Christ and those who do not—but is a salvation division based on a personal quality along those lines. Perhaps because of the pronoun's prime location in this case, some manuscripts "corrected" the neuter *what* to the masculine (οὓς) to express the traditional division based on a personal *who*, which would express the expected salvation of persons, not personal traits, and which was clearly the more comfortable understanding for these scribes (as it is for modern exegetes).⁴⁵ The scribes' attempted fix, however, draws out John's original point—a personal quality, not a person group, is with Christ.

The NT also uses adjectives or participles, rather than nouns, for the saved and the doomed. "Both righteousness [δικαίων] and unrighteousness [ἀδίκων] are next to be resurrected" (Acts 24:15). "The Lord knows how to rescue reverence [εὐσεβεῖς] from trial and to reserve unrighteousness [ἀδίκους] for punishing into a day of judgment" (2 Pet 2:9–10). These

---

40. Keener, *John*, II: 1053.
41. Carson, *John*, 555; Morris, *John*, 636–37 n.9.
42. Carson, "Matthew," 326.
43. Kostenberger, *John*, 1.
44. Morris, *John*, 651 n.75.
45. Carson, *John*, 571; Metzger, *Textual Commentary*, 214.

substantive adjectives, unlike nouns, linguistically stress qualities, not persons.[46] They are also here anarthrous, which is abnormal and further stresses the qualities.[47] So, given the grammar used, that which is saved and that which is doomed are literally personal qualities, not persons. Participles reflect the same distinction: "He not being [ὢν] with me is against me, and he not gathering [συνάγων] to me scatters" (Matt 12:30// Luke 11:23). The usual understanding is that this "divides humanity simply into two groups; there is no middle ground,"[48] and this is because an individual must be "heaven bound or hell bound," "pro-Jesus or con-Jesus," "righteous or unrighteous," but not both.[49] Even if such a binary humanity was, notwithstanding chapter 6, in accord with what is scripturally described and commonly observed, the participles undermine this reading by denoting the qualities in motion, not the actors.[50]

In short, Scripture often expresses salvation of a personal quality, not of a person altogether, and this is well expressed if individuals are ultimately divisible, not one from the other, but as to a quality pertaining to them. To avoid this conclusion, Scripture must in several places be taken as grammatically wayward.

c. Experiencing Binary Outcomes

The NT sometimes says the eschatological binaries are applied to the full range of humanity in such a way that those binaries are experienced in nonbinary ways. That is, eternal life and perishing, despite unmistakably being either-or, are said to be experienced by humans, not as either-or, but to an extent. The joyful binary, to begin with, is experienced variously according to the mina parable—different performances receive different eschatological rewards (Luke 19:11–27).[51] Similarly, the rich will *hardly* (δυσκόλως) enter God's reign (Matt 19:23//Mark 10:23//Luke 18:24), where the adverb means *degree* of difficulty.[52] Also, according to the church fathers, the various glories in the cosmos that Paul identified

---

46. Turner, *Grammar*, III: 13; Wallace, *Greek Grammar*, 233.
47. Porter, *Idioms*, 105; Robertson, *Grammar*, 794; Wallace, *Greek Grammar*, 294.
48. France, *Matthew*, 481.
49. Stein, *Luke*, 332.
50. Robertson, *Grammar*, 1100; Wallace, *Greek Grammar*, 613, 616.
51. Bock, *Luke 9:51—24:53*, 1536–37, 1540–43.
52. Balz, "Δυσκόλως," 361; France, *Mark*, 404; Morris, *Matthew*, 492–93.

(1 Cor 15:39–44) and the many eschatological mansions that Jesus referred to (John 14:2) suggest that the blessed have different grades of holiness in the afterlife.[53]

The negative binary is likewise said to be experienced diversely. Some people are *twice* as hellish[54] as others (Matt 23:15), the damnation of some is *more bearable*[55] than others (10:15, 11:22, 24; Luke 10:12, 14), and some are condemned *more*[56] than others (20:47//Mark 12:40). Each of these rare comparative adjectives plainly expresses "degree, not kind."[57] Finally, eschatological destiny in the faithful servant parable involves some flayed *much* and others flayed *little*,[58] depending on their degree of unfaithfulness (Luke 12:47–48), and the tormentors get *as much*[59] torment in their eschatological destiny as they gave in life (Rev 18:6–7).

Though these expressions of degrees of blessedness and damnation might all be hyperbolic,[60] only a resolve that the binaries be experienced either-or requires that the expressed variability in the afterlife be figurative. Suggesting otherwise does not change the scriptural insistence *that* the outcomes are binary, but the idea that the binary outcomes are experienced variably challenges the typical understanding of *how* they are experienced. Without some other element, these descriptions of eschatological variability lack their literal meaning because someone cannot have eternal life, wonderful at the extreme, and someone else have more, nor can someone have absolute negation, God-less eternity, and someone else have less.[61] On the other hand, when individual divisibility is allowed for, the expressions express reality because they depict these two either-or outcomes as variously experienced.

---

53. Augustine, "Homilies on John," 121 [67, 2]; Gregory I, "Moral Teachings," 315 [4, 36, 70]; Perkins, *First Corinthians*, 187.

54. Διπλότερον is the comparative of διπλοῦς, "double." BDAG, 251–52.

55. Ἀνεκτότερον is the comparative of ἀνεκτός, "bearable, endurable." BDAG, 76.

56. Περισσότερον as the comparative of περισσός, "abundant," means "even more." BDAG, 805–6.

57. Wallace, *Greek Grammar*, 296–98.

58. These are plurals of πολύς, "much," and ὀλίγος, "little." BDAG, 702–3, 847–50.

59. Τοσοῦτον is the correlative demonstrative pronoun "so much." BDAG, 1012.

60. Hagner, *Matthew 14–28*, 669.

61. Holten, "Traditional View of Hell," 475; N. T. Wright, *Surprised by Hope*, 179.

d. "To the Extent"

English typically expresses binary conditions with "if." Greek does this with εἰ. To express binary conditions that are applied in nonbinary ways, English uses "to the extent (that)," and this can be more truthful than "if." For instance, *if I laugh, the comedy is funny* is less accurate than *to the extent I laugh, the comedy is funny*. The phrase *to the extent* acts like *if* so as to identify the condition, but makes the triggering of the condition also conditional in its application so that it is not either/or but variable. According to paradoxism, such variability applies to salvation's extent in that eternal life is *to the extent* godly. Unfortunately, though common in English, koine Greek supposedly uses no such fully scalable conditional in this or any other context. Instead, given what contemporary grammarians manage to finagle from the NT's conditionals, Greek conditions can apparently only express the odds of the condition obtaining (or not), ranging from likely to hypothetical.[62] Each NT condition, therefore, is basically limited to the formula, "Given certain conditions, certain results follow."[63] As a result, the NT authors are seemingly incapable of stating what English speakers state effortlessly, "*To the extent* of certain conditions, certain results follow."

Two Greek terms almost achieve what English achieves with "to the extent." The first is καθότι, which blends *according to* (κατά), *what* (ὅ), and *thing* (τι) and in classical Greek meant "to the degree,"[64] but this adverb, which is not a condition at all, is saying that the would-be condition is obtained to *an* extent, which is unlike "to *the* extent" because only the latter phrase retains the conditionality of "if." Regardless of this distinction here, καθότι is, however, entirely unhelpful on this issue because it had merely become in Hellenistic Greek a variant of ὅτι (because), and this is how it was used all six times in the NT, all by one author (Luke 1:7; 19:9; Acts 2:24, 45; 4:35; 17:31).[65]

The second Greek word that could be confused for "to the extent" is the adverbial pronoun ὅσος (*insofar, inasmuch*), but the distinction between "to the extent" and its near homonyms of "to an extent" and "to such an extent" is important here. In its 110 NT uses and in koine Greek generally, ὅσος expresses the dependent relationship of correlation

---

62. Robertson, *Grammar*, 1004–27.
63. Moule, *Idiom Book*, 148.
64. Marshall, *Luke*, 53; Plummer, *Luke*, 10.
65. Plummer, *Luke*, 10; Porter, *Idioms*, 237.

or comparison, not an either-or condition.⁶⁶ As an example, the groomsmen mourn *as long as* (ἐφ' ὅσον) the groom is with them (Matt 9:15), which means the groom is there for some amount of time definitely, *not* conditionally. The confusion in English with *to <u>the</u> extent* comes from how the correlation relationship of ὅσος resembles *to <u>an</u> extent*, which is not a condition but a definite reality that has obtained partly, and *to <u>such an</u> extent*, which is not a condition but a definite reality that has obtained extremely.⁶⁷ The New American Standard Bible, a typically literal translation, demonstrates this by twice rendering ἐφ' ὅσον as *to the extent* (Matt 25:40, 45), despite precisely rendering the same phrase elsewhere (9:15; Rom 11:13).⁶⁸ Regardless of translation and its similarity to *to the extent*, ὅσος by definition and every NT usage is, not an actual condition like *to the extent*, but a correlation that definitely obtains (albeit variously).⁶⁹

Admittedly, any NT lacuna regarding *to the extent* is manageable because the Greek authors had other writing strategies that could compensate, such as an expressive puzzle (*e.g.*, "I believe; help my unbelief") or odd grammar (*e.g.*, neuter nouns for people) to imply an underlying non-binary conditional. Any *to the extent* lacuna could in part be from the Scripture's apparent lack of interest in drawing fine distinctions between the character of persons. This is seen in how rarely Scripture uses comparative or superlative adjectives even when they are meant; instead, it even then usually uses positive adjectives.⁷⁰ Though Scripture occasionally makes explicit the absoluteness of a character assessment (1 Thess 5:23), it mostly avoids character gradations even in non-conditionals.⁷¹ As examples, Noah, Job, Lot, the NT Josephs, and Paul are each said to be "blameless" or "righteous" without being absolutely so because the terms are intended to be relatively, not absolutely, descriptive (Gen 6:9; Job 1:1, 8; Matt 1:19; Luke 23:50; Phil 3:6; 2 Pet 2:7–8).⁷² Even if making clear character gradations were ever desired, the precision of *to the extent*

---

66. Balz, "Ὅσος," 537; *BDAG*, 729; *LSJ*, "Ὅσος," 1262; Montanari, "Ὅσος," 1494; Thayer, "Ὅσος," 457.

67. These idiomatic distinctions are described in Merriam-Webster's Learner's Dictionary, "extent," http://learnersdictionary.com/definition/extent.

68. Dunn, *Romans 9–16*, 655; Nolland, *Matthew*, 40.

69. Nolland, *Matthew*, 1031; Robertson, *Grammar*, 733.

70. Wallace, *Greek Grammar*, 296–97.

71. Clines, *Job 1–20*, 12.

72. Blomberg, *Matthew*, 58; Demarest, *Cross and Salvation*, 416–19; Mathews, *Genesis 1–11:26*, 358–59.

can sound clinical, and its prolixity contrasts with *if*'s bite. Still, these workarounds and excuses fail to explain why the NT talents omit entirely nonbinary conditionals, which English speakers express with such ease by using "to the extent that."[73]

While admittedly not apparent from its translation or even its ordinary exegesis, one Greek word in the NT could, in conjunction with the conditional "if [εἰ]," express "to the extent." It is the particle ἄν. It unquestionably adds contingency to what it modifies, though this is usually unrenderable in English.[74] When the ἄν modifies a main verb, English translators can try to reflect its presence by adding "would" (*they have gone* can become *they would have gone*), or, when ἄν modifies a particle, the translators can add "ever" (*what do you mean* can become *whatever do you mean*).[75] The contingency that ἄν adds is entirely lost, however, when it modifies the already contingent "if [εἰ]" in their blend ἐάν, which just means "if" too.[76]

In ἐάν's 351 NT appearances, most of them are as a marker of condition paired with a subjunctive verb to indicate a third-class condition, which is a condition whose odds of obtaining range among likely, possible, or hypothetical,[77] but this is what the subjunctive mood means anyway.[78] And, of course, εἰ is conditional without ἄν at all. So, the ἄν in ἐάν does nothing but merely express opaquely and redundantly the odds of the condition, which defies literary criticism's insight that each scriptural bit counts.[79] Though no jot should fail (Luke 16:17),[80] the ἄν in ἐάν seems to be an exception—"if" plus ἄν equals "if."[81] But it need not be that way. By combining "if" with the further contingency of ἄν, ἐάν could truly express a conditional in both kind (from "if") and degree (from

---

73. The phrase is "often used" to describe conceptual relationships. Merriam-Webster's Learner's Dictionary, "extent," http://learnersdictionary.com/definition/extent.

74. BDAG, 56; Carson, "Matthew," 397; Moulton, *Grammar*, I: 165.

75. BDAG, 56.

76. Robertson, *Grammar*, 1007.

77. Balz, "Ἐάν," 367. Technically, the apodosis also must not be in the present indicative, and, when it is, it is actually a fifth class condition—present general condition (simple if-then). Wallace, *Greek Grammar*, 470.

78. Wallace, *Greek Grammar*, 461–63.

79. Waltke, *Genesis*, 33.

80. Gregory of Nazianzus, "In Defence of His Flight," 28 [2, 105]; Jerome, "Ephesians," Bk II, 591 (3:5–7, p. 147); Luther, *Galatians*, 480 [WA 402,57 (5:12)].

81. Weima, *1–2 Thessalonians*, 224.

ἄν), and this combination could thereby accomplish what "to the extent" accomplishes in English.

Before considering the NT usages of ἐάν as they pertain to paradoxism and risking the accusation that its novel rendering here is makeshift, the appropriate interpretation of the word can be tested by substituting wherever in the NT ἐάν is rendered "if" with "to the extent" or, in the negative, "except to the extent." The proposed meaning works generally, though proving so is impractical here given that it happens hundreds of times. By way of consolation, forty instances will be given below in the context of paradoxism, and a half dozen examples have previously appeared in this discourse without comment (*e.g.*, Mark 9:43–49; 1 John 4:10–11). Instead, using a single archetypically disputed example as a test exercise is more workable, and one of the more theologically significant uses of ἐάν is: *Works do not justify <u>except/unless</u> through faith* (Gal. 2:16), where the *except* or *unless* is the traditional rendering of ἐάν in the negative (μή). The conditional phrase has doctrinal repercussions because, when understood as "except," the verse is said to mean that justification is from faith and *not* works, and, when understood as "unless," it is said to mean that justification is from faith *along with* works.[82] Both traditions, however, are only employing the "if" within the ἐάν, and, so, they are treating the sentence as a basic if-not conditional—*Works do not justify <u>if not</u> through faith*. Yet, if the contribution of ἄν were restored to the verse, faith's necessity and work's value become apparent either way: *Works do not justify <u>except/unless to the extent</u> through faith*.

The import of ἐάν is implicated especially in NT passages addressing paradoxism's issues. This can be shown in mostly canonical order with ἐάν rendered as *to the extent* or, in the negative, *except to the extent*. The word's use begins in the NT's first book, which employs ἐάν's conditioning to express the idea that humans can forgive on a spectrum: "*To the extent* you release others their trespasses, your heavenly Father will release you too, but, *to the extent* you release no others, your Father won't release your trespasses" (Matt 6:14–15). "In wrath, his lord gave him over to the torturers till he paid all he owed. So will my heavenly Father do to you *except to the extent* you release your brother from your heart" (18:34–35). Unlike the proffered "to the extent" understanding of ἐάν, which denotes a relationship between receiving forgiveness and giving it, the typical "if" rendering implies that forgiving is one and done rather than what it is,

---

82. Hunn, "'Ἐὰν Μή in Galatians," 281–82; Longenecker, *Galatians*, 83–84.

ongoing and rarely complete.[83] Similarly, "*except to the extent* you turn to become as little children, you'll never enter the heavens' reign" (18:3) reflects the reality that an adult's childlikeness is not either-or but varies, which is unlike the relationship expressed by the usual "if" formulation.[84]

Luke makes the same connection with repentance: "*Except to the extent* you repent, all will perish" (13:3, 5). With ἐάν's conventional meaning, the condition is third class (repentance might not happen),[85] which, while it indicates the odds of repentance, leaves the extent of repentance unsaid, but repentance is not just either-or but has amplitude.

Building on what the Synoptics have expressed regarding what happens with the failure to be godly, Luke's sequel expresses the positive side: "All *to the extent* calling on the Lord's name will be saved" (Acts 2:21). The conditional phrase in this verse is literally "all who ἐάν call," which is commonly taken as leaving unspecified who calls,[86] but the subjunctive phrase, "all who . . . call," does that without ἐάν at all. Proficient authors add words to add meaning, and ἐάν does that as "to the extent," unlike its conventional meaning.

John's gospel often uses ἐάν in expressing the relationship between godliness and salvation. "*Except to the extent* one is born above once, he can't see God's reign," and, "*except to the extent* one is born of water and Spirit, he can't enter God's reign" (3:3, 5). Although literal birth is binary, only by ignoring ἄν's added contingency is God's reign likewise read by exegetes as "bipolar."[87] Retaining ἄν's contribution, however, recognizes that God's reign runs through us, not necessarily throughout us (Luke 17:21).[88] This salvation continuum is a recurring expression in John:

> No one can come to me *except to the extent* the Father who sent me drags him, and I'll raise him on the last day. . . . I Am the living bread that descended from heaven. Anyone *to the extent* eating of this bread will live into the age. . . . [E]xcept *to the extent* you eat the Son of Man's flesh and drink his blood, you've no life in you. . . . By this I told you no one can come to me *except to the extent* given by the Father. (6:44, 51, 53–54, 65)

---

83. France, *Matthew*, 252.
84. France, *Matthew*, 678.
85. Bock, *Luke 9:51—24:53*, 1206.
86. Bock, *Acts*, 119.
87. Carson, *John*, 439.
88. Ziegler, *Militant Grace*, 92–94.

Christianity's Divisible Individual

> *[T]o the extent* you believe not that I Am, you die in your sins.... *[T]o the extent* the Son frees you, you'll be truly free.... My word *to the extent* anyone keeps, death he'll never ever note. (8:24, 36, 51)
>
> Through me anyone *to the extent* entering will be saved. (10:9)
>
> *[T]o the extent* you believe, you'll see God's glory. (11:40)
>
> *[E]xcept to the extent* the wheat kernel falling to the ground dies, it remains alone, but, *to the extent* it dies, it bears much fruit. He loving his soul annihilates it, while he hating his soul in this world will keep it into eternal life. Anyone *to the extent* serving me must follow me.... *To the extent* anyone serves me, my Father will honor him. (12:24–26)

Given its full meaning, the ἐάν in these verses appreciates that individuals are not exclusively either godly or not, and this finding continues in the Farewell Discourse:

> *To the extent* you love me, keep my commands.... *To the extent* anyone loves me, he'll keep my word, my Father will love him, and we'll come to him to make accommodation within him. (14:15, 23)
>
> As the branch itself can bear no fruit—it must abide in the vine—neither can you bear fruit except *to the extent* you abide in me.... Anyone *to the extent* not abiding in me is like the branch cast away to wither; they're gathered, cast into the fire, and burned.... *To the extent* you keep my commands, you'll abide in my love, as I've kept my Father's commands and abide in his love. (15:4, 6, 10)

The traditional understanding of these conditions as meaning either-or sees these statements as what is literally relevant to no one because precisely no one entirely keeps God's commands or entirely abides in his love. Thus, exegetes must assume the conditions are not really as absolute as the traditional "if" conditions are saying they are,[89] but this resort is unnecessary when ἄν contributes its nuance to the conditions.

The Pauline corpus has similar expressions: "*To the extent* you confess in your mouth Jesus 'Lord' and believe in your heart God raised him from among the dead, you will be saved" (Rom 10:9–10). Confessing and believing, in addition to being present or not, are scalable in intensity and frequency, which "to the extent," but not "if," actually expresses here.

---

89. Carson, *John*, 520–21.

Galatians adds, "*to the extent* man reaps, that also he sows" (6:7). The condition, which is set by "ὃ . . . ἐάν," is often understood as "whatever" and thereby establishes a "direct correlation between a person's sowing and reaping."[90] This, however, is literally and obviously false. One can reap without ever having sowed at all because someone else could have done the sowing (Matt 25:26//Luke 19:22), and, regardless, seed that is sown reaps not seed but fruit, which is momentously different (Mark 4:3–9// Matt 13:3–9//Luke 8:5–8; 1 Cor 15:36–38). The audience can of course intuit the point of the proverb that Paul is using, but this obvious connection is what validates the meaning, though typically unrecognized, of ἐάν as something like "to the extent" and not merely "if." Finally, Ephesians relates goodness to divine justice: "*To the extent* anyone . . . does good, this the Lord will repay"[91] (6:8). A person is repaid, if it is truly a repayment, based on the extent of the liability, not merely if there is a liability.

The general epistles productively use ἐάν too. One is the staggering claim in James: "Anyone *to the extent* resolving to befriend the world is appointed God's hater" (4:4). When the conditional is understood as expressing the normal *if*, the auditors are warranted in taking this as "the dualism of Qumran" with "no middle point"; "one must be '100 percent,'" "either God's friend or his enemy."[92] Because such a monochrome view of humanity is as unreal as chapter 6 showed, exegetes familiar with reality are forced to treat the statement in James as *amounting* to a nuanced relationship between befriending the world and hating God,[93] but, giving effect to ἄν allows the scriptural author himself to express that subtlety, which does not make his literal claim any less staggering, just less dubious.

John's main epistle, like the gospel of that name, frequently applies ἐάν to godliness' extent:

> *To the extent* we say "we have community with him" yet walk in the darkness, we falsify and practice not the truth, but, *to the extent* we walk in the light, we have community with others, and his Son Jesus' blood purifies us from all sin. *To the extent* we say "we have no sin," we mislead ourselves and the truth is not in us. *To the extent* we confess our sins, he, faithful and righteous,

---

90. Longenecker, *Galatians*, 280.

91. The verb κομίσεται is *provide* in the middle voice and means something like *recover* or *receive back*. BDAG, 557.

92. Davids, *James*, 161.

93. Moo, *James*, 187.

releases our sins and purifies us from all unrighteousness. *To the extent* we say "we have not sinned," we make him a liar and his word is not in us. (1:6–10)

In this we know we have known him: *To the extent* we obey his commands.... *To the extent* anyone loves the world, the Father's love is not in him.... *To the extent* what you heard since beginning abides in you, you too will abide in the Son and the Father, and this is the promise he promised us—eternal life. (2:3, 15, 24–25)

[T]*o the extent* we love others, God abides in us and his love is being completed in us.... *To the extent* anyone confessed that Jesus is the Son of God, God abides in him and he in God. (4:12–13, 15–16)

The ἐάνs in these verses are typically taken as expressing uncertainty about the subject they reference,[94] but the ἐάνs almost never have here a written Greek subject at all. Instead, the ἐάνs always appear proximate to a Greek verb. This makes their connection with the unstated Greek subject, rather than the actual Greek verbs, hardly the most natural. More importantly, merely expressing uncertainty about the subject gives ἄν no meaning at all because *if* alone creates that uncertainty. Thus, without any real meaning for John's ἄνs, the exegetes must again come to the rescue, as Stephen Smalley exemplifies: "John is not saying that the Christian must be perfectly obedient before he can in any way know God.... Obedience is not the *condition* for knowing God; but 'obeying orders' should *characterize* that knowledge (normally, if not without exception) ...."[95] The multidimensional contingency of ἐάν, however, obviates the need to salvage what was canonized. That is, the ἐάνs that the Elder actually wrote avoid by themselves what I. Howard Marshall noted were otherwise "absolute... conditions," which of course "would surely be ... unreasonable,"[96] or, more accurately, uninformative.

❦

The Greek of the NT might not, after all, have had a lacuna of "to the extent." In using ἐάν, many NT writers might have eluded the simplicity of an unmitigated if-then construction and found a way to express salvation as a conditional continuum.

---

94. Jobes, *1,2&3 John*, 67–68; Wallace, *Greek Grammar*, 698–99.
95. Smalley, *1,2,3 John*, 45.
96. Marshall, *Epistles of John*, 123.

e. Divisibility in the Restoration

Of the several scriptural depictions of the universal consummation, among the first is Isaiah's prophetic image for eschatological salvation in that book's last two chapters.[97] Set out there is the by-now timeworn phrases for the binary outcomes—*the new heaven and the new earth* for the positive outcome and *the undying worm and the unquenchable fire* for the negative one (65:17; 66:22, 24). Mark's Jesus and John the Revelator explicitly use this Isaian framework (Mark 9:43–48; Rev 21:1).[98] Despite clearly expressing the standardized *two* eschatological outcomes, Isaiah just as clearly, but discordantly, expresses those experiencing the outcomes as falling into *three* categories:

1. the faith*ful* endure into the positive eschatological outcome (66:22),
2. the faith*less* perish in the negative eschatological outcome (65:2, 12; 66:4, 16, 24), and
3. "all flesh" endures in the end to worship God and see the second category perish in the negative eschatological outcome (66:23–24).

Because the second and third categories are literally incongruent, the portrayal is paradoxical—the faithless perish but somehow everyone also abides worshipfully.[99] Walter Brueggemann notes that this is "a profound tension between magnanimous *inclusiveness* and intensely felt *exclusiveness*."[100]

Tradition, as represented by John Oswalt, resolves this tension by recognizing "only two categories of people," "those who fall down before him in worship, and those who foolishly rebel against him,"[101] but this tension-free interpretation effaces Isaiah's third category, which says "all flesh" will live on to see the perishing and to worship God.[102] For Isaiah, like communicators as a rule, "all flesh" refers to everyone, at least those, such as humans, who are perishable.[103] Therefore, like the paradox of

---

97. Bulgakov, *Orthodox Church*, 176; Hanson, *OT Apocalyptic*, 35–38.
98. Tonstad, *Revelation*, 304–5; Williamson, *Death and the Afterlife*, 136.
99. Stromberg, "Inner-Isaianic Reading," 271.
100. Brueggemann, *Isaiah 40–66*, 260.
101. Oswalt, *Isaiah: Chapters 40–66*, 691.
102. Motyer, *Isaiah*, 460–61.
103. Knight, *New Israel*, 119; Oswalt, *Isaiah 40–66*, 313 n.93; Schultz, "Nationalism and Universalism," 130, 137.

salvation's extent, Isaiah is saying that some humans perish and also that every human lives, which, if not meant to be a paradox, requires the sort of exegetical repair suggested by Oswalt to avoid the contradiction. Paradoxism's divisible individual, however, allows Isaiah's three categories to work with its two outcomes. The faithless both perish and live on.

John the Baptist, using a different Isaiah declaration (Isa 40:5 LXX), echoed the observation that everyone will seemingly be in on the two outcomes, "All flesh will see God's salvation" (Luke 3:6). "All flesh" again clearly refers to every human, and "will see" translates the future tense of ὁράω, which in the transitive here means *perceive* or *experience*.[104] So, in spite of the Baptist's contemporaneous stress on God's destructive wrath that is coming in the end (3:7–9), he is implying that everyone will nevertheless experience salvation.[105] These two outcomes, perishing and salvation, are obvious concurrent opposites, but having human lives end *and* every human live on is intelligible if each of them is divisible after this life. All flesh will experience God's salvation in eternal life and, to the extent ungodly, also experience his wrath in the perishing.

4. Theologians Approach Paradoxism

While Scripture may suggest the unforeseen idea that the individual can be divisible in the afterlife, theologians have not. That much is almost clear, though a few theologians, as will be shown here, have offered descriptions of the afterlife that are nearly suggestive of individual divisibility. Some theologians, especially potentialists, can agree with paradoxism's *premise* that no traditional position on salvation's extent has properly handled Scripture's salvation paradox, but, on paradoxism's *answer* of afterlife individual divisibility, no scholar has yet truly ventured there, at least not in such a way that anyone has noticed. And such a position would presumably get noticed. That said, several theologians have nearly given that answer in such a way that paradoxism is not as alien to orthodoxy as its innovation might indicate because, without endorsing its model, these theologians have portrayed afterlife purging so colorfully that the individual is nearly divided then. That is, in trying to make sense of this world where we are thoroughly both godly and ungodly and of the ultimate world where we will be thoroughly godly only, these theologians

---

104. *BDAG*, 719–20.
105. Bock, *Luke 1–9:50*, 295; Morris, *Luke*, 105.

have described a metaphorical meatgrinder so brutal that the divisibility of the individual would be compatible. Extended quotes from them must often be added to avoid the claim that they are being defamed.

a. Universal Purging

All salvation-extent positions have found purging useful in explaining how nonbinary individuals will be able to adapt ultimately to the binary outcomes, but universalism to achieve its definitional universality must subject most people, if not all of them, to purging so that all evil ends in the end without any evil people also coming to an end.[106] Origen argued, in "the day of judgment," "the good will be separated from the evil and the righteous from the unrighteous and every individual soul will by the judgment of God be allotted to that place of which his merits have rendered him worthy...." God destroys "evil thoughts of the mind, shameful deeds and longings after sin" such that everyone "advances and comes to higher degrees of perfection" until "all stains" are "purged."[107] Athanasius too realized that, for salvation to be universal, "evil should be entirely consumed in all men" so as to have their "soul purified."[108] In fact, most universalists, whether Gregory of Nyssa,[109] Cassian,[110] Eriugena,[111] Tillich,[112] or Moltmann,[113] make explicit that afterlife purging is what discontinues evil in the end without discontinuing evil people in the end, but the universalist whose described purging most nearly fits afterlife individual divisibility is Bulgakov.

Bulgakov saw the individual as a "mixture of good and evil," which is sifted in afterlife judgment.[114]

> Every human being sees himself in Christ and measures the extent of his difference from this proto-image.... Love is the Holy

---

106. Ramelli, *Christian Doctrine of Apokatastasis*, 252.
107. Origen, *On First Principles*, I,1,2, 2,4, 3,8, II,10,5, 9,8 III,6,3 (pp. 7, 17, 38–39, 136, 143, 248).
108. Athanasius, "Letter III," 4 (p. 514).
109. Zachhuber, *Human Nature in Gregory*, 1–2, 188, 191–92, 210, 241–42.
110. Cassian, "Conferences," XIII, chs 7, 9, 11 (pp. 425–28).
111. John, *Periphyseon*, Bk V, chs 36, 38 (pp. 334–40, 352).
112. Tillich, *ST*, III: 397–401.
113. Moltmann, *Coming of God*, 76, 97, 255.
114. Bulgakov, *Bride of the Lamb*, 359–60, 457, 497, 504.

> Spirit.... But this love ... is also the judgment of the individual upon himself, his vision of himself ... in conflict with himself, that is, outside Christ ....
>
> [T]his ontological condemnation ... is ... the metaphysical annihilation of what is condemned ... [,] not to personal being ..., but to his mortal ... content, which is consumed by the divine fire. The inner division of every human being, his separation into mortal and immortal parts, ... is ... the judgment of God.... Everything that is not in conformity with this image falls into the outer darkness, into nonbeing.... *The spiritual sword cuts a human being asunder to his very depths.*
>
> This partial nonbeing ... is experienced as fire.... Every human being experiences this ... in conformity with his wrong state and to the degree it is wrong.... But ... "Annihilation" ... does not extend to the entire being of a person. *It is a separation or a spiritual amputation, so to speak* ....[115]

Bulgakov's universalism, as discussed in chapter 4, governs eventually, but, until then:

> *We must ... conclude that the very separation into heaven and hell ... is internal and relative.* Every human being bears within himself the principle of the one and the other, depending upon the measure of his personal righteousness.
>
> [T]he very distinction between heaven and hell exists only for our limited earthly condition. But since every human sins, the two states inevitably coexist in one the same person.... The *mixture* of good and evil that is proper to the overwhelming majority of human beings compels us to postulate not a simple but a complex sum total of God's judgment, which unites blessing and condemnation.
>
> [T]he fundamental antinomic postulate of eschatology is that *eternal life ... can coexist with ... perdition. Both, to different degrees, are included in being. When it is conceived statically, this antinomy becomes a direct contradiction. When it is conceived dynamically, it can be grasped livingly.*[116]

Bulgakov thus depicted purging similar to divisibility, but, as a universalist, he concluded that no one can ever be damned; rather, it is through the penultimate scrubbing that he so vividly described that the

---

115. Bulgakov, *Bride of the Lamb*, 459, 463 (emphasis added).
116. Bulgakov, *Bride of the Lamb*, 465, 476–77 (emphasis added except "mixture").

individual is ultimately unified in universalism, not divided.[117] Because in the end everyone is saved and no one is doomed, universalists must leave the scriptural expression of the salvation paradox unworked. In contrast to universalism's purgation, which picks *out* what is *foreign* to the person so as to save the person, paradoxism's division picks *apart* what *is* the person so as to save the paradox. Universalists like Bulgakov nonetheless realize that we each tend to be godly-ungodly composites that must be ferociously separated in the end.

b. Orthodox Catharsis

Mainstream theologians can nearly divide an individual after this life too, but this is to prepare the saved for the positive ultimate to the extent of their ungodliness. The certainly mainstream Ratzinger, aka Pope Benedict XVI, sees an individual conflicted in degrees based on conflicting personal orientations: "The borderline between Sheol and life runs through our very midst, and those who are in Christ are situated on the side of life, and that everlastingly." As a result, "Christ inflicts pure perdition on no one," "but comes to be wherever a person distances himself from Christ." "Christ's word, the bearer of the offer of salvation, then lays bare the fact that the person who is lost *has himself drawn the dividing line* and separated himself from salvation." "One is in heaven when, *and to the degree*, that one is in Christ."[118]

Balthasar, as part of his potentialist position discussed in chapter 4, expresses himself similarly. For him, the individual is "torn into two opposite values," part of which is "receptive to salvation" and "part that is not," and this separation in each of us amounts to a personal "bifurcation"; yet, the Son, who "both grounds and surpasses all we mean by separation," brings about its resolution.[119] Balthasar once explained this personal bifurcation consistent with individual divisibility:

> Ambrose came up with the daring statement: "*Idem homo et salvatur ex parte, et condemnatur ex parte*" [Every sinner will hear both "Begone into eternal fire" and "Come ye blessed of my Father"],[120] man is somehow both to the right and to the left of

---

117. Blosser, *Become Like the Angels*, 31.
118. Ratzinger, *Eschatology*, 94, 117, 205–6, 234–36 (emphasis added).
119. Balthasar, *Theo-Drama*, IV: 223–24, 325.
120. Ambrose's statement is literally, "the same human, both saved partly and

the Judge. Accordingly, . . . it takes the entire courage of Christian hope for a man to . . . trust that . . . what is damnable in him has been separated from him and thrown out with the unusable residue that is incinerated outside the gates of the Holy City.[121]

Balthasar later exposited this notion by reference to the visionary experiences of Christ's death that his muse von Speyr explained to him: Christ "experiences . . . the whole ambiguity of his human nature," including the "dispositions to the good" and "dispositions to evil" that exist in "every man," where "the evil will lies" close to "the good will," but, at death, Christ goes "in two opposite directions: . . . toward paradise and . . . into deep hell." And it is in the latter that Christ encounters human "effigies," which "consist of what a man has given from his own substance to the sin he has committed." As for each human in general, Balthasar wrote, quoting von Speyr: "'as a sinner, he is copied, in negative,'" and "his dead copy in hell regains a sort of life . . . ; 'he knows as a saved person: Hell holds his copy.'"[122]

Despite appearances, these remarks do not reflect an individual being split nor do they attempt to address the salvation paradox.[123] This is, of course, unfortunate for a thesis in need of a senior partner on its primary contribution, even if the supportive reasoning is from a mystic's visions. Instead of supporting the individual's divisibility of the thesis, Balthasar, in applying von Speyr's annual visionary crucifixions, saw the sinner not as split into two, but saw the subjective *sinner* as differentiated from her objectified *sins*.[124] That is, the sins are removed from the sinner rather than the individual being divided between sinner and saint. This is because Balthasar did not understand the individual as essentially both godly and ungodly, but as either one or the other based on what was primarily the case: "the particular direction taken depends on the individual's personal and primary direction for or against Jesus, which means that he chooses either the path toward God or the path toward chaos."[125]

---

condemned partly," and pertains to the unworthy works of the saved (1 Cor 3:15). "Expositio in Psalmum CXVIII," 1238 ¶ 58 (col. 1580).

121. Balthasar, *Theo-Drama*, V: 321 & n.27.
122. Balthasar, *Theo-Logic*, II: 285, 351, 355–57.
123. Brotherton, "Possibility of Universal Conversion," 319.
124. Miles, "Obedience of a Corpse," 180–81; Sutton, *Heaven Opens*, 15–16, 25, 172–73, 178, 184–85. See Speyr, *Farewell Discourses*, 81, 208, 237, 269; *Gates of Eternal Life*, 60, 112; *The Word*, 31.
125. Balthasar, *Theo-Drama*, IV: 433–34.

This fundamentally binary choice was also how von Speyr understood what happened to the conflicted individual.[126] This understanding of an essential unity corresponds to the well-recognized indivisibility of the personal identity, which paradoxism also uses, but it does not fit the divisibility of the personal character, which is what paradoxism purports to contribute.

Protestants too can understand that individuals are saved in degrees, though not divisibly. Barth in particular noted, "Man is . . . on the way to eternal life to the degree that he lives *by* the grace of God . . . ."[127] The person's inner "frontier" reflects "the degree" to which the person is godly: One side of the person is for God and the other is against him, and this two-sided person is judged "divisive[ly]" such that the anti-God side "tears away." God's judgment "locks up the one in order to . . . free him from his identification with the first man and his wrong," a division "between the man of sin and man himself." "It is this man . . . that He condemns and . . . causes . . . to perish as such, . . . aiming thereby to separate him completely from this unfaithful man. . . . *This separation has to take place in him.*" For Barth, despite applying terms of internal divisiveness and separation in God's ultimate judgment for the person's life, this is not describing the divisibility of the individual because "God's sentence on him pronounces all this as an indivisible whole,"[128] which is why, as seen in chapter 4, everyone is entirely saved potentially.

Pannenberg also sees the eschatological judgment of a dually oriented individual similar to divisibility: "confrontation with eternity means judgment *only insofar* as" people make "themselves autonomous in relation to God, separated themselves from him," "and our existence as sinners makes shipwreck on this *inner contradiction* . . . ." "At issue already in this life is identity," which is "integration of the moments of life into the unity of life as a whole." "In the sphere of the eternal present, . . . all things that make up the content of life sound forth together . . . ." "The word of Christ as the offer of salvation will then make clear that the lost drew the line themselves and separated themselves from salvation."[129] What follows is the individual's extreme purging:

---

126. Speyr, *Confession*, 55, 58; *Farewell Discourses*, 164; *Passion from Within*, 157.
127. Barth, *CD II/2*, § 37.2 (p. 576).
128. Barth, *CD IV/1*, §§ 58.1, 61.3 (pp. 82, 568–69, 574, 593) (emphasis added).
129. Pannenberg, *ST*, III: 610–11, 614 (emphasis added).

> Holding fast to his purpose in creation implies that [God] will not let his creatures make shipwreck on the dissonances of their existence as these are disclosed in the sphere of the eternal present.... It is the fire that purges out everything in the life of the creature that is incompatible with the eternal God....[130]
>
> The separation between good and evil remains, since such a separation is the essence of judgment. But it is a separation that applies to each one of us. Each person is to be purified from everything that is incompatible with God's eternal life, though the extent of such purification may be different in each individual case.[131]

This purging mitigates exclusivism without succumbing to universalism:

> How the life of an individual may emerge from the contradiction that fills it ... to stand as a whole before God's eyes is something that no one can know. However, even if our life is not destroyed in the contradiction between selfhood and openness to the world, it is only beyond death that we can hope for the life in which the ego itself lives out of God instead of living in tension with him...[132]

Notwithstanding such copious commentary about an individual's internal conflict and how it is to be ultimately resolved through a severe purgation, Pannenberg's position is that the individual is unqualifiedly unitary, the opposite of divisible.[133]

As promised, no orthodox theologian offers the afterlife divisibility of the individual that paradoxism proposes, but many draw near to this its most disturbing feature. Theologians have done this through an extreme form of purging to account for how each conflicted individual can eternally live with God, and this explains how mixed creatures end up in bliss. These theologians, however, do not explain, nor do they purport to explain, how Scripture's salvation paradox is unreservedly true. Regardless, they understand the force of the afterlife purging as similar to dividing in order to understand how those who we know best can have eternal life despite our ungodliness.

---

130. Pannenberg, *ST*, III: 637–38.
131. Pannenberg, "Task of Christian Eschatology," 9–10.
132. Pannenberg, *What Is Man?* 67.
133. Turner, *Theology, Psychology and Plural Self*, 151–61.

The immoderate recourse of remodeling the individual as divisible to preserve the paradox of salvation's extent is, therefore, not as foreign to Christianity as it seems. Scripture hints at afterlife divisibility, and many theologians come close to dividing the individual with afterlife purging. With paradoxism now justified, explained, and defended, it remains to be applied in the last chapter to other Christian doctrines.

9

Systemic Truth

> *I can't believe that, when we have all been changed and put on the incorruptibility, we will forget our fantastic condition of mortality and impermanence, the great bright dream of procreating and perishing that meant the whole world to us.*
>
> —Robinson, *Gilead*

THE NEED THAT PARADOXISM addresses was detailed through chapter 5, and the chapters since have given paradoxism's basis and rationale. One defense remains. Paradoxism should, if true, accommodate other truths and, if false, contravene them (1 John 2:21).[1] The premise that truths cohere with other truths powers systematic theology,[2] if not reasoning more basically.[3] Conflicting facts are generally not all facts. For instance, consistency is how we distinguish, when we do, the reality that we encounter in our life from the realities that we encounter in our dreams.

So, the current chapter confronts the truths with which paradoxism most directly transacts, such as the doctrines of anthropology, theistic

---

1. Balthasar, *Theo-Logic*, I: 39, 127; Hume, *Treatise of Human Nature*, I.III.9 (p. 77); Wiles, *Making of Christian Doctrine*, 141–42.
2. Dunning, *Grace, Faith, and Holiness*, 39.
3. Elster, *Sour Grapes*, 1.

atonement, infant salvation, and divine justice and grace, and what these confrontations find is that dividing the individual imperils only its target, the individual. Though possibly unexpected, this follows from paradoxism modeling all the data without writing off as false whatever threatens the starting worldview, which is what avoids the collateral damage that comes from pre-selecting the data before trying to understand what is happening. "What at first seems totally new, even disruptive," von Speyr spotted, will, if true, "find the place reserved for it in tradition and be woven together with related truths and integrate itself organically into the age-old teachings."[4]

1. Paradoxism Conserves Anthropology

The divisibility of the individual might seem to undermine traditional Christian anthropology, but, as often with paradoxes, what seems misleads. Christian anthropology rightly deals primarily with this earthly life,[5] which any divisibility afterwards affects not at all. Therefore, no matter how irreversibly unified we are in this life, division afterwards cannot be to the contrary.[6] Paradoxism also leaves intact whatever the Christian understanding of afterlife anthropology happens to be, despite paradoxism modeling its proposed division as of then, because nothing about anthropology in the afterlife requires *in*divisibility then. This earthly life, which is unitary, obviously has continuity with the next life as the individual does not end with biological death, at least that is how Christians understand such death,[7] but whatever a person's afterlife continuity consists of, whether spirit or something else, remains the case with paradoxism. That is, whoever we are without paradoxism is whoever we are with it, out of which paradoxism fashions afterlife individual divisibility, which is hardly a greater wonder than God pulling off our living after dying.[8]

While tradition lacks individual divisibility and this is clearly paradoxism's supplement, Christian anthropology nevertheless requires that we be thoroughly mutable or else we could not be transformed from the

---

4. Speyr, *Gates of Eternal Life*, 64.
5. Gooder, *Heaven*, 81; White, *Life Beyond Death*, 65–66.
6. Lowe, *Subjects of Experience*, 36.
7. Polkinghorne, *God of Hope*, xxiii, 77, 149; Speyr, *Mystery of Death*, 65.
8. Balthasar, *Life out of Death*, 38; Davis, "Physicalism and Resurrection," 239; MacDonald, *History of the Concept*, 102.

old self to the new self, and individual mutability is especially part of the afterlife, where the individual experiences eschatological purging and glorification. Because it is this mutable individual who is called upon to endure divisibility in the afterlife, paradoxism does not even alter Christian anthropology except for what is anticipated from the afterlife process: The traditional division, which is what divides individuals between those who are to some extent godly, whether wholly, amply, sufficiently, or particularly, and those who are not godly to the obverse extent, becomes understood as a divisibility for each individual who is godly and who is not. Apart from this intra-individual division, no other change in the individual is necessitated by the model.

2. The Good News Remains God's for Us

This discourse has not imposed much on the doctrine of God because the topic has been who is saved, not who does the saving,[9] or, in grammatical constituents, the discourse has addressed salvation's direct object, not its subject.[10] A limited focus is required when the writer (or his reader) is limited. Besides, humans writing to humans about humans naturally feature humans.[11] No apology is required for that. Even such God-oriented writings as creeds and catechisms are apt to be built around the first person.[12] That said, in seeking the self we find God[13] and see Christ in other selves.[14] Humans seeking truth thus secretly prioritize Christology, Hamann understood,[15] and humans see life from their perspective, Paul understood.[16] "Amidst the shreds of my talents I began to search for my self, amidst the manifold for the One," Rosenzweig noted.[17]

The doctrine of God has here been sidelined partly because salvation results from something, and this result, if treated causally, can take

---

9. Ward, "Hegel and the Grandeur," 262; Wiles, *Making of Christian Doctrine*, 106.

10. Robinson, *In the End, God . . .* , 72.

11. Berkouwer, *Man: Image of God*, 10, 356–57; McCombs, *Paradoxical Rationality*, 56.

12. Davies, *Early Christian Church*, 198–99; Torrance, ed., *School of Faith*, xlvii-viii.

13. Calvin, *Institutes*, I,1 (p. 4); Cunningham, "Suspending the Natural Attitude," 281.

14. Montemaggi, *Reading Dante's Commedia*, 26.

15. Milbank, "Theological Critique of Philosophy," 29–30.

16. Boer, *Defeat of Death*, 179 (discussing 1 Cor 15 and Rom 5).

17. Rosenzweig, "Life," 95 (30 Aug. 1920 letter to Meinecke).

salvation as part of a divine routine.[18] For universalists, salvation is the inevitable result of an individual being created, and, for exclusivists, salvation follows from binary distinctives like baptism/atonement, election, or faith.[19] Von Speyr went so far as to claim that salvation is the "Power to compel God"—that is, to "demand eternal life."[20] If God were a mechanism, salvation as a proximate causality would compute, but, since he is not, it does not. Like any understanding of causality, particularly that involving the Divine, causation in salvation can easily devolve into the mechanical. Paradoxism, happily, does not suffer especially from this mechanistic urge.

Counting as ultimately meaningful everything in life is not only personal and realistic, but dovetails with the doctrine of *God*, which in Trinitarian salvation is *with the Father through the Son in the Spirit*.[21] Irenaeus explained, "The Spirit prepares humanity in the Son of God, and the Son leads humanity to the Father, while the Father confers incorruption for eternal life, which comes to all those who see God."[22] Salvation is the Son and Spirit reestablishing godly relations.[23] It is Christ's victory,[24] transforming us for a restored life.[25] "God Himself," Cabasilas noted, joined "human nature," "thus removing the separation between Godhead and manhood." Christ "slays the evil life" while giving goodness,[26] drawing us towards reconciliation and away from resistance,[27] uniting life's brokenness,[28] gathering our annihilation and being.[29] The Spirit correlates to this, filling from the inside rather than leading from the outside.[30] To the extent the individual is Spirit-filled, the individual's will bends from

---

18. Bonhoeffer, *Christ the Center*, 44.
19. Marshall, "Divine and Human Punishment," 225.
20. Speyr, *The Word*, 119.
21. Balthasar, *Theo-Logic*, III; Cyril, *John*, I: Bk IV, ch 1 [500] (p. 223).
22. Irenaeus, *Against Heresies*, 4:20,5 (p. 115).
23. Gunton, *Father, Son and Holy Spirit*, 90.
24. Schwarz, *Human Being*, 175.
25. Henry, *Words of Christ*, 110.
26. Cabasilas, *Life in Christ*, Bk II § 7, Bk III § 2, Bk IV §§ 16–17 (pp. 78, 105, 140–41).
27. Guardini, *World and the Person*, 154, 157; Lossky, *Mystical Theology*, 153.
28. Behr, *Mystery of Christ*, 92.
29. Ratzinger, *Eschatology*, 65.
30. Spezzano, *Glory of God's Grace*, 4.

ungodly to godly[31] and has eternal life.[32] The Spirit's "multiple densities," Tom Greggs observed, "avoid[s] the binaries of saved-damned or heaven-hell while still creating room for . . . the importance of the decision of faith."[33] Paradoxism relies on this same Trinitarian understanding.

Paradoxism not only leaves the doctrine of God as it should be, but also leaves untouched the issue of *how* God achieves salvation. The ecumenically unresolved theory of atonement, from Irenaeus through Tertullian, Cyprian, Athanasius, Augustine, Anselm, Abelard, Luther, and Calvin, and into modernity to now, has despite all the disputes tended to cluster around two foci: 1) Christ has released us from the doom, such as the ransom model where his sacrifice redeems humanity, the Christus Victor model where he overcomes Satan, the satisfaction model where Christ satisfies humanity's debt, or the penal substitution model where Christ suffers for humanity, or 2) Christ has changed us from people who were previously doomed, such as the union, imputation, therapeutic, or influence models, where he restores humanity.[34] All the theories, notwithstanding all the variety, recognize that Christ atoned with effect, and each theory can be used under both universalism and exclusivism. Perhaps obviously, when both universalism and exclusivism can handle a theory, paradoxism can handle that theory too. Each atonement theory has Christ achieve salvation at least to an extent, which occurs under paradoxism as well.

Paradoxism's acceptance of Scripture's exclusivism along with its acceptance of Scripture's universalism can raise an issue that neither conventional position alone shares. Accepting both accounts of salvation's extent may suggest that everyone is damned to an extent, which may seem to conflict with the incontestable principle that Christ has atoned with effect. That paradoxism has everyone damned, even to an extent, is untrue, however. No saved personal identity is, for instance, damned under the model; so, everyone being damned under paradoxism is to that extent misleading.

Even as to the personal character, damning everyone to an extent is not part of the model. Anyone who is sinlessly faithful, such as how

---

31. Berkouwer, *Man: Image of God*, 163.
32. Pannenberg, *ST*, III: 622.
33. Greggs, *Barth, Origen, and Universalism*, 14–15.
34. Eddy and Beilby, "Atonement," 9–20; Grenz, *Theology for the Community*, 340–53.

Catholicism or Orthodoxy envision Mary,[35] needs no division because any such persons are not damned at all. The same would be true for the fully penitent or any otherwise unconflicted character, which is clearly what is desired for us (Deut 6:5; Ps 119:113; Mat 22:37//Mark 12:30//Luke 10:27; 1 Thess 5:23; Jas 1:8, 4:8). "Beware, brothers, lest unbelief's evil heart be in any of you, turning from the living God" (Heb 3:12). As noted in chapter 7, theologians like Cabasilas, Luther, and Finney argue that dividedness is not possible for a true believer. To the extent they are right and the faithful are genuinely without conflict, the unconflicted would not suffer damnation to any extent and would thereby not be divided to any extent. Also, any of the saved, even if conflicted, could, as tradition has it, be purged of any ungodliness in the afterlife, and, once purged, any division becomes unnecessary for them as well. More fundamentally, the division of *the saved* is not a required part of the model at all, and this is because the salvation paradox does not require their division. According to Scripture, everyone is saved; it does not say everyone is damned, but only that some are. Thus, in understanding the salvation paradox, only the damned must suffer division under the model so as to be saved to an extent. The saved can be excused.

Even if none of this were true and the model damned everyone to an extent, Christ would still atone with effect. He would still redeem us, restore us, prevail over Satan, satisfy our divine debt, and take our place for our transgressions. That the model also damns to an extent is no less (or more) troubling than that humanity is damned to an extent as the orthodoxy of exclusivism has it already. That salvation is less than a hundred percent undermines no atonement theory just as no atonement theory undermines exclusivism. The gospel, as it always has, divides its audience between godly and ungodly.[36] Paradoxism's only difference in this regard is that salvation's extent can be among *each* individual, not between *groups* of them. So, with paradoxism, God's news is still good entirely, but its human reception remains not so much.

3. Paradoxism Handles Binary Problems

As orthodoxy understands the negative ultimate, whether eternity's inferno or its oblivion, the concept wears tolerably on those actively

---

35. Lossky, *Mystical Theology*, 141, 193; Wallenfang, *Human and Divine Being*, 147.
36. Colijn, *Images of Salvation*, 74, 77.

responsible for it, but there is "insurmountable doubt," Bulgakov pointed out, "for the overwhelming majority," such as "children who die at an early age," "pagans and members of other religions," "the mentally retarded, severely handicapped, idiots, and all those whose life is marked by the 'karma' of heredity and lack of consciousness."[37] A classic conundrum at least since Augustine ruthlessly applied baptism's significance has been unbaptized infants.[38] Condemning them to perdition repulses, but their salvation regardless of anything at all means infanticide strangely assures that salvation. Accordingly, infant salvation puts exclusivism to a decisive test because being saved from merely being alive is exactly what universalism is,[39] and no one takes the position that exclusivism is only true after our first birthday. Automatic salvation for infants would ignore the clear call to faith, which they have not truly answered, would diminish the clear promise of hope, which they have not truly lived, and would disregard the clear command to love, which they have not truly heeded.[40] Exclusivists thus lack consensus on the issue.[41]

In addition to damning the seemingly undamnable, consistently applying exclusivism gives the persistently godly the same destiny as those briefly so, such as those taking on the deathbed whatever the necessary salvation step is determined to be.[42] Avoiding these sorts of predicaments is part of universalism's appeal, but universalism just eliminates the second ultimate altogether, which creates the opposite problem: This life matters ultimately not at all. With universalism, no matter how horrible life is lived, God shakes his cosmic Etch-a-Sketch and restores everyone to the original image that conforms to his will. In other words, being regenerate is all that is ultimately relevant for exclusivism, and for universalism it is just being generate.

In contrast, the entirety of divine grace and the human response informs paradoxism. To the extent godly, the individual has eternal life; to the extent not, the individual has perishing. Under paradoxism, therefore, nothing in this life is ultimately irrelevant because there is nothing worthwhile in this life that is outside of being godly or ungodly.

37. Bulgakov, *Bride of the Lamb*, 369–70.
38. Augustine, "On Merit and Forgiveness," 15–43 (Bk I). See Geisler, *ST*, 984, 999.
39. D. Hart, *That All Shall Be Saved*, 145.
40. Timpe, "Argument for Limbo," 286.
41. J. Sanders, *No Other Name*, 305.
42. Nichols, *Death and Afterlife*, 188–89.

Thus, infants, returning to that quandary, are, as expected, like everyone else, both God-oriented and self-oriented and can thus be saved and not saved. The only ultimate distinctive for those who die as infants is what truly distinguishes them as a group from everyone else—they have been deprived of life's primary character-building chapters.[43] Paradoxism similarly nuances other doctrines that deal with salvation's determinants, which tend to be binary given the binary ultimate. Instead of identifying either-or indicators of eternal life, whether rebirth for exclusivism or just birth for universalism, everything in this life ultimately matters.[44] Paradoxism, as a result, does deserve to be condemned for blurring the absolute demarcation between godly humans and ungodly humans into which tradition has tended to compartmentalize them—not as much as Jesus deserved it,[45] but condemned nonetheless.

4. Proportional Justice Survives

Another salvation-extent vexation is that God's eschatological menu has only two entrées, and extreme ones at that. The selection of paradise, hell, and nothing else seems far too short and unimaginative for the Infinite One, especially when his reign is at its maximum. As applied to all of humanity's variety, the choices limited to either eternal life or perdition challenge exclusivism's justice, and the variety of the universalist menu, with just its one ultimate, is only worse. Humanity's farrago, even when aggregated into approximate categories, certainly seems to call for more than one or two outcomes. Plato, apparently the first to write clearly on afterlife judgment, had enough fecundity to provide for four outcomes.[46] God should be no less resourceful than Plato, especially since God's justice so clearly entails proportionality and even reflexivity.[47]

Proportional justice was one of God's first principles: "Whoever sheds man's blood, by man his blood will be shed" (Gen 9:6), and this proportionality was later broadened to all corporeal harm (Exod 21:12,

---

43. Carter and Frith, *Mapping the Mind*, 19–22; Come, *Kierkegaard as Theologian*, 164–66, 173.

44. Ludlow, *Universal Salvation*, 15–16.

45. Bornkamm, *Paulus*, 235.

46. Plato, *Phaedo*, 113d-114c. See Bernstein, *Formation of Hell*, 55, 61.

47. Bernstein, *Formation of Hell*, 237; Kvanvig, "Hell," 419; Pinnock, "Annihilationism," 471.

23–25; Lev 24:17–20). Because God prefers that human justice be proportional, his justice should reflect this, and it does.[48] God gives what is due to each individual (Pss 28:4–5; 62:12; Prov 24:12; Isa 3:10–11; Jer 17:9–10; 32:19; Ezek 14:12–14, 20). God adjudicates impartially (Deut 1:17; 11:26–28; Eccl 12:14; Jer 18:20) and judges equitably (*bĕmêšārîm*,[49] Ps 96:10; also 75:2), both with his chosen and to the ends of the earth (Amos 3:2; Obad 1:15; Ezek 18:30; 39:24). "I will judge each as befits his ways" (33:20). When people complained that the divine justice as God had announced it should be more communal and less individualized, God defended it as superior precisely because of its proportionality, because it is "adjusted to the standard [*yittākēn*]"[50] (18:5–29; 33:8–20).

God repeatedly applies justice that is proportional. When humanity spoiled the earth, God spoiled humanity (Gen 6:11–13). Those blessing Abram are blessed; those cursing him are cursed (12:2–3). When the people sought meat and turned their nose up to God, God gave the people meat until it came out their nose (Num 11:19–20). When the forty-day patrol reported to the people that the promised land was deadly, the people had to patrol forty years outside the promised land until dead (14:28–34). When the people faced away from God, God hid his face (Deut 31:18). When they violated the ban, he banned them (Josh 7:12). Those glorifying God are glorified; those disdaining God are disdained (1 Sam 2:30). The righteous are righted; the condemnable are condemned (1 Kgs 8:23; 2 Chr 6:23). God pillaged the people who pillaged God's people (Jer 30:16, 50:15; Ezek 39:10; Joel 3:4–8; Hab 2:8), and, when the people rejected God, God rejected the people, "They sow the wind and reap the whirlwind" (Hos 4:6; 8:7).

Thus far only the Hebrew Scriptures have been cited, but not because the NT diminishes the proportionality in God's justice.[51] It is still the case that "Your standard's measure will measure you" (Luke 6:38//Matt 7:2; also Mark 4:24). Afflicters are afflicted (2 Thess 1:5–9),[52] and "Anyone corrupting God's sanctuary, God will corrupt" (1 Cor 3:17), "for we all must be revealed before Christ's bench, so each may be repaid for the

---

48. Basil, "Asketikon," LR Pro. ¶ 4 (p. 158); N. G. Wright, "Kinder, Gentler Damnation?" 232.

49. This is the always plural noun for the verb "smooth" that literally means "evenness." BDB, 449.

50. BDB, 1067.

51. Schreiner, "Penal Substitution View," 79.

52. Weima, *1–2 Thessalonians*, 464–66, 475.

deeds in the body, whether good or evil" (2 Cor 5:10).[53] The only creditable change is that the NT seems to stress particularly the proportionality of justice in the eschaton, which is of course the fulcrum of ultimate salvation. This proportionality is not merely in the notorious images of Revelation, where God punishes blood for blood and, in the end, will "render to each his deed" (2:23; 11:18; 14:13; 16:6; 22:12),[54] but Christ's minas parable has proportional eschatological judgment too (Luke 19:11–27), as does even the contrasting parable of the talents: Though the Master expresses equal pleasure for various achievements, better achievers still finish better (Matt 25:14–30). God's justice, even when not symmetrical, is proportional, whether sevenfold (Gen 4:15; Lev 26:18) or double (Isa 40:2; Jer 16:18; Rev 18:6).

Unlike universalism, where merely having a life determines ultimate salvation, and unlike exclusivism, where a certain threshold in life does, God's ultimate judgment reflects all of this life, not just particular moments.[55] Universalism prioritizes a person's first moment because as of then salvation is guaranteed, and exclusivism prioritizes either a special moment such as the last one because by then whatever is thought to be decisive occurs or a few special moments such as baptism and atonement. Yet, Christianity generally gives every moment ultimate priority.[56] God "will light up the secrets in darkness and expose the hearts' resolves. Each will then receive his recognition from God" (1 Cor 4:5; also 1 Tim 5:24–25). For the ungodly, "the end will correspond to their works" (2 Cor 11:15), and the saved are not exempt (1 Cor 3:12–15; 2 Tim 4:8). God, "the impartial judge of each man's work" (1 Pet 1:17), judges individually (Rom 14:10–12; 2 Cor 5:10). Jesus' eschatological judgment repays for an entire life (Matt 16:27). The unrighteous have God's wrath; the rest, eternal life (Rom 1:29–31; 2:2, 5–10). We have in the next life what we cultivate in this one.[57]

While eternal life and perishing are the only scripturally stated outcomes, those obtaining them clearly fail to categorize that neatly.[58] Universalism's solution is to eliminate proportion altogether in ultimate

---

53. Guthrie, *2 Corinthians*, 290.
54. Koester, *Revelation*, 473, 521.
55. Lewis, "Weight of Glory," 28.
56. Caputo, *Radical Hermeneutics*, 15.
57. Gregory of Nyssa, *Life of Moses*, Bk II (pp. 73–74).
58. Harrison, *God's Many-Splendored Image*, 18; Ludlow, *Universal Salvation*, 14.

judgment, one for all, and exclusivism, with only two outcomes, is just one better. Universalists explain that the ultimate lacks proportion because God's nature lacks proportion,[59] but God's purely good nature has existed all along and evil has been around for quite a while. Exclusivists also must rationalize, offering two apologies for how non-binary humanity receives binary ultimate justice. One is that God's election is just inexplicable, but this implies arbitrariness.[60] While no deal breaker, it does not comport with God's concern for proportion. The second is that eternal life is always gratuitous, which means perdition is always deserved.[61] This too, while coherent, still leaves the ultimates outside God's bias for proportion. Both rationalizations based on divine entropy deplete the ultimate of meaning nearly as well as motile definitions deplete words of meaning.[62]

Paradoxism, in contrast, allows proportion in the ultimate without repudiating either the binary outcomes or the ultimate meaning of every moment in life. Whatever is godly lives ultimately, and whatever is ungodly perishes ultimately. Christian eschatology is thus no refuge because eternity's judgment is not so much a fascinating reckoning for what all one has done but a holy recognition of what all one has become.[63] Henry described the typical "reproach: the invention of a fantastic (or even phantasmagoric) other world, a place of imaginary satisfaction of all the desires and all the aspirations that a person cannot realize here below . . . ." "The problem was not its ideals but that by projecting them into an empty heaven it reduced them to pious wishes instead of bringing them into daily life, through struggle and contradictions in the difficult history of humankind." This fantasy is not Christian, whose "decisive thesis" "is that there exists only one reality," "nothing other than life,"[64] and, with paradoxism, all in this life matters after all.

5. Paradoxism Values Grace

Bonhoeffer famously villainized cheap salvation, where "grace alone does everything" so "everything can stay in its old ways," which is "the mortal

---

59. D. Hart, *That All Shall Be Saved*, 47, 53, 58, 69–70, 78, 202–3.
60. James, *Varieties of Religious Experience*, 323; Ludlow, *Universal Salvation*, 14.
61. Calvin, *Institutes*, III,11–13 (pp. 473–501).
62. Pannenberg, *Anthropology in Theological Perspective*, 333.
63. Bultmann, *Theology of the NT*, I: 2.2 (p. 15).
64. Henry, *I Am the Truth*, 234–35, 238.

enemy of the church." The grace that has been cheapened in this way contrasts with the grace that remains worthy and thus real; true grace costs a life of discipleship, "a genuine, simple obedience in faith in the righteousness of Christ."[65] Any understanding of an afterlife risks contributing to the cheapening of this grace,[66] if for no other reason than that the afterlife tends to pale in comparison to the earthy life.[67] Anticipating the life that is in God's unmediated presence is bound to dazzle, and this can cause us to lose sight of the life we are living now.

To retain the ultimate importance of this life, the various doctrines of salvation can freeze-facture life into critical moments, but, to the extent that any part of this life does not affect the ultimate, that moment is to that extent free of any ultimate cost at all. Universalism can cheapen grace because nothing from this life, which is all we can offer, matters ultimately to salvation other than that there was one, and exclusivism can be similar in that nothing matters ultimately to salvation beyond whatever select set of events split humanity into saved and damned. The response to grace is not like that. As Kierkegaard noted, faith is "a task for a whole lifetime,"[68] practicing throughout life "the earnest thought of death."[69] Understanding this life, or any part of it, as irrelevant to the end is dispiriting to that extent. The end that occurs without regard for the life that has been led is like the *deus ex machina* that ends a play, which is not a problem because of the *deus* or the *machina*, but because of how such an end cheapens the rest of the play.

While both universalism and exclusivism can depreciate the cost of grace in this way, this is not the case if the individual is ultimately divisible between godly and ungodly. In that case, nothing about God's grace is cheapened, and every moment matters to its pricing.[70] Bonhoeffer knew, "One takes from life what it offers, not all or nothing, but good things and bad," which means the Christian life "includes choosing something relatively better over something relatively worse." It is "a concrete ethic" encompassing "all of life,"[71] and that is what ultimately matters. "For

---

65. Bonhoeffer, *Discipleship*, 43, 45, 120, 144 [29, 31, 121, 148].
66. Feuerbach, *Essence of Christianity*, I,XVII (p. 161).
67. Brunner, *Eternal Hope*, 91.
68. Kierkegaard, *Fear and Trembling*, 23.
69. Kierkegaard, "At a Graveside," 77.
70. Cabasilas, *Life in Christ*, Bk I § 1 (p. 44).
71. Bonhoeffer, *Ethics*, 92, 98–100, 159, 261, 378 [79, 86–88, 151, 260, 381].

nothing is hidden but to be brought to light, or secreted but to have come into light" (Mark 4:22).

6. Afterlife Decision-Making Is Unneeded

Both exclusivists and universalists, to alleviate a theological problem with their respective positions, have hypothesized that those betraying this life can about-face afterwards. Exclusivists, so no one is judged too hastily before losing out forever on eternal life, can postulate that each of us is given further chances after this life to decide rightly, whether through a purgatory or otherwise.[72] These exclusivists do not see an impassable abyss like in Luke's Lazarus parable that separates eschatological perishing from its paradise based on the earthly life, but instead see an everlasting offer like in C. S. Lewis' *The Great Divorce* allegory that theoretically allows the damned to cross over out of hell. Similarly, some universalists, in recognition of the fact that eternal life involves true love, which cannot be forced, postulate that the afterlife involves God outlasting the naysayers who are given endless choices until everyone is eventually induced "freely" to have the required loving mindset.[73] God uses in the ultimate what amounts to a divine water-drip torture to obtain a godly confession from everyone, no matter how recalcitrant.[74] Under either exclusivism or universalism's do-over approach, Brian Hebblethwaite explained, we are to "free ourselves from the old idea that opportunities to repent and respond to God's love are restricted to a single life span on earth."[75] And once one afterlife opportunity is added, a second opportunity, a third one, ad infinitum, are as supposable.[76] Like Kantian immortality, Philip Ziegler perceived, "we are not so much saved by the bell as saved by the fact that the bell never rings."[77]

And it is not merely perpetual choices that are added in the afterlife because more choices do not always, or even usually, produce the desired choice. Not only may the choice never change to the correct one, it is

---

72. Griffiths, "Purgatory," 427.

73. Bulgakov, *Bride of the Lamb*, 363; Ludlow, *Universal Salvation*, 106; Talbott, "Universalism," 451–52.

74. McClymond, *Devil's Redemption*, II: 956.

75. Hebblethwaite, *Christian Hope*, 215.

76. Kvanvig, "Hell," 418.

77. Ziegler, *Militant Grace*, 98.

sometimes the first choice that is correct and the later one that is wrong. So, given that more choices may not make things better and could even make them worse, the afterlife cannot be truly reimagined as one of further choosing, but must be seen as having only the choice that is the correct one, otherwise known as no choice at all. Such an afterlife Groundhog Day is affirmed only by treating this one life as just the first among many opportunities, which denies this life its criticality, if not its purpose.[78]

God, on the other hand, takes the invitation in this life seriously. Every Christian branch, following Scripture's clear read, has recognized that death is a finality, particularly in the context of salvation.[79] The parables of the bridesmaids, of the talents, and of the minas all reflect that it is this life that matters to the ultimate (Matt 25:1–30; Luke 19:11–27). The Lazarus parable makes this point especially: Although Dives begs for mercy after his death, this is denied because his one life was sufficient (16:19–31).[80] What we do in the earthly body judges us (2 Cor 5:10), and judgment "into salvation" occurs after "dying once" (Heb 4:1, 6–7, 9–11; 9:27–28). The time for deciding for or against God therefore runs out when this life does.[81] There is a literal *dead*line.[82] No individual, Kierkegaard discerned, can try out another identity in eternity to see if it fits.[83] Those ungodly in little—in this life—will be ungodly in much—in the next (Luke 16:10). "What God does for us, He does in us," C. S. Lewis reminded, in "the daily and hourly repeated exercises of my own will . . . ."[84]

Christians nonetheless acknowledge that, to live in God's presence, we must lose from this life whatever is unsuitable for the next. Catholics hold that this afterlife purging happens over a span of time, and this has matured into their doctrine of purgatory.[85] They acknowledge Scripture hardly justifies the doctrine, and, so, Catholics principally base it on praying for the dead: If the dead are instantaneously in God's presence,

---

78. Daley, *Hope of the Early Church*, 95, 108; Martin, *Will Many Be Saved?* 154; Schwarz, *Eschatology*, 346–47; Williamson, *Death and the Afterlife*, 191–92; Yates, *Between Death and Resurrection*, 225.

79. Bulgakov, *Bride of the Lamb*, 362; Ludlow, *Universal Salvation*, 163; Ratzinger, *Eschatology*, 216–17.

80. Bernstein, *Formation of Hell*, 241.

81. Balthasar, *Theo-Drama*, I: 22; V: 413.

82. Caldecott, *Radiance of Being*, 243.

83. Kierkegaard, *Upbuilding Discourses*, 66; "At a Graveside," 84.

84. Lewis, "Slip of the Tongue," 191–92.

85. Goff, *Birth of Purgatory*, 41, 271.

prayers for people after they die would be tardy, but, since the prayers have been efficacious, purging must be durational.[86] Other Christians reject purgatory as foreign to Scripture, but they still have an afterlife purging, except it is nontemporal.[87] Purging that is instantaneous, however, devalues the God-given duration of this life; if the personal character can be what it should be instantaneously, a life*time* is superfluous, if not ridiculous.[88] This is not the case, of course. A person's character comes to be that person's character only through duration.[89] In contrast to universalism and exclusivism, paradoxism has no need to resort to an afterlife do-over, whether from a chronological purgatory,[90] which is not from Scripture, or from an instantaneous character development, which is not from living. The individual division of paradoxism preserves, not nullifies, the import of this life in the next.

7. The Community Is Eternal

Individuality only thrives within relationality.[91] Christianity has known this at least since Augustine,[92] and modernity has known this at least since Hegel.[93] The individual's web of relationships in this life—collectively called the community—is accordingly indispensable, and this should be no less true in the eschaton, which is also a community.[94] A universalist advantage, therefore, is that by definition the entire community perdures in the end, but, as has been discussed, among its weaknesses is that the ungodly are obliged to become who they have not lived to be in order to make their appearance then.[95] Universalism, to save the village, must

---

86. Nichols, *Death and Afterlife*, 171–76; Ratzinger, *Eschatology*, 218–33; Rausch, *ST*, 283–84.

87. Calvin, *Institutes*, III,2,28, 4,31, 5,2 (pp. 373, 427, 436); Grenz, *Theology for the Community*, 591–92.

88. Nichols, *Death and Afterlife*, 175; Stackhouse, "Terminal Punishment Response," 181.

89. Lewis, *Mere Christianity*, 51.

90. Chronological duration is not necessary to the purgatory doctrine. Benedict XVI, *Spe Salvi*, 47.

91. Barresi and Martin, "History as Prologue," 54.

92. Augustine, *Confessions*, 1,6,10 (p. 8).

93. Hegel, *Phenomenology of Spirit*, ¶¶ 166–99 (pp. 104–19).

94. Buber, *I and Thou*, 63; Grenz, *Theology for the Community*, 603, 611.

95. D. Hart, *That All Shall Be Saved*, 150–58.

destroy who the villagers are. In contrast, exclusivism in order to be exclusivist must eliminate any engagement with those outside salvation, meaning some of those with whom the saved have been in community are inevitably lost to the eternal community. So, through either universalism's compulsion or exclusivism's expulsion, some life-giving communal relations from this life must go missing in the next.

Paradoxism, however, retains in eternal life the entire web of personal relations. The eschatological community, as paradoxism understands it, consists of everyone being in the community to the extent godly, and this is unlike exclusivism. Similarly, with paradoxism, everyone to the extent they are in the eschatological community are there because they identify with it, and this is unlike universalism. Paradoxism's focus on the individual might have at the outset seemed hostile to the community, but the opposite has proven to be true. Every individual is subject to division, and, therefore, no matter what else happens, every individual remains ultimately in community. That is, individual divisibility allows the eternal to include everyone, unlike exclusivism, and does so without necessitating the Stepford replacements of the ungodly, unlike universalism. Instead, with paradoxism, the open issue, and the critical one, is the extent to which all this occurs.

☙❧

While adversely affecting no doctrine, paradoxism unsettles humanity's ultimates. Antonio Lopez describes the "excruciating" concept that "requires the ungrateful person to let go of his own idea of perfection and of the predilection for his own coherence...."[96] Paradoxism strives to be like Christianity itself, which is Kierkegaard's "turbulent thing."[97] "Experiencing God can be likened to falling down the rabbit hole," Gabelman concluded, "all manner of things become believable which were previously thought impossible."[98] Paradoxism fundamentally alters the individual, just as Christianity does.[99] *Who* brings ultimate salvation is worshipped, but *what* yields ultimate salvation is not, at least it shouldn't be; and it is the *what*, at least whatever certitude attaches to it, that paradoxism defies. Just being a creature, which is sufficient for universalism, is not taken as

---

96. Lopez, *Gift and Unity*, 295.
97. Kierkegaard, *For Self-Examination*, 14.
98. Gabelman, *Theology of Nonsense*, 203.
99. Ziegler, *Militant Grace*, 167.

ultimately so. Whatever threshold exclusivism finds ultimately sufficient, whether conversion, election, or deeds, is not taken that way either. Rather, every moment is important, and no moment is all-important. Everything is necessary; nothing is sufficient.[100] As Barth wrote, "to Christianity," "no problem of life, be it great or small, is trivial or irrelevant."[101] At the center of each led life, whether among the great or small, is whether the person identifies with God, and, as C. S. Lewis noted, he is "an acquired taste."[102]

---

100. Barth, *Romans*, 361 (9:24–29); Hoff, "Rise and Fall," 185; Kierkegaard, *The Moment*, 290.

101. Barth, *Romans*, 463 (12:16).

102. Lewis, *Problem of Pain*, 55.

Concludings

The thought of the life beyond the grave distracts me to anguish, to terror . . . And now I am so bold as to ask you. Oh, God! What will you think of me now?

—Dostoevsky, *The Brothers Karamazov*

Chapters 1 and 2 framed the predicament that chapter 3 presented, which is that Scripture by imparting both exclusivist and universalist accounts is in paradox on salvation's extent. Chapter 4 documented how the church has responded to this predicament, which, according to every position that has so far been taken on the subject, is that Scripture is in contradiction and, as a result, one account on salvation's extent must be hollowed out so that the preferred account may be hallowed. After centuries of mostly ineffectual debate about which account to prefer, the church has decided conclusively but precipitously on exclusivism, which includes potentialism, but many Christians, particularly after Origen and of late, have favored universalism. Chapter 5 found that each competing position is incomplete primarily because each side, so as to brevet one scriptural account to doctrine, must cashier the other scriptural account to misconception, and, not only must each side do violence to what Scripture says to achieve pellucidity, each position is in the ultimate noetically unbalanced: universalism seems Pollyanna, exclusivism seems savage, and potentialism seems disingenuous.

This unsatisfactory state of affairs led to chapter 6's disquisition that the individual is divisible, which, as chapter 7 explained, allows Scripture's portrayal of salvation's extent to be paradoxical—that is, seemingly contradictory but actually true. As a consequence of everyone being ultimately divisible, both are true: everyone is saved, and not everyone is. Chapters 8 and 9 offered additional reasons for this strange understanding. The stances that have been argued with conviction throughout the book's second half have been offered mostly to suggest the viability of preserving Scripture's salvation paradox through individual division. Those so inclined are invited to jettison any number of the stances taken, such as those which concern who we are, the scriptural exegesis, or the doctrinal influences, and this should not undermine the primary stance of the thesis, which, at the end here, can be singled out from the *obiter dicta*.

The thesis originated with what cannot be fairly disputed: Scripture says that everyone will be saved and also that not everyone will be. If the text of Scripture did not itself make both accounts clear enough, the church's many first-rate proponents have confirmed each account on salvation's extent. Denying either account is effectively unavailable until one of them is exegeted with extreme prejudice—the favored account, whichever one that happens to be, is used to justify reinterpreting the other so that just the favorite survives. The only alternative has been to claim that actual contradictions are true, but this view does not survive contact with reality except perhaps under dictatorial doublethink. In contrast, the impetus of the thesis has been that Scripture's portrayal of salvation's extent should be as it appears, paradoxical.

The gist of the thesis has been to show *how* this scriptural paradox need not be treated as an actual contradiction, which means to say something false, and the insight proposed has been that of the divisible individual. Though *individual* has been around for nearly as long as cogitation, Descartes famously highlighted its indivisibility. Those disputing Cartesian anthropology have largely challenged its dualism or its stringency, but the eligible anthropological alternatives, whether before or after Descartes, still model the living individual as generally indivisible thanks to this life's naturally unitary corporeality and the first-person's inherently unitary perspective. The thesis, regardless of whatever dependence our thinking has on Descartes, also uses this understanding of the individual for two reasons. First, the in-itself individual has clearly been the most common understanding since antiquity and remains so until today, and, given our unitary perspective, it is also the most reasonable.

This is why Descartes' position, even if wrong at the physical or metaphysical level, has been so credible at the practical level. Second, the in-itself individual, which emphasizes the integrity of the entity, actually imposes the most stress on paradoxism's divisibility. So, those of us with less Cartesianesque views can, if persuaded by them, consider their alternatives for *individual* (or *self* or *human*) and should have an easier time with the paradox. Regardless of how indivisible we are each understood to be, the salvation paradox had best remain as it is scripturally presented—a paradox. Even if our understanding of the individual changes, the issue will remain whether dividing an individual, to whatever extent it might be Cartesian, risks less than enfeebling one scriptural account. If the dividing of the individual as modeled here does not display the salvation paradox, some other model should.

Long before the thesis, Scripture's adherents have struggled with its paradoxes. In those struggles, the church has typically imbibed Scripture entirely, marginalizing as heresy only the sublations, even when dressed up as sublimations, and, to avoid subjecting Scripture to such reductions, the church modeled new theological insights. An interminable exception, however, has been the paradox of salvation's extent. Instead of accepting, as Scripture asserts, that both everyone is ultimately saved and not everyone is, Christians have accepted only the account deemed best. The exclusivist position, which has been dominant, is based on Scripture unmistakably describing two actual, populated ultimate destinies, one of which is perdition. The universalist position, which competed early on and resurges today, is based on Scripture clearly declaring that God, who is through and in everyone, reconciles and saves everyone, dragging everyone to himself, even the ungodly. Given the inescapable principle of noncontradiction, whether reasoned out or intuitively lived, the church felt obliged, despite the evident presence of both scriptural accounts, to pick one. This unraveling of the contradiction, once it was taken as a contradiction, required no insight, just a cleanup of the other scriptural account.

The church in its first several centuries tentatively split on which contradicting account to clean up. In deciding more vital issues, each involving seemingly contradictory scriptural accounts, the church had resisted the alluring simplicity of contradiction and preserved the paradoxes that Scripture presented, but it had not decided on how best to understand the paradox of salvation's extent by the time the church had begun to see paradoxy as a threat. By then, a "coating of dust" had fallen,

Bornkamm described, "on the holy writings like a pall."[1] So, the sixth-century church, lacking the appetite for more incongruities, opted for exclusivism, though universalism subsequently persisted as a heresy and has, as Christianity's bona fides have waned, now regained popularity. Both sides in the debate, despite reaching opposite conclusions on salvation's extent, have agreed on one fundamental, which is that the salvation paradox is a contradiction in need of reform.

In contrast, paradoxism takes salvation's extent as what Scripture says it is, which means taking the salvation-extent accounts not as untruthful or as unartful but as paradoxical. If both scriptural accounts are taken as true, the accounts cannot contradict, and it is this that invites the individual's divisibility. It can be admitted at the end that this, despite being unexpected, is as should be expected. Absolute truth claims, such as those that Scripture makes about eternal life, are bound to be particularistic *and* universalistic because such claims are exceptional without exception.[2] Paradoxism, to the extent elegant, is, however, no anodyne for the salvation paradox because to preserve the paradox the model exposes the individual as divisible into two, not merely purged into clarity.

The healthy among us naturally question how this can be, an individual that is divisible. The model, in answer, relies on how little we know about the individual. Much of what we suspect to be the case does not contribute in our context, and, so, unspecified here are whatever the substances are, if any, that continue from this life to the next. Nonetheless, the Christian consensus delivers, and the model employs, two unavoidable axioms that *are* relevant. First, as corpses prove relentlessly, our bodies suffer an erasure when life ends that is, at least eventually, as thorough as unused words wiped into dust from the chalkboard. Second, beyond the corporeal dust left behind, there are at least two other personal aspects that perdure from this life to the next if there is to be an afterlife: Our personal identity continues because any afterlife to be ours must be *experienced* by us, and our personal character continues because any afterlife to be ours must *be* us. While the personal identity is our first-person awareness and is thereby unitary, the personal character is what our led life renders and is thereby chronically conflicted between what is basically godly and ungodly. From this, paradoxism's understanding of the salvation paradox follows: The individual is ultimately saved to the

---

1. Bornkamm, *Paulus*, xxv.
2. Stuurman, *Invention of Humanity*, 113.

extent godly and doomed to the extent ungodly, dividing (if necessary) the two orientations of the personal character, and our personal identity experiences the personal character with which it identifies.

As a result, because no one is nothing ultimately, everyone in God's mercy is remade ultimately while also remaining oneself, reunifying God with the singular, but anyone opposing God's mercy deserts the self.[3] In the paradox of salvation's extent, as with most other Christian paradoxes, what coincides is identity and difference, the singular and the plural.[4] Divisibility, therefore, contrary to expectation, unifies because everything in this life matters for the next, notwithstanding that the next life, by general agreement, radically differs.[5] The next is not merely this life plus extras, just as the eternal is not dying plus overtime. Rather, Christ unifies this life with the next,[6] and, while everything now will matter to the next, not everything now will be in the next.[7]

This began as an effort to understand what Scripture means when it says that everyone is saved and that not everyone is saved. Paradoxism accepts both as true, but this is reckless, even perilous, because it domesticates neither salvation proposition. Preserving Scripture's salvation paradox means that what ultimately matters is how we face every moment, not any particular moment or two, and the choice we face is the lifelong one between the sinfully earthy and the earthly Divine.[8] "The man under grace is engaged unconditionally in a conflict," Barth saw, "a war of life and death, a war in which there can be no armistice—and no peace." "Upon the threshold of my existence there appears . . . the new man in Christ Jesus, . . . endowed with attributes which are not mine . . . This new man is . . . no other, second person with whom I may be compared; he claims to be me myself, my existential, unobservable ego," but this internal dissension means only "that an abyss is disclosed between myself and—myself."[9] The question heard in the abyss is, With whom do I identify? Hamann answered rightly, "Unbelief in the most essential, historical sense of the word is thus the only sin against the spirit of the

---

3. Lopez, *Gift and Unity*, 290, 293, 302.
4. Stang, *Our Divine Double*, 253.
5. Lopez, *Gift and Unity*, 303.
6. Gregor, *Philosophical Anthropology*, 124.
7. Speyr, *Mystery of Death*, 74, 108.
8. Speyr, *Passion from Within*, 136–37.
9. Barth, *Romans*, 225, 229, 262.

true religion, whose heart is in heaven and whose heaven is in the heart." "As a result, there is no mediating concept left ... except to believe with all their heart, with all their soul, with all their mind: For God so loved the world—This faith is the victory that overcomes the world."[10]

"God is love," which is not our love for him, but his for us, namely his love revealed in us (1 John 4:8–10, 16). This in Wordsworth's words is "the sustaining thought."[11] "[T]he glory of God," Irenaeus noted, "is a living man; and the life of man consists in beholding God."[12] Cabasilas advanced the idea, "It is those in whom this noble passion is nourished who truly live, just as all things are dead for those in whom it is absent."[13] No one escapes this passion entirely, just as no mere mortal nourishes it thoroughly. The "dangerous condition of being human," McConville reminds us, involves "the perpetual tension between flourishing and degradation."[14] "In redemption, as in creation," Käsemann knew, "everything is differentiated" because "God does not want stereotypes."[15] Yet too, "Nothing differentiates" (Rom 3:22).[16] We are therefore encouraged not to differentiate people as either godly or ungodly, but to recognize that we each are both.[17] God's love certainly does not differentiate among us, but every great love, even his, knows absolute differentiation at its most lived, which is the yearning difference between the lover and the beloved.[18]

When all is done, I want to be "counted worthy of God's reign" (2 Thess 1:5). I do not know if I can try more—I certainly can—or how much that counts—I question that—but I will try more, because "nothing entering man from outside can defile," only "what comes out of man" (Mark 7:18, 20//Matt 15:17–18). "I do not wish the Word to save only half of me," Gregory of Nazianzus foresaw.[19] I alone am guilty, Kierkegaard judged, which brings the joy that the fault lies in me alone and that my

---

10. Hamann, "Golgotha and Sheblimini!," 193–95.
11. Wordsworth, *The Prelude*, XIV,204–5
12. Irenaeus, "Against Heresies [1994]," 4:20,7 (p. 490).
13. Cabasilas, *Life in Christ*, Bk VII § 15 (p. 228).
14. McConville, *Being Human*, 192.
15. Käsemann, *Perspectives on Paul*, 4.
16. Barth, *Romans*, 99–102.
17. Hutson, *First . . . Timothy*, 174.
18. Cunningham, *Genealogy of Nihilism*, 188, 222.
19. Gregory of Nazianzus, "Concerning His Own Life," 58–59 (ln 626).

task alone remains.[20] Therefore, even when assured of salvation,[21] I doubt the extent to which I abide in it.[22] "God will call to account the pursuit" (Eccl 3:15). Though the good news is God's grace to humanity, I live the paradox of a loving but an alienating response.[23] I am, therefore, sure and unsure of salvation. I hear distinctly Yes and No, but the voices sound different. It is as if I am divided. Sure, God loves *me entirely*, but if only *I entirely* returned the favor. Kierkegaard again writes for *me*: "now, for the first time, I understand and can see the whole of it—but then of course I cannot say 'I.'"[24] "What is this mystery in me?" the original Climacus asked. "Speak to me, my yoke-fellow, my nature! I cannot ask anyone else about you," he insisted. "How can I escape the danger of my own nature? I have made a promise to Christ that I will fight you, yet how can I defeat your tyranny?"[25] I—no, we—should fight this fight, not because we want to live eternally, but because we want to be there when we do.

20. Kierkegaard, *Upbuilding Discourses*, 275, 277, 280.
21. Luther, *Galatians*, 364–65, 370 [WA 401, 577–78, 586 (4:6)].
22. Demarest, *Cross and Salvation*, 379.
23. Schwobel, "Human Being as Relational," 161.
24. Kierkegaard, *JP*, VI: 287 (NB13.21).
25. Climacus, *Ladder*, 186 (step 15).

Bibliography

Abraham, William J. "Eschatology and Epistemology." In *Oxford Handbook of Eschatology*, edited by Jerry L. Walls, 581–95. Oxford: Oxford University Press, 2008.
Acts and Decrees of the Synod of Jerusalem. Translated by J. N. W. B. Robertson. London: Thomas Baker, 1899.
Adorno, Theodor. *Minima Moralia*. Translated by E. F. N. Jephcott. London: NLB, 1974.
Al-Ghazali, Muhammad. "Deliverance from Error." Translated by R. J. McCarthy. In *Al-Ghazali's Path to Sufism*, 17–80. Louisville: Fons Vitae, 2000.
Alexander, W. M. *Johann Georg Hamann: Philosophy and Faith*. The Hague: Martinus Nijhoff, 1966.
Allen, David L. *The Extent of Atonement*. Nashville: B&H, 2016.
Alvaro, Pascual-Leone, Amedi Amir, Fregni Felipe, and B. Merabet Lotfi. "The Plastic Human Brain Cortex." *Annual Review of Neuroscience* 28.1 (2005) 377–401.
Ambrose. "Expositio in Psalmum CXVIII." In *Sancti Ambrosii Mediolanensis Episcopi Opera Omnia*, 971–1238 (cols. 1261–1580). Paris: Migne, 1887.
———. "On the Christian Faith." In *Nicene and Post-Nicene Fathers: Second Series*, edited by Philip Schaff and Henry Wace, 199–314. Peabody, MA: Hendrickson, 1995.
The Ambrosiaster. "Commentaries on Thirteen Pauline Epistles." Translated by William A. Jurgens. In *The Faith of the Early Fathers (vol. 2)*, edited by William A. Jurgens, 177–79. Collegeville, MN: Liturgical, 1979.
Andreopoulos, Andreas. "Eschatology in Maximus the Confessor." In *The Oxford Handbook of Maximus the Confessor*, edited by Pauline Allen and Bronwen Neil, 322–40. Oxford: Oxford University Press, 2015.
Ansell, Nik. "Annihilation of Hell and Perfection of Freedom." In *All Shall Be Well*, edited by Gregory MacDonald, 417–39. Eugene, OR: Cascade, 2011.
Anselm. *Cur Deus Homo*. Translated by Sidney Norton Deane. Fort Worth, TX: RDMc, 2005.
Anthony the Great. *The Letters*. Translated by Derwas J. Chitty. Oxford: SLG, 1975.

Aquinas, Thomas. *Compendium of Theology*. Translated by Richard J. Regan. Oxford: Oxford University Press, 2009.

———. *De Potentia* [The Power of God]. Translated by Richard J. Regan. Oxford: Oxford University Press, 2012.

———. *The Division and Methods of the Sciences*. Translated by Armand Maurer. 3rd rev. ed. Toronto: Pontifical Institute of Mediaeval Studies, 1963.

———. *Faith, Reason and Theology*. Translated by Armand Maurer. Toronto: Pontifical Institute of Mediaeval Studies, 1987.

———. *Quaestiones De Anima* [Questions on the Soul]. Translated by James H. Robb. Milwaukee: Marquette University Press, 2009.

———. *Summa Theologiae, 1a*. Translated by Timothy Suttor. Vols. XI, XIII. New York: Blackfriars with McGraw-Hill, 1970, 1964.

———. *Summa Theologica, Parts I, II, II-II*. Translated by Fathers of the English Dominican Province. London: Burns Oates & Washbourne, 1920.

———. *Summa Theologica, Part III (Suppl.)*. Translated by Fathers of the English Dominican Province. Vols. XX, XXI. London: Burns Oates & Washbourne, 1921, 1922.

———. *Tertia Pars Summae Theologiae a Quaestione 60-90*. Opera Omnia, Iussu Impensaque Leonis XIII. P.M. Edita. Tome: Romae Typographia Polyglotta, 1882.

Arendt, Hannah. "Karl Jaspers: Citizen of the World?" In *Men in Dark Times*, 81–94. New York: Harcourt, Brace, 1968.

———. *Love and St Augustine*. Chicago: University of Chicago Press, 1996.

———. "Thinking." In *The Life of the Mind*, edited by Mary McCarthy, 3–238. San Diego: Harcourt, 1978.

———. "Willing." In *The Life of the Mind*, edited by Mary McCarthy, 3–240. San Diego: Harcourt, 1978.

Aristotle. "Ethica Nicomachea." Translated by W. D. Ross. In *Introduction to Aristotle*, edited by Richard McKeon, 308–543. New York: Modern Library, 1947.

———. *De Anima* [On the Soul]. Translated by R. D. Hicks. New York: Cosimo, 2008.

———. *Metaphysics: Books 1–9*. Translated by Hugh Tredennick. Cambridge: Harvard University Press, 1989.

———. *Rhetoric*. Translated by W. Rhys Roberts. South Bend, IN: Infomotions, 2000.

Arnold, Bill T. "OT Eschatology and the Rise of Apocalypticism." In *Oxford Handbook of Eschatology*, edited by Jerry L. Walls, 23–39. Oxford: Oxford University Press, 2008.

Athanasius. "Against Arianism." Translated by John Henry Newman. In *Select Treatises of St Athanasius*, 155–428. New York: AMS, 1978.

———. "Letter III." In *Nicene and Post-Nicene Fathers: Second Series*, edited by Philip Schaff and Henry Wace, 512–15. Peabody, MA: Hendrickson, 1994.

———. "Letter X." In *Nicene and Post-Nicene Fathers: Second Series*, edited by Philip Schaff and Henry Wace, 527–32. Peabody, MA: Hendrickson, 1994.

———. "Tomus Ad Antiochenos." In *Nicene and Post-Nicene Fathers: Second Series*, edited by Philip Schaff and Henry Wace, 481–86. Peabody, MA: Hendrickson, 1994.

Athenagoras of Athens. "Supplication for the Christians." Translated by William A. Jurgens. In *The Faith of the Early Fathers (vol. 1)*, edited by William A. Jurgens, 69–71. Collegeville, MN: Liturgical, 1970.

Auden, W. H. *The Double Man*. New York: Random House, 1941.

Bibliography

Augustine. "Against an Adversary of the Law and the Prophets." Translated by William A. Jurgens. In *The Faith of the Early Fathers (vol. 3)*, edited by William A. Jurgens, 142–43. Collegeville, MN: Liturgical, 1979.

———. "Against Faustus the Manichean." Translated by William A. Jurgens. In *The Faith of the Early Fathers (vol. 3)*, edited by William A. Jurgens, 58–60. Collegeville, MN: Liturgical, 1979.

———. *City of God*. Translated by Henry Bettenson. London: Penguin, 2003.

———. *Confessions*. Translated by Henry Chadwick. Oxford: Oxford University Press, 1992.

———. "Enchiridion." In *Nicene and Post-Nicene Fathers: First Series*, edited by Philip Schaff, 237–76. Peabody, MA: Hendrickson, 1995.

———. "Enchiridion Ad Laurentium." In *De Doctrina Christiana Libri Quatuor, Et Enchiridion Ad Laurentium*, edited by Carl Hermann Bruder, 166–252. Leipzig: Tauchnitz, 1838.

———. *Enchiridion on Faith, Hope and Charity*. Translated by Bruce Harbert. Hyde Park: New City, 2011.

———. "Grace and Free Will." Translated by Robert P. Russell. In *Fathers of the Church*, edited by R. J. Deferrari. Washington, DC: Catholic University Press, 1968.

———. "Homilies on the Gospel of John." Translated by William A. Jurgens. In *The Faith of the Early Fathers (vol. 3)*, edited by William A. Jurgens, 115–24. Collegeville, MN: Liturgical, 1979.

———. "Letters." Translated by J. G. Cunningham. *From Nicene and Post-Nicene Fathers, First Series*, Vol. 1. Edited by Philip Schaff. Buffalo, NY: Christian Literature, 1887. Revised and edited for New Advent by Kevin Knight. <http://www.newadvent.org/fathers/1102082.htm>.

———. *On Christian Teaching*. Translated by R. P. H. Green. Oxford: Oxford University Press, 2008.

———. "On Merit and the Forgiveness of Sins, and the Baptism of Infants." Translated by Peter Holmes and Robert Ernest Wallis, and revised by Benjamin B. Warfield. From *Nicene and Post-Nicene Fathers: First Series*, Vol. 5. Edited by Philip Schaff. Buffalo, NY: Christian Literature, 1887. Revised and edited for New Advent by Kevin Knight. <http://www.newadvent.org/fathers/15011.htm>.

———. "On the Morals of the Manichaeans." In *Nicene and Post-Nicene Fathers: First Series*, edited by Philip Schaff, 95–107. Peabody, MA: Hendrickson, 1995.

———. "On Rebuke and Grace" ["De Correptione Et Gratia"]. Translated by Peter Holmes and Robert Ernest Wallis, and revised by Benjamin B. Warfield. From *Nicene and Post-Nicene Fathers, First Series*, Vol. 5. Edited by Philip Schaff. Buffalo, NY: Christian Literature, 1887. Revised and edited for New Advent by Kevin Knight. <http://www.newadvent.org/fathers/1513.htm>.

———. *The Retractions (Fathers of the Church, Vol. 60)*. Translated by Sister Mary Inez Bogan. Washington, DC: Catholic University of America Press, 1991.

Ayres, Lewis. *Augustine and the Trinity*. Cambridge: Cambridge University Press, 2010.

———. *Nicaea and Its Legacy*. Oxford: Oxford University Press, 2009.

Badham, Paul. *Christian Beliefs about Life after Death*. London: SPCK, 1978.

Bailer-Jones, Daniela M. "Models, Metaphors and Analogies." In *Blackwell Guide to Philosophy of Science*, edited by Peter Machamer and Michael Silberstein, 108–27. Oxford: Blackwell, 2002.

Baillie, John. *And the Life Everlasting*. London: Oxford University Press, 1934.

Baker, Lynne Rudder. "Materialism with a Human Face." In *Soul, Body, and Survival*, edited by Kevin J. Corcoran, 159–80. Ithaca, NY: Cornell University Press, 2001.

———. *Persons and Bodies*. Cambridge: Cambridge University Press, 2000.

———. "Persons and the Metaphysics of Resurrection." *Religious Studies* 43.3 (2007) 333–48.

Ballou, Hosea. *Treatise on Atonement*. Bennington, VT: Walbridge, 1811.

Balthasar, Hans Urs von. *Dare We Hope 'That All Men Be Saved'?* Translated by David Kipp and Lothar Krauth. San Francisco: Ignatius, 1988.

———. "Epilogue: Apokatastasis." In *Dare We Hope 'That All Men Be Saved'?* translated by David Kipp and Lothar Krauth, 223–54. San Francisco: Ignatius, 1988.

———. *Life out of Death*. Translated by Davis Perkins. Philadelphia: Fortress, 1985.

———. *Mysterium Paschale*. Translated by Aidan Nichols. San Francisco: Ignatius, 1990.

———. "Short Discourse on Hell." In *Dare We Hope 'That All Men Be Saved'?* translated by David Kipp and Lothar Krauth, 161–221. San Francisco: Ignatius, 1988.

———. *Theo-Drama*. Translated by Graham Harrison. 5 vols. Vols. I-V, San Francisco: Ignatius, 1988–98.

———. *Theo-Logic*. Translated by Adrian J. Walker. 3 vols. Vols. I-III, San Francisco: Ignatius, 2000–2005.

Balz, Horst. "Δυσκόλως." In *Exegetical Dictionary of the NT*, edited by Horst Balz and Gerhard Schneider, 361. Grand Rapids: Eerdmans, 1990.

———. "Ἐάν." In *Exegetical Dictionary of the NT*, edited by Horst Balz and Gerhard Schneider, 367. Grand Rapids: Eerdmans, 1990.

———. "Ὅσος." In *Exegetical Dictionary of the NT*, edited by Horst Balz and Gerhard Schneider, 537. Grand Rapids: Eerdmans, 1990.

Barclay, William. *A Spiritual Autobiography*. Grand Rapids: Eerdmans, 1977.

Bardesan. "Book of the Laws of Divers Countries." In *Ante-Nicene Fathers*, edited by Alexander Roberts and James Donaldson, 723–34. Peabody, MA: Hendrickson, 1995.

Barna Group. "What Americans Believe about Universalism and Pluralism." https://www.barna.com/research/what-americans-believe-about-universalism-and-pluralism/.

Barnett, Paul. *Second Epistle to the Corinthians*. New International Commentary of the NT. Edited by Gordon D. Fee. Grand Rapids: Eerdmans, 1997.

Barresi, John, and Raymond Martin. "History as Prologue." In *Oxford Handbook of the Self*, edited by Shaun Gallagher, 33–56: Oxford: Oxford University Press, 2014.

Barth, Karl. *Church Dogmatics I/1*. Translated by Geoffrey W. Bromiley. 2nd ed. London: T. & T. Clark, 2008.

———. *Church Dogmatics I/2*. Translated by G. T. Thomson and Harold Knight. Edinburgh: T. & T. Clark, 1956.

———. *Church Dogmatics II/1*. Translated by Geoffrey W. Bromiley. London: T. & T. Clark, 1957.

———. *Church Dogmatics II/2*. Translated by Geoffrey W. Bromiley, et al. Edinburgh: T. & T. Clark 2001.

———. *Church Dogmatics III §43–44*. Translated by Geoffrey W. Bromiley, et al. Study ed. London: T. & T. Clark, 2010.

———. *Church Dogmatics IV/1–3.1*. Translated by Geoffrey W. Bromiley. London: T. & T. Clark, 2004.

———. *Epistle to the Romans*. Translated by Edwyn C. Hoskyns. 6th ed. Oxford: Oxford University Press, 1976.

———. "Preface to the First Edition." Translated by Edwyn C. Hoskyns. In *The Epistle to the Romans*, 1–2. Oxford: Oxford University Press, 1976.

———. "Preface to the Second Edition." Translated by Edwyn C. Hoskyns. In *The Epistle to the Romans*, 2–15. Oxford: Oxford University Press, 1976.

Barton, John. "Source Criticism (OT)." In *Anchor Bible Dictionary*, edited by David Noel Freedman, 162–65. New York: Doubleday, 1992.

Basil the Great. "The Asketikon." Translated by Anna M. Silvas. In *The Asketikon of St Basil the Great*, edited by Anna M. Silvas, 151–451: Oxford: Oxford University Press, 2007.

———. *Commentary on the Prophet Isaiah*. Translated by Nikolai Lipatov. Cambridge: Edition Cicero, 2001.

———. "De Spiritu Sancto." In *Nicene and Post-Nicene Fathers: Second Series*, edited by Philip Schaff and Henry Wace, 1–50. Peabody, MA: Hendrickson, 1994.

———. "Letters." In *Nicene and Post-Nicene Fathers: Second Series*, edited by Philip Schaff and Henry Wace, 109–327. Peabody, MA: Hendrickson, 1994.

Bates, Matthew W. *Salvation by Allegiance Alone*. Grand Rapids: Baker Academic, 2017.

Bauckham, Richard. *Jude, 2 Peter*. Word Biblical Commentary. Waco, TX: Word, 1983.

———. "Universalism: Historical Survey." *Themelios* 4 (1979) 48–54.

Bavinck, Herman. *The Last Things*. Translated by John Bolt. Grand Rapids: Baker, 1996.

———. *Reformed Dogmatics*. Translated by John Vriend. Vol. IV, Grand Rapids: Baker, 2008.

Beale, G. K. *Book of Revelation*. New International Greek Testament Commentary. Grand Rapids: Eerdmans, 2013.

———. *Colossians and Philemon*. Baker Exegetical Commentary on the NT. Grand Rapids: Baker Academic, 2019.

Beavis, Mary Ann. *Mark*. Paideia Commentaries on the NT. Grand Rapids: Baker Academic, 2011.

Becker, Ernest. *The Denial of Death*. New York: Free, 1973.

Behr, John. *Irenaeus of Lyons*. Oxford: Oxford University Press, 2013.

———. "Life and Death in the Age of Martyrdom." In *The Role of Death in Life*, edited by John Behr and Conor Cunningham, 79–95. Eugene, OR: Cascade, 2015.

———. *The Mystery of Christ*. Crestwood, NY: St Vladimir's Seminary Press, 2006.

Bell, Richard H. "The Corrupt Mind and the Renewed Mind." In *Grandeur of Reason*, edited by Peter M. Candler, Jr. and Conor Cunningham, 197–217. London: SCM, 2010.

———. "Rom 5.18–19 and Universal Salvation." *New Testament Studies* 48.3 (2002) 417–32.

Bell, Rob. *Love Wins*. San Francisco: Harper Collins, 2011.

Benedetto, Dario, et al. "The Puzzle of Basil's Epistula 38." *Journal of Quantitative Linguistics* 20.4 (2013) 267–87.

Benedict XVI. *Spe Salvi*. Encyclical Letter of 30 Nov. 2007. Boston: Pauline, 2007.

Beougher, Timothy K. "Are All Doomed to Be Saved?" In *Who Will Be Saved?* edited by Paul R. House and Gregory A. Thornbury, 83–110. Wheaton, IL: Crossway, 2000.

Berdyaev, Nicolas. *The Fate of Man in the Modern World*. Translated by D. A. Lowrie. Ann Arbor, MI: University of Michigan Press, 1961.

Bergson, Henri. *Time and Free Will*. Translated by F. L. Pogson. New York: Humanities, 1971.

———. *The Two Sources of Morality and Religion*. Translated by Ashley Audra and Cloudesley Brereton. Garden City, NY: Doubleday, 1935.

Berkhof, Hendrikus. *The Christian Faith.* Translated by Sierd Woudstra. Grand Rapids: Eerdmans, 1980.

Berkouwer, G. C. *Man: Image of God.* Translated by Dirk W. Jellema. Grand Rapids: Eerdmans, 1972.

Bernstein, Alan E. *Formation of Hell.* Ithaca, NY: Cornell University Press, 1993.

Bettis, Joseph P. "Was Karl Barth a Universalist." *Scottish Journal of Theology* 20 (1967) 423–36.

Betz, Hans Dieter. *Galatians.* Hermeneia. Edited by Helmut Koester. Philadelphia: Fortress, 1979.

Betz, John R. *After Enlightenment: Post-Secular Vision of J. G. Hamann.* Chichester, UK: Wiley-Blackwell, 2009.

———. "A Radically Orthodox Reformer: J. G. Hamann." *Modern Theology* 33.4 (2017) 640–77.

Bishop, Jeffrey P. "On Medical Corpses." In *The Role of Death in Life*, edited by John Behr and Conor Cunningham, 164–778. Eugene, OR: Cascade, 2015.

Black, Max. "More about Metaphor." In *Metaphor and Thought*, edited by Andrew Ortony, 19–41. Cambridge: Cambridge University Press, 1979.

Blomberg, Craig L. *Matthew.* New American Commentary. Edited by David S. Dockery. Nashville: Broadman, 1992.

———. "The Unity and Diversity of Scripture." In *New Dictionary of Biblical Theology*, edited by T. Desmond Alexander and Brian S. Rosner, 64–72. Downers Grove, IL: InterVarsity, 2000.

Blondel, Maurice. *Action (1893).* Translated by Oliva Blanchette. South Bend, IN: University of Notre Dame Press, 1984.

———. "History and Dogma." In *Letter on Apologetics & History and Dogma*, 219–87. Grand Rapids: Eerdmans, 1964.

———. "Letter on Apologetics." In *Letter on Apologetics & History and Dogma*, 125–208. Grand Rapids: Eerdmans, 1964.

Blosser, Benjamin P. *Become Like the Angels.* Washington, DC: Catholic University of America Press, 2012.

Blowers, Paul M. *Maximus the Confessor.* Oxford: Oxford University Press, 2016.

Bobonich, Christopher. *Plato's Utopia Recast.* Oxford: Clarendon, 2002.

Bock, Darrell L. *Acts.* Baker Exegetical Commentary on the NT. Grand Rapids: Baker, 2007.

———. *Luke 1—9:50, Luke 9:51—24:53.* Baker Exegetical Commentary on the NT. Grand Rapids: Baker, 1994, 1996.

de Boer, Martinus C. *The Defeat of Death.* Sheffield, UK: JSOT, 1988.

Boethius. "Contra Eutychen." Translated by H. F. Stewart, et al. In *The Theological Tractates and the Consolation of Philosophy*, 73–129. Cambridge, MA: Loeb, 1973.

Bonhoeffer, Dietrich. *Christ the Center.* Translated by John Bowden. New York: Harper, 1960.

———. *Discipleship.* Translated by Barbara Green and Reinhard Krauss. Minneapolis: Fortress, 2003.

———. *Ethics.* Translated by Reinhard Krauss et al. Minneapolis: Fortress, 2009.

———. *Letters and Papers from Prison.* Translated by Reginald Fuller et al. Enlarged ed. New York: Touchstone, 1997.

———. *Life Together.* Translated by John W. Doberstein. New York: HarperOne, 1954.

Borges, Jorge Luis. "Borges and I." Translated by Andrew Hurley. In *Collected Fictions*, 324. New York: Penguin, 1998.

Boring, M. Eugene. "Language of Universal Salvation in Paul." *Journal of Biblical Literature* 105.2 (1986) 269–92.

Bornkamm, Günther. *Paulus*. Translated by D. M. G. Stalker. New York: Harper & Row, 1971.

Bourget, David, and David Chalmers. "What Do Philosophers Believe?" *Philosophical Studies* 170.3 (2014) 465–500.

Bovon, Francois. *Commentary on the Gospel of Luke 9:51—19:27*. Translated by Donald S. Deer. Hermeneia. Minneapolis: Fortress, 2013.

———. "The Soul's Comeback." *Harvard Theological Review* 103.4 (2010) 387–406.

Bowles, Ralph G. "Does Revelation 14:11 Teach Eternal Torment?" In *Rethinking Hell*, edited by Christopher M. Date et al., 138–54. Eugene, OR: Cascade, 2014.

Boyd, Gregory A. "Christus Victor View." In *The Nature of Atonement*, edited by James Beilby and Paul R. Eddy, 23–49. Downers Grove, IL: InterVarsity Academic, 2006.

Brant, Jo-Anna A. *John*. Paideia Commentaries on the NT. Edited by Mikeal C. Parsons and Charles H. Talbert. Grand Rapids: Baker Academic, 2011.

Bray, Gerald L. *God Has Spoken*. Wheaton, IL: Crossway, 2014.

Bridges, Carl B. "Degrees of Punishment and Reward in the Gospels." *Stone-Campbell Journal* 14.1 (2011) 81–86.

Brontë, Charlotte. *Jane Eyre*. New York: Knopf, 1991.

Brookins, Timothy A. "Greco-Roman Perspectives on Anthropology." In *Anthropology and NT Theology*, edited by Jason Maston and Benjamin E. Reynolds, 43–63. London: T. & T. Clark, 2019.

Brotherton, Joshua R. "The Possibility of Universal Conversion in Death." *Modern Theology* 32.3 (2016) 307–24.

Brower, Jeffrey E. *Aquinas's Ontology of the Material World*. Oxford: Oxford University Press, 2017.

Brown, Colin. "Spirit." In *New International Dictionary of NT Theology*, 689–708. Grand Rapids: Zondervan, 1986.

Brown, Peter. *The Rise of Western Christendom*. Rev. ed. Chichester, UK: Wiley-Blackwell, 2013.

Brown, Raymond E. *The Death of the Messiah*. 2 vols. New York: Doubleday, 1994, 1998.

Bruce, F. F. *Epistle of Paul to the Romans*. Tyndale NT Commentaries. Grand Rapids: Eerdmans, 1985.

———. *Epistles to the Colossians, to Philemon, and to the Ephesians*. New International Commentary of the NT. Edited by Gordon D. Fee. Grand Rapids: Eerdmans, 1984.

———. *Epistle to the Galatians*. New International Greek Testament Commentary. Grand Rapids: Eerdmans, 1982.

Brueggemann, Walter. *Isaiah 40–66*. Westminster Biblical Companion. Louisville: Westminster John Knox, 1998.

Brunner, Emil. *Eternal Hope*. Translated by Harold Knight. London: Lutterworth, 1954.

Buber, Martin. *Between Man and Man*. Translated by Ronald Gregor Smith. London: Kegan Paul, 1927.

———. *I and Thou*. Translated by Ronald Gregor Smith. Edinburgh: T. & T. Clark, 1950.

———. "Religion and Philosophy." Translated by Maurice S. Friedman. In *Eclipse of God*, 25–46. Amherst, MA: Humanity Books, 1996.

———. "God and the Spirit of Man." Translated by Maurice S. Friedman. In *Eclipse of God*, 93–111. Amherst, MA: Humanity Books, 1996.

———. "Religion and Ethics." Translated by Eugene Kamenka and Maurice S. Friedman. In *Eclipse of God*, 121–29. Amherst, MA: Humanity Books, 1996.

———. *Ten Rungs*. New York: Citadel, 1995.

———. *The Way of Man*. Secaucus, NJ: Citadel, 1966.

Buckareff, Andrei A., and Joel S. Van Wagenen. "Surviving Resurrection." *International Journal for Philosophy of Religion* 67 (2010) 123–39.

Bulgakov, Sergius. *Bride of the Lamb*. Translated by Boris Jakim. Neviesta Agntsa. Grand Rapids: Eerdmans, 2002.

———. "By Jacob's Well." Translated by Natalie Duddington and James Pain. In *A Bulgakov Anthology*, edited by James Pain and Nicolas Zernov, 100–113. Philadelphia: Westminster, 1976.

———. "Heroism and Otherworldliness." Translated by Natalie Duddington and James Pain. In *A Bulgakov Anthology*, edited by James Pain and Nicolas Zernov, 51–53. Philadelphia: Westminster, 1976.

———. "The Lamb of God." Translated by Natalie Duddington and James Pain. In *A Bulgakov Anthology*, edited by James Pain and Nicolas Zernov, 114–18. Philadelphia: Westminster, 1976.

———. *The Orthodox Church*. Translated by Lydia Kesich. Crestwood, NY: St Vladimir's Seminary Press, 1988.

———. "Vladimir Solovyov: Scholar and Seer." Translated by Natalie Duddington and James Pain. In *A Bulgakov Anthology*, edited by James Pain and Nicolas Zernov, 42–48. Philadelphia: Westminster, 1976.

Bullivant, Stephen. *The Salvation of Atheists and Catholic Dogmatic Theology*. Oxford: Oxford University Press, 2012.

Bultmann, Rudolf. "New Testament and Mythology." In *New Testament and Mythology*, edited by Schubert M. Ogden, 1–43. Philadelphia: Fortress, 1989.

———. "On the Problem of Demythologizing (1961)." In *New Testament and Mythology*, edited by Schubert M. Ogden, 155–63. Philadelphia: Fortress, 1989.

———. "Theology as Science." In *New Testament and Mythology*, edited by Schubert M. Ogden, 45–67. Philadelphia: Fortress, 1989.

———. *Theology of the NT*. Translated by Kendrick Grobel. 2 vols.: Waco, TX: Baylor University Press, 2007.

Burdett, Michael S. "Transcendence and Human Enhancement." In *Transhumanism and Transcendence*, edited by Ronald Cole-Turner, 19–35. Washington, DC: Georgetown University Press, 2011.

Butler, Joseph. *Analogy of Religion*. New York: Robert Carter, 1750.

Butler, Samuel. *The Way of All Flesh*. New York: Random House, 1950.

Butterfield, Herbert. *Whig Interpretation of History*. New York: Norton, 1965.

Butterworth, G. W. "Introduction." In *Origen on First Principles*, i–xxxix. Eugene, OR: Wipf & Stock, 1936.

Bynum, Caroline Walker. "Material Continuity, Personal Survival, and the Resurrection of the Body." *History of Religions* 30.1 (1990) 51–85.

———. *The Resurrection of the Body*. New York: Columbia University Press, 1995.

Cabasilas, Nicholas. *The Life in Christ*. Translated by Carmino J. deCatanzaro. Crestwood, NY: St Vladimir's Seminary Press, 1974.

Caird, G. B., and L. D. Hurst. *New Testament Theology*. Oxford: Oxford University Press, 1995.

Caldecott, Stratford. *The Radiance of Being*. Tacoma, WA: Angelico, 2013.

Calvin, John. *Epistle of Paul the Apostle to the Romans and to the Thessalonians.* Translated by R. Mackenzie. Grand Rapids: Eerdmans, 1960.
———. *Institutes of the Christian Religion.* Translated by Henry Beveridge. Peabody, MA: Hendrickson, 2012.
Campbell, John. "Personal Identity." In *Oxford Handbook of the Self*, edited by Shaun Gallagher, 339–51: Oxford: Oxford University Press, 2014.
Candler, Peter M., Jr. *Theology, Rhetoric, Manuduction.* Grand Rapids: Eerdmans, 2006.
Candler, Peter M., Jr., and Conor Cunningham, eds. *The Grandeur of Reason.* London: SCM, 2010.
"Canons of 543." Translated by Richard Price. In *The Acts of the Council of Constantinople of 553*, 281. Liverpool: Liverpool University Press, 2012.
"Canons of 553." Translated by Richard Price. In *The Acts of the Council of Constantinople of 553*, 284–86. Liverpool: Liverpool University Press, 2012.
Caputo, John. *Radical Hermeneutics.* Bloomington, IN: Indiana University Press, 1987.
Carson, D. A. *Divine Sovereignty and Human Responsibility.* Grand Rapids: Baker, 1994.
———. *Gospel according to John.* Pillar NT Commentary. Grand Rapids: Eerdmans, 1991.
———. "Matthew." In *Expositor's Bib. Commentary*, edited by Frank E. Gaebelein, 2–599. Grand Rapids: Zondervan, 1984.
Carter, Rita, and Christopher Frith. *Mapping the Mind.* Rev. ed. Los Angeles: University of California Press, 2010.
Casimir, Brother. "When (the Father) Will Subject All Things to (the Son)." *Greek Orthodox Theological Review* 28.1 (1983) 1–25.
Cassara, Ernest, ed. *Universalism in America.* Boston: Beacon, 1971.
Cassian, John. "The Conferences." In *Nicene and Post-Nicene Fathers: Second Series*, edited by Philip Schaff and Henry Wace, 291–545. Peabody, MA: Hendrickson, 1994.
Cassirer, Ernst. *The Myth of the State.* New Haven, CT: Yale University Press, 1946.
Catholic Church. *Catechism of the Catholic Church.* New York: Doubleday, 1995.
Catullus, Valerius. "Poem 85." *Carmina.* Perseus Project, accessed 1 Aug. 2020.
Cavanaugh, William T. "Beyond Secular Parodies." In *Radical Orthodoxy*, edited by John Milbank et al., 182–200. London: Routledge, 1999.
Cavell, Marcia. "The Self: Growth, Integrity, and Coming Apart." In *Oxford Handbook of the Self*, edited by Shaun Gallagher, 592–605: Oxford: Oxford University Press, 2014.
Celsus. *On the True Doctrine.* Translated by R. Joseph Hoffman. Oxford: Oxford University Press, 1987.
Chadwick, Henry. *Augustine of Hippo.* Oxford: Oxford University Press, 2010.
———. *The Church in Ancient Society.* Oxford: Oxford University Press, 2008.
———. *Early Christian Thought and the Classical Tradition.* Oxford: Oxford University Press, 1984.
———. *The Early Church.* New York: Penguin, 1977.
Chapman, Mark D. *Anglican Theology.* London: T. & T. Clark, 2012.
Charlton, James. *Non-Dualism in Eckhart, Julian of Norwich and Traherne.* London: Bloomsbury, 2014.
Chauncy, Charles. *The Salvation of All Men.* New Haven, CT: A. Morse, 1784.
Chesterton, Gilbert K. *Orthodoxy.* No loc.: Cavalier Classics, 2015.
———. *St Thomas Aquinas.* New York: Angelico, 2011.
Chomsky, Noam. *Reflections on Language.* New York: Pantheon, 1975.

Christian Universalist Association. "History of the CUA." https://christianuniversalist.org/history/.

Christensen, Michael J. "The Problem, Promise, and Process of Theosis." In *Partakers of the Divine Nature*, edited by Michael J. Christensen and Jeffrey A. Wittung, 23–31. Grand Rapids: Baker, 2008.

Chrysostom, John. "Commentary on the Epistle to the Galatians." Translated by William A. Jurgens. In *The Faith of the Early Fathers (vol. 2)*, edited by William A. Jurgens, 119. Collegeville, MN: Liturgical, 1979.

———. *Homilies on First Corinthians*. Translated by Talbot W. Chambers. From *Nicene and Post-Nicene Fathers, First Series*, Vol. 12. Edited by Philip Schaff. Buffalo, NY: Christian Literature, 1889. Revised and edited for New Advent by Kevin Knight. <http://www.newadvent.org/fathers/220141.htm>.

———. *Homilies on Matthew*. Translated by George Prevost and revised by M. B. Riddle. From *Nicene and Post-Nicene Fathers, First Series*, Vol. 10. Edited by Philip Schaff. Buffalo, NY: Christian Literature, 1888. Revised and edited for New Advent by Kevin Knight. <http://www.newadvent.org/fathers/200136.htm>.

———. "Homilies on the Epistle to the Ephesians." Translated by William A. Jurgens. In *The Faith of the Early Fathers (vol. 2)*, edited by William A. Jurgens, 120–21. Collegeville, MN: Liturgical, 1979.

———. "Homily 11 (on Ephesians)." Translated by Wendy Mayer and Pauline Allen. In *John Chrysostom*, 60–72 (Field 214–27). London: Routledge, 2000.

———. "Victory over Death." Translated by Thomas P. Halton. In *The Paschal Mystery*, edited by Adalbert Hamman, 98–106 [PG 46, 65–681]. New York: Alba House, 1969.

Clark, Mary T. "An Inquiry into Personhood." *Review of Metaphysics* 46.1 (1992) 3–28.

Clarke, W. Norris. *Person and Being*. Milwaukee: Marquette University Press, 2008.

von Clausewitz, Carl. *On War*. Translated by J. J. Graham. London: N. Trübner, 1909.

Clement of Alexandria. "Fragments from Cassiodous." In *Ante-Nicene Fathers*, edited by Alexander Roberts and James Donaldson, 571–77. Peabody, MA: Hendrickson, 1995.

———. "The Stromata." In *Ante-Nicene Fathers*, edited by Alexander Roberts and James Donaldson, 299–568. Peabody, MA: Hendrickson, 1995.

Clendenin, Dan. "Freedom and Universal Salvation." *Ellul Studies Bulletin*, Aug. 1988, 3.

Climacus, John. *The Ladder of Divine Ascent*. Translated by Colm Luibheid and Norman Russell. Mahwah, NJ: Paulist, 1982.

Clines, David J. A. *Job 1–20*. Word Biblical Commentary. Dallas: Word, 1989.

Clymer, Wayne K. "Union with Christ." In *All Shall Be Well*, edited by Gregory MacDonald, 116–40. Cambridge: James Clarke, 2011.

Cole, G. A. "Justice: Retributive or Reformative." *Reformed Theological Review* 45.1 (1986) 5–12.

Colic, Ahmo, and Hrustem Smailhodzic. "The Study of Light." Paper presented at the AIP Conference Proceedings 899, 2007.

Colijn, Brenda B. *Images of Salvation in the NT*. Downers Grove, IL: InterVarsity Academic, 2010.

Come, Arnold B. *Kierkegaard as Theologian*. Montreal: McGill-Queen's University Press, 1997.

Commission on Christian Doctrine appointed by the Archbishops of Canterbury and York in 1922. "Doctrine in the Church of England." London: SPCK, 1938.

Congdon, David W. *The God Who Saves*. Eugene, OR: Cascade, 2016.
Connell, Matt F. "Georg Wilhelm Friedrich Hegel." In *From Kant to Levi-Strauss*, edited by Jon Simons, 33–49. Edinburgh: Edinburgh University Press, 2002.
Connolly, John M. *Living without Why*. Oxford: Oxford University Press, 2014.
Constable, Henry. "Divine Justice." In *Rethinking Hell*, edited by Christopher M. Date et al., 198–206. Eugene, OR: Cascade, 2014.
Cook, Stephen L. *Ezekiel 38–48*. Anchor Yale Bible. New Haven, CT: Yale University Press, 2018.
Cooper, Adam G. *Holy Eros*. Kettering, UK: Angelico, 2014.
———. *Naturally Human, Supernaturally God*. Minneapolis: Fortress, 2014.
Cooper, John W. "Biblical Anthropology and the Body-Soul Problem." In *Soul, Body, and Survival*, edited by Kevin J. Corcoran, 218–28. New York: Cornell University Press, 2001.
———. *Body, Soul, and Life Everlasting*. Grand Rapids: Eerdmans, 1989.
———. "Whose Interpretation? Which Anthropology?" In *Neuroscience and the Soul*, edited by Thomas M. Crisp et al., 238–57. Grand Rapids: Eerdmans, 2016.
Copi, Irving M. *Introduction to Logic*. 6th ed. New York: Macmillan, 1982.
Corcoran, Kevin J. "Persons and Bodies." *Faith and Philosophy* 15.3 (1998) 324–40.
Corcoran, Kevin J., and Kevin Sharpe. "Neuroscience and the Human Person." In *Neuroscience and the Soul*, edited by Thomas M. Crisp et al., 121–36. Grand Rapids: Eerdmans, 2016.
Cranfield, C. E. B. *Romans 1–8, Romans 9–16*. International Critical Commentary. Edinburgh: T. & T. Clark, 1985 (Repr. ed.), 1994 (Corr. ed.).
Crick, Francis. *The Astonishing Hypothesis*. New York: Simon & Schuster, 1995.
Crisp, Oliver D. "'I Do Teach It, but I Also Do Not Teach It': Universalism of Karl Barth." In *All Shall Be Well*, edited by Gregory MacDonald, 305–24. Eugene, OR: Cascade, 2011.
Crisp, Oliver D., and Fred Sanders, eds. *Christian Doctrine of Humanity*. Grand Rapids: Zondervan, 2018.
Crockett, William, ed. *Four Views on Hell*. Grand Rapids: Zondervan, 1996.
Croft, Alice Thompson. "Didymus the Blind on 1 Corinthians 15." MA diss., Waterloo, ON: Wilfrid Laurier University, 1987.
Crosby, John F. *Selfhood of the Human Person*. Washington, DC: Catholic University of America Press, 1996.
Crouzel, Henri. *Origen*. Translated by A. S. Worrall. Edinburgh: T. & T. Clark, 1989.
Cunningham, Conor. *Genealogy of Nihilism*. London: Routledge, 2002.
———. "Is There Life before Death?" In *The Role of Death in Life*, edited by John Behr and Conor Cunningham, 120–51. Eugene, OR: Cascade, 2015.
———. "Suspending the Natural Attitude." In *Transcendence and Phenomenology*, edited by Conor Cunningham and Peter M. Candler, Jr., 260–87. London: SCM, 2007.
Cyprian of Carthage. "Letter of Cyprian to the People of Thibar." Translated by William A. Jurgens. In *The Faith of the Early Fathers (vol. 1)*, edited by William A. Jurgens, 231. Collegeville, MN: Liturgical, 1970.
———. "The Unity of the Catholic Church." Translated by William A. Jurgens. In *The Faith of the Early Fathers (vol. 1)*, edited by William A. Jurgens, 219–22. Collegeville, MN: Liturgical, 1970.

———. "To Demetrian." Translated by William A. Jurgens. In *The Faith of the Early Fathers (vol. 1)*, edited by William A. Jurgens, 223. Collegeville, MN: Liturgical, 1970.

Cyril of Alexandria. *Commentary on John*. Translated by David R. Maxwell. Ancient Christian Texts. Edited by Thomas C. Oden and Gerald L. Bray. 2 vols. Vol. I-II, Downers Grove, IL: InterVarsity, 2013, 2015.

———. "Festal Letter Seven." Translated by Philip R. Adimon. In *Fathers of the Church*, edited by Thomas P. Halton, 125–36. Washington, DC: Catholic University of America Press, 2009.

Cyril of Jerusalem. "Catechetical Lectures." Translated by William A. Jurgens. In *The Faith of the Early Fathers (vol. 1)*, edited by William A. Jurgens, 347–71. Collegeville, MN: Liturgical, 1970.

Czachesz, Istvan. "Why Body Matters in the Afterlife." In *The Human Body in Death and Resurrection*, edited by Tobias Nicklas, et al., 391–411. Berlin: de Gruyter, 2009.

Dahl, M. E. *The Resurrection of the Body*. Naperville: Allenson, 1962.

Daley, Brian E. *The Hope of the Early Church*. Grand Rapids: Baker, 1991.

Dalferth, Ingolf U. *Creatures of Possibility*. Translated by Jo Bennett. Grand Rapids: Baker Academic, 2016.

Davids, Peter H. *Epistle of James*. New International Greek Testament Commentary. Grand Rapids: Eerdmans, 1982.

———. *Letters of 2 Peter and Jude*. Pillar NT Commentary. Grand Rapids: Eerdmans, 2006.

Davies, Brian. *Thomas Aquinas on God and Evil*. Oxford: Oxford University Press, 2011.

Davies, Douglas J. "Immortality." In *The Role of Death in Life*, edited by John Behr and Conor Cunningham, 31–41. Eugene, OR: Cascade, 2015.

Davies, J. G. *The Early Christian Church*. Grand Rapids: Baker, 1987.

Davis, Stephen T. "Eschatology and Resurrection." In *Oxford Handbook of Eschatology*, edited by Jerry L. Walls, 384–98. Oxford: Oxford University Press, 2008.

———. "Physicalism and Resurrection." In *Soul, Body, and Survival*, edited by Kevin J. Corcoran, 229–48. New York: Cornell University Press, 2001.

———. *Risen Indeed*. Grand Rapids: Eerdmans, 1993.

Deikman, Arthur J. "'I' = Awareness." In *Models of the Self*, edited by Shaun Gallagher and Jonathan Shear, 421–27. Thorverton, UK: Imprint, 1999.

Demarest, Bruce. *The Cross and Salvation*. Wheaton, IL: Crossway, 2006.

Dennett, Daniel C. *Elbow Room*. New ed.: MIT Press, 2015.

Denzinger, Henry, and Karl Rahner, eds. *The Sources of Catholic Dogma*. 30th ed. St Louis: B. Herder, 1957.

Dickens, Charles. *A Tale of Two Cities*. New York: Barnes & Noble, 1993.

Dickinson, Emily. "Life." In *Collected Poems*, 3–72. New York: Barnes & Noble, 1993.

Dilthey, Wilhelm. *Introduction to the Human Sciences*. Translated by Ramon J. Betanzos. Detroit, MI: Wayne State University Press, 1988.

Dilworth, Craig. *Metaphysics of Science*. 2nd ed. Dordrecht: Springer, 2007.

Dinesen, Isak. "The Dreamers." In *Seven Gothic Tales*, 337–442. New York: Modern Library, 1994.

Doble, Peter. *The Paradox of Salvation*. Cambridge: Cambridge University Press, 1996.

Donahue, John R., and Daniel J. Harrington. *Gospel of Mark*. 2 vols. Vol. II, Sacra Pagina. Collegeville, MN: Liturgical, 2002.

Doniger, Wendy. *Splitting the Difference*. Chicago: University of Chicago Press, 1999.
Dostoevsky, Fyodor. *The Brothers Karamazov*. Translated by Constance Garnett. New York: Barnes & Noble, 1995.
Driver, John. *Images of the Church in Mission*. Scottdale, PA: Herald, 1997.
Drury, M. O'C. "Conversations with Wittgenstein." In *Ludwig Wittgenstein: Personal Recollections*, edited by Rush Rhees, 112–89. Totowa, NJ: Rowman & Littlefield, 1981.
Dulles, Avery. "The Population of Hell." *First Things* 133, May 2003, 36–41.
Dunn, James D. G. *Epistles to the Colossians and to Philemon*. New International Greek Testament Commentary. Grand Rapids: Eerdmans, 1996.
———. *Romans 1–8, Romans 9–16*. Word Biblical Commentary. Edited by David A. Hubbard. Dallas: Word, 1988.
Dunning, H. Ray. *Grace, Faith, and Holiness*. Kansas City: Beacon Hill, 1988.
Eastman, Susan Grove. *Paul and the Person*. Grand Rapids: Eerdmans, 2017.
Eckhart, Meister. "Book of 'Benedictus.'" Translated by Bernard McGinn. In *Meister Eckhart*, 240–47. New York: Paulist, 1981.
———. "Commentary on John." Translated by Edmund Colledge. In *Meister Eckhart*, 122–73. New York: Paulist, 1981.
Eddy, Paul R., and James Beilby. "The Atonement." In *The Nature of Atonement*, 9–21. Downers Grove, IL: InterVarsity Academic, 2006.
Edwards, David L. *After Death?* New York: Cassell, 1999.
Edwards, James R. *Gospel according to Mark*. Pillar NT Commentary. Grand Rapids: Eerdmans, 2002.
Edwards, Jonathan. "The Miscellanies." In *Works of Jonathan Edwards*, edited by Paul Ramsey, 833–1152. New Haven, CT: Yale University Press, 1957.
———. *The Works*. 2 vols. Vol. I. London: Westley, 1834.
Eliot, George. *Middlemarch*. New York: Barnes & Noble, 1996.
Eliot, T. S. *Four Quartets*. San Diego: Harcourt, 1971.
———. *Murder in the Cathedral*. San Diego: Harcourt, 1963.
Ellis, E. Earle. "New Testament Teaching on Hell." In *Rethinking Hell*, edited by Christopher M. Date et al., 116–37. Eugene, OR: Cascade, 2014.
Ellul, Jacques. *Apocalypse*. Translated by George W. Schreiner. New York: Seabury, 1977.
———. *The Ethics of Freedom*. Translated by Geoffrey W. Bromiley. London: Mowbrays, 1976.
———. *What I Believe*. Translated by Geoffrey W. Bromiley. Grand Rapids: Eerdmans, 1989.
Elster, Jon. *Sour Grapes*. Cambridge: Cambridge University Press, 1983.
Elwell, Walter A., ed. *Scripture*. 4 vols. Vol. IV. Baker Encyclopedia of the Bible. Grand Rapids: Baker, 1988.
Engel, S. Morris, and Angelika Soldan. *The Study of Philosophy*. 6th ed. Lanham, MD: Rowman & Littlefield, 2008.
Epictetus. *Discourses*. Translated by William A. Oldfather. 2 vols. Cambridge: Harvard University Press, 1956, 1959.
———. "Fragments." Translated by William A. Oldfather. In *Discourses*, 439–73. Cambridge, MA: Harvard University Press, 1959.
Epicurus. "Letter to Menoeceus." Translated by George K. Stodach. In *Philosophy of Epicurus*, edited by George K. Stodach, 178–95. Evanston, IL: Northwestern University Press, 1963.

Erasmus. "De Libero Arbitrio." Translated by E. Gordon Rupp and A. N. Marlow. In *Luther and Erasmus: Free Will and Salvation*, 35–97. Philadelphia: Westminster, 1969.

Erickson, Millard J. *Christian Theology*. 2nd ed. Grand Rapids: Baker, 1998.

Erskine, Thomas. *Doctrine of Election*. London: Duncan, 1837.

Eshleman, Andrew. "Moral Responsibility." In *Stanford Encyclopedia of Philosophy*, edited by Edward N. Zalta, 2016. <https://plato.stanford.edu/archives/win2016/entries/moral-responsibility/>

Euclid. *Elements*. 3rd ed. Dublin: Hodges, Figgis, 1885.

Eusebius of Caesarea. "Against Marcellus." Translated by Kelley McCarthy Spoerl and Markus Vinzent. In *Fathers of the Church*, 75–155. Washington, DC: Catholic University of America Press, 2017.

———. *Commentary on Isaiah*. Translated by Jonathan J. Armstrong. Downers Grove, IL: InterVarsity, 2013.

———. "On Ecclesiastical Theology." Translated by Kelley McCarthy Spoerl and Markus Vinzent. In *Fathers of the Church*, 159–337. Washington, DC: Catholic University of America Press, 2017.

Evans, C. Stephen, and Robert C. Roberts. "Ethics." In *Oxford Handbook of Kierkegaard*, edited by John Lippitt and George Pattison, 211–29: Oxford: Oxford University Press, 2013.

Fabro, Cornelio. *God in Exile*. Translated by Arthur Gibson. Westminster, MD: Newman, 1968.

Fabry, Heinz-Josef. "Ṣēlā." In *Theological Dictionary of the OT*, edited by G. Johannes Botterweck et al., 400–405. Grand Rapids: Eerdmans, 2003.

Fagerberg, David W. "Foreword." In *Holy Eros*. Kettering, UK: Angelico, 2014.

Fairley, Barker. "Goethe's Last Letter." *University of Toronto Quarterly* 27.1 (1957) 1–9.

Fee, Gordon D. *First Epistle to the Corinthians*. New International Commentary of the NT. Grand Rapids: Eerdmans, 1987.

Felix, Minucius. "Octavius." Translated by William A. Jurgens. In *The Faith of the Early Fathers (vol. 1)*, edited by William A. Jurgens, 109–11. Collegeville, MN: Liturgical, 1970.

Ferguson, Niall. *Civilization*. New York: Penguin, 2011.

Ferre, Nels F. S. *Christian Understanding of God*. New York: Harper, 1951.

Feuerbach, Ludwig. *Essence of Christianity*. Translated by George Eliot. New York: Harper, 1957.

Fichte, Johann Gottlieb. *The Vocation of Man*. Translated by Peter Preuss. Indianapolis: Hackett, 1987.

Finlan, Stephen. "Can We Speak of Theosis in Paul?" In *Partakers of the Divine Nature*, edited by Michael J. Christensen and Jeffrey A. Wittung, 68–80. Grand Rapids: Baker, 2008.

Finney, Charles G. *The Memoirs*. Complete Restored ed. Grand Rapids: Zondervan, 1989.

———. *Systematic Theology*. Abr. ed. Minneapolis: Bethany House, 1976.

Fitzmyer, Joseph A. *Gospel according to Luke*. 2 vols. Vol. II: Anchor Yale Bible. New Haven, CT: Yale University Press, 1985.

Fitzpatrick, Antonia. *Thomas Aquinas on Bodily Identity*. Oxford: Oxford University Press, 2017.

Forsyth, Peter Taylor. *The Principle of Authority*. London: Independent Press, 1952.

Foster, John. "Brief Defense of the Cartesian View." In *Soul, Body, and Survival*, edited by Kevin J. Corcoran, 15–29. New York: Cornell University Press, 2001.
van Fraassen, Bas C. *The Empirical Stance*. New Haven, CT: Yale University Press, 2002.
———. *Scientific Representation*. Oxford: Clarendon, 2013.
France, R. T. *Gospel of Mark*. New International Greek Testament Commentary. Grand Rapids: Eerdmans, 2002.
———. *Gospel of Matthew*. New International Commentary of the NT. Grand Rapids: Eerdmans, 2007.
Francis of Assisi. "Words of Admonition." Translated by Paschal Robinson. In *The Writings of St Francis of Assisi*, 3–19. Philadelphia: Dolphin, 1905.
Frankfurt, Harry. "Freedom of the Will and the Concept of a Person." *Journal of Philosophy* 68 (1971) 5–20.
Frankl, Viktor E. *Man's Search for Meaning*. Boston: Beacon, 2006.
Freud, Sigmund. *The Future of an Illusion*. Translated by James Strachey. New York: Norton, 1961.
Fromm, Erich. *Man for Himself*. New York: Henry Holt, 1990.
———. "Modern Man and the Future." Translated by Lance W. Garmer. In *On Being Human*, edited by Rainer Funk, 15–31. New York: Continuum, 2005.
Froom, LeRoy E. "Conditionalism in the Early Church." In *Rethinking Hell*, edited by Christopher M. Date et al., 260–75. Eugene, OR: Cascade, 2014.
Frost, Robert. "The Trial by Existence." In *Complete Poems*, 19–20. New York: Holt, 1967.
———. "Ten Mills." In *Complete Poems*, 405–7. New York: Holt, 1967.
Frost, Stanley Brice. "Death of Josiah." *Journal of Biblical Literature* 87.4 (1968) 369–82.
Fudge, Edward William. *The Fire That Consumes*. 3rd ed. Eugene, OR: Cascade, 2012.
Fulgence of Ruspe. "The Forgiveness of Sins." Translated by William A. Jurgens. In *The Faith of the Early Fathers (vol. 3)*, edited by William A. Jurgens, 292. Collegeville, MN: Liturgical, 1979.
———. "The Rule of Faith." Translated by William A. Jurgens. In *The Faith of the Early Fathers (vol. 3)*, edited by William A. Jurgens, 294–99. Collegeville, MN: Liturgical, 1979.
Fuyarchuk, Andrew. *Gadamer's Path to Plato*. Eugene, OR: Wipf & Stock, 2010.
Gabelman, Josephine. *A Theology of Nonsense*. Eugene, OR: Pickwick, 2016.
Gallagher, Shaun. "Introduction: Diversity of Selves." In *Oxford Handbook of the Self*, 1–29: Oxford: Oxford University Press, 2014.
Gallup, Gordon G., Jr., James R. Anderson, and Steven M. Platek. "Self-Recognition." In *Oxford Handbook of the Self*, edited by Shaun Gallagher, 80–110: Oxford: Oxford University Press, 2014.
Gammie, John G. "Spatial and Ethical Dualism in Jewish Wisdom and Apocalyptic Literature." *Journal of Biblical Literature* 93.3 (1974) 356–85.
Gardiner, Eileen. *Medieval Visions of Heaven and Hell*. New York: Garland, 1993.
Garff, Joakim. "Formation and the Critique of Culture." Translated by George Pattison. In *Oxford Handbook of Kierkegaard*, edited by John Lippitt and George Pattison, 252–72: Oxford: Oxford University Press, 2013.
Garland, David E. *1 Corinthians*. Baker Exegetical Commentary on the NT. Grand Rapids: Baker, 2003.
———. *2 Corinthians*. New American Commentary. Nashville: B&H, 1999.
Gassar, Georg, and Matthias Stefan, eds. *Personal Identity*. Cambridge: Cambridge University Press, 2015.

Gavrilyuk, Paul L. "The Judgment of Love." In *All Shall Be Well*, edited by Gregory MacDonald, 280–304. Eugene, OR: Cascade, 2011.

Geisler, Norman L. *Systematic Theology*. One vol. ed. Minneapolis: Bethany House, 2011.

Gendler, Tamar Szabo. "Exceptional Persons." In *Models of the Self*, edited by Shaun Gallagher and Jonathan Shear, 447–65. Thorverton, UK: Imprint, 1999.

George, Timothy and Denise George, eds. *Baptist Confessions, Covenants, and Catechisms*. Nashville: Broadman & Holman, 1999.

Gergen, Kenneth J. "The Social Construction of Self." In *Oxford Handbook of the Self*, edited by Shaun Gallagher, 633–53: Oxford: Oxford University Press, 2014.

Gerontology Research Group. "GRG World Supercentenarian Rankings List: Validated Living Supercentenarians." http://www.grg.org/SC/WorldSCRankingsList.html.

Gerson, Lloyd P. *Knowing Persons*. Oxford: Oxford University Press, 2003.

Gillman, Neil. *The Death of Death*. Woodstock, VT: Jewish Lights, 2006.

Gilson, Étienne. *Being and Some Philosophers*. 2nd ed. Toronto: Pontifical Institute of Mediaeval Studies, 2016.

———. *The Spirit of Mediaeval Philosophy*. Translated by A. H. C. Downes. South Bend, IN: University of Notre Dame Press, 2009.

Glasser, Arthur F., Charles E. Van Engen, Dean S. Gilliland, and Shawn B. Redford. *Announcing the Kingdom*. Grand Rapids: Baker, 2003.

Glicksberg, Charles I. *Ironic Vision in Modern Literature*. The Hague: Nijhoff, 1969.

Gockel, Matthias. *Barth and Schleiermacher on the Doctrine of Election*. Oxford: Oxford University Press, 2006.

Goddard, Andrew. "The Totality of Condemnation Fell on Christ." In *All Shall Be Well*, edited by Gregory MacDonald, 325–54. Eugene, OR: Cascade, 2011.

Goddard, Cliff. "The Natural Semantic Metalanguage Approach." In *Oxford Handbook of Linguistic Analysis*, edited by Bernd Heine and Heiko Narrog, 459–84: Oxford: Oxford University Press, 2010.

von Goethe, Johann Wolfgang. *Faust: A Tragedy*. Translated by Martin Greenberg. New Haven, CT: Yale University Press, 1992.

———. *Wilhelm Meister's Apprenticeship*. Translated by Eric A. Blackall and Victor Lange. New York: Suhrkamp, 1989.

Goetz, Stewart. "Substance Dualism." In *In Search of the Soul*, edited by Joel B. Green, 33–60. Eugene, OR: Wipf & Stock, 2010.

———. "Substance Dualist Response to Nonreductive Physicalism." In *In Search of the Soul*, edited by Joel B. Green, 139–42. Eugene, OR: Wipf & Stock, 2010.

Gonzalez, Justo L. *The Story of Christianity*. Rev. ed. New York: HarperOne, 2010.

Gooder, Paula. *Heaven*. London: SPCK, 2011.

Gorman, Michael J. *Inhabiting the Cruciform God*. Grand Rapids: Eerdmans, 2009.

Gouvea, Fernando Q. "Godliness." In *Evangelical Dictionary of Theology*, edited by Walter A. Elwell, 508–9. Grand Rapids: Baker, 2007.

Gracia, Jorge J. E. *Individuality*. Alban, NY: State University of New York Press, 1988.

Graham, Billy. *The Holy Spirit*. Nashville: Thomas Nelson, 1988.

Grant, Jamie A. "What Is Man?" In *Anthropology and NT Theology*, edited by Jason Maston and Benjamin E. Reynolds, 5–25. London: T. & T. Clark, 2019.

Green, Michael. *2 Peter and Jude*. Tyndale NT Commentaries. Edited by Leon Morris. Rev. ed. Grand Rapids: Eerdmans, 2000.

Greene, Graham. *The Power and the Glory*. New York: Penguin, 1991.

Bibliography

Greggs, Tom. *Barth, Origen, and Universal Salvation*. Oxford: Oxford University Press, 2009.

———. "Christian Universalist View." In *Five Views on the Extent of Atonement*, edited by Adam J. Johnson, 197–217. Grand Rapids: Zondervan, 2019.

Gregor, Brian. *Philosophical Anthropology of the Cross*. Bloomington, IN: Indiana University Press, 2013.

Gregory I (the Great). "Moral Teachings Drawn from Job." Translated by William A. Jurgens. In *The Faith of the Early Fathers (vol. 3)*, edited by William A. Jurgens, 313–18. Collegeville, MN: Liturgical, 1979.

Gregory of Nazianzus. "Concerning His Own Life." Translated by Carolinne White. In *Autobiographical Poems*, edited by Carolinne White, 11–154. Cambridge: Cambridge University Press, 1996.

———. *Festal Orations*. Translated by Nonna Verna Harrison. Crestwood, NY: St Vladimir's Seminary Press, 2008.

———. "In Defence of His Flight to Pontus after His Ordination." Translated by William A. Jurgens. In *The Faith of the Early Fathers (vol. 2)*, edited by William A. Jurgens, 28. Collegeville, MN: Liturgical, 1979.

———. *On God and Man*. Translated by Peter Gilbert. Crestwood, NY: St Vladimir's Seminary Press, 2001.

———. "Orations." In *Nicene and Post-Nicene Fathers: Second Series*, edited by Philip Schaff and Henry Wace, 203–434. Peabody, MA: Hendrickson, 1994.

———. "Second Theological Oration." Translated by William A. Jurgens. In *The Faith of the Early Fathers (vol. 2)*, edited by William A. Jurgens, 30–31. Collegeville, MN: Liturgical, 1979.

Gregory of Nyssa. "The Catechetical Oration." Translated by J. H. Srawley. In *Catechetical Oration of St Gregory of Nyssa*, edited by J. H. Srawley, 23–120. London: SPCK, 1917.

———. "In Illud: Tunc Et Ipse Filius." In *Gregorii Nysseni Opera III/2*, edited by Joseph Kenneth Downing, 44–50. Leiden: Brill, 1982.

———. "Letter 34." Translated by Anna M. Silvas. In *The Letters*, edited by Anna M. Silvas, 246–47. Boston: Brill, 2007.

———. "Letter 35." Translated by Anna M. Silvas. In *The Letters*, edited by Anna M. Silvas, 249–59. Boston: Brill, 2007.

———. *The Life of Moses*. Translated by Abraham J. Malherbe and Everett Ferguson. New York: Harper, 2006.

———. "The Life of Moses." Translated by William A. Jurgens. In *The Faith of the Early Fathers (vol. 2)*, edited by William A. Jurgens, 45. Collegeville, MN: Liturgical, 1979.

———. *On the Soul and Resurrection*. Translated by Catharine P. Roth. Crestwood, NY: St Vladimir's Seminary Press, 1993.

Gregory Thaumaturgus. "Address of Thanksgiving to Origen." Translated by Michael Slusser. In *Fathers of the Church*, edited by Thomas P. Halton, 91–126. Washington, DC: Catholic University of America Press, 1998.

Gregory the Great. *Forty Gospel Homilies*. Translated by Dom David Hurst. Kalamazoo, MI: Cistercian, 1990.

Grenz, Stanley J. *Theology for the Community of God*. Grand Rapids: Eerdmans, 2000.

Griffiths, Paul J. "Purgatory." In *Oxford Handbook of Eschatology*, edited by Jerry L. Walls, 427–45. Oxford: Oxford University Press, 2008.

Gschwandtner, Christina M. "Fully Alive?" In *The Role of Death in Life*, edited by John Behr and Conor Cunningham, 56–75. Eugene, OR: Cascade, 2015.

Guardini, Romano. *Freedom, Grace, and Destiny*. Translated by John Murray. New York: Pantheon, 1961.

———. *The World and the Person*. Translated by Stella Lange. Chicago: Regnery, 1965.

Guarini, Marcello, Amy Butchart, Paul Simard Smith, and Andrei Moldovan. "Resources for Research on Analogy." *Informal Logic* 29.2 (2009) 84–197.

Guhrt, Joachim. "Time-αἰών." In *New International Dictionary of NT Theology*, edited by Colin Brown, 826–33. Grand Rapids: Zondervan, 1986.

Guignon, Charles. "Heidegger and Kierkegaard on Death." In *Kierkegaard and Death*, edited by Patrick Stokes and Adam Buben, 184–203. Bloomington, IN: Indiana University Press, 2011.

Gulley, Philip, and James Mulholland. *If Grace Is True*. New York: HarperOne, 2003.

Gundry, Robert H. *Soma in Biblical Theology*. Cambridge: Cambridge University Press, 1976.

Gunton, Colin E. *Father, Son and Holy Spirit*. London: T. & T. Clark, 2003.

———. "Trinity, Ontology and Anthropology." In *Persons, Divine and Human*, edited by Christoph Schwobel and Colin E. Gunton, 47–61. Edinburgh: T. & T. Clark, 1991.

Guthrie, George H. *2 Corinthians*. Baker Exegetical Commentary on the NT. Grand Rapids: Baker, 2015.

Hacking, Ian. "Our Neo-Cartesian Bodies in Parts." *Critical Inquiry* 34.1 (2007) 78–105.

Haeckel, Ernst. *The Riddle of the Universe*. Translated by Josephy McCabe. New York: Harper, 1900.

Hafner, Verena V., Pontus Loviken, Antonio Pico Villalpando, and Guido Schillaci. "Prerequisites for an Artificial Self." *Front. Neurorobot* 14.5 (2020) 1–10.

Haggard, Patrick. "Do We Have Conscious Free Will." In *Mapping the Mind*, edited by Rita Carter, 192–93. Los Angeles: University of California Press, 2010.

Hagner, Donald A. *Matthew 1–13, Matthew 14–28*. Word Biblical Commentary. Dallas: Word Books, 1993, 1995.

De Haan, Daniel D., and Brandon Dahm. "Thomas Aquinas on Separated Souls as Incomplete Human." *The Thomist* 83.4 (2019) 589–637.

Hahn, Hans-Cristoph. "Conscience." In *New International Dictionary of NT Theology*, edited by Colin Brown, 348–51. Grand Rapids: Zondervan, 1986.

Hamann, Johann Georg. "Aesthetica in Nuce." Translated by Kenneth Haynes. In *Hamann: Writings on Philosophy and Language*, edited by Kenneth Haynes, 60–95. Cambridge: Cambridge University Press, 2009.

———. "Cloverleaf of Hellenistic Letters." Translated by Kenneth Haynes. In *Hamann: Writings on Philosophy and Language*, edited by Kenneth Haynes, 33–59. Cambridge: Cambridge University Press, 2009.

———. "Essay on an Academic Question." Translated by Kenneth Haynes. In *Hamann: Writings on Philosophy and Language*, edited by Kenneth Haynes, 9–19. New York: Cambridge University Press, 2009.

———. "Golgotha and Sheblimini!" Translated by Kenneth Haynes. In *Hamann: Writings on Philosophy and Language*, edited by Kenneth Haynes, 164–204. Cambridge: Cambridge University Press, 2009.

———. "The Last Will and Testament of the Knight of the Rose-Cross." Translated by Kenneth Haynes. In *Hamann: Writings on Philosophy and Language*, edited by Kenneth Haynes, 96–110. Cambridge: Cambridge University Press, 2009.

———. "Letter to Jacobi 27 Apr. 1787." In Friedrich Heinrich Jacobi, *Werke Vol. 4, Pt. 3*, 255. Leipzig: Fleischer, 1819.

———. "Letter to Lindner 9 Aug. 1759 (Excerpt)." Translated by Ronald Gregor Smith. In *J. G. Hamann*, edited by Ronald Gregor Smith, 67. New York: Harper, 1960.

———. "Philological Ideas and Doubts about an Academic Prize Essay." Translated by Kenneth Haynes. In *Hamann: Writings on Philosophy and Language*, edited by Kenneth Haynes, 111–36. Cambridge: Cambridge University Press, 2009.

———. "Socratic Memorabilia." Translated by Gwen Griffith Dickson. In *Johann Georg Hamann's Relational Metacriticism*, edited by Gwen Griffith Dickson, 375–407. New York: de Gruyter, 1995.

Hammett, John S. "Multiple-Intentions View of the Atonement." In *Perspectives on the Extent of Atonement*, edited by Andrew David Naselli and Mark A. Snoeberger, 143–94. Nashville: B&H, 2015.

———. "Response to General Atonement View." In *Perspectives on the Extent of Atonement*, edited by Andrew David Naselli and Mark A. Snoeberger, 134–41. Nashville: B&H, 2015.

Hanson, Paul D. *OT Apocalyptic*. Nashville: Abingdon, 1987.

Harari, Yuval Noah. *Sapiens*. New York: Harper, 2015.

Harder, Gunther. "Soul." In *New International Dictionary of NT Theology*, edited by Colin Brown, 676–86. Grand Rapids: Zondervan, 1986.

Harding, Sarah. *Paul's Eschatological Anthropology*. Minneapolis: Fortress, 2015.

Harmon, Steven R. "Subjection of All Things in Christ." In *All Shall Be Well*, edited by Gregory MacDonald, 47–65. Eugene, OR: Cascade, 2011.

Harre, Rom. *Principles of Scientific Thinking*. Chicago: University of Chicago Press, 1970.

Harris, Murray J. "Salvation." In *New Dictionary of Biblical Theology*, edited by T. Desmond Alexander and Brian S. Rosner, 762–67. Downers Grove, IL: InterVarsity, 2000.

———. *Second Epistle to the Corinthians*. New International Greek Testament Commentary. Grand Rapids: Eerdmans, 2005.

Harrison, Jonathan. "The Logical Function of 'That'." *Philosophy* 79.1 (2004) 67–96.

Harrison, Nonna Verna. *God's Many-Splendored Image*. Grand Rapids: Baker, 2010.

Hart, David Bentley. "Christ's Rabble." *Commonweal* 143.16 (2016) 18–21.

———. "Death, Final Judgment, and the Meaning of Life." In *Oxford Handbook of Eschatology*, edited by Jerry L. Walls, 476–89. Oxford: Oxford University Press, 2008.

———. *The Experience of God*. New Haven, CT: Yale University Press, 2013.

———. *The New Testament*. New Haven, CT: Yale University Press, 2017.

———. *That All Shall Be Saved*. New Haven, CT: Yale University Press, 2019.

Hart, Trevor. "In the End, God." In *All Shall Be Well*, edited by Gregory MacDonald, 355–81. Eugene, OR: Cascade, 2011.

———. "Redemption and Fall." In *Cambridge Companion to Christian Doctrine*, edited by Colin E. Gunton, 189–206: Cambridge: Cambridge University Press, 1998.

Hartshorne, Charles. *The Logic of Perfection*. Lasalle, IL: Open Court, 1962.

Hasker, William. "Do My Quarks Enjoy Beethoven." In *Neuroscience and the Soul*, edited by Thomas M. Crisp et al., 13–40. Grand Rapids: Eerdmans, 2016.

———. *The Emergent Self*. Ithaca, NY: Cornell University Press, 2001.

———. "Persons as Emergent Substances." In *Soul, Body, and Survival*, edited by Kevin J. Corcoran, 107–19. New York: Cornell University Press, 2001.

Haub, Carl. "How Many People Have Ever Lived on Earth?" Population Reference Bureau, http://www.prb.org/Publications/Articles/2002/HowManyPeopleHaveEverLivedonEarth.aspx.

Hawking, Stephen, and Leonard Mlodinow. *The Grand Design*. New York: Bantam, 2010.

Healy, Nicholas J. *Eschatology of Hans Urs von Balthasar*. Oxford: Oxford University Press, 2007.

Hebblethwaite, Brian. *The Christian Hope*. Rev. ed. Oxford: Oxford University Press, 2010.

Hegel, Georg W. F. *Lectures on the Philosophy of Religion*. Translated by E. B. Spiers and J. B. Sanderson. 3 vols. Vol. I. New York: Humanities, 1968.

———. *Logic*. Translated by William Wallace. Oxford: Clarendon, 1978.

———. *Phenomenology of Spirit*. Translated by A. V. Miller. Oxford: Oxford University Press, 1981.

Heidegger, Martin. "Being and Time: Introduction." Translated by Joan Stambaugh. In *Basic Writings*, edited by David Farrell Krell, 41–89. New York: Harper & Row, 1977.

———. "The End of Philosophy and the Task of Thinking." Translated by Joan Stambaugh. In *Basic Writings*, edited by David Farrell Krell, 193–242. New York: Harper & Row, 1977.

———. "Letter on Humanism." Translated by Frank A. Capuzzi. In *Basic Writings*, edited by David Farrell Krell, 247–86. New York: Harper & Row, 1977.

———. "Modern Science, Metaphysics, and Mathematics." Translated by W. B. Barton, Jr. and Vera Deutsch. In *Basic Writings*, edited by David Farrell Krell, 345–67. New York: Harper & Row, 1977.

———. "The Origin of the Work of Art." Translated by Albert Hofstadter. In *Basic Writings*, edited by David Farrell Krell, 149–87. New York: Harper & Row, 1977.

———. "What Calls for Thinking?" Translated by Fred D. Wieck and J. Glenn Gray. In *Basic Writings*, edited by David Farrell Krell, 373–92. New York: Harper & Row, 1977.

Hemming, Laurence Paul. "Heidegger and the Grounds of Redemption." In *Radical Orthodoxy*, edited by John Milbank et al., 91–108. London: Routledge, 1999.

Hendrik, Lorenz. *The Brute Within*. Oxford: Clarendon, 2006.

Hennessey, Lawrence R. "The Place of Saints and Sinners after Death." In *Origen of Alexandria*, edited by Charles Kannengiesser and William L. Petersen, 295–312. South Bend, IN: University of Notre Dame Press, 1988.

Henry, Carl F. H. *God, Revelation and Authority*. 6 vols. Vol. I. Wheaton, IL: Crossway, 1999.

Henry, Michel. *Barbarism*. Translated by Scott Davidson. London: Continuum Impacts, 2012.

———. *The Essence of Manifestation*. Translated by Girard Etzkorn. The Hague: Nijhoff, 1973.

———. *I Am the Truth*. Translated by Susan Emanuel. Stanford, CA: Stanford University Press, 2003.

———. *Incarnation*. Translated by Karl Hefty. Evanston, IL: Northwestern University Press, 2015.

———. *Material Phenomenology*. Translated by Scott Davidson. New York: Fordham University Press, 2008.

———. "Phenomenology of Life." Translated by Nick Hanlon. In *Transcendence and Phenomenology*, edited by Conor Cunningham and Peter M. Candler, Jr., 241–59. London: SCM, 2007.

———. *Words of Christ*. Translated by Christina M. Gschwandtner. Cambridge: Eerdmans, 2012.

Henze, Matthias. "On the Anthropology of Early Judaism." In *Anthropology and NT Theology*, edited by Jason Maston and Benjamin E. Reynolds, 27–42. London: T. & T. Clark, 2019.

Heraclitus. *Fragments*. Translated by Brooks Haxton. New York: Viking, 2001.

Hermans, Hubert J. M. "Dialogical Self." In *Oxford Handbook of the Self*, edited by Shaun Gallagher, 654–80: Oxford: Oxford University Press, 2014.

Hershenov, David B., and Rose Koch-Hershenov. "Personal Identity and Purgatory." *Religious Studies* 42 (2006) 439–51.

Hesiod. "Works and Days." In *Theogony, Works and Days, Testimonia*, edited by Glenn W. Most, 86–153. Cambridge: Harvard University Press, 2010.

Hick, John. *Death and Eternal Life*. New York: Harper, 1976.

———. *Evil and the God of Love*. London: Macmillan, 1966.

Hickman, Louise. "Love Is All and God Is Love." In *All Shall Be Well*, edited by Gregory MacDonald, 95–115. Eugene, OR: Cascade, 2011.

Highet, Gilbert. *Man's Unconquerable Mind*. New York: Columbia University Press, 1954.

Hilary of Poitiers. *Tractatus Super Psalmos I-XCI*. Edited by J. Doignon. Turnhout: Brepols, 1997.

Hilborn, David, and Don Horrocks. "Universalistic Trends in the Evangelical Tradition." In *Universal Salvation?* edited by Robin A. Parry and Christopher H. Partridge, 219–44. Carlisle, UK: Paternoster, 2003.

Hill, Claire Ortiz. *Rethinking Identity and Metaphysics*. New Haven, CT: Yale University Press, 1997.

Hillerbrand, Hans J. *The Division of Christendom*. Louisville: Westminster, 2007.

Hippolytus of Rome. "Against the Greeks." Translated by William A. Jurgens. In *The Faith of the Early Fathers (vol. 1)*, edited by William A. Jurgens, 172. Collegeville, MN: Liturgical, 1970.

Hobbes, Thomas. *Leviathan*. South Bend, IN: Infomotions, 2000.

Hobson, Peter R. "Autism and the Self." In *Oxford Handbook of the Self*, edited by Shaun Gallagher, 571–91. Oxford: Oxford University Press, 2014.

Hoehner, Harold W. *Ephesians: Exegetical Commentary*. Grand Rapids: Baker, 2004.

Hoff, Johannes. "The Rise and Fall of the Kantian Paradigm." In *Grandeur of Reason*, edited by Peter M. Candler, Jr. and Conor Cunningham, 167–96. London: SCM, 2010.

Hofstadter, Douglas. *Metamagical Themas*. New York: Basic, 1985.

Holmes, Thomas Scott. *Origin and Development of the Christian Church*. London: Macmillan, 1911.

van Holten, Wilko. "Can the Traditional View of Hell Be Defended?" *Anglican Theological Review* 85.3 (2003) 457–76.

———. "Hell and the Goodness of God." *Religious Studies* 35 (1999) 37–55.

Honko, Lauri. "The Problem of Defining Myth." *Scripta Instituti Donneriani Aboensis* 6.1 (1972) 7–19.

Hooke, Robert. *Micrographia*. 1664. Project Gutenberg eBook, 2005.

Horne, Brian L. "Person as Confession." In *Persons, Divine and Human*, edited by Christoph Schwobel and Colin E. Gunton, 65–73. Edinburgh: T. & T. Clark, 1991.

Horrocks, Don. "Postmortem Education." In *All Shall Be Well*, edited by Gregory MacDonald, 198–218. Eugene, OR: Cascade, 2011.

Horst, Steven. *Cognitive Pluralism*. Cambridge: MIT Press, 2016.

Horton, Michael S. "Traditional Reformed View." In *Five Views on the Extent of Atonement*, edited by Adam J. Johnson, 112–33. Grand Rapids: Zondervan, 2019.

Hudson, Hud. "The Morphing Block and Diachronic Personal Identity." In *Personal Identity*, edited by Georg Gassar and Matthias Stefan, 236–48: Cambridge: Cambridge University Press, 2015.

Hughes, Peter. "Universalism, Universalists." In *Encyclopedia of Christianity*, edited by Erwin Fahlbusch et al., 638–42. Grand Rapids: Eerdmans, 2008.

Hughes, Philip E. "Is the Soul Immortal?" In *Rethinking Hell*, edited by Christopher M. Date et al., 185–97. Eugene, OR: Cascade, 2014.

Hume, David. *Treatise of Human Nature*. Mineola, NY: Dover, 2014.

Hunn, Debbie. "'Ἐὰν Μή in Galatians 2:16." *Novum Testamentum* 49.3 (2007) 281–90.

Husserl, Edmund. "Author's Preface to English Ed." In *Ideas*, 5–22. New York: Collier, 1967.

———. *Cartesian Meditations*. Translated by Dorion Cairns. The Hague: Nijhoff, 1960.

———. *The Crisis of European Sciences*. Translated by David Carr. Evanston, IL: Northwestern University Press, 1970.

———. *The Idea of Phenomenology*. Translated by Lee Hardy. Dordrecht: Kluwer, 1999.

———. *Ideas*. Translated by W. R. Boyce Gibson. New York: Collier, 1967.

Hutson, Christopher. *First and Second Timothy and Titus*. Paideia Commentaries on the NT. Grand Rapids: Baker Academic, 2019.

Huxley, Aldous. *Brave New World*. New York: HarperCollins, 1998.

Ignatius. "Epistle to the Romans." In *Ante-Nicene Fathers*, edited by Alexander Roberts and James Donaldson, 73–78. Peabody, MA: Hendrickson, 1994.

———. "Epistle to the Smyrnaeans." In *Ante-Nicene Fathers*, edited by Alexander Roberts and James Donaldson, 86–92. Peabody, MA: Hendrickson, 1994.

———. "Letter to the Ephesians." Translated by William A. Jurgens. In *The Faith of the Early Fathers (vol. 1)*, edited by William A. Jurgens, 17–19. Collegeville, MN: Liturgical, 1970.

International Theological Commission. "Some Current Questions on Eschatology." 1992. http://www.vatican.va/roman_curia/congregations/cfaith/cti_documents/rc_cti_1990_problemi-attuali-escatologia_en.html

Irenaeus. *Against Heresies*. Translated by James R. Payton, Jr. Irenaeus on the Christian Faith ed. Cambridge: James Clarke, 2012.

———. "Against Heresies." Translated by William A. Jurgens. In *The Faith of the Early Fathers (vol. 1)*, edited by William A. Jurgens, 84–104. Collegeville, MN: Liturgical, 1970.

———. "Against Heresies." Translated by Alexander Roberts and William Rambaut. In *Ante-Nicene Fathers*, edited by Alexander Roberts, et al., 309–567. Peabody, MA: Hendrickson, 1994.

Isaac of Nineveh. *The Second Part*. Translated by Sebastian Brock. 2 vols. Vol. I. Leuven: Peeters, 1995.

Jacob, Francois. *The Logic of Life*. Translated by Betty Spillman. New York: Pantheon, 1973.

Bibliography

Jacobi, Friedrich Heinrich. *Werke Vol. 4, Pt. 3.* Leipzig: Fleischer, 1819.

Jaeger, Luc. "A Biochemical Perspective." In *The Role of Death in Life*, edited by John Behr and Conor Cunningham, 14–28. Eugene, OR: Cascade, 2015.

Jaeger, Werner. *Early Christianity and Greek Paideia*. Cambridge, MA: Belknap, 1961.

James, William. *Essays in Radical Empiricism*. The Works. Edited by Frederick H. Burkhardt et al. Cambridge: Harvard University Press, 1976.

———. *Principles of Psychology*. 2 vols. Vol. I, New York: Henry Holt, 1890.

———. *The Varieties of Religious Experience*. New York: Random House, 1902.

Jenson, Robert W. *Systematic Theology*. 2 vols. Oxford: Oxford University Press, 1997, 1999.

Jerome. "Commentary on the Epistle to the Ephesians." Translated by Ronald E. Heine. In *Commentaries of Origen and Jerome on St Paul's Epistle to the Ephesians*, edited by Ronald E. Heine, 75–272. Oxford: Oxford University Press, 2002.

Jobes, Karen H. *1,2&3 John*. Zondervan Exegetical Commentary on the NT. Grand Rapids: Zondervan, 2014.

———. "Remember These Things." In *Anthropology and NT Theology*, edited by Jason Maston and Benjamin E. Reynolds, 189–203. London: T. & T. Clark, 2019.

John of Damascus. "Fount of Knowledge." Translated by Frederic H. Chase, Jr. In *St John of Damascus Writings*, 3–406. New York: Fathers of the Church, 1958.

John the Scot. *Periphyseon*. Translated by Myra L. Uhlfelder. Eugene, OR: Wipf & Stock, 2011.

Johnson, Adam J., ed. *Five Views on the Extent of Atonement*. Grand Rapids: Zondervan, 2019.

Johnson, Luke Timothy. *Letter of James*. AB. New York: Doubleday, 1995.

———. *Writings of the NT*. Rev. ed. Minneapolis: Fortress, 1999.

Johnson, P.S. "Life, Disease and Death." In *Dictionary of the OT: Pentateuch*, edited by T. Desmond Alexander and David W. Baker, 532–36. Downers Grove, IL: InterVarsity, 2003.

Johnson, Thomas. "A Wideness in God's Mercy." In *Universal Salvation?* edited by Robin A. Parry and Christopher H. Partridge, 77–102. Carlisle, UK: Paternoster, 2003.

Johnston, Mark. *Surviving Death*. Princeton: Princeton University Press, 2010.

Jopling, David A. *Self Knowledge and the Self*. London: Routledge, 2000.

Joyce, James. *Ulysses*. New York: Random House, 1961.

Jukes, Andrew. *Second Death and the Restitution of All Things*. 4th ed. London: Longmans, Green, 1875.

Julian of Norwich. *Book of Showings*. 2 vols. Vol. II. Toronto: Pontifical Institute of Mediaeval Studies, 1978.

Jung, C. G. *Modern Man in Search of a Soul*. Translated by W. S. Dell and Cary F. Baynes. Orlando, FL: Harvest, 1933.

Jüngel, Eberhard. *God as the Mystery of the World*. Translated by Darrell L. Guder. Grand Rapids: Eerdmans, 1983.

Kallistos (Ware) of Diokleia. "Unity of the Human Person according to the Greek Fathers." In *Philosophical Theology and the Christian Tradition*, edited by David Bradshaw, 67–76. Washington, DC: Council for Research in Values and Philosophy, 2012.

Kant, Immanuel. "Preface to Second Edition." Translated by Norman Kemp Smith. In *Critique of Pure Reason*, 17–37. New York: St Martin's Press, 1965.

Kapriev, Georgi. "Conceptual Apparatus of Maximus the Confessor and Contemporary Anthropology." Translated by Stoyan Tanev. In *Maximus the Confessor as a*

European Philosopher, edited by Sotiris Mitralexis et al., 166–92. Eugene, OR: Cascade, 2017.

Karkkainen, Veli-Matti. *Christology: Global Introduction*. Grand Rapids: Baker, 2003.

———. "Multidimensional Monism." In *Neuroscience and the Soul*, edited by Thomas M. Crisp et al., 201–27. Grand Rapids: Eerdmans, 2016.

Käsemann, Ernst. *Jesus Means Freedom*. Philadelphia: Fortress, 1968.

———. *Perspectives on Paul*. Translated by Margaret Kohl. Philadelphia: Fortress, 1978.

Kayser, Wolfgang. *The Grotesque in Art and Literature*. Translated by Ulrich Weisstein. New York: Columbia University Press, 1957.

Keating, Daniel A. *Deification and Grace*. Naples: Sapientia, 2007.

Keats, John. *Selected Letters*. Cambridge: Harvard University Press, 2005.

Keener, Craig S. *Gospel of John: Commentary*. 2 vols. Vol. II. Peabody, MA: Hendrickson, 2003.

Kelly, J. N. D. *Early Christian Doctrines*. 5th ed. New York: Continuum, 2012.

Kelsey, David H. "Personal Bodies." In *Personal Identity in Theological Perspective*, edited by Richard Lints et al., 139–58. Grand Rapids: Eerdmans, 2006.

Kempis, Thomas à. *The Imitation of Christ*. Translated by William Benham. London: George Routledge & Sons, 1886.

Kenny, Anthony. *The Legacy of Wittgenstein*. Oxford: Blackwell, 1987.

Kierkegaard, Søren. "At a Graveside." Translated by Howard V. and Edna H. Hong. In *Three Discourses on Imagined Questions*, edited by Howard V. and Edna H. Hong. Princeton: Princeton University Press, 2009.

———. *Attack Upon "Christendom."* Translated by Walter Lowrie. Princeton: Princeton University Press, 1991.

———. *Book on Adler*. Translated by Howard V. and Edna H. Hong. Princeton: Princeton University Press, 2009.

———. *Christian Discourses*. Translated by Howard V. and Edna H. Hong. Princeton: Princeton University Press, 1997.

———. *The Concept of Anxiety*. Translated by Reidar Thomte. Princeton: Princeton University Press, 1980.

———. *Concluding Unscientific Postscript to Philosophical Fragments*. Translated by Howard V. and Edna H. Hong. 2 vols. Vol. I. Princeton: Princeton University Press, 1992.

———. *Eighteen Upbuilding Discourses*. Translated by Howard V. and Edna H. Hong. Princeton: Princeton University Press, 1990.

———. *Either/Or*. Translated by Howard V. and Edna H. Hong. 2 vols. Vol. I. Princeton: Princeton University Press, 1987.

———. *Either/Or*. Translated by David F. Swenson and Lillian Marvin Swenson. Rev. ed. 2 vols. Vol. II. Garden City: Doubleday, 1959.

———. *Fear and Trembling*. Translated by Walter Lowrie. Princeton: Princeton University Press, 1970.

———. *For Self-Examination*. Translated by Howard V. and Edna H. Hong. Minneapolis: Augsburg, 1952.

———. *Journal and Papers*. Translated by Howard V. and Edna H. Hong. 7 vols. Bloomington, IN: Indiana University Press, 1967–78.

———. *The Moment and Late Writings*. Translated by Howard V. and Edna H. Hong. Princeton: Princeton University Press, 1998.

———. *Philosophical Fragments or a Fragment of Philosophy*. Translated by Howard V. and Edna H. Hong. Princeton: Princeton University Press, 1985.

———. *The Point of View*. Translated by Howard V. and Edna H. Hong. Princeton: Princeton University Press, 1998.
———. *Practice in Christianity*. Translated by Howard V. and Edna H. Hong. Princeton: Princeton University Press, 1991.
———. *Purity of Heart Is to Will One Thing*. Translated by Douglas V. Steere. New York: Harper, 1956.
———. "Repetition." Translated by M. G. Piety. In *Repetition and Philosophical Crumbs*, edited by Edward F. Mooney, 1–82. Oxford: Oxford University Press, 2009.
———. *The Sickness unto Death*. Translated by Howard V. and Edna H. Hong. Princeton: Princeton University Press, 1980.
———. *Stages on Life's Way*. Translated by Howard V. and Edna H. Hong. Princeton: Princeton University Press, 1988.
———. *Training in Christianity*. Translated by Walter Lowrie. Princeton: Princeton University Press, 1967.
———. *Two Ages*. Translated by Howard V. and Edna H. Hong. Princeton: Princeton University Press, 1978.
———. *Upbuilding Discourses in Various Spirits*. Translated by Howard V. and Edna H. Hong. Princeton: Princeton University Press, 1993.
———. *Works of Love*. Translated by Howard V. and Edna H. Hong. Princeton: Princeton University Press, 1995.
Kimel, Aidan. "Did the Fifth Ecumenical Council Condemn Universal Salvation?" https://afkimel.wordpress.com/2020/05/31/did-the-fifth-ecumenical-council-condemn-universal-salvation/
Kind, Amy. *Persons and Personal Identity*. Cambridge: Polity, 2015.
Klein, Carolina A., and Soniya Hirachan. "The Masks of Identities." *Journal of the America Academy of Psychiatry and the Law* 42 (2014) 369–78.
Klink, Edward W., III. *John*. Zondervan Exegetical Commentary on the NT. Grand Rapids: Zondervan, 2016.
Knight, George A.F. *The New Israel: Commentary on the Book of Isaiah 56–66*. Grand Rapids: Eerdmans, 1985.
Knight, George W., III. *Pastoral Epistles*. New International Greek Testament Commentary. Grand Rapids: Eerdmans, 1992.
Koehn, Daryl. *Nature of Evil*. New York: Palgrave MacMillan, 2005.
Koester, Craig R. *Revelation*. Anchor Yale Bible. New Haven, CT: Yale University Press, 2014.
van Kooton, George H.. *Paul's Anthropology in Context*. Tübingen: Mohr Siebeck, 2008.
———. "St Paul on Soul, Spirit and the Inner Man." In *The Afterlife of the Platonic Soul*, edited by Maha Elkaisy-Friemuth and John M. Dillon, 25–44. Leiden: Brill, 2009.
———. "The 'Two Inclinations' and the Double-Minded Human Condition in the Letter of James." In *The Evil Inclination in Early Judaism and Christianity*, edited by J. Aiken, H. M. Patmore, and I. Rosen-Zvi, 143–58. Cambridge: Cambridge University Press, 2021.
Kostenberger, Andreas J. *John*. Baker Exegetical Commentary on the NT. Grand Rapids: Baker, 2004.
Krapiec, Mieczylaw. *I-Man*. Translated by Marie Lescoe et al. New Britain, PNG: Mariel, 1983.
Krell, David Farrell. "General Introduction: Question of Being." In *Martin Heidegger Basic Writings*, edited by J. Glenn Gray, 3–35. New York: Harper & Row, 1977.
Kreppner, Jana M., Michael Rutter, Celia Beckett, Jenny Castle, Emma Colvert, Christine Groothues, Amanda Hawkins. "Normality and Impairment Following

Profound Early Institutional Deprivation." *Developmental Psychology* 43.4 (2007) 931–46.

Kristensen, Johanne Stubbe Teblgjaerg. *Body and Hope*. Tübingen: Mohr Siebeck, 2013.

Kruse, Colin G. *Letters of John*. Pillar NT Commentary. Grand Rapids: Eerdmans, 2000.

Kugel, James. *Traditions of the Bible*. Cambridge: Harvard University Press, 1998.

Küng, Hans. *Eternal Life?* Translated by Edward Quinn. London: SCM, 1991.

Kvanvig, Jonathan L. "Hell." In *Oxford Handbook of Eschatology*, edited by Jerry L. Walls, 413–26. Oxford: Oxford University Press, 2008.

Lafer-Sousa, et al. "Striking Individual Differences in Color Perception." *Current Biology* 25 (2015) R545–46.

Lakoff, George, and Mark Johnson. *Metaphors We Live By*. Chicago: University of Chicago Press, 2003.

Lane, William L. *Gospel according to Mark*. New International Commentary of the NT. Grand Rapids: Eerdmans, 1974.

Lange, John. "The Argument from Silence." *History and Theory* 5.3 (1966) 288–301.

Lanzillotta, Lautato Roig. "One Human Being, Three Early Christian Anthropologies." *Vigiliae Christianae* 61 (2007) 414–44.

———. "Spirit, Soul and Body in Nag Hammadi Literature." *Gnosis: Journal of Gnostic Studies* 2 (2017) 15–39.

Lash, Nicholas. *Easter in Ordinary*. Charlottesville, VA: University Press of Virginia, 1988.

Lawlor, Leonard. "The Postmodern Self." In *Oxford Handbook of the Self*, edited by Shaun Gallagher, 696–714: Oxford: Oxford University Press, 2014.

Le Goff, Jacques. *Birth of Purgatory*. Translated by Arthur Goldhammer. Chicago: University of Chicago Press, 1986.

LeDoux, Joseph. *Synaptic Self*. New York: Penguin, 2002.

Lee, Eric Austin. "Standing Accused: Analogy and Dialogue as the Personhood of Substance." PhD Diss., University of Nottingham, 2003.

Leftow, Brian. "Souls Dipped in Dust." In *Soul, Body, and Survival*, edited by Kevin J. Corcoran, 120–38. New York: Cornell University Press, 2001.

Leget, Carlo. "Eschatology." In *Theology of Thomas Aquinas*, edited by Rik van Nieuwenhove and Joseph Wawrykow, 365–85. South Bend, IN: University of Notre Dame Press, 2005.

Legrand, Dorothee. "Phenomenological Dimensions of Bodily Self-Consciousness." In *Oxford Handbook of the Self*, edited by Shaun Gallagher, 204–27: Oxford: Oxford University Press, 2014.

Lemmon, E. J. *Beginning Logic*. Indianapolis: Hackett, 1978.

Lenski, R. C. H. *Interpretation of St Matthew's Gospel*. Minneapolis: Augsburg, 1964.

"Letter to Diognetus." Translated by William A. Jurgens. In *The Faith of the Early Fathers (vol. 1)*, edited by William A. Jurgens, 40–42. Collegeville, MN: Liturgical, 1970.

"Letter of Justinian to the Holy Council." Translated by Richard Price. In *The Acts of the Council of Constantinople of 553*, 282–84. Liverpool: Liverpool University Press, 2012.

Levering, Matthew. *Proofs of God*. Grand Rapids: Baker, 2016.

———. "Response to Andrew Louth." In *Five Views on the Extent of Atonement*, edited by Adam J. Johnson, 223–26. Grand Rapids: Zondervan, 2019.

———. "Response to Professor Greggs." In *Five Views on the Extent of Atonement*, edited by Adam J. Johnson, 223–26. Grand Rapids: Zondervan, 2019.

Lewis, Alan E. *Between Cross and Resurrection*. Grand Rapids: Eerdmans, 2003.

Lewis, C. S. *The Great Divorce*. New York: HarperOne, 1973.
———. "Is Theology Poetry?" In *The Weight of Glory and Other Addresses*, 116–40. New York: HarperOne, 2001.
———. "Membership." In *The Weight of Glory and Other Addresses*, 158–76. New York: HarperOne, 2001.
———. *Mere Christianity*. New York: Collier, 1960.
———. *The Problem of Pain*. New York: Harper, 1996.
———. "A Slip of the Tongue." In *The Weight of Glory and Other Addresses*, 184–92. New York: HarperOne, 2001.
———. "Transposition." In *The Weight of Glory and Other Addresses*, 91–115. New York: HarperOne, 2001.
———. "The Weight of Glory." In *The Weight of Glory and Other Addresses*, 25–46. New York: HarperOne, 2001.
———. "Why I Am Not a Pacifist." In *The Weight of Glory and Other Addresses*, 64–90. New York: HarperOne, 2001.
Lewontin, R. C. *Biology as Ideology*. New York: HarperPerennial, 1991.
Lincoln, Andrew T. *Ephesians*. Word Biblical Commentary. Dallas: Word, 1990.
Locke, John. *Essay concerning Human Understanding*. Oxford: Clarendon, 1975.
Lockwood, Michael. "Consciousness and the Quantum World." In *Consciousness*, edited by Quentin Smith and Aleksandar Jokic, 447–67. Oxford: Clarendon, 2003.
Lohr, Hermut. "The Role of Eschatology in NT Moral Thought." In *Eschatology of the NT and Some Related Documents*, edited by Jan G. van der Watt, 644–65. Tübingen: Mohr Siebeck, 2011.
Lombard, Peter. *The Sentences: Book 3; on the Incarnation of the Word*. Translated by Giuolio Silano. Toronto: Pontifical Institute of Medieval Studies, 2008.
Lonergan, Bernard J. F. *Insight*. London: Longmans, Green, 1957.
———. *Method in Theology*. London: Darton, Longman & Todd, 1971.
Long, D. Stephen. *The Perfectly Simple Triune God*. Minneapolis: Fortress, 2016.
Longenecker, Richard N. *Galatians*. Word Biblical Commentary. Dallas: Word, 1990.
Lopez, Antonio. *Gift and the Unity of Being*. Eugene, OR: Cascade, 2014.
Lossky, Vladimir. *The Mystical Theology of the Eastern Church*. Translated by Fellows of St Alban and St Sergius. Crestwood, NY: St Vladimir's Seminary Press, 2002.
Louth, Andrew. "Eastern Orthodox Eschatology." In *Oxford Handbook of Eschatology*, edited by Jerry L. Walls, 233–47. Oxford: Oxford University Press, 2008.
———. "Response to Tom Greggs." In *Five Views on the Extent of Atonement*, edited by Adam J. Johnson, 218–22. Grand Rapids: Zondervan, 2019.
Lowe, E. J. "The Probable Simplicity of Personal Identity." In *Personal Identity*, edited by Georg Gassar and Matthias Stefan, 137–55: Cambridge: Cambridge University Press, 2015.
———. *Subjects of Experience*. Cambridge: Cambridge University Press, 1996.
de Lubac, Henri. *Catholicism*. Translated by Lancelot C. Sheppard and Elizabeth Englund. San Francisco: Ignatius, 1988.
———. *Theological Fragments*. Translated by R. H. Balinski. San Francisco: Ignatius, 1984.
Lucretius. *On the Nature of Things*. Translated by Anthony M. Esolen. Baltimore: John Hopkins University Press, 1995.
Ludlow, Morwenna. *Universal Salvation*. Oxford: Oxford University Press, 2000.

———. "Universalism in the History of Christianity." In *Universal Salvation?* edited by Robin A. Parry and Christopher H. Partridge, 191–218. Carlisle, UK: Paternoster, 2003.

Luther, Martin. *Commentary on Genesis*. Translated by J. Theodore Mueller. 2 vols. Vol. II, Grand Rapids: Zondervan, 1958.

———. *Commentary on St Paul's Epistle to the Galatians*. Translated by Erasmus Middleton and Philip S. Watson. Westwood, CT: Revell, 1953.

———. "De Servo Arbitrio." Translated by Philip S. Watson and B. Drewery. In *Luther and Erasmus: Free Will and Salvation*, 101–334. Philadelphia: Westminster, 1969.

———. *Word and Sacrament II*. American ed. 36 vols. Philadelphia: Fortress, 1959.

MacDonald, George. *Unspoken Sermons Sermons I, II, III*. Whitehorn: Johannesen, 1997.

MacDonald, Gregory. "Introduction: Between Heresy and Dogma." In *All Shall Be Well*, 1–25. Eugene, OR: Cascade, 2011.

MacDonald, Paul S. *History of the Concept of Mind*. Burlington, VT: Ashgate, 2003.

Macquarrie, John. *Principles of Christian Theology*. New York: Scribner's Sons, 1966.

Maimonides, Moses. *The Guide for the Perplexed*. Translated by Michael Friedländer. BN, 2007.

Maritain, Jacques. *Existence and the Existent*. Translated by Lewis Galantiere and Gerald B. Phelan. New York: Pantheon, 1948.

Marks, Tamara Monet. "Kierkegaard's Understanding of the Afterlife." In *Kierkegaard and Death*, edited by Patrick Stokes and Adam Buben, 274–97: Bloomington, IN: Indiana University Press, 2011.

Marshall, Christopher D. "Divine and Human Punishment in the NT." In *Rethinking Hell*, edited by Christopher M. Date et al., 207–27. Eugene, OR: Cascade, 2014.

Marshall, I. Howard. *Epistles of John*. New International Commentary of the NT. Grand Rapids: Eerdmans, 1978.

———. *Gospel of Luke*. New International Greek Testament Commentary. Grand Rapids: Paternoster, 1995.

———. "The New Testament Does Not Teach Universal Salvation." In *Universal Salvation?* edited by Robin A. Parry and Christopher H. Partridge, 55–76. Carlisle, UK: Paternoster, 2003.

Marsilius of Padua. *The Defensor Pacis*. Translated by Alan Gewirth. 2 vols. Vol. II. New York: Columbia University Press, 1956.

Martens, Paul. "Kierkegaard and the Bible." In *Oxford Handbook of Kierkegaard*, edited by John Lippitt and George Pattison, 150–65: Oxford: Oxford University Press, 2013.

Martin, Dale B. *The Corinthian Body*. New Haven, CT: Yale University Press, 1995.

Martin, G. W. "Faith." In *New Dictionary of Theology*, edited by Sinclair B. Ferguson and David F. Wright, 246–47. Downers Grove, IL: InterVarsity, 1988.

Martin, Ralph. *Will Many Be Saved?* Grand Rapids: Eerdmans, 2012.

Martin, Ralph P. *2 Corinthians*. Word Biblical Commentary. Edited by David A. Hubbard. Waco, TX: Word, 1986.

Martyr, Justin. *First and Second Apologies*. Translated by Leslie William Barnard. New York: Paulist, 1997.

Marx, Karl. "A Contribution to the Critique of Political Economy: Introduction." Translated by Annette Jolin and Joseph O'Malley. In *Critique of Hegel's Philosophy of Right*, edited by Joseph O'Malley, 129–42. Cambridge: Cambridge University Press, 1982.

———. "Economic and Philosophical Manuscripts." In *Karl Marx Selected Writings*, edited by David McLellan, 75–112: Oxford: Oxford University Press, 1978.

Mason, Alistair. "Universalism." In *Oxford Companion to Christian Thought*, edited by Adrian Hastings, 733. Oxford: Oxford University Press, 2000.

Maston, Jason. "Enlivened Slaves." In *Anthropology and NT Theology*, edited by Jason Maston and Benjamin E. Reynolds, 141–59. London: T. & T. Clark, 2019.

Mateiescu, Sebastian. "Counting Natures and Hypostases." In *Studia Patristica LXXXIX*, edited by Markus Vinzent and Sotiris Mitralexis, 63–78. Leuven: Peeters, 2017.

Matera, Frank J. *Romans*. Paideia Commentaries on the NT. Grand Rapids: Baker Academic, 2010.

Mathews, Kenneth A. *Genesis 1—11:26*. New American Commentary. Nashville: Broadman & Holman, 1996.

Maximus the Confessor. *Ambigua*. Translated by Nicholas Constas. 2 vols. Cambridge: Harvard University Press, 2014.

———. "Ambiguum 7." Translated by Paul M. Blowers and Robert Louis Wilken. In *On the Cosmic Mystery of Jesus Christ*, 45–74. Crestwood, NY: St Vladimir's Seminary Press, 2003.

———. "Opusculum 6." Translated by Paul M. Blowers and Robert Louis Wilken. In *On the Cosmic Mystery of Jesus Christ*, 173–76. Crestwood, NY: St Vladimir's Seminary Press, 2003.

Mazza, Edmund J. *The Scholastics and the Jews*. Kettering, UK: Angelico, 2017.

Mazzolini, Elizabeth. "Food, Waste, and Judgment on Mount Everest." *Cultural Critique* 76 (Fall 2010) 1–27.

McClymond, Michael J. *The Devil's Redemption*. 2 vols. Grand Rapids: Baker, 2018.

McCombs, Richard. *The Paradoxical Rationality of Søren Kierkegaard*. Bloomington, IN: Indiana University Press, 2013.

McConville, J. Gordon. *Being Human in God's World*. Grand Rapids: Baker, 2016.

McCormack, Bruce L. "So That He May Be Merciful to All." In *Karl Barth and American Evangelicalism*, edited by Bruce L. McCormack and Clifford B. Anderson, 227–49. Grand Rapids: Eerdmans, 2011.

McCoy, Timothy A. "The Gospel Truth." In *Who Will Be Saved?* edited by Paul R. House and Gregory A. Thornbury, 167–77. Wheaton, IL: Crossway, 2000.

McDonald, William. "Kierkegaard and Romanticism." In *Oxford Handbook of Kierkegaard*, edited by John Lippitt and George Pattison, 94–111: Oxford: Oxford University Press, 2013.

McFarland, Ian A. "The Upward Call." In *Christian Doctrine of Humanity*, edited by Oliver D. Crisp and Fred Sanders, 217–36. Grand Rapids: Zondervan, 2018.

McFarlane, Graham. "Strange News from Another Star." In *Persons, Divine and Human*, edited by Christoph Schwobel and Colin E. Gunton, 98–119. Edinburgh: T. & T. Clark, 1991.

McGilchrist, Iain. *The Master and His Emissary*, Exp. ed. New Haven, CT: Yale University Press, 2019.

McGowan, John. *Postmodernism and Its Critics*. Ithaca, NY: Cornell University Press, 1992.

McGuckin, J. A. "Strategic Adaptation of Deification in the Cappadocians." In *Partakers of the Divine Nature*, edited by Michael J. Christensen and Jeffrey A. Wittung, 95–114. Grand Rapids: Baker, 2008.

McInroy, Mark. *Balthasar on the Spiritual Senses*. Oxford: Oxford University Press, 2014.

McIntosh, J. R., and M. P. Koonce. "Mitosis." *Science* 246.4930 (1989) 622–28.

McKnight, Scot. *Letter of James*. New International Commentary of the NT. Grand Rapids: Eerdmans, 2011.

Meillassoux, Quentin. "The Immanence of the World Beyond." Translated by Peter M. Candler, Jr. et al. In *Grandeur of Reason*, edited by Peter M. Candler, Jr. and Conor Cunningham, 444–78. London: SCM, 2010.

Merleau-Ponty, Maurice. *Signs*. Translated by Richard C. McCleary. Evanston, IL: Northwestern University Press, 1987.

Merricks, Trenton. "How to Live Forever without Saving Your Soul." In *Soul, Body, and Survival*, edited by Kevin J. Corcoran, 183–200. New York: Cornell University Press, 2001.

———. "The Resurrection of the Dead and the Life Everlasting." In *Reason for the Hope Within*, edited by Michael Murray, 261–86. Grand Rapids: Eerdmans, 1999.

Merton, Thomas. *The Seven Storey Mountain*. 50th anniversary ed. Orlando, FL: Harcourt, 1998.

Methodius. "Banquet of the Ten Virgins." In *Ante-Nicene Fathers*, edited by Alexander Roberts and James Donaldson, 309–55. Peabody, MA: Hendrickson, 1994.

Metzger, Bruce M. *Textual Commentary on the Greek NT*. 2nd ed. Stuttgart: German Bible Society, 2007.

Metzinger, Thomas. *Being No One*. Cambridge: MIT Press, 2003.

———. "The No-Self Alternative." In *Oxford Handbook of the Self*, edited by Shaun Gallagher, 279–96: Oxford: Oxford University Press, 2014.

Milavec, Aaron, ed. *The Didache*. Collegeville, MN: Liturgical, 2003.

Milbank, John. *Beyond Secular Order*. Chichester, UK: Wiley-Blackwell, 2013.

———. "The Double Glory." In *The Monstrosity of Christ*, edited by Creston Davis, 110–233. Cambridge: MIT Press, 2009.

———. "The Mystery of Reason." In *Grandeur of Reason*, edited by Peter M. Candler, Jr. and Conor Cunningham, 68–117. London: SCM, 2010.

———. "Theological Critique of Philosophy in Hamann and Jacobi." In *Radical Orthodoxy*, edited by John Milbank et al., 21–37. London: Routledge, 1999.

———. *Theology and Social Theory*. Cambridge: Blackwell, 2003.

———. *The Word Made Strange*. Cambridge: Blackwell, 1997.

Miles, Lois M. "Obedience of a Corpse: The Key to the Holy Saturday Writings of Adrienne von Speyr." PhD Diss., University of Aberdeen, 2013.

Mitchell, Jason A. *Being and Participation*. 2 vols. Vol. I. Rome: Ateneo Pontificio Regina Apostolorum, 2012.

Molnar, Paul D. "Thomas F. Torrance and the Problem of Universalism." *Scottish Journal of Theology* 68.2 (2015) 164–86.

Moltmann, Jürgen. *The Coming of God*. Translated by Margaret Kohl. Minneapolis: Fortress, 2004.

———. *The Crucified God*. Translated by R. A. Wilson and John Bowden. New York: Harper & Row, 1974.

———. *Theology of Hope*. Translated by James W. Leitch. London: SCM, 2002.

Monk of the West. *Christianity and the Doctrine of Non-Dualism*. Translated by Alvin Moore, Jr. and Marie M. Hansen. Hillsdale, NY: Sophia Perennis, 2004.

de Montaigne, Michel. *Complete Works*. Translated by Charles Cotton. Philadelphia: William T. Amies, 1879.

———. "Essays." Translated by Donald M. Frame. In *Complete Works*, 1–857. Stanford: Stanford University Press, 1967.

Montanari, Franco. "Ὅσος." In *The Brill Dictionary of Ancient Greek*, edited by Madeleine Goh and Chad Schroder, 1493-94. Boston: Brill, 2015.

Montemaggi, Vittorio. *Reading Dante's Commedia as Theology*. Oxford: Oxford University Press, 2016.

Montero, Barbara. "Post-Physicalism." *Journal of Consciousness Studies* 8.2 (2001) 61-80.

Moo, Douglas J. *Epistle to the Romans*. New International Commentary of the NT. Edited by Joel B. Green. 2nd ed. Grand Rapids: Eerdmans, 2018.

———. *Letter of James*. Pillar NT Commentary. Grand Rapids: Eerdmans, 2000.

Mooney, Edward F. "Pseudonyms and 'Style.'" In *Oxford Handbook of Kierkegaard*, edited by John Lippitt and George Pattison, 191-210: Oxford: Oxford University Press, 2013.

Mooney, Timothy. "On the Critiques of Pairing and Appresentation by Merleau-Ponty and Levinas." In *Transcendence and Phenomenology*, edited by Conor Cunningham and Peter M. Candler, Jr., 448-94. London: SCM, 2007.

Moore, Peter. *Where Are the Dead?* London: Routledge, 2017.

Morris, Leon. *Gospel according to John*. New International Commentary of the NT. Grand Rapids: Eerdmans, 1995.

———. *Gospel according to Matthew*. Pillar NT Commentary. Grand Rapids: Eerdmans, 1992.

———. *Luke*. Tyndale NT Commentaries. Rev. ed. Grand Rapids: Eerdmans, 2000.

Morrison, Margaret. *Reconstructing Reality*. Oxford: Oxford University Press, 2015.

Mostert, Christiaan. *God and the Future*. London: T. & T. Clark, 2002.

Motyer, J. Alec. *Isaiah*. Tyndale Old Testament Commentaries. Downers Grove, IL: InterVarsity, 2009.

Moule, C. F. D. *Idiom Book of NT Greek*. 2nd ed. Cambridge: Cambridge University Press, 1990.

Moulton, James Hope. *Grammar of NT Greek*. 3rd ed. 4 vols. Vol. I. Edinburgh: T. & T. Clark, 1978.

Mounce, Robert H. *Book of Revelation*. New International Commentary of the NT. Rev. ed. Grand Rapids: Eerdmans, 1998.

Mounce, William D. *Pastoral Epistles*. Word Biblical Commentary. Nashville: Thomas Nelson, 2000.

Mountcastle, Vernon B. "Brain Science at the Century's Ebb." *Daedalus* 127.2 (1998) 1-36.

Mouw, Richard J. "The Relevance of Biblical Eschatology." In *Christian Doctrine of Humanity*, edited by Oliver D. Crisp and Fred Sanders, 61-69. Grand Rapids: Zondervan, 2018.

Mulder, Jack, Jr. "Must All Be Saved?" *International Journal for Philosophy of Religion* 59 (2006) 1-24.

Mullin, Amy. "Selves, Diverse and Divided." *Hypatia* 10.4 (1995) 1-31.

Murphy, Nancey. *Bodies and Souls, or Spirited Bodies?* Cambridge: Cambridge University Press, 2012.

———. "Nonreductive Physicalist Response to Substance Dualism." In *In Search of the Soul*, edited by Joel B. Green, 65-68. Eugene, OR: Wipf & Stock, 2010.

Musurillo, Herbert. *Acts of the Christian Martyrs*. London: Oxford: Oxford University Press, 1972.

Nabokov, Vladimir. *Lolita*. New York: Knopf, 1992.

———. *Pale Fire*. New York: Quality Paperback Book Club, 1993.

Naselli, Andrew David. "Conclusion." In *Perspectives on the Extent of Atonement*, edited by Andrew David Naselli and Mark A. Snoeberger, 213–27. Nashville: B&H, 2015.

Nebe, Gottfried. "Μέρος." In *Exegetical Dictionary of the NT*, edited by Horst Balz and Gerhard Schneider, 409–10. Grand Rapids: Eerdmans, 1990.

Nelson, Paul, and Joanna Masel. "Inevitability of Multicellular Aging." *PNAS* 114.49 (2017) 12982–87.

Netland, Harold. "The Question of Criteria." *Calvin Theological Journal* 31.2 (1996) 495–503.

Nemes, Steven. "Praying Confidently for the Salvation of All." *Heythrop Journal* 61.2 (2016) 285–96.

Neuhof, Moran, Michael Levin, and Oded Rechavi. "Vertically and Horizontally Transmitted Memories." *Biology Open* 5 (2016) 1177–88.

Nicholas of Cusa. "Learned Ignorance." Translated by Jasper Hopkins. In *Nicholas of Cusa on Learned Ignorance*, edited by Jasper Hopkins, 49–158. Minneapolis: Banning, 1981.

Nichols, Terence. *Death and Afterlife*. Grand Rapids: Brazos, 2010.

Nickelsburg, George W. E. *Resurrection, Immortality, and Eternal Life*. Expanded ed. Cambridge: Harvard Divinity, 2006.

Niebuhr, Helmut Richard. *The Meaning of Revelation*. Louisville: Westminster John Knox, 2006.

Nietzsche, Friedrich. "The Anti-Christ." Translated by Judith Norman. In *The Anti-Christ and Other Writings*, edited by Aaron Ridley and Judith Norman, 1–67. Cambridge: Cambridge University Press, 2005.

———. *The Gay Science*. Translated by Josefine Nauckhoff. Cambridge: Cambridge University Press, 2001.

———. "The Genealogy of Morals." Translated by Francis Golffing. In *The Birth of Tragedy and the Genealogy of Morals*, 158–299. Garden City, NY: Doubleday, 1956.

———. *Thus Spoke Zarathustra*. Translated by R. J. Hollingdale. New York: Penguin, 1981.

———. *The Will to Power*. Translated by Walter Kaufmann. New York: Vintage, 1968.

———. *Writings from the Late Notebooks*. Translated by Kate Sturge. Cambridge: Cambridge University Press, 2003.

Noll, Mark A. *History of Christianity in the United States and Canada*. Grand Rapids: Eerdmans, 1992.

Nolland, John. *Gospel of Matthew*. New International Greek Testament Commentary. Grand Rapids: Eerdmans, 2005.

———. *Luke 9:21—18:34*. Word Biblical Commentary. Dallas: Word, 1993.

Noonan, Harold W. *Personal Identity*. 2nd ed. London: Routledge, 2003.

———. "Personal Identity and Its Perplexities." In *Personal Identity*, edited by Georg Gassar and Matthias Stefan, 82–101: Cambridge: Cambridge University Press, 2015.

Nordmeyer, Ann. E., and Michael C. Frank. "The Role of Context in Young Children's Comprehension of Negation." *Journal of Memory and Language* 77 (2014) 25–39.

Northrop, F. S. C. "Introduction." In *Werner Heisenberg's Physics and Philosophy*, 1–26. Amherst, MA: Prometheus, 1999.

Novakovic, Lidija. *Resurrection*. London: Bloomsbury, 2016.

de la Noval, Roberto J. "Divine Drama or Divine Disclosure?" *Modern Theology* 36.1 (2020) 201–10.

Novello, Henry L. "New Life as Life out of Death." In *The Role of Death in Life*, edited by John Behr and Conor Cunningham, 96–119. Eugene, OR: Cascade, 2015.

O'Brien, Peter T. *Colossians, Philemon*. Word Biblical Commentary. Waco, TX: Word Books, 1982.

O'Collins, Gerald G. "Salvation." In *Anchor Bible Dictionary*, edited by David Noel Freedman, 907–14. New York: Doubleday, 1992.

O'Flaherty, James C. *Unity and Language*. Chapel Hill, NC: University of North Carolina, 1952.

O'Meara, Thomas Franklin. *Thomas Aquinas Theologian*. South Bend, IN: University of Notre Dame Press, 1997.

O'Laughlin, Michael. "Anthropology of Evagrius Ponticus and Its Sources." In *Origen of Alexandria*, edited by Charles Kannengiesser and William L. Petersen, 357–73. South Bend, IN: University of Notre Dame Press, 1988.

Oakes, Edward T. "Christ's Descent into Hell." In *All Shall Be Well*, edited by Gregory MacDonald, 382–99. Eugene, OR: Cascade, 2011.

———. *A Theology of Grace in Six Controversies*. Grand Rapids: Eerdmans, 2016.

Oakes, Peter. *Galatians*. Paideia Commentaries on the NT. Grand Rapids: Baker Academic, 2015.

Oepke, Albrecht. "Ἀποκατάστασις." In *Theological Dictionary of the NT*, edited by Gerhard Kittel, 389–93. Grand Rapids: Eerdmans, 1964.

Oliver, Simon. "Radical Orthodoxy." In *Cambridge Dictionary of Christian Theology*, edited by Ian A. McFarland, 428–29: Cambridge: Cambridge University Press, 2011.

Olson, Eric T. "A Compound of Two Substances." In *Soul, Body, and Survival*, edited by Kevin J. Corcoran, 73–88. New York: Cornell University Press, 2001.

Olson, Roger E. *The Mosaic of Christian Belief*. Downers Grove, IL: InterVarsity, 2002.

Origen. *Commentary on the Epistle to the Romans Books 1–5*. Translated by Thomas P. Scheck. Fathers of the Church. Washington, DC: Catholic University of America Press, 2001.

———. "Dialogue with Heraclides." Translated by Robert J. Daly. In *Treatise on the Passover and Dialogue with Heraclides*, 57–78. New York: Paulist, 1992.

———. "Homilies on Luke." Translated by William A. Jurgens. In *The Faith of the Early Fathers (vol. 1)*, edited by William A. Jurgens, 200–201. Collegeville, MN: Liturgical, 1970.

———. *On First Principles*. Translated by G. W. Butterworth. Eugene, OR: Wipf & Stock, 1936.

Orlow, Dietrich. "The Conversion of Myths into Political Power." *America Historical Review* 72.3 (1967) 906–24.

Orwell, George. *1984*. New York: New America Library, 1961.

Osborne, Grant R. "General Atonement View." In *Perspectives on the Extent of Atonement*, edited by Andrew David Naselli and Mark A. Snoeberger, 81–127. Nashville: B&H, 2015.

———. *Revelation*. Baker Exegetical Commentary on the NT. Edited by Moises Silva. Grand Rapids: Baker, 2004.

Osiek, Carolyn. *Shepherd of Hermas*. Hermeneia. Edited by Helmut Koester. Minneapolis: Fortress, 1999.

Oswalt, John N. *Book of Isaiah: Chapters 40–66*. New International Commentary on the Old Testament. Grand Rapids: Eerdmans, 1998.

Owen, John. *The Death of Death in the Death of Christ*. The Works. Edited by William Gould. Carlisle, PA: Banner of Truth Trust, 1967.
Pabst, Adrian. *Metaphysics: Creation of Hierarchy*. Grand Rapids: Eerdmans, 2012.
———. "Sovereign Reason Unbound." In *Grandeur of Reason*, edited by Peter M. Candler, Jr. and Conor Cunningham, 135–66. London: SCM, 2010.
Pacherie, Elisabeth. "Self-Agency." In *Oxford Handbook of the Self*, edited by Shaun Gallagher, 442–64: Oxford: Oxford University Press, 2014.
Pinker, Steven. *Enlightenment Now*. New York: Viking, 2018.
Panksepp, Jaak. *Affective Neuroscience*. Oxford: Oxford University Press, 1998.
Pannenberg, Wolfhart. *Anthropology in Theological Perspective*. Translated by Matthew J. O'Connell. Philadelphia: Westminster, 1985.
———. "Constructive and Critical Functions of Christian Eschatology." *Harvard Theological Review* 77.2 (1984) 119–39.
———. "Faith and Reason." Translated by George H. Kehm. In *Basic Questions in Theology*, vol. 2, 46–64. Philadelphia: Westminster, 1971.
———. *Human Nature, Election, and History*. Philadelphia: Westminster, 1977.
———. "Modernity, History, and Eschatology." In *Oxford Handbook of Eschatology*, edited by Jerry L. Walls, 493–99. Oxford: Oxford University Press, 2008.
———. *Systematic Theology*. Translated by Geoffrey W. Bromiley. 3 vols. Vols. II-III. Edinburgh: T. & T. Clark, 1994, 1998.
———. "The Task of Christian Eschatology." In *The Last Things*, edited by Carl E. Braaten and Robert W. Jenson, 1–13. Grand Rapids: Eerdmans, 2002.
———. *What Is Man?* Translated by Duane A. Priebe. Philadelphia: Fortress, 1970.
Parfit, Derek. *Reasons and Persons*. Oxford: Oxford University Press, 1986.
———. "The Unimportance of Identity." In *Oxford Handbook of the Self*, edited by Shaun Gallagher, 419–41. Oxford: Oxford University Press, 2014.
Parnas, Josef, and Louis A. Sass. "Structure of Self-Consciousness in Schizophrenia." In *Oxford Handbook of the Self*, edited by Shaun Gallagher, 521–46: Oxford: Oxford University Press, 2014.
Parry, Robin A. "Universalist View." In *Four Views on Hell*, edited by Preston Sprinkle, 101–27. Grand Rapids: Zondervan, 2016.
Parry, Robin A., and Christopher Partridge, eds. *Universal Salvation?* Carlisle, UK: Paternoster, 2003.
Parry, Robin A., with Ilaria L. E. Ramelli. *A Larger Hope?* 2 vols. Vol. II. Eugene, OR: Cascade, 2019.
Parsenios, George L. *First, Second, and Third John*. Paideia Commentaries on the NT. Edited by Mikeal C. Parsons, Charles H. Talbert, and Bruce W. Longenecker. Grand Rapids: Baker Academic, 2014.
Parsons, Mikeal C. *Body and Character in Luke and Acts*. Grand Rapids: Baker, 2006.
Pascal, Blaise. *Pensees*. Translated by W. F. Trotter. New York: Dutton, 1958.
Pater, Walter. *Marius the Epicurean*. New York: Penguin, 1985.
Pearson, Carlton. *The Gospel of Inclusion*. New York: Atria, 2009.
Peeler, Amy L. B. "The Eschatological Son." In *Anthropology and NT Theology*, edited by Jason Maston and Benjamin E. Reynolds, 162–75. London: T. & T. Clark, 2019.
Peguy, Charles. *Temporal and Eternal*. Translated by Alexander Dru. London: Harvill, 1958.
Perkins, Pheme. *First Corinthians*. Paideia Commentaries on the NT. Grand Rapids: Baker Academic, 2012.

Perl, Eric D. *Theophany: Neoplatonic Philosophy of Dionysius the Areopagite*. Albany, NY: State University of New York Press, 2007.
Perry, John. *Identity, Personal Identity, and the Self*. Indianapolis: Hackett, 2002.
———. "On Knowing One's Self." In *Oxford Handbook of the Self*, edited by Shaun Gallagher, 372–93. Oxford: Oxford University Press, 2014.
Pfuetze, Paul. *Self, Society, Existence*. New York: Harper, 1961.
Phan, Peter C. "Roman Catholic Theology." In *Oxford Handbook of Eschatology*, edited by Jerry L. Walls, 215–32. Oxford: Oxford University Press, 2008.
Pieper, Josef. *Death and Immortality*. Translated by Richard Winston and Clara Winston. South Bend, IN: St Augustine's, 2000.
Pinnock, Clark H. "Annihilationism." In *Oxford Handbook of Eschatology*, edited by Jerry L. Walls, 462–75. Oxford: Oxford University Press, 2008.
Piper, John. *Let the Nations Be Glad*. 2nd ed. Grand Rapids: Baker Academic, 2007.
Plato. *Phaedo*. Translated by R. S. Bluck. London: Routledge, 2014.
———. *Phaedrus*. Translated by Tom Griffith. In *Symposium and Phaedrus*, 89–180. New York: Knopf, 2000.
———. *Phaedrus*. Translated by Chris Emlyn-Jones and William Preddy. In *Euthyphro, et al.*, edited by Chris Emlyn-Jones and William Preddy, 412–579. Cambridge: Harvard University Press, 2017.
———. *The Republic*. Translated by G. M. A. Grube. Indianapolis: Hackett, 1974.
———. *Sophist*. Translated by Harold North Fowler. In *Theaetetus Sophist*. Cambridge: Harvard University Press, 1921.
———. *Symposium*. Translated by Tom Griffith. In *Symposium and Phaedrus*, 5–85. New York: Knopf, 2000.
———. *Theaetetus*. Translated by Harold North Fowler. In *Theaetetus Sophist*. Cambridge: Harvard University Press, 1921.
Plotinus. *Plotinus: The Six Enneads*. Translated by Stephen MacKenna and B. S. Page. Great Books of the Western World, vol. 17. Chicago: Encyclopedia Britannica US, 1952.
Plummer, Alfred. *Gospel according to S. Luke*. International Critical Commentary. Edinburgh: T. & T. Clark, 1981.
Polkinghorne, John. *The God of Hope and the End of the World*. New Haven, CT: Yale University Press, 2002.
Polycarp. "Martyrdom of Polycarp." Translated by Alexander Roberts and William Rambaut. In *Ante-Nicene Fathers*, edited by Alexander Roberts et al., 39–44. Peabody, MA: Hendrickson, 1994.
Pope, Alexander. "Essay on Man." In *The Works*, 190–228. Ware, UK: Wordsworth, 1995.
Porter, Stanley E. *Idioms of the Greek NT*. Biblical Languages: Greek. 2nd ed. Sheffield, UK: Sheffield Academic Press, 1996.
Portmann, Adolf. *Essays in Philosophical Zoology*. Translated by E. B. Carter. Lampeter, UK: Mellen, 1990.
Poythress, Vern Sheridan. "Meaning of Malista in 2 Tim 4:13 and Related Verses." *Journal of Theological Studies* 53 (2002) 523–32.
Presbyterian Church (USA). "Constitution of the Presbyterian Church (USA) Book of Confessions." Louisville: Office of the General Assembly, 2004.
Price, Richard. *The Acts of the Council of Constantinople of 553*. Liverpool: Liverpool University Press, 2012.

Priest, Christopher. *The Prestige*. New York: St Martin's, 1996.
Priest, Graham, J. C. Beall, and Bradley Armour-Garb, eds. *The Law of Noncontradiction*. Oxford: Oxford University Press, 2004.
"Proceedings." Translated by Richard Price. In *The Acts of the Council of Constantinople of 553*, 106–39. Liverpool: Liverpool University Press, 2012.
Proust, Marcel. *In Search of Lost Time*. Translated by C. K. Scott Moncrieff et al. 6 vols. London: Folio Society, 2001.
Przywara, Erich. *Analogia Entis*. Translated by John R. Betz and David Bentley Hart. Grand Rapids: Eerdmans, 2014.
Pseudo-Dionysius the Areopagite. "The Divine Names." Translated by Colm Luibheid. In *The Complete Works*, 47–131. New York: Paulist, 1987.
Purkiser, W. T., Richard S. Taylor, and William H. Taylor. *God, Man, and Salvation*. Kansas City: Beacon Hill, 1977.
Radden, Jennifer. "Multiple Selves." In *Oxford Handbook of the Self*, edited by Shaun Gallagher, 547–70: Oxford: Oxford University Press, 2014.
———. "Pathologically Divided Minds." In *Models of the Self*, edited by Shaun Gallagher and Jonathan Shear, 343–58. Thorverton, UK: Imprint, 1999.
Radner, Ephraim. "The Mystery of Christian Anthropology." In *Anthropology and NT Theology*, edited by Jason Maston and Benjamin E. Reynolds, 243–62. London: T. & T. Clark, 2019.
Rae, Murray. "Salvation in Community." In *All Shall Be Well*, edited by Gregory MacDonald, 171–97. Eugene, OR: Cascade, 2011.
Rahner, Karl. "Eschatology." In *Encyclopedia of Theology: Concise Sacramentum Mundi*, 434–39. New York: Seabury, 1975.
———. *Foundations of Christian Faith*. Translated by William V. Dych. New York: Crossroad, 1985.
———. "The Hermeneutics of Eschatological Assertions." Translated by Kevin Smith. In *Theological Investigations*, 401–28. Baltimore: Helicon, 1960.
———. "Mystery." In *Encyclopedia of Theology: Concise Sacramentum Mundi*, 1000–1004. New York: Seabury, 1975.
Ramelli, Ilaria L. E. *Christian Doctrine of Apokatastasis*. Leiden: Brill, 2013.
———. *A Larger Hope?* 2 vols. Vol. I, Eugene, OR: Cascade, 2019.
———. "Origen, Bardaisan, and the Origin of Universal Salvation." *Harvard Theological Review* 102.2 (2009) 135–68.
———. "Procus and Apokatastasis." In *Proclus and His Legacy*, edited by David D. Butorac, 95–122. Boston: de Gruyter, 2017.
Ramelli, Ilaria L. E., and David Konstan. *Terms for Eternity*. Piscataway, NJ: Gorgias, 2013.
Ramm, Bernard. *The Pattern of Authority*. Grand Rapids: Eerdmans, 1957.
Rankin, David. *The Early Church and the Afterlife*. London: Routledge, 2018.
Ratzinger, Joseph. *Behold the Pierced One*. Translated by Graham Harrison. San Francisco: Ignatius, 1986.
———. *Eschatology: Death and Eternal Life*. Translated by Michael Waldstein. 2nd ed. Washington, DC: Catholic University of America Press, 1988.
———. *Theological Highlights of Vatican II*. Translated by Henry Traub, Gerard C. Thormann and Werner Barzel. New York: Paulist, 1966.
———. *Truth and Tolerance*. Translated by Henry Taylor. San Francisco: Ignatius, 2004.
Rausch, Thomas P. *Systematic Theology: Roman Catholic Approach*. Collegeville, MN: Liturgical, 2016.

Rawls, John. *A Theory of Justice*. Cambridge: Belknap, 1978.
Reddy, Vasudevi. *How Infants Know Minds*. Cambridge: Harvard University Press, 2008.
Reitan, Eric. "Human Freedom and the Impossibility of Eternal Damnation." In *Universal Salvation?* edited by Robin A. Parry and Christopher H. Partridge, 125–42. Carlisle, UK: Paternoster, 2003.
Richardson, Alan. *Christian Apologetics*. New York: Harper, 1947.
Riches, Aaron. *Ecce Homo*. Grand Rapids: Eerdmans, 2016.
Ringgren, Helmer. "Rab, Inclusive Plural." In *Theological Dictionary of the OT*, edited by G. Johannes Botterweck, et al., 293. Grand Rapids: Eerdmans, 2004.
Rips, Lance J., et al. "Tracing the Identity of Objects." *Psychological Review* 113.1 (2006) 1–30.
Rist, John M. "Plato Says That We Have Tripartite Souls." Chap. I In *Man, Soul and Body*. Brookfield: Variorum, 1996.
Robertson, A. T. *Grammar of the Greek NT*. Nashville: Broadman, 1934.
Robinson, David. *The Unitarians and the Universalists*. Westport, CT: Greenwood, 1985.
Robinson, John A. T. *In the End, God . . . .* Special ed. Eugene, OR: Cascade, 2011.
Robinson, Marilynne. *Gilead*. New York: Picador, 2004.
Rochat, Philippe. "What Is It Like to Be a Newborn?" In *Oxford Handbook of the Self*, edited by Shaun Gallagher, 57–79: Oxford: Oxford University Press, 2014.
Rosenzweig, Franz. "The Life." In *His Life and Thought*, edited by Nahum N. Glatzer, 1–176. New York: Schocken, 1953.
———. "The New Thinking." Translated by Paul W. Franks and Michael L. Morgan. In *Philosophical and Theological Writings*, edited by Paul W. Franks and Michael L. Morgan, 109–39. Indianapolis: Hackett, 2000.
———. *The Star of Redemption*. Translated by Barbara E. Galli. Madison, WI: University of Wisconsin Press, 2005.
Rosner, Brian S. "Son of God at the Centre." In *Anthropology and NT Theology*, edited by Jason Maston and Benjamin E. Reynolds, 225–41. London: T. & T. Clark, 2019.
Rousseau, Jean-Jacques. "The Social Contract." Translated by Christopher Betts. In *Discourse on Political Economy and the Social Contract*, 43–168: Oxford: Oxford University Press, 2009.
Rousseau, Mary F. "Elements of a Thomastic Philosophy of Death." *The Thomist* 43.4 (1979) 581–602.
Rowell, Geoffrey. *Hell and the Victorians*. Oxford: Clarendon, 1974.
Rowland, Christopher. "Eschatology of the NT Church." In *Oxford Handbook of Eschatology*, edited by Jerry L. Walls, 56–72. Oxford: Oxford University Press, 2008.
Russell, Norman. *Doctrine of Deification in the Greek Patristic Tradition*. Oxford: Oxford University Press, 2006.
Sachs, John R. "Apocatastasis in Patristic Theology." *Theological Studies* 54 (1993) 617–40.
Sanders, Fred. "Response to Matthew Levering." In *Five Views on the Extent of Atonement*, edited by Adam J. Johnson, 101–5. Grand Rapids: Zondervan, 2019.
———. "Response to Tom Greggs." In *Five Views on the Extent of Atonement*, edited by Adam J. Johnson, 235–39. Grand Rapids: Zondervan, 2019.
———. "Wesleyan View." In *Five Views on the Extent of Atonement*, edited by Adam J. Johnson, 156–76. Grand Rapids: Zondervan, 2019.

Sanders, John. "Freewill Theist's Response to Talbott's Universalism." In *Universal Salvation?* edited by Robin A. Parry and Christopher H. Partridge, 169–87. Carlisle, UK: Paternoster, 2003.

———. *No Other Name*. Grand Rapids: Eerdmans, 1992.

———. "Raising Hell about Razing Hell." *Perspectives in Religious Studies* 40.3 (2013) 267–81.

Sartre, Jean-Paul. *Between Existentialism and Marxism*. Translated by John Mathews. New York: William Morrow, 1976.

Schaff, Adam. *Marxism and the Human Individual*. Translated by Olgierd Wogjasiewicz. New York: McGraw-Hill, 1970.

Schechtman, Marya. *Staying Alive*. Oxford: Oxford University Press, 2014.

Scheffler, Samuel. *Death and the Afterlife*. Oxford: Oxford University Press, 2013.

Schiller, Friedrich. "Letters on the Aesthetical Education of Man." Translated by Nathan Haskell Dole. In *Aesthetical and Philosophical Essays*, 33–125. New York: Collier, 1902.

———. "On the Sublime." Translated by Nathan Haskell Dole. In *Aesthetical and Philosophical Essays*, 135–49. New York: Collier, 1902.

———. "Philosophical Letters." Translated by Nathan Haskell Dole. In *Aesthetical and Philosophical Essays*, 379–441. New York: Collier, 1902.

Schindler, D. C. *The Perfection of Freedom*. Eugene, OR: Cascade, 2012.

Schleiermacher, Friedrich. *Christian Faith*. Translated by Terrence N. Tice et al. 2 vols. Vol. II. Louisville: Westminster John Knox, 2016.

Schreiner, Thomas R. *1,2 Peter, Jude*. New American Commentary. Nashville: Broadman & Holman, 2003.

———. "Penal Substitution View." In *The Nature of Atonement*, edited by James Beilby and Paul R. Eddy, 67–98. Downers Grove, IL: InterVarsity Academic, 2006.

———. *Romans*. Baker Exegetical Commentary on the NT. Grand Rapids: Baker, 2003.

Schroeder, Gerald L. *The Hidden Face of God*. New York: Touchstone, 2002.

Schultz, Richard L. "Nationalism and Universalism in Isaiah." In *Interpreting Isaiah*, edited by David G. Firth and H. G. M. Williamson, 122–44. Downers Grove, IL: InterVarsity, 2009.

Schumacher, Bernard N. *Death and Mortality in Contemporary Philosophy*. Translated by Michael J. Miller. Cambridge: Cambridge University Press, 2011.

Schwarz, Hans. *Eschatology*. Grand Rapids: Eerdmans, 2000.

———. *Evil: Historical and Theological Perspective*. Minneapolis: Fortress, 1995.

———. *The Human Being*. Grand Rapids: Eerdmans, 2013.

Schwobel, Christoph. "Human Being as Relational Being." In *Persons, Divine and Human*, edited by Christoph Schwobel and Colin E. Gunton, 141–65. Edinburgh: T. & T. Clark, 1991.

———. "Introduction." In *Persons, Divine and Human*, edited by Christoph Schwobel and Colin E. Gunton, 1–29. Edinburgh: T. & T. Clark, 1991.

———. "Last Things First?" In *The Future as God's Gift*, edited by David Fergusson and Marcel Sarot, 217–41. Edinburgh: T. & T. Clark, 2000.

Scott, Mark S. M. *Journey Back to God*. Oxford: Oxford University Press, 2012.

Secker, Philip J. "Martin Luther's Views on the State of the Dead." *Concordia Theological Monthly* 38.7 (1967) 422–35.

Sedgwick, Henry Dwight. *Life of Marcus Aurelius*. New Haven, CT: Yale University Press, 1922.

Seifrid, Mark A. "Righteousness, Justice and Justification." In *New Dictionary of Biblical Theology*, edited by T. Desmond Alexander and Brian S. Rosner, 740–45. Downers Grove, IL: InterVarsity, 2000.

Shaw, Gregory. *Theurgy and the Soul*. 2nd ed. Kettering, UK: Angelico, 2014.

Shakespeare, William. "Hamlet, Prince of Denmark." In *The Complete Works of William Shakespeare*, by William James Craig, 1006–49. Oxford: Oxford University Press, 1919.

———. "The Tragedy of King Richard II." In *The Complete Works of William Shakespeare*, by William James Craig, 437–69. Oxford: Oxford University Press, 1919.

Shelley, Bruce L. *Church History in Plain Language*. 3rd ed. Nashville: Thomas Nelson, 2008.

Shelley, Mary. *Frankenstein*. New York: Norton, 1996.

Sherman, Jacob Holsinger. *Partakers of the Divine*. Minneapolis: Fortress, 2014.

Shields, Christopher, and Robert Pasnau. *Philosophy of Aquinas*. 2nd ed. Oxford: Oxford University Press, 2016.

Shoemaker, Sydney. "On What We Are." In *Oxford Handbook on the Self*, edited by Shaun Gallagher, 352–71. Oxford: Oxford University Press, 2014.

Silouan, Staretz. "The Writings." Translated by Rosemary Edmonds. In *Saint Silouan the Athonite*, edited by Archimandrite Sophrony, 269–504. Crestwood, NY: St Vladimir's Seminary Press, 1991.

Silva, Moises. *Philippians*. Baker Exegetical Commentary on the NT. 2nd ed. Grand Rapids: Baker, 2005.

Silvas, Anna M. *The Asketikon of St Basil the Great*. Oxford: Oxford University Press, 2007.

———. *Gregory of Nyssa: The Letters*. Boston: Brill, 2007.

Simmons, Michael. *Universal Salvation in Late Antiquity*. Oxford: Oxford University Press, 2015.

Sloterdijk, Peter. *Critique of Cynical Reason*. Translated by Michael Eldred. Minneapolis: University of Minnesota Press, 1987.

Smalley, Stephen S. *1,2,3 John*. Word Biblical Commentary. Waco, TX: Word, 1984.

Smith, Janet E. "Plato's Use of Myth in the Education of Philosophic Man." *Phoenix* 40.1 (1986) 20–34.

Snyder, Laura J. "William Whewell." In *Stanford Encyclopedia of Philosophy*, edited by Edward N. Zalta: Stanford: Stanford University, 2019. <https://plato.stanford.edu/archives/spr2021/entries/whewell/>

"The So-Called Second Letter of Clement of Rome to the Corinthians." Translated by William A. Jurgens. In *The Faith of the Early Fathers (vol. 1)*, edited by William A. Jurgens, 42–44. Collegeville, MN: Liturgical, 1970.

Solomon of Akhlat. *Book of the Bee*. Translated by Ernest A. Wallis Budge. Oxford: Clarendon, 1886.

Song, Robert. *Covenant and Calling*. London: SCM, 2014.

Sophrony, Archimandrite. "The Staretz' Life and Teaching." Translated by Rosemary Edmonds. In *Saint Silouan the Athonite*, 9–259. Crestwood, NY: St Vladimir's Seminary Press, 1991.

Sorabji, Richard. *Self: Ancient and Modern Insights*. Oxford: Clarendon, 2006.

Sorg, Theo. "Heart." In *New International Dictionary of NT Theology*, edited by Colin Brown, 180–84. Grand Rapids: Zondervan, 1986.

Soskice, Janet Martin. *Metaphor and Religious Language*. Oxford: Clarendon, 1985.
Spaemann, Robert. *Essays in Anthropology*. Translated by Guido de Graaff and James Mumford. Eugene, OR: Cascade, 2010.
von Speyr, Adrienne. *The Christian State of Life*. Translated by Mary Frances McCarthy. San Francisco: Ignatius, 1986.
———. *Confession*. Translated by Douglas W. Stott. San Francisco: Ignatius, 1985.
———. *The Farewell Discourses*. Translated by E. A. Nelson. San Francisco: Ignatius, 1987.
———. *Gates of Eternal Life*. Translated by Corona Sharp. San Francisco: Ignatius, 1983.
———. *Mystery of Death*. Translated by Graham Harrison. San Francisco: Ignatius, 1988.
———. *The Passion from Within*. Translated by Lucia Wiedenhover. San Francisco: Ignatius, 1998.
———. *The Word*. Translated by Alexander Dru. San Francisco: Ignatius, 2019.
Spezzano, Daria. *The Glory of God's Grace*. Sapientia Press of Ave Maria Univ., 2015.
Spicq, Ceslas. *Theological Lexicon of the NT*. Translated by James D. Ernest. 3 vols. Vol. I. Peabody, MA: Hendrickson, 1994.
Spitz, L. "Conjoined Twins." *British Journal of Surgery* 83 (1996) 1028–30.
Sprinkle, Preston, ed. *Four Views on Hell*. 2nd ed. Grand Rapids: Zondervan, 2016.
Stackhouse, John G., Jr. "Terminal Punishment." In *Four Views on Hell*, edited by Preston Sprinkle, 61–81. Grand Rapids: Zondervan, 2016.
———. "Terminal Punishment Response to Hell and Purgatory." In *Four Views on Hell*, edited by Preston Sprinkle, 179–89. Grand Rapids: Zondervan, 2016.
Stang, Charles. *Apophasis and Pseudonymity in Dionysius the Areopagite*. Oxford: Oxford University Press, 2012.
———. *Our Divine Double*. Cambridge: Harvard University Press, 2016.
———. "The Two 'I's of Christ." *Anglican Theological Review* 94.3 (2012) 529–47.
Stark, Rodney. *The Rise of Christianity*. Princeton: Princeton University Press, 1996.
Starr, James. "Does 2 Peter 1:4 Speak of Deification?" In *Partakers of the Divine Nature*, edited by Michael J. Christensen and Jeffrey A. Wittung, 81–92. Grand Rapids: Baker, 2008.
Stein, Edith. *Potency and Act*. Translated by Walter Redmond. Washington, DC: ICS, 2009.
Stein, Robert H. *Luke*. New American Commentary. Nashville: Broadman, 1992.
———. *Mark*. Baker Exegetical Commentary on the NT. Grand Rapids: Baker, 2008.
Stephens, Mark B. *Annihilation or Renewal?* Tübingen: Mohr Siebeck, 2011.
Stern, Daniel N. *The Interpersonal World of the Infant*. New York: Basic, 1985.
Stevenson, Robert Louis. *The Strange Case of Dr. Jekyll and Mr. Hyde*. New York: Dover, 1991.
Stott, John R. W. *Epistles of John*. Tyndale NT Commentaries. Edited by R. V. G. Tasker. Grand Rapids: Eerdmans, 1987.
Strange, Daniel. "Calvinist Response to Talbott's Universalism." In *Universal Salvation?* edited by Robin A. Parry and Christopher H. Partridge, 145–68. Grand Rapids: Eerdmans, 2004.
Strawson, Galen. "The Minimal Subject." In *Oxford Handbook of the Self*, edited by Shaun Gallagher, 253–78: Oxford: Oxford University Press, 2014.

———. "The Self." In *Models of the Self*, edited by Shaun Gallagher and Jonathan Shear, 1–24. Thorverton, UK: Imprint, 1999.
Stromberg, Jacob. "Inner-Isaianic Reading of Isaiah 61:1–3." In *Interpreting Isaiah*, edited by David G. Firth and H. G. M. Williamson, 261–72. Downers Grove, IL: InterVarsity, 2009.
Stuurman, Siep. *Invention of Humanity*. Cambridge: Harvard University Press, 2017.
Sudhaile, Stephanus Bar. *Book of the Holy Hierotheos*. Translated by Fred Shipley Marsh. Amsterdam: APA-Philo, 1979.
Sutton, Matthew Lewis. *Heaven Opens*. Minneapolis: Fortress, 2014.
Sweetman, Robert. "Sin Has Its Place, but All Shall Be Well." In *All Shall Be Well*, edited by Gregory MacDonald, 66–92. Eugene, OR: Cascade, 2011.
Swinburne, Richard G. "The Future of the Totally Corrupt." In *Rethinking Hell*, edited by Christopher M. Date et al., 234–40. Eugene, OR: Cascade, 2014.
———. "How to Determine Which Is the True Theory of Personal Identity." In *Personal Identity*, edited by Georg Gassar and Matthias Stefan, 105–22. Cambridge: Cambridge University Press, 2015.
Talbott, Thomas. "Christ Victorious." In *Universal Salvation?* edited by Robin A. Parry and Christopher H. Partridge, 15–31. Carlisle, UK: Paternoster, 2003.
———. *The Inescapable Love of God*. 2nd ed. Eugene, OR: Cascade, 2014.
———. "Pauline Interpretation of Divine Judgment." In *Universal Salvation?* edited by Robin A. Parry and Christopher H. Partridge, 32–52. Carlisle, UK: Paternoster, 2003.
———. "Reply to My Critics." In *Universal Salvation?* edited by Robin A. Parry and Christopher H. Partridge, 247–73. Carlisle, UK: Paternoster, 2003.
———. "Towards a Better Understanding of Universalism." In *Universal Salvation?* edited by Robin A. Parry and Christopher H. Partridge, 3–14. Carlisle, UK: Paternoster, 2003.
———. "Universalism." In *Oxford Handbook of Eschatology*, edited by Jerry L. Walls, 446–61. Oxford: Oxford University Press, 2008.
Taliaferro, Charles. "Human Nature, Personal Identity, and Eschatology." In *Oxford Handbook of Eschatology*, edited by Jerry L. Walls, 534–47. Oxford: Oxford University Press, 2008.
Tanner, Kathryn. *Christ the Key*. Cambridge: Cambridge University Press, 2010.
Tappert, Theodore G., ed. *Book of Concord: Confessions of the Evangelical Lutheran Church*. Philadelphia: Fortress, 1959.
Taylor, Charles. *Hegel*. Cambridge: Cambridge University Press, 1995.
———. *A Secular Age*. Cambridge: Belknap Press of Harvard University, 2007.
———. *Sources of the Self*. Cambridge: Cambridge University Press, 2000.
Taylor, Mark C. *Journeys to Selfhood*. Berkeley: University of California Press, 1980.
Taylor, Stephen S. "Faith, Faithfulness." In *New Dictionary of Biblical Theology*, edited by T. Desmond Alexander and Brian S. Rosner, 487–93. Downers Grove, IL: InterVarsity, 2000.
Taylor, Walter F., Jr. "Humanity, NT View." In *Anchor Bible Dictionary*, edited by David Noel Freedman, 321–25. New York: Doubleday, 1992.
Temple, William. *Nature, Man and God*. Edinburgh: R. & R. Clark, 1940.
Teresa, Mother. *Come Be My Light*. New York: Doubleday, 2007.
Tertullian. "Apology." Translated by William A. Jurgens. In *The Faith of the Early Fathers (vol. 1)*, edited by William A. Jurgens, 112–18. Collegeville, MN: Liturgical, 1970.

———. "On the Resurrection of the Flesh." In *Ante-Nicene Fathers*, edited by Alexander Roberts and James Donaldson, 545–94. Peabody, MA: Hendrickson, 1994.

———. "Prescription against Heretics." In *Ante-Nicene Fathers*, edited by Alexander Roberts and James Donaldson, 243–68. Peabody, MA: Hendrickson, 1994.

Thayer, Joseph H. "'Οσος." In *Thayer's Greek-English Lexicon of the NT*, 456–57. Peabody, MA: Hendrickson, 1996.

Theodoret of Cyrus. *Commentary on the Letters of St Paul*. Translated by Robert Charles Hill. 2 vols. Vol. I. Brookline, NY: Holy Cross Orthodox, 2001.

Theophilus of Antioch. "To Autolycus." Translated by William A. Jurgens. In *The Faith of the Early Fathers (vol. 1)*, edited by William A. Jurgens, 73–77. Collegeville, MN: Liturgical, 1970.

Thigpen, Paul. *Saints Who Saw Hell*. Charlotte, NC: Tan, 2019.

Thiselton, Anthony C. *First Epistle to the Corinthians*. New International Greek Testament Commentary. Grand Rapids: Eerdmans, 2000.

Thompson, James W. "Philippians." In *Philippians and Philemon*, 3–147. Paideia Commentaries on the NT. Grand Rapids: Baker Academic, 2016.

Tillich, Paul. *Systematic Theology*. 3 vols. Chicago: University of Chicago Press, 1973–76.

Timpe, Kevin. "An Argument for Limbo." *Journal of Ethics* 19 (2015) 277–92.

Tolstoy, Leo. *Anna Karenina*. Translated by Richard Pevear and Larissa Volokhonsky. New York: Penguin, 2000.

———. *The Death of Ivan Ilyich and Other Stories*. Translated by Rosemary Edmondson. London: Penguin, 1960.

Toner, Patrick. "St Thomas Aquinas on Death and the Separated Soul." *Pacific Philosophical Quarterly* 91 (2010) 587–99.

Tononi, Giulio. *Phi*. New York: Pantheon, 2012.

Tononi, Giulio, and Christof Koch. "Consciousness: Here, There, and Everywhere?" *Philosophical Transactions of the Royal Society B: Biological Sciences* 370: 201440167 (2015).

Tonstad, Sigve K. *Revelation*. Paideia Commentaries on the NT. Grand Rapids: Baker Academic, 2019.

Torrance, Thomas F. *Atonement*. Downers Grove, IL: InterVarsity, 2009.

———, ed. *The School of Faith*. Eugene, OR: Wipf & Stock, 1996.

Towner, Philip H. *Letters to Timothy and Titus*. New International Commentary of the NT. Grand Rapids: Eerdmans, 2006.

Trabbic, Joseph G. "Can Aquinas Hope 'That All Men Be Saved'?" *Heythrop Journal* LVII (2016) 337–58.

Trueman, Carl R. "Definite Atonement View." In *Perspectives on the Extent of Atonement*, edited by Andrew David Naselli and Mark A. Snoeberger, 19–61. Nashville: B&H, 2015.

Trumbower, Jeffrey A. *Rescue for the Dead*. Oxford: Oxford University Press, 2001.

Tseng, Shao Kai. "Condemnation and Universal Salvation: Karl Barth's 'Reverent Agnosticism' Revisited." *Scottish Journal of Theology* 71.3 (2018) 324–38.

Turner, James T., Jr. "No Explanation of Persons." *International Journal for Philosophy of Religion* 76 (2014) 297–317.

Turner, Leon. *Theology, Psychology and the Plural Self*. Burlington, VT: Ashgate, 2008.

Turner, Nigel. *Grammar of NT Greek: J. H. Moulton*. 4 vols. Vol. III, Edinburgh: T. & T. Clark, 1998.

de Unamuno, Miguel. *Tragic Sense of Life*. Translated by J. E. Crawford Flitch. New York: Dover, 1954.
U.S. Census Bureau, "Historical Estimates of World Population." https://www.census.gov/data/tables/time-series/demo/international-programs/historical-est-worldpop.html.
Vanhoozer, Kevin. "Human Being, Individual and Social." In *Cambridge Companion to Christian Doctrine*, edited by Colin E. Gunton, 158–88. Cambridge: Cambridge University Press, 1998.
———. "The Origin of Paul's Soteriology." In *Reconsidering the Relationship between Biblical and Systematic Theology*, edited by Benjamin E. Reynolds et al., 177–212. Tübingen: Mohr Siebeck, 2014.
Vatican Council. "Dogmatic Constitution on the Church: Lumen Gentium, Solemnly Promulgated by His Holiness, Pope Paul VI on November 21, 1964." Boston: St Paul Eds., 1965.
Vaught, Carl G. *Access to God in Augustine's Confessions: Books X-XIII*. Albany, NY: State University of New York Press, 2005.
Vidal, Fernando. "Brains, Bodies, Selves, and Science." *Critical Inquiry* 28.4 (2002) 930–74.
de Villiers, Pieter G. R. "In the Presence of God: Eschatology of 1 Thessalonians." In *Eschatology of the NT and Some Related Documents*, edited by Jan G. van der Watt, 302–32. Tübingen: Mohr Siebeck, 2011.
Vincent of Lerins. "A Commonitory." In *Nicene and Post-Nicene Fathers: Second Series*, edited by Philip Schaff and Henry Wace, 131–59. Peabody, MA: Hendrickson, 1994.
Vinson, Richard B. "Godly." In *The New Interpreter's Dictionary of the Bible*, edited by Katharine Doob Sakenfeld, 620–21. Nashville: Abingdon, 2007.
Visala, Aku. "Human Cognition and the Image of God." In *Christian Doctrine of Humanity*, edited by Oliver D. Crisp and Fred Sanders, 91–109. Grand Rapids: Zondervan, 2018.
Vishnevskaya, Elena. "Divinization as Perichoretic Embrace in Maximus the Confessor." In *Partakers of the Divine Nature*, edited by Michael J. Christensen and Jeffrey A. Wittung, 132–45. Grand Rapids: Baker, 2008.
Vogeley, Kai, and Shaun Gallagher. "Self in the Brain." In *Oxford Handbook of the Self*, edited by Shaun Gallagher, 111–36: Oxford: Oxford University Press, 2014.
Volf, Miroslav. *After Our Likeness*. Grand Rapids: Eerdmans, 1998.
———. *The End of Memory*. Grand Rapids: Eerdmans, 2006.
Walker, Adrian J. "The Lived Body as the Organ of Theology." *Communio* 33 (2006) 203–14.
Wall, Robert W. "Conscience." In *Anchor Bible Dictionary*, edited by David Noel Freedman, 1128–30. New York: Doubleday, 1992.
Wallace, Daniel B. *Greek Grammar*. Grand Rapids: Zondervan, 1996.
Wallenfang, Donald. *Human and Divine Being*. Eugene, OR: Cascade, 2017.
Walls, Jerry L. "Hell and Purgatory Response to Eternal Conscious Torment." In *Four Views on Hell*, edited by Preston Sprinkle, 55–59. Grand Rapids: Zondervan, 2016.
———. *Hell: Logic of Damnation*. South Bend, IN: University of Notre Dame Press, 1992.
———, ed. *Oxford Handbook of Eschatology*. Oxford: Oxford University Press, 2008.

———. "Philosophical Critique of Talbott's Universalism." In *Universal Salvation?* edited by Robin A. Parry and Christopher H. Partridge, 105–24. Carlisle, UK: Paternoster, 2004.

Walsh, Maureen L. "Re-Imagining Redemption." *Horizons* 39.2 (2012) 189–207.

Walsh, Sylvia. *Living Christianly*. Philadelphia: Pennsylvania University Press, 2005.

Walter, Tony. *Eclipse of Eternity*. New York: St Martin's, 1996.

Waltke, Bruce K. *Genesis: Commentary*. Grand Rapids: Zondervan, 2001.

Wanamaker, Charles A. *Epistles to the Thessalonians*. New International Greek Testament Commentary. Grand Rapids: Eerdmans, 1990.

Ward, Graham. "The Displaced Body of Jesus Christ." In *Radical Orthodoxy*, edited by John Milbank et al., 163–81. London: Routledge, 1999.

———. "Hegel and the Grandeur of Reason." In *Grandeur of Reason*, edited by Peter M. Candler, Jr. and Conor Cunningham, 232–63. London: SCM, 2010.

Wasserman, Ryan. "Personal Identity, Indeterminacy and Obligation." In *Personal Identity*, edited by Georg Gassar and Matthias Stefan, 63–81. Cambridge: Cambridge University Press, 2015.

Watkin, Julia. "Kierkegaard—Dying and Eternal Life as Paradox." PhD diss., University of Bristol, 1979.

———. "Kierkegaard's View of Death." *History of European Ideas* 12.1 (1990) 65–78.

Watson, Nicholas. "Visions of Incusion." *Journal of Medieval and Early Modern Studies* 27.2 (1997) 145–87.

Weima, Jeffrey A.D. *1–2 Thessalonians*. Baker Exegetical Commentary on the NT. Grand Rapids: Baker Academic, 2014.

Welz, Claudia. *Humanity in God's Image*. Oxford: Oxford University Press, 2016.

Wenger, J. C. "Dordrecht Confession of Faith." In *The Mennonite Encyclopedia*, edited by Harold S. Bender, 92–93. Scottdale, PA: Mennonite, 1956.

Westphal, Merold. *Becoming a Self*. West Lafayette, IN: Purdue University Press, 1996.

White, Vernon. *Life beyond Death*. London: Darton, Longman & Todd, 2006.

Whitehead, Alfred North. *Process and Reality*. New York: Free, 1969.

Whitman, Walt. "Song of Myself." In *Leaves of Grass*, 33–115. New York: Modern Library, 2001.

Wiener, Norbert. *The Human Use of Human Beings*. Rev. ed. New York: Da Capo, 1954.

Wild, Robert. *Catholic Reading Guide to Universalism*. Eugene, OR: Resource, 2015.

Wilde, Oscar. *De Profundis*. New York: Modern Library, 2000.

Wiles, Maurice. *The Making of Christian Doctrine*. Cambridge: Cambridge University Press, 1967.

Wilkes, Kathleen V. "Know Thyself." In *Models of the Self*, edited by Shaun Gallagher and Jonathan Shear, 25–38. Thorverton, UK: Imprint, 1999.

———. *Real People*. Oxford: Clarendon, 1988.

Willard, Dallas. *The Divine Conspiracy*. New York: Harper, 1998.

Williams, A. N. *Architecture of Theology*. Oxford: Oxford University Press, 2011.

Williams, Bernard. *Moral Luck*. Cambridge: Cambridge University Press, 1993.

———. *Problems of the Self*. Cambridge: Cambridge University Press, 1973.

Williams, Rowan. *On Christian Theology*. Malden, MA: Blackwell, 2000.

Williams, Stephen N. *The Election of Grace*. Grand Rapids: Eerdmans, 2015.

Williams, Thomas D., and Jan Olof Bengtsson. "Personalism." In *Stanford Encyclopedia of Philosophy*, edited by Edward N. Zalta, 2016. <https://plato.stanford.edu/archives/spr2020/entries/personalism/>

Bibliography

Williamson, Paul R. *Death and the Afterlife*. Downers Grove, IL: Apollos, 2018.
Wilson, John Cook. *Statement and Inference and Other Philosophical Papers*. 2 vols. Vol. II. Oxford: Clarendon, 1969.
Winchester, Elhanan. *The Universal Restoration*. 4th ed. London: n.p., 1799.
Winslow, Donald F. *Dynamics of Salvation*. Cambridge: Philadelphia Patristic Foundation, 1979.
Wippel, John F. *Metaphysical Thought of Thomas Aquinas*. Washington, DC: Catholic University of America Press, 2000.
Witherington, Ben, III. "Equally Orthodox Christians." In *Rethinking Hell*, edited by Christopher M. Date et al., 292–303. Eugene, OR: Cascade, 2014.
Wittgenstein, Ludwig. "Philosophie Der Psychologie—Ein Fragment." Translated by G. E. M. Anscombe et al. In *Philosophische Untersuchungen*, edited by P. M. S. Hacker and Joachim Schulte, 182–243. Chichester, UK: Wiley-Blackwell, 2009.
———. *Philosophische Untersuchungen* [Philosophical Investigations]. Translated by G. E. M. Anscombe et al. 4th ed. Chichester, UK: Wiley-Blackwell, 2009.
Wojtyla, Karol. *The Acting Person*. Translated by Andrzej Potocki. Dordrecht: Reidel, 1976.
Wolinski, Joseph. "Trinity: Theological History." In *Encyclopedia of Christian Theology*, edited by Jean-Yves Lacoste, 1606–16. London: Routledge, 2005.
Wollheim, Richard. *The Thread of Life*. Cambridge: Harvard University Press, 1984.
Woodhouse, Sidney Chawner. *English-Greek Dictionary: A Vocabulary of the Attic Language*. London: Routledge, 1910.
Wordsworth, William. *The Prelude*. New York: Rinehart, 1954.
Wright, Christopher J. H. *The Mission of God*. Downers Grove, IL: InterVarsity, 2006.
Wright, N. T. *Epistles of Paul to the Colossians and to Philemon*. Tyndale NT Commentaries. Edited by Leon Morris. Grand Rapids: Eerdmans, 2000.
———. *The Resurrection of the Son of God*. Minneapolis: Fortress, 2003.
———. "Righteousness." In *New Dictionary of Theology*, edited by Sinclair B. Ferguson and David F. Wright, 590–92. Downers Grove, IL: InterVarsity, 1988.
———. *Surprised by Hope*. New York: HarperOne, 2008.
———. "Towards a Biblical View of Universalism." *Themelios* 4.2 (1979) 54–58.
Wright, Nigel G. "A Kinder, Gentler Damnation?" In *Rethinking Hell*, edited by Christopher M. Date et al., 228–33. Eugene, OR: Cascade, 2014.
Wycliffe, John. *On the Truth of Holy Scripture*. Translated by Ian Christopher Levy. Kalamazoo, MI: Medieval Institute, 2001.
Yates, Stephen. *Between Death and Resurrection*. London: Bloomsbury, 2017.
Yu, Carver T. *Being and Relation*. Edinburgh: Scottish Academic, 1987.
Zachhuber, Johannes. *Human Nature in Gregory of Nyssa*. Leiden: Brill, 2014.
Zahavi, Dan. "Unity of Consciousness and the Problem of Self." In *Oxford Handbook of the Self*, edited by Shaun Gallagher, 316–35: Oxford: Oxford University Press, 2014.
Zaleski, Carol. "Near-Death Experiences." In *Oxford Handbook of Eschatology*, edited by Jerry L. Walls, 614–28. Oxford: Oxford University Press, 2008.
Zalta, Edward N. "In Defense of the Law of Noncontradiction." In *The Law of Noncontradiction*, edited by Graham Priest et al., 418–36: Oxford: Oxford University Press, 2004.
Ziegler, Philip G. *Militant Grace*. Grand Rapids: Baker, 2018.

Zimmerman, Dean W. "Compatibility of Materialism and Survival." *Faith and Philosophy* 16.2 (1999) 194–212.

———. "Materialism, Dualism, and 'Simple' Theories of Personal Identity." In *Personal Identity*, edited by Georg Gassar and Matthias Stefan, 206–35. Cambridge: Cambridge University Press, 2015.

Zizioulas, John D. *Being as Communion*. Crestwood, NY: St Vladimir's Seminary Press, 1985.

———. "On Being a Person." In *Persons, Divine and Human*, edited by Christoph Schwobel and Colin E. Gunton, 33–46. Edinburgh: T. & T. Clark, 1991.

www.ingramcontent.com/pod-product-compliance
Lightning Source LLC
Chambersburg PA
CBHW052143300426
44115CB00011B/1499